SEX AND EROTICISM IN MESOPOTAMIAN LITERATURE

Sex and Eroticism in Mesopotamian Literature allows a glimpse of a world with a sexual culture and erotic values very different from our own, through exploration of the earliest preserved written evidence on the subject – the Sumero-Akkadian cuneiform sources of the 21st to 5th centuries BC.

Drawing on sophisticated and astonishing literary texts – courtly love poems and bridal songs, myths, narratives and incantations – Gwendolyn Leick uncovers a fascinating range of perspectives on the subject of passion and pleasure. The reader is treated to eloquent and freely-expressed views on topics from prostitution, love magic and deviant sexual practice to gender, fertility and potency.

This revealing and candid volume celebrates a wealth of erotic material from one of the world's earliest literate civilisations, and encompasses archaeological, religious, historical, anthropological and gender-based themes and approaches. It will be of interest to students and teachers in all these disciplines.

Gwendolyn Leick is author of several books on the ancient Near East, including *The Babylonians* (2003), *Who's Who in the Ancient Near East* (Routledge 2001), *A Dictionary of Ancient Near Eastern Mythology* (Routledge 1988) and *Mesopotamia: The Invention of the City* (2002).

SEX AND EROTICISM IN MESOPOTAMIAN LITERATURE

Gwendolyn Leick

Routledge
Taylor & Francis Group

LONDON AND NEW YORK

First published 1994 by Routledge
11 New Fetter Lane, London EC4P 4EE

Simultaneously published in the USA and Canada
by Routledge
29 West 35th Street, New York, NY 10001

Routledge is an imprint of the Taylor & Francis Group

First published in paperback 2003

© 1994 and 2003 Gwendolyn Leick

Typeset in Garamond by Solidus (Bristol) Limited
Printed and bound in Great Britain by
Biddles Ltd, Guildford, Surrey

British Library Cataloguing in Publication Data
A catalogue record for this book is available from the
British Library

Library of Congress Cataloging in Publication Data
A catalog record for this book has been requested

ISBN 0–415–06534–8 (hbk)
ISBN 0–415–31161–6 (pbk)

This book is dedicated to Ibrahim Gürcan

CONTENTS

CONTENTS

Part II Sources from the later second and first millennia

PLATES

PREFACE

For some years, the main concern of my publications has been to make the results of Assyriological research accessible for the non-specialist. Since the great wave of popular interest in the subject during the Victorian and Edwardian era, when the curly-bearded, giant bull-men drew the crowds in London, Berlin and Paris, the general awareness of Mesopotamian scholarship, even within academic circles, has dwindled remarkably. Although public enthusiasm for the ancient Near East never matched that for Pharaonic Egypt, in spite of the often spectacular archaeological discoveries, there was also a remarkable lack of communication between the specialists, toiling at the rock-face of the tablets, and the wider audience. The pressures of contemporary academic life make such a mediating role even more difficult. Consequently, most of the astonishing data of one of the great early and literate civilizations remains practically unknown outside the world of cuneiformists and biblical scholars.

The present work brings together as many original texts on love and sexuality, or relevant excerpts, as are available in published form. There has been considerable activity during the last twenty years in translating and collecting Mesopotamian love poetry. After all, the Old Akkadian, Sumerian and Old Babylonian sources are the oldest literary documents about love, predating the Egyptian material of the Middle Kingdom by several hundred years. But while in other academic disciplines, especially in the Classics, the subject has received a good deal of scholarly attention over the last twenty years, to some extent inspired by feminist thinking,[1] there has so far been no attempt to synthesize the available data from Mesopotamian sources. They are, as will become apparent, far from naïve or primitive. Not all of them are poetry, some are myths, rituals, or incantations.

PREFACE

Formally, this book is a collection of essays that focus on particular aspects of erotic love that are common to or characteristic of certain genres of Mesopotamian literature. I have approached the compositions from various angles, in order to offer different perspectives, but without feeling committed to a particular mode of interpretation, whether exclusively feminist, structuralist, psychoanalytical, or deconstructionist. I have sometimes used cross-cultural comparisons, based on anthropological data from very different cultures, in order to widen the customary conceptual constraint of Ancient Near Eastern scholarship. My comments on the text sometimes differ considerably from those of their editors, but such deviations are acknowledged in the notes. These refer the reader to the original sources, and also sometimes tackle linguistic matters for the attention of my colleagues.

My use of the term 'literature' is not meant to convey the notion of fiction or poetry as an aesthetic category as in the German *Belletristik*, but as a general corpus of written material that is not bureaucratic, documentary, or used for direct communication like letters, receipts, etc. By the word 'text' I mean the original written work or document without any deconstructionist or exegetic dimension.

It is not possible to write about sexuality in the Ancient Near East. We know very little about people's private lives. But literature can tell us about cultural aspirations, general norms of thinking, and articulates emotion and desire. This book is only an attempt to do some justice to the complexity, ambiguity and subtlety of Mesopotamian literature on love and I hope that it will stimulate the debate within the field, and deepen the interest of the general reader.

ACKNOWLEDGEMENTS

To each of the following for the permission to reproduce photographs as indicated: the Musée de Louvre (nos 3, 4–11) and the Bildarchiv Preußischer Kulturbesitz, Vorderasiatisches Museum Berlin (nos 1–2).

My thanks go to my anthropologist colleague and friend, Teri Brewer, for her suggestions and comments; to Jeremy Black for his critical reading of the manuscript, to Bendt Alster for letting me see drafts of some forthcoming articles and for his encouragement; to Professor W.G. Lambert and Tzvi Abusch for bibliographical assistance; to Tan Pearson for drawing the map; and to my friends Freya and Franz Krummel for their support and inspiration.

Cardiff, 1993

NOTES FOR
NON-ASSYRIOLOGIST
READERS

Due to the fact that German scholars composed the first lexical works on Akkadian and Sumerian, their principles of transliteration were influenced by German phonetics. The question of the actual pronunciation of both languages is of course, unanswerable, especially in the case of Sumerian, which is not related to any other linguistic group. Assyriologists meanwhile read transliterations, by convention, as if they were written in German.

Hence the vowel 'a' is as in English 'far'; 'e' as in English 'hence', 'i' as in 'is', and 'u' as in 'full'.

The letter 'š' stands for 'sh', 'ḫ' is pronounced as in Scottish 'loch'.

The grave and acute accents on certain syllables in transliterations, as well as subscripted numbers, indicate to the cuneiformist which sign, out of a group of homophones, is written in the text. It does not refer to pronunciation. Length-marks and circumflexes in Akkadian transliterations indicate either vowel-length or contractions.

In the translations, square brackets [ ] indicate gaps in the text, due to some damage of the tablet; text within square brackets is restored from other versions. Round brackets ( ) contain words not in the actual text, inserted to facilitate the understanding of the sentence in English. Dots ... mean that the translator does not attempt to render a word or passage. A question mark following a word denotes that the chosen English equivalent is considered doubtful by the translator. When a word is written in capital letters this means that the phonetic value is uncertain.

All dates are BC unless otherwise stated.

ABBREVIATIONS

AHw   W. von Soden, *Akkadisches Handwörterbuch*
CAD   *Chicago Assyrian Dictionary*
CH   Code of Hammurabi
CT   *Cuneiform Texts from the British Museum*
MSL   *Materialien zum Sumerischen Lexikon*
RA   *Reallexikon der Assyriologie*

Abbreviations for cuneiform text editions follow *CAD*.

CHRONOLOGICAL CHART

BC	Periods in Mesopotamia	
3500		
	Uruk period	first pictographic texts
3000		
	Early Dynastic period (c.2800–2270)	Old Sumerian literature
2500		
	Sargonic dynasty (c.2270–2083) Neo-Sumerian period (c.2100–2004)	Old Akkadian
2000	Third Dynasty of Ur/Isin–Larsa	royal hymns, courtly love poetry
	Old Babylonian period (c.2000–1760)	
	Middle Babylonian period (c.1600–1000)	
1500	Kassite dynasty	
1000	Second Dynasty of Isin Neo-Assyrian period	
500	Neo-Babylonian period	Fall of Nineveh: 621 Babylon captured by Cyrus: 539

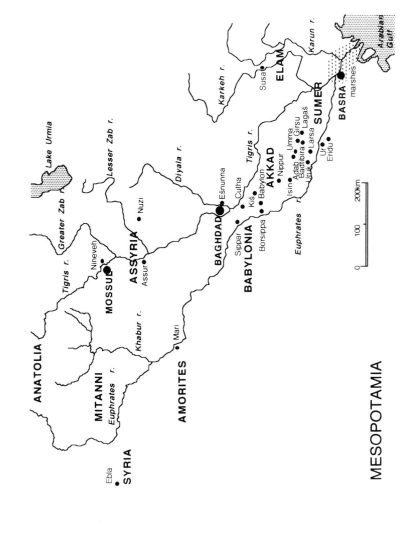

MESOPOTAMIA

ANATOLIA

Lake Urmia

Greater Zab r.

Lesser Zab r.

Tigris r.

SYRIA

Ebla

MITANNI

Euphrates r.

Khabur r.

Mari

AMORITES

Nineveh

MOSSUL

ASSYRIA

Assur

Nuzi

Diyala r.

BAGHDAD

Ešnunna

Cutha

Kiš

Sippar

Babylon

Borsippa

BABYLONIA

AKKAD

Nippur

Isin

Adab

Umma

Badtibira

Girsu

Lagaš

Uruk

Larsa

Ur

Eridu

Euphrates r.

Tigris r.

SUMER

BASRA

marshes

Susa

ELAM

Karkeh r.

Karun r.

Arabian Gulf

0   100   200 km

INTRODUCTION

And the woman was arrayed in purple and scarlet colour, and decked with gold and precious stones and pearls, having a golden cup in her hand full of abominations and filthiness of her fornication:
And upon her forehand was a name written, MYSTERY, BABYLON THE GREAT, THE MOTHER OF HARLOTS AND ABOMINATIONS OF THE EARTH.

These lines from the seventeenth chapter of the Book of Revelation associate Babylon with depravity of the senses and the iniquities of fornication. When Luther attacked the Roman Church for her low moral standards he compared her to the Whore of Babylon.[1] Seen through the perspective of post-exilic Hebrew literature, the civilization of Mesopotamia became synonymous with vice, and even Herodotus, though not generally given to moral judgements, remarks on the strangeness of local customs, especially what he believed to be the enforced, temporary prostitution of all women (I, 180).

It is only some hundred and sixty years ago that the modern world rediscovered the tangible remains of Assyria and Babylon. Since then, archaeologists and epigraphists, historians and linguists have been evaluating the reality of Mesopotamian civilization.

Through a fortunate historical coincidence, the discovery of a trilingual rock-inscription on the Iranian hills, the key to the decipherment of Akkadian was achieved almost simultaneously (1851 by Rawlinson).[2] Layard's find of the remains of Ashurbanipal's great library, with its useful lists of signs, words, synonyms, etc. considerably furthered the advancement of epigraphy. The understanding of Akkadian texts is to some extent helped by the fact that

1

the language is part of the Semitic group, and shares grammatical structures and vocabulary with related languages such as Hebrew and Arabic. The situation is quite different in respect to Sumerian, which has no discernible relation to any known language. We still have to some degree to rely on the attempts by ancient Akkadian grammarians to make sense of the Sumerian texts, as they provided the indispensable bilingual texts and lexical lists. The study of Akkadian has therefore progressed further and more rapidly. At the present time, the dictionary project undertaken by the University of Chicago is nearing completion for the Assyrian dictionary, while work on the Sumerian dictionary will continue until well into the next century. There is also no absolute agreement yet over the grammatical description of Sumerian, and the interpretation of literary texts is by no means unanimous.

The main reason for these difficulties is the medium of cuneiform writing itself. It is now clear that the impetus for the invention of writing in Mesopotamia was a desire not to communicate ideas but to facilitate bookkeeping. Some of these accounting tools are preserved in the form of marked tokens which referred to the standard commodities of exchange, sheep, grain, oil and cloth. The signs on these tokens represented the nature of the merchandise.[3] The use of seals, stamps as well as cylinders, widened the repertoire of communicable symbols, including now 'signs' for cities and individuals. The next step was to extend the semantic range of primary symbols by combining and juxtaposing individual signs. So, for instance, the sign for HEAD + sign for BOWL near the mouth part of HEAD means FOOD, or, by implication, TO EAT. Already at this stage, which is called pictographic because the references are primarily pictorial, the possibilities of some signs transcend the direct reference to the object depicted; as indicated above, the sign can include an activity as well as a commodity, a verbal idea as well as a noun. These texts were able to convey a message without reference to a particular language, in the same way as international traffic signs or mathematical notation can be 'understood' without having to be 'read'. A crucial development was the use of a sign representing a tangible object for its phonetic value. In Sumerian, the word AN meant 'heaven', but the sound corresponding to the syllable an had a variety of grammatical uses too. The sign AN could therefore stand for 'heaven', and also for 'God', or 'above', in a conceptual extension of the original symbol, as well as for the sound an, which would derive meaning from its grammatical or syntactic context only. This exploitation of homophony made it possible to express a particular spoken language, with the exclusion of others. When the Semitic inhabitants of Mesopotamia adapted this system for their quite different language, they encountered serious problems and ultimately contributed to its increased complexity and polyvalence. Because they took over the syllabic value of each sign, as well as its logographic meaning, they had to transfer the semantic value of the logographs by translating them into their language, which in turn provided additional syllabic values. This writing system is implicitly ambiguous, as meaning can be conveyed either by symbols (logographs) or phonetic signs (syllables). To alleviate the confusion of the reader, the scribes could indicate the context of a cluster of signs by specific markers, the so-called determinatives. These were related to the conceptual backbone of cuneiform scribal education, the lists of words arranged under acrographic headings which denoted a common frame of reference (personal names, professions, cities, rivers, mountains, animals, stars, as well as the complete repertoire of material culture: things made of wood, reed, cloth, metal, clay, etc.). The Egyptian hieroglyphic system of writing was essentially similar, with a preference for logographic spellings glossed abundantly with determinatives. Chinese script, on the other hand, eliminates the ambiguity caused by a phonetic representation of the spoken word by concentrating on the meaning conveyed by symbols only. This system proved to be a uniting force in a vast country with many different local dialects. The so-called alphabetic scripts (this includes here also those with an inherent vowel, as in Devanagari, or implied vowels, as in the Hebrew and Arabic scripts), on the other hand, abstract the meaning of words from the representation of their sounds alone; as each word is seen as the sum of its constituent phonemes, and the individual signs have no meaning as such.[4] In comparison with the more or less totally logographic system (e.g. Chinese) and the more or less totally alphabetic system (e.g. Italian), cuneiform writing is polyvalent and multi-dimensional because it allows meaning to be expressed in several ways. The use of logographs allows the symbolic to be integrated in the written text. In those texts which we call literary, in so far as they are not concerned with the communication of messages, the polyvalence of this writing system is exploited to great effect. The author disposed of a whole range of artifices that went beyond the spoken language and were only discernible to the reader. The choice of expression between logograph and syllable allowed a complex interplay of ambiguities and allusions. By referring to the symbolic order of language in writing by the deliberate use of logographs, the written text made the complex system of references transparent and thereby gained an advantage over the spoken word.

This multi-dimensionality of the text has a physical correlate in the tablet itself. The medium of cuneiform writing is clay. In the process of writing, the scribe pressed his stylus into the soft surface of his tablet. The marks appear therefore below the surface. To read the sign, one has to hold up the tablet and move it this way or that, in order to determine the original slant of the stylus. This slant is caused by the direction of the hand holding the instrument and constitutes the salient feature of the various strokes of which each sign is composed. Cuneiform writing is therefore physically three-dimensional. It was ideally suited for the medium of soft clay as the signs could be impressed with considerable speed. On a hard material, as on ceremonial inscriptions on stone, metals, etc., the signs were chiselled into the surface, laboriously, in low relief. The modern epigraphist rarely makes copies in clay. Copying a cuneiform tablet means reproducing its aspect on a two-dimensional surface, usually a piece of paper, drawing the signs with a pen to make a perspective of the original. The next step consists in the transcription or transliteration, whereby the signs are rendered into the modern alphabet with the help of sign-lists that are to some extent based on original cuneiform compilations. Invariably, the epigraphist offers his or her personal perception of the sign, and only the experienced colleague will be able to deduce the original shape of the sign from this transcribed value. The range of inherent meaning becomes even narrower in translation, when the trans-literated text is expressed in a particular modern language. Most translations are stylistically unsatisfactory because Sumerologists especially stick to a kind of unofficial and idiosyncratic code of alluding to cuneiform signs and expressions. The initiate is well able to deduce from Kramer's or Jacobsen's turns of phrase their Sumerian equivalent, but for any reader untrained in the conventions of this discipline it is quite impossible to form any idea of the text's original complexity and polyvalence. The bulky corpus of footnotes which invariably accompany the scholarly edition of texts do to some extent make up for the lost 'depth', but they are generally excluded from the 'popular' editions. It is therefore not surprising that this astonishing corpus of literature is hardly known, and has not received much attention from cultural linguists, students of literature, historians or even psychoanalysts, who, since Freud, are attracted to ancient sources. By reducing the plasticity of the originals to one-dimensional and practically meaningless texts, the conscientious scholar ensures, in spite of his best intentions, that they remain as unread as when they were still buried in the sands.

But in spite of all the problems that the modern scholar and the modern reader encounter, we have to acknowledge that the system of cuneiform writing was ideally suited to literature as an art form. In fact it remained the most successful of the arts in Mesopotamia; its visual style, compared to the assured elegance of Egypt, is at best grandiose.

This study is concerned with a particular aspect of this literature, the subject of eroticism and sexuality. I believe that the inherent possibilities of cuneiform for expressing layers of meaning are particularly interesting here. In spite of Foucault's contention that the very concept 'sexuality' is an invention of the nineteenth century AD, the ambiguous nature of sexual love was well understood in ancient and traditional societies, but was obviously subject to different cultural values.

The language of love, the erotic metaphor, was used to write about many different topics, from cosmogony to the function of kingship, in keeping with the 'anthropomorphistic' perspective of thought current at the time. Other genres of literature deal directly with the subject of sexual relationships, mainly between men and women. I am not concerned with a history of sexuality (like Foucault), or of sexual behaviour or moral attitudes, as there is not enough material from non-literary texts. We have law-codes regulating divorce and concubinage, sanctioning adultery and rape, but the legal implications of such codes are still debated. Closer to real life are the actual court documents which record the decisions arrived at by the official judiciary. Most are concerned with contractual problems over ownership, and divorces meriting the expense of a court-case were invariably tied up with the division of property and inheritance. Then we have some private letters, but rarely do we find expression of personal feeling in these letters, let alone passion. As very few people were literate, letters had to be read out aloud, hardly a private form of communication.

The literary texts are our main form of information on the cultural value of love and sensuality. When they were first translated, Sir

James Frazer's *Golden Bough* had an enormous impact on the interpretation of these works. Every love-song, every hymn that mentioned Inanna and Dumuzi, as well as all the archaeological artefacts with sexual scenes, were automatically classified as being pertinent to a 'Sacred Marriage' ritual, with the aim of perpetuating 'fertility'. The notion is still current among contemporary and eminent Assyriologists. But this simplifies the complexity of the subject far too much. The texts themselves did not form a coherent genre, say 'romantic fiction', 'courtly love poetry', or even 'pornography'. An Akkadian catalogue of songs did group together those whose titles suggest a primarily erotic content, but this is an exception.

The majority of these compositions have divine protagonists. We hear of the courtship of the goddess Inanna and her young lover, the shepherd Dumuzi, of sensuous Enki, gentle Lugalbanda, and the jealousy of Ṣarpānîtu, the wife of Marduk. We have intimate poetic dialogues between gods and their spouses which ritually evoke their conjugal sex-life. Some may not have been intended for any ritual use at all, while others, which appear quite secular to our understanding, may have been used in initiations to cultic functions. The scholars affiliated to the famous 'Tablet Houses', the scribal training centres of the Old Babylonian period, collected texts from previous times, and no doubt composed new works, which in turn became literary classics. There is also the influence of the oral medium of song, proverb and narrative, which contributed to the development of cuneiform literature. The distinctions between a religious content (supplied by the presence of divine names) and a secular intention (e.g. entertainment at court) is not always clear. Our conceptual categories do not fit the material, and we find little enlightenment in the native librarian system (what exactly is a 'tigi' or a 'bal-bal-e'?).

For this book I have tried to group together texts with some internal coherence of subject-matter and context. I have also ordered the sources, very broadly, according to the date of their composition.[5] The reason for this division is the fact that many Sumerian compositions were only transmitted until the first centuries of the second millennium, but did not become assimilated into the traditional canon of Mesopotamian literature, for which the library of Ashurbanipal is our main source. A number of those that were not passed on have a strong erotic component. I also believe that there is a certain ideological coherence in the earlier Sumero-Akkadian tradition, which is different from the later, primarily Akkadian sources, although I admit that this is hard to substantiate with any precision.

I have further grouped the older materials into those texts that deal primarily with the male perspective on sexuality, and those that present the subject mainly from a feminine point of view. However, this should not suggest a dualistic system, or that there was a general opposition between male and female attitudes, merely that a number of literary works primarily concern men, while others are concerned with women. In those given over to the female perspective, I have separated, sometimes provisionally, the different 'voices' of women. I found that the 'bride' expresses a certain view of the erotic, distinct from that of the older woman, be she now a 'wife', or a 'professional lover'. These variant perspectives allow us to appreciate the subtle variations of perception and the literary artifices applied to convey them.

Some topics, such as Sex in the Underworld, the Divine Marriage, and Deviant Sexuality, were treated in both Sumerian and Akkadian texts. The chapters discussing these issues integrate this material. The later chapters deal primarily with Akkadian sources from the later second and early first millennia. For the later, primarily Akkadian sources, I have used literary categories rather than those of perspective; this reflects the specialization of Akkadian literature. Narratives, or epic works, with human rather than divine protagonists, were an important new genre. The development of magic texts, incantations and rituals is also better represented in Akkadian, as are omen texts. The tendency to allocate the subject of love and sexuality to a ritualistic, magic context is also typical for this material.

I have tried to sketch out the cultural–historical background to the various categories, and to quote appropriate sources from non-literary texts in order to illuminate their meaning. Occasionally I have found it useful to introduce cross-cultural comparisons, or adopt a perspective of cultural anthropology, to approach the topic from another angle and to introduce the methods of the social sciences into the somewhat isolated discipline of Assyriology. I have also quoted parallels from various languages and historical periods, because of their literary relevance. The main reason for such digressions is to raise a point and stimulate the debate.

I have also allowed myself to use intuition, to listen to an echo in my own imagination, to let the texts reach my understanding beyond the philological barrier. A subject like eroticism inevitably involves the researcher's personal attitudes. I wanted these texts to probe my sensibilities, and they have in turn affected the way I think about these matters now. I agree with Camille Paglia that we have to acknowledge not only the intellectual references of our respective disciplines, but own up to the impact of the whole cultural background of our generation, post-Freudian, post-Jungian, post-modern, post-feminist, post-1960s liberalism, *actualiter* AIDS-awareness, etc.

Aware as I am of the dangers of distorting the sources to suit my interpretations, I have refrained from making my own translations, except for rendering original French or German into English, or occasionally choosing a different synonym. My limited linguistic competence in Sumerian would not have made such attempts advisable for the sources in this language. I have therefore used the translations made by reputable epigraphists in their editions, and allowed the different styles of translation to stand as evidence for the variety of solutions offered.

I have added a short glossary, which explains some of the historical and archaeological terms used throughout the book. For further background information see Hallo and Simpson 1971, the *Cambridge Ancient History*, Hrouda, 1971, Redman 1978, Nissen 1988, Milroop 1992.

Part I

THE SUMERO-AKKADIAN TRADITION OF THE THIRD AND EARLY SECOND MILLENNIA

1

THE COSMOLOGICAL
ARTICULATION OF
SEXUALITY

At some point every culture formulates beliefs about the origin of
the familiar world. Sometimes, especially in literate societies, these
concepts are worked into a coherent theory to account for the
primary dynamics of the universe, the earth and 'all that is therein'.
But even when only certain aspects of life or society are traced to a
primary stage, the patterns of thought involved reflect specific
cultural conditions as well as experience common to all humanity
that are projected into a primordial Other Time or Past.

Unlike the Greeks, Mesopotamian writers did not describe some
of their literary works as 'myths' and they did not set out to
compose 'cosmogonies'. But many texts that concern the function
and the deeds of deities or the origin of institutions have a
mythological and cosmological framework. By beginning this exam-
ination of eroticism and sexuality with a section on cosmology I am
honouring a hallowed Mesopotamian scribal tradition.

Scribes employed by a temple tended to focus on the god/dess
they served and their cosmogonic speculations were related to the
prevalent theological thought associated with these deities. The
relative currency of their cosmological pattern varied with the rise
and fall in the political fortunes of the gods' cities and temples. There
were also regional differences. All this is common to literary
production in polytheistic systems. We need only think of the
various creation myths in ancient Egypt, Greece or India.

In this chapter I shall not attempt to offer a comprehensive survey
of all relevant cuneiform texts,[1] but concentrate on the use of the
sexual metaphor as it occurs in the various cosmogonic models.

In some aetiological narratives or 'myths of origin' the texts begin
with the phrase 'when so-and-so did not yet exist' or 'when so-and-

11

so did not have a name'. The consequences of this absence are then described. For instance, before the appearance of cattle and grain, the gods had only grass to eat. We are then told of how an institution or commodity to remedy this situation was introduced. By elaboration this process can be taken further back to arrive at a primary stage of creation. This is generally characterized as undifferentiated and formless, but not Nothing. Mesopotamian cosmogonies, like those of most traditional cultures, do not invisage a *creatio ex nihilo*, but stress the inert potentiality of some *prima materia*. The beginning of creation is the beginning of a process of division and subdivision, the setting in motion of a dynamic principle. While in Egypt or India we find several analogies for this unfolding divergence, from the biological to the abstract, the Cosmic Egg to the Word of the Demiurge, the Mesopotamian systems have a strong anthropomorphic component and within this conceptual framework the most persistent pattern is that of sexual reproduction. The descent of generations of human beings has its equivalent in the sphere of divine beings and the forces of nature. Many ancient Near Eastern texts are therefore structured as retrogressive genealogies. The Book of Genesis, for instance, begins with the creation of Heaven and Earth, and then the organization of the world progresses to the first human couple, Adam and Eve, and their descendants down to the twelve sons of Joseph, who in turn are the ancestors of the Twelve Tribes of Israel.

But one must not take the strictly patrilinear structure of the Hebrew composition as the only possible model for integrating sexual metaphor in the cosmogonic process. The following models demonstrate that there was much more variation in the constituents of the primal scenario and the function and nature of reproduction and sexual roles.

THE SOUTHERN OR ERIDU MODEL

Without trying to submit Mesopotamian mythology to a geographical reductionism it is worth considering that the natural features of a landscape do at times inform the imagery of mythical language. This is very obviously the case in much of the Australian or Native American material, but the impact of mountain peaks, rivers, lakes and springs, etc. is almost ubiquitous.

My division of the Mesopotamian system into a 'southern' and 'northern' model tries to correlate the terms 'Eridu' and 'Nippur' theology[2] with their geographical situation. But it should not be taken as the basis of a binary orientation affecting Mesopotamian thought. Sumerian tradition held that 'after kingship had descended from Heaven, Eridu became the first seat of kingship'.[3]

Eridu (the modern name of the site is Abu Shahrein) was situated at the edge of the great marshes. With their characteristic reed thickets and wide lagoons, they survive precariously in southern Iraq.[4] The marshes have water in abundance but little stable land which can be used for large-scale growing of crops. Survival depends on a careful adaptation to the peculiar ecological conditions, and is not conducive to significant increase of population. The classical Mesopotamian civilization, however, was based on surplus production of cereals, made possible by putting normally arid zones under the plough and irrigating the land by an intricate system of canals, dikes and ditches. In these basically desert conditions, water was of fundamental importance to the economy. It became one of the most significant symbols for representing well-being, fertility and creation. The marshes of the South may well have actually been one of the oldest habitats of Mesopotamia (Green 1975: 47–50), as the native tradition always maintained. Their proximity to the wide lagoons contributed to the formulation of the so-called Eridu theology. The basic symbol associated with Eridu is ENGUR (Labat No. 484); its main temple was called E. engura. The same sign preceded by the symbol for 'water' was used as a determinative for waterways, river, canal, lake, etc. The realm of the divine in this context is not the sky or the earth, but water. The sign ENGUR can also be read as nammu. This is a synonym of abzu, which is usually translated as the 'watery deep' or 'sweet water ocean' and defined as the subterranean source of water that emerges from the ground, from wells and springs, not rain-water. The importance of the abzu was recognized in the ritual. Temples throughout Mesopotamia and throughout history had basins or pools to symbolize and represent the abzu. Sumerian texts describe the abzu as lying below the surface of the earth, where the water deity lives. In later mythological texts, most notably in the Babylonian *Enuma eliš* (see below pp. 14–15), Apsû (the Akkadian form of abzu) is personified as male.

The Sumerian personification of ENGUR was female and called Nammu. God-lists and other texts describe her as 'the mother who gave birth to Heaven and Earth', 'mother, first one, who gave birth to the gods of the universe'[5] or as 'Mother of Everything'. She is a goddess without a spouse, the self-procreating womb, the primal matter, the inherently fertile and fertilizing waters of the abzu. Nammu stands for the female sex as the one apparently able to create spontaneously, as expressed in a hymn to the temple of Eridu; 'E. engura, womb of abundance'.[6] Nammu does not play a significant role in the corpus of texts that has survived, nor was she much of a mythological personality. She may either belong to an older stratum of Sumerian or pre-Sumerian deities who did not become subjects of literary compositions, or owe her appearance in the hymns and god-lists to a tendency to anthropomorphize general concepts such as abzu or ENGUR and thereby integrate it into the Sumerian pantheon but without really becoming a 'character'.

In Eridu itself, the archaeologists discovered a long series of shrines and temples.[7] The first solid structure, a little room made of mud-brick, dates from the late sixth millennium. We do not know who was worshipped there, since the earliest cuneiform records date from the first quarter of the third millennium, and they associate Eridu with a male deity, Enki. Enki's name bears no obvious connection with water, unless one concedes that ki can also stand for 'below'. He is known as the son of Nammu and there has been some argument that Nammu's divine functions had at some stage been transferred to her son,[8] as he is never considered to be at the origin of creation himself. Enki always remains the Son. His mythological personality is very complex, partly because of the many associations with water: he became a god of wisdom, crafts and magic, also of fertility; and we shall see that he even achieved some status as a phallic and creator god. At any rate, he sometimes appears as a Trickster.

In the Babylonian tradition, ENGUR, the self-contained *prima materia*, is split into two components, Apsû and Tiāmat. Grammatically speaking, Apsû is masculine and Tiāmat (etymologically related to the Semitic word for 'sea') is feminine. The 'Single Mother' matrix is hereby replaced by a couple to represent the primary constituents of the universe. The important Babylonian text from the late second millenium, called *Enuma eliš* after its initial words, describes the beginning of the universe:

> When on high heaven had not (yet) been created,
> Earth below had not (yet) been brought into being,
> When Apsû primeval, their begetter,
> Primal Tiāmat, their progenitress,
> (Still) mingled their waters together,

When no grassland had been formed, no reed thicket laid out,
When no gods whatever been brought into being,
Were not yet existent, their destinies undetermined,
(At that time) the gods were created within them.

(Held 1976: 231)

The Assyrian version specifies that Ea (the Sumerian equivalent of Enki) and his wife Damkina were the first pair of gods created, while the Babylonian text has the sequence Lahmû-Lahāmu, Anšar-Kišar, followed by Ea. The text explicitly states that the Apsû and Tiāmat 'mingled their waters'. This might mean that they constitute *de facto* one element (though, as often explained, probably as a mixture of sweet and salty waters). On the other hand, this mingling has been interpreted as a metaphor for sexual procreation (Lambert 1981: 220), although this text generally avoids sexual metaphors. The first generations of gods were torn within the undifferentiated body of water, and even the later deities just emerge, complete, with their respective spouses. For the sake of symmetry and perhaps for the benefit of an audience no longer familiar with matrilinear references, the primal matter was artificially divided into complementary, male–female elements. But the older model of a singular source of life is still easily recognizable. It is also interesting that, in the course of the narrative, it is the female of the original couple, Tiāmat, who poses the most serious threat to the younger generation of gods, after her husband, Apsû, had been vanquished by his own 'grandson', Ea-Enki. The ensuing events, especially the ideas that the ordering of the universe could only take place after the violent overthrow of Tiāmat, is quite another subject and cannot concern us here.

The Eridu model assumes the primacy of the watery element, represented by the symbol of ENGUR = Abzu = Nammu, the sweet-salty, mud-marsh lagoon, teeming with life. The mythological signifier of the dynamic creative aspect is Nammu, while Apsû stands for the inert, permeable ubiquity that characterizes the physical element. Subsequent differentiation within creation occurs spontaneously and randomly. It is important to note that reproduction depending on heterosexual mating is not a primary metaphor in this model. However, this does not exclude erotic connotations: the marshes were the proverbial locus for sexual encounters (see later) and the connotations of abundance, seeping moisture, soft mud, etc. have sensuous overtones of a feminine and/or autoerotic kind. There is an interesting parallel in the ancient Lower Egyptian cosmogony

15

of Heliopolis, which was also situated in a marshy delta. The creator deity Atum sits on his island surrounded by water, masturbates and thereby initiates a heterosexual lineage.

THE NORTHERN MODEL

The lagoon and marsh situation of southern Mesopotamia contributed to the formation of the primary symbol of the Eridu system, the fertile and fertilizing Abzu. Further north, in the alluvial plain, the vista is dominated by a huge sky and the wide, flat earth. Consequently, the duality of Sky and Earth features more prominently in the works associated with the city of Nippur, the home of the Sumerian national god Enlil:

> Heaven was born of its own accord, Earth was born of its own accord. Heaven was abyss (= ENGUR), Earth was abyss.
> (Lambert 1981: 219)

Heaven and Earth are here both regarded as *prima materia* and generators of life; this is made explicit by the fact that they are both equated with the symbol ENGUR. In this particular passage Heaven and Earth emerge at the same time, but other texts make one exist before the other. In the god-list An = Anum, for example, Earth existed before Heaven: An, the sky-god is said to be the offspring of Earth (here Uraš, masculine) and Earth (Ninuraš, feminine). The division of Earth into a couple recalls the scholarly redaction of the *Enuma eliš* and the pair Tiāmat-Apsû.

A genealogy of Enlil also considers the Earth as the source of all life but uses the maternal, agricultural metaphor: 'Earth where barley sprouted', generating life on her own accord (Lambert 1981: 220). In another text, however, Enlil and his consort Ninlil derive descent from an ancestral and rather shadowy couple, Enki and Ninki.[9]

Sometimes Sky comes first. So we read in a text that traces the ancestry of the toothworm:

> After Anu [had created heaven], Heaven had created Earth, Earth had created rivers, rivers created canals, canals created the marsh, the marsh created the worm.
> (Heidel 1951: 72)

However, one does get the impression that the composer of this text was not very particular about the exact order of cosmic events; he rushes to get to the aetiological point of his narrative. Since 'Sky' could also stand for the deity An, whose position in the Mesopotamian pantheon was that of a patriarch of all gods, the text might refer here to the hierarchical structure of command rather than a cosmological proposition.

The third variation, which is in fact more widespread than any of the other two, has Heaven and Earth joined in primordial unity. But unlike the artificial distinction between Apsǔ and Tiāmat or Uraš and Ninuraš, who both symbolize the same element, the difference between Heaven and Earth exists in reality; they are seen as complementary opposites. In Mesopotamian cosmology, the earth is floating above water (the abzu) and the vault of the sky is suspended like an inverted bowl above her. But this could only take place after their initial union had been broken. The separation of Heaven and Earth became the first dynamic event in cosmogony. In some aetiological myths this deed is ascribed to Enlil (in the myth about the Pickaxe), but the text does not elaborate on how this was achieved. In *Gilgameš, Enkidu and the Netherworld*, 'Anu took over the Sky and Enlil the Earth'; this refers to a political division of spheres of influence rather than a cosmic event (Kramer 1944: 33–7). The most elaborate description of the separation of Heaven and Earth occurs in the *Enuma eliš*, when Marduk splits the body of vanquished Tiāmat in two halves like an oyster, then lifts the upper part to form the sky while the lower part becomes the earth. The Babylonian composition manages to weave both cosmogonic models into one coherent sequence of events: the separation of Heaven and Earth signals the beginning of Marduk's organization of the world. As a demiurge he assigns to the planets their courses, fashions rivers and mountains, and creates mankind. The forceful separation is also alluded to in the Hurrian myth of Ullikummi, where the implement used to cut them apart is of some importance to the plot (Güterbock 1951–2).

Heaven and Earth, irrespective as to the manner of their original state, united or not, are sometimes described as a couple. This is a practically universal metaphor, but one that had comparatively little currency in Mesopotamia. It occurs in an archaic text from about the middle of the third millennium, a small fragment of a larger composition (van Dijk 1964: 34ff.). The language is metaphorical and the interpretation of the passage remains provisional. The vulva of Earth is mentioned, and a hole in the earth is to be filled with water. An, the Sky, 'stood up like a young man (and) An and Ki roared together'.

More explicit, indeed highly lyrical, is the 'Disputation between Wood and Reed', another essentially aetiological composition (van Dijk 1964: 45).

> The great Earth (Ki) made herself glorious, her body
>   flourished with greenery.
> Wide Earth put on silver metal and lapis-lazuli ornaments,
> Adorned herself with diorite, calcedony, cornelian and
>   diamonds.
> Sky (An) covered the pasture with (irresistible) sexual
>   attraction, presented himself in majesty,
> The pure young woman (Earth) showed herself to the pure
>   Sky,
> The vast Sky copulated with the wide Earth,
> The seed of the heroes Wood and Reed he ejaculated into her
>   womb.
> The Earth, the good cow, received the good seed of Sky in her
>   womb.
> The Earth, for the happy birth of the plants of Life, presented
>   herself.

Like a young bride, Earth reveals herself in all her splendour to Sky. An makes love to Ki and pours his 'fluid' into her body. The sign a can stand for water as well as for male semen; in this cosmic act of sex the sperm of Sky is the rain falling on the Earth, a rare motif in Mesopotamian mythology, as Lambert justly noticed. It is also interesting that the Mother symbolism in Mesopotamian thought is more often related to the watery element (Nammu), as a source of all life and fertility, than the Earth, who in this part of the world only yields fruit when irrigated.

SEXUAL REPRODUCTION AS THE SOURCE OF DIVERSITY

Whether the *prima materia* is defined as one single substance which at some point generates living beings, or as a whole composed of two complementary elements, a sort of Yin and Yang as in Chinese thought, the actual process of diversification begins with sexual reproduction. In the myth about the 'Marriage of Martu' we have a prologue that refers specifically to the primordial existence of a city called Ninab. This is juxtaposed with the non-, or rather not-yet existence of another locality:

> Ninab existing, Kiritab not existing,
> The holy existing, the holy aga not existing,
> Holy herbs existing, holy cedars not existing,
> Holy salt existing, holy naga not existing,
> Copulation, [kissing] existing,
> Birth-giving in the meadows existing.
>
> (lines 1–6; Kramer 1993: 11)

With the statement that sexuality and reproduction were in place, the actual narrative begins which concerns the marriage of the nomad god Martu with a Sumerian, city-dwelling, goddess called Adnigkidu.

The general diversification of creation may happen right at the beginning (Heaven and Earth) or after some androgynous or autoerotic phase, but at some point heterosexual relations are the normal procedure. A number of divine genealogies and god-lists express the progressive differentiation of deities by male–female couples who each produce another pair, and so forth. The pattern for ancestral lineages of deities derives from patrilinear genealogies. The model of sexual reproduction within a patrilinear structure has one major problem, that of incest. In this scheme the sexual partner of the mother equals the father of her children and the resulting pair of offspring are *ipso facto* brother and sister. Lambert (1981: 221) has pointed out that the sibling incest taboo in Mesopotamia may have influenced the phraseology of some cosmogonic texts, especially the move towards abstraction. It was said that the generations of gods did evolve in parallel pairs, as it were, but they were 'manifestations of evolution' rather than a sequence of incestuous generations.

There is one text which tackles the incest problem from a different angle. It is a curious and rather fragmentary tale of uncertain provenance, called the Theogony of Dunnu (Jacobsen 1984). It describes a sequence of divine ancestors who practised incest and parricide as well as matricide. Then the text becomes unintelligible, although later parts mention well-known Babylonian gods such as Ellil, Nusku and Ninurta. It is thought that the disorderly and outrageous pattern of behaviour was made to contrast with more 'civilized' norms, but as the relevant portions of the tablets are missing it is impossible to speculate on the structure of this change.

It is clear from this brief survey of cosmological ideas that there were various different ideas about the primal scenario. The notion of a watery matrix was the most widely accepted one and it is generally linked with a female creative principle. But while the actual control over the process of primary creation could be ascribed to various agents or gods, depending on the theological slant of the text, the dynamic process of creation, the unfolding diversification, is always symbolized by a male–female pair who mate to produce further offspring, and so on. This view recognizes the fundamental purpose of sexuality as a means of reproduction and creative organization of the universe. Modern theorists of genetics and biology have come to very similar conclusions (Jones 1993).

2

MASCULINE SEXUALITY IN SUMERIAN LITERATURE

ERECTING THE PHALLUS: ENKI[1] AND CREATION

Instead of presenting the available cuneiform sources on sexuality and eroticism in Mesopotamian literature in chronological order, I have found it useful to divide the material according to its content, and furthermore into a group of those texts that deal with the male perspective and those that express primarily the feminine experience. The former is the subject of several fairly long and complex narratives, the latter is mainly found in the poetic repertoire.

Both perspectives are represented by a paradigmatic mythological figure: Enki and the goddess Inanna. Enki is the only Mesopotamian deity with explicit phallic characteristics, although one must remember that phallicism never flourished in this culture the way it did after the Aryan invasion of India, or even in Pharaonic Egypt or classical antiquity. The relative rarity of phallic symbolism is also evident in the archaeological remains, where nude male figures or phallic symbols are comparatively rarer than naked females and depictions of the vulva. Inanna, though as complex a mythic personality as Enki, retained her unequivocal association with eroticism in spite of periodical shifts of emphasis in the texts, while Enki's phallic associations were decidedly more in evidence in Sumerian literature than in Akkadian texts, where his counterpart Ea was mainly revered for his wisdom and magic power. I shall use these deities as parameters in our discussion, on the understanding that I am singling out particular aspects of their character for the specific context of this book. Other gods and goddesses will be integrated into this framework as appropriate.

✻

21

Enki's background was, as we have seen, Eridu, close to the marshes, where he resided in his temple, the E-engura. Archaeologists uncovered thick deposits of fish bones from daily offerings to him. Eridu was never the seat of a dynasty and had little obvious political impact, its prestige being mainly derived from the antiquity of the site itself. Enki's own functions and powers stem from his association with water. We have already explored the cosmological aspect of this element in Mesopotamian thought. We have also seen that Enki is a secondary personification, taking over, as it were, from his mother, Nammu, the Mother of All Gods. This shift of generations is significant. Nammu, and the Babylonian equivalent couple Apsû and Tiāmat, represent the primeval potential of the element in an as yet undifferentiated form. Enki, however, is also called Nudimmud, which means 'the one who creates'. He does not create the way Nammu created, by inherent fertility, but by force of his intelligence and his word. His most popular epithet is the 'wise' or, better, 'crafty' one, as his wit does not exclude deviousness. Other male gods, notably An and Enlil, also create through the power of their utterance, but they are associated more with the cosmic organization, while Enki is credited with having made the world a place fit for human beings, having invented them to begin with. We shall see below how he organized the world.

He made the Apsû his home, having tamed and subdued the dangerous aspects of the unruly watery deep, as the *Enuma eliš* so vividly describes. But he is powerless against the forces of nature, the storm and flood, which are in the possession of Enlil, the most uncompromising and forceful of gods. Enki controls the waters within the context of Sumerian civilization, where the intelligent management of the element provided the economic basis for its very existence.

The purifying power of water, like that of fire, is an essential substance in magic rituals and by the second millennium Enki's intelligence was mainly associated with efficacious spells.

The source of Enki's creative and reproductive potential was also linked to water. There is the inherent fecundity of muddy water, usually referred to as the 'fathering mud of the Apsû' – with its self-generating force we encountered in context with cosmogony – and there is the *semen virile*, the 'fluid' of the penis, as the Sumerian expresses it. We shall see how all these various aspects underline the construction of Enki's theological personality and his demand for authority.

Enki and the World Order is the modern title of a highly polemical text, written like most literary compositions during the third dynasty of Ur or just before it (Benito 1969). It is quite a long text; some 445 lines are preserved, the last 20 are lost. It will be quoted here at some length to show how the god's claims to authority are built up.

> Exalted master of Heaven and Earth, the self-reliant,
> Father Enki, engendered by a bull, begotten by a wild bull,
> Prized by Enlil, the Great Mountain, loved by holy An.

These first few lines establish the tenor of the composition, to integrate Enki as a full member of the great Sumerian triad of male deities. 'Wild bull' or 'bison' is a common epithet for gods, stressing untamed masculinity and strength. Here it stands for An, the patriarch of the gods. Enki is claimed as the product of his seed. He is also the younger brother of Enlil, who himself is the undisputed 'first-born', very much the 'managing director' of the pantheon and national god of Sumer. Significantly, Nammu, his mother, is never mentioned once in the whole text. Enki's credentials take up the first 150 or so lines. They include the establishment of his temple in Eridu and its effect on the furthest reaches of the land, the power of his word to bring fruitfulness and vigour, to keep the inhabitants safe, to fertilize the land and its herds. With all these accomplishments he sees himself fit to be 'the great brother of the gods' (line 71), and fit 'to decree the fates' (line 76) with An and Enlil. The assembled Anunna gods, a sort of chorus in Sumerian poetry, take up his praise; he joins in joyfully and sets out to organize his temple and its rituals. On his sacred boat he embarks on a voyage through his newly established domain to try out the power of his command. He blesses the various regions, and he organizes the basis of Sumerian civiliz-ation by appointing a particular deity to be in charge of each sector: irrigation, the marshlands, rain, agriculture; brick-making and architecture; the steppe and pastoralism; boundaries and justice as well as weaving, 'the woman's art'. The tenor of the composition changes with the appearance of the goddess Inanna who complains that she has been left out. Enki points to her already considerable powers, especially those concerning warfare, although the final blessings of Inanna are not preserved.

In this text, the erection of Enki's potency, in the political sense, proceeds by several stages. First, through patrilinear descent: he is begotten and 'beloved' by An and supported by his older brother, Enlil, which legitimizes his position within the Sumerian pantheon at the time of composition. But in order to function fully as a god, Enki has to put his generative power to the test. He begins with 'logos', the efficacy of his spoken command:

> [A word from you] – and heaps and piles stack high with
> grain.
> [In the land] be it fat, be it milk, the stalls and sheepfolds
> produce it.
> (lines 27–8, Kramer and Maier 1989: 40)

It also affects the vitality of human beings:

> Your word invigorates the young man's heart,
> (impatiently) he gores in the yard like a thick-horned bull.
> Your word beautifies the young woman's countenance,
> They gaze at her in wonder in the cities.
> (lines 32–5)

Next, his physical presence influences the fertility of land and flocks:

> Father Enki, come close to the seeded land: let it bear healthy
> seed.
> Nudimmud, come close to the pregnant (or fecund) ewe: let it
> give birth to a healthy lamb.
> (lines 52–3, Kramer and Maier 1989: 40)

The enigmatic lines 195–6 refer to the mysterious inner source of Enki's potency, the place where the gods are born. It is significant that this sign written with the divine determinative stands for the mother-goddess Mummu; maybe in this context it is a reference to the maternal origin of Enki: ENGUR as personified by Nammu. In this text, which stresses the male aspects of power, this reference is only made obliquely.

In the middle of the section where Enki delegates authority to various minor deities there are some lines which are in marked contrast to the rest of the composition:

> After Father Enki lifted his eyes over the Euphrates,
> He stood up full of lust like an attacking bull,
> Lifted his penis, ejaculated,

Filled the Tigris (*sic*: meaning the Euphrates) with flowing
water

(lines 251–4)

and he does likewise with the Tigris:

He lifted (his) penis, he brought the bridal gifts,
Like a great wild bull he thrilled the heart of the Tigris, [stood
by] as it gave birth.

(lines 257–8)

The scenario is one of primordial absurdity: rivers without water. As
we noted before, it was a common literary device to introduce acts
of creation with a statement of an elementary deficiency – a river
without water is not a river. And how does the water god remedy
this situation? Quite simply, with his 'fluid'; remember that Sumerian a stands for 'water', 'sperm' and 'urine'. The passage has sexual
overtones through the reference to the 'bridal gifts' and the
metaphor of the 'lusty bull', but it also evokes the image of the god
releasing a powerful jet of urine. However, the instrument in either
case is his penis. The life-giving waters of the river are thereby firmly
associated with the masculine organ of Enki. At the same time, he
imitates his father An, the 'wild bull' who *illo tempore* made love to
Earth. So in lines 257–8, Enki 'brings the bridal gifts' and 'thrills' the
'inside' (the sign can also mean 'womb') of the Tigris, here presented
as a female partner who is inseminated. In this manner Enki
identifies with the phallus of the father and takes on the role of the
Phallus as the signifier of the Other (in the case of the river bereft
of water, water – his a). Seen in this light, these lines appear to stem
from an earlier level of tradition, or at least a deeper level of the
unconscious.[2]

The last section of the text deals with the confrontation between
Inanna and Enki. This has been regarded as the main motive of the
composition, to explain the extraordinary powers of the goddess.
But the fact is that Inanna has to come to Enki for her share of divine
prerogatives and although he rhetorically protests, 'what more could
we possibly add to you?' (line 424), he manages to assign her some
functions, although the bad state of the tablets does not allow us to
specify what these were. Inanna's request adds to Enki's status, and
she regards herself as one of the female deities who were allocated
their spheres of competence by him (like Nanše, Ašnan, Uttu, and
in Inanna's speech also Aruru, Ninisina, Ninmug and Nidaba). All

25

this implies that Enki in his role as representative of the 'Law of the Father' controls the realm of women as much as any other. Inanna never challenges Enki's authority, she merely worries about her share of divine prerogatives (me). The fact that she, the most powerful of goddesses, is dependent on Enki's largess underlines his absolute authority. His credentials are impeccable: as the son of An and the younger brother of Enlil he has his place in the hierarchy, he is able to use his command and intelligence effectively to manage the affairs of the world in a senior position and he controls the element water in a clearly masculine manner through the equation a/water = sperm/urine = fertility = Phallus.

Enki and Ninmah[3] has the same Sumerian classification, a 'praise' (za-mí), as *Enki and the World Order*, it develops the argument by a set of narratives rather than hymnic descriptions of utterances and actions. The main topic is the creation of mankind and its capacity to reproduce itself. But Enki is seen to assert his authority *vis-à-vis* a female representative of the pantheon. The second part of the text especially is a straightforward competition with a final judgement between Enki and Ninmah.

The question of sexuality is treated here primarily in relation to reproduction. Enki appears as the wise creator god Nudimmud, who, through his authority over the potential fertility of the Apsû, presides over the creation of mankind. The text is also concerned with the fundamental difference between humans and gods. Although humankind was destined to toil for the gods, the latter are responsible for its ability to procreate.[4]

The text begins with a rather fragmentary cosmogonic prelude which presents Heaven and Earth as the primal parents. Their offspring reproduce sexually; the goddesses were 'distributed between heaven and earth' (line 6), 'taken in marriage' and gave birth to other gods. At this stage the gods still had to do hard menial work and they asked Enki to provide them with substitutes who would liberate them from their toil. Enki is asleep in the depth of the Apsû and his mother Nammu has to wake him.[5] Enki oversees the task of creating Man, which is carried out by a team of female deities who use the clay of the Apsû as their raw material. The process is fairly complicated and involves various ritual proceedings.[6] The important fact is that Man was fabricated and was not the result of divine intercourse, although Enki is recognized as the virtual father.[7]

The gods assemble and praise the Enki's intelligence for having

26

freed them from their heavy workload. In the course of the celebrations Enki and Ninmah, the representative of the mother-goddesses, drink beer and get drunk. The following section of the text is usually understood as a contest between the two intoxicated deities. Ninmah creates at whim, and Enki has to decree a suitable fate for each creation. Ninmah proceeds to create six beings from the clay of the Apsû who all have congenital defects, such as lameness, blindness, sterility and absence of genitals. In each case Enki finds a solution. With the exception of the man who cannot retain his a (translated as 'urine' by Jacobsen or 'semen' by Benito and Kramer), whom he cures with blessed a (water), he finds social positions for the afflicted people. The aetiological message is clear: such beings were fashioned by a drunk goddess but their employment is sanctioned by Enki's wisdom. Then it is Enki's turn to create something for Ninmah to deal with. Unfortunately, the relevant passage is damaged; but Enki declares:

'The semen which the male member is emitting,
When discharged into a woman's womb that woman gives
    birth to it from her womb.

(Jacobsen 1987a: 162)

Jacobsen reconstructed the next few lines to mean that a woman was brought to Enki to give birth but that she aborted the foetus before its time. He did not elaborate as to whether it is Enki's sperm that should provide the fertilizing agent. In any case, a creature results whose name is Udmul ('My day is far off') and who is totally unviable; he is unable to eat, drink, sit, stand or even lie down. Ninmah declares herself unable to do anything for this unfortunate being, which causes Enki to recount once more how successfully he had dealt with her creations. Ninmah's reaction is still unclear, because of the poor state of preservation of the tablet at this point. She seems to lament her fate, or possibly curses Enki (as in *Enki and Ninhursag*). The final parts of the text are also fragmentary and far from completely intelligible. Jacobsen proposed that it contained a speech by Enki consoling Ninmah and reminding her that what the creature lacked was *her*, i.e. the woman's, contribution in successful gestation. Line 134 praises his penis; the rest is broken, except for the doxology which states that Ninmah could not rival the great lord Enki, whose 'praise is sweet'.

As the text is so badly preserved in crucial passages it is difficult to assign it any particular interpretation. It has been analysed in various different ways and the function of Udmul has attracted most attention (Draffkorn-Kilmer 1976). Kramer and Maier in their latest translation refrain from a reconstruction of the missing lines. This was attempted by Jacobsen, who reads the section concerning Udmul as a very complex description of an unsuccessful gestation. He regards Udmul as 'the phenomenon of abortion, the male seed (...) prematurely ejected' (Jacobsen 1987a: 153). He also regards Ninmah as the 'power in gestation' and Udmul's creation 'amounts to a nullification of her powers' (ibid.).

There are difficulties with these proposals, especially with Jacobsen's tendency to assign the gods the numinous powers of institutions or natural phenomena. Also, the description of Udmul does not tally with those in texts that deal with miscarriages.[8] However, the creation of human beings and their reproductive abilities are a major concern of this work. The first part gives the usual Mesopotamian *raison d'être* for mankind's existence: to alleviate the labour of the gods.[9] The second part concerns the imperfection of at least some sections of the population[10] and the origin of human reproduction. The gods took the goddesses 'in marriage' and thus the next generation was generated. Mankind is not related to the gods by direct or indirect descent, but has been fashioned separately. Although the substance, the 'clay' of the Apsû, is 'holy' and the stuff of all creation, the point is made that human beings were purpose-made. They also had to be able to continue their line spontaneously. The solution was to make them capable of reproducing by the same mechanism as the gods. The lines in the centre of the text comprise the theory of conception and birth: the germ of life, the male semen, is received by the womb, which gives birth. This is a decree of fate uttered by Enki. The male semen is able to create life; hence it is a divine substance, endowed on mankind by Enki.[11] The contest scene, with its deliberate creation of monstrosities, seems to function like a non-liability clause: human reproduction is fraught with things that can go wrong, and while some deformed people can be accommodated by society, others are simply unviable; even Ninmah, the representative of the mother-goddesses, is unable to rectify this. To what extent Enki crated Udmul to outsmart Ninmah is a moot point, considering the framework of a contest. Benito makes this intent the prime purpose of the text: 'Ninmah's incapability of performing the same actions as Enki, she has lost any chance to be in the pantheon with the same privileges. Her pretensions and efforts to be recognized as equal to Enki were unfruitful' (Benito

1969: 18). Kramer and Maier's point that it may also have political undertones, to justify Enki's and his city's superiority over Kesh, the city of the Mother-goddess, is impossible to substantiate: Kesh is never mentioned (Kramer and Maier 1989: 31). These views rely on the widespread assumption that Sumerian goddesses are after 'power' and 'positions of privilege in the pantheon'. There is absolutely no indication in this composition that this was indeed Ninmah's motive. Disputations were a favourite rhetorical device in the Sumerian curriculum and we have examples of all sorts of protagonists, the Hoe and Pickaxe, Cattle and Grain, Summer and Winter, etc. Nobody suggests that either of these contestants were after a supreme place in the hierarchy. But when it comes to a disputation between a goddess and a god, this is almost automatically suggested as the underlying reason.

The final passages of the work are again very damaged and the context is far from clear, but it concludes with the line 'may my phallus be praised'. It would seem that this refers to the source not only of Enki's creative powers, but of the procreative ability of human beings too. Mankind has a share in the divine because of sexual reproduction; just as the gods in the beginnings of time made love and gave birth, so do mortals; but the essential substance came from the male.[12]

3

ENKI AND NINHURSAGA
A myth of male lust?[1]

While *Enki and the World Order* describes the whole range of Enki's powers and considers the legitimacy of his position in the established Sumerian pantheon, *Enki and Ninhursaga* concerns Enki's relationship with female deities and aspects of sexuality and fertility. Both works are classed as 'praise' (za. mì) of Enki, but where the former was programmatic and unanimous in the eulogy of Enki's suitability, the latter introduces a threat to the god's very survival and there is an element of tension in the composition. As Enki's sexuality is an important theme, the language is full of word plays, allusions and *doubles entendres*. The innuendo here suits the personality of Enki, who is a witty as well as a sexy god. Present understanding of Sumerian seriously limits our appreciation of these linguistic displays and no translation can possibly do justice to the original.[2] In the following synopsis I am trying to highlight the ambiguity of key passages.

The setting of the story is not Eridu, Enki's traditional home, but Dilmun, a city famous for its springs of clear water and a prosperous international trading post.[3] The first episode is an aetiological account of Dilmun's origin (lines 1–63). It is a 'pure' and 'holy' place, where Enki lies with Ninsikila, the Maiden.[4] Alster contended that the gods were literally 'sleeping', 'but [that] there is no sexual relation between them'. However, there is nothing in the text to confirm this assumption[5] and it is more in keeping with the whole tenor of the work to begin with a scene where the gods are amorously entwined.

Dilmun, though 'holy', is strangely lacking in essential commodities, and the behaviour of people and animals differs from that of later times. These descriptions were probably meant to be funny and absurd. Ninsikila is obviously aware of the anomalous situation when she tells Enki:

> 'You have a given city!
> What good is your gift?
> A [city] that has no river quay?
> A city that has no fields, fallow and arable land.
> You have given a city.
> [You have given a city that has no ponds of sweet water!]'
>
> (29–39)

This seems to imply that Dilmun was Enki's (bridal?) gift to Ninsikila and she is quick to detect its flaw. But how could 'wise' Enki have made such a mistake? One possible clue is to remember that Enki is easy prey to intoxication, as is well known from other texts.[6] In this text his judgement is clouded not by drink but by sensuality: lying with the young goddess he has forgotten to provide water for the city! But he rises to the challenge with great aplomb and makes a magnificent speech, very much in the style of the blessings in *Enki and the World Order*, but probably satirical for all its pomposity. He not only promises abundant water but blesses Dilmun with everlasting agricultural and trade superiority (lines 39–50, plus fragment). Enki achieves all this by the power of his divine word; whatever he utters becomes reality:

> Dilmun became a (store)house on the quay for the country's produce.
> At this moment, on this day, and (under this) sun, thus is verily became.
>
> (62–3)

After this impressive display of verbal command, Enki turns to the physical expression of his vigour. The actual passage is ambiguous and different interpretations have been proposed for some of the lines. Before the goddess, now called Nintu(r),[7] he uses his penis.

> (He) was digging his phallus into the levee,
> plunging his phallus into the canebrake.
>
> (Jacobsen 1987a: 189)

Kramer and Maier (1989: 24) translate:

> Has his phallus fill the ditches full with semen,
> has his phallus glut the reeds with an overflow of sperm

while Attinger (1985: 15) renders the lines as:

avec son pénis, creuse un fossé pour l'eau,
avec son pénis, fait beigner les roseaux dans l'eau.[8]

Alster (ibid.: 17) concluded that these lines amount to masturbation 'among the reeds of the ditches' and refers to the passage in *Enki and the World Order* where Enki fills the Tigris and Euphrates with the effluent of his penis. But that passage is an isolated instance of phallic display, where the sexual aspect is only implied, with the river representing the female. Here the presence of the goddess and the whole atmosphere of the composition provide a very definitely erotic situation.[9] Jacobsen (1987a: 183) understood the passage as Enki trying to make love to Nintur 'by pushing his phallus into the canebrake, which is probably to be understood mythopoeically as the pubic hairs of the earth mother'. But the marshes and reed-beds were generally considered to have erotic associations.[10] Any activity there can be a metaphor for sex, and Enki uses his phallus quite explicitly. The female body itself was often likened to the earth and the damp area of the marshes especially provided an apt metaphor for female genitals.[11] The 'filling of canals' is also mentioned in the Akkadian potency incantations (Biggs 1967: Nos. 15 and 16). Then Enki calls out: 'No man walks in the marshland!' (line 69). Kramer and Maier (1989: 210, note 17) suggested that Enki may have wanted to reassure Ninhursag that no one was observing their intercourse so as not to embarrass her. Alster (1978: 17), pursuing his theory of 'unnatural sex', said that it is 'because he is afraid of the consequences of his own sexual powers. He does not want anyone to take possession of his semen.' I am inclined to read Enki's injunction as another ironic reference. At any rate he commands the goddess to lie down (line 73). Line 74 complicates matters by introducing a new name for the goddess, Damgalnunna, literally the Great Spouse of the Prince; it was the official name of Enki's wife:

Enki pours semen into Damgalnunna, lying in the marshes.

In line 75 the name of the goddess changes again, to that of Ninhursaga, the well known mother-goddess, and the text is now quite straightforward:

Enki ejaculates sperm into the womb of Ninhursaga,
She received the sperm into her womb, the sperm of Enki.

(74–5)

These two lines amount to the technical description of impregnation, as we have seen in *Enki and Ninmah*. The twofold change of names for Enki's female partner has given rise to the assumption that different goddesses were involved and that the sperm designed for Damgalnunna was received or removed by Ninhursaga (so Kramer and Maier, and Alster). But there is nothing beyond the change of names, or rather epithets, to suggest that more than one goddess was meant. Her pregnancy, as befitting a goddess, is miraculously short, lasting only nine days. The delivery is also remarkably easy ('like butter, like oil') and she gives birth to a daughter, Ninnisiga, 'Lady Verdure', as Jacobsen calls her.

The next episode concerns Enki's continuous desire for any female who ventures into his territory, the marshland. The names of the goddesses change, but otherwise the text is repeated practically verbatim four times.[12] There is no doubt as to the identity of each of the goddesses because we are told that they are the offspring of the goddess born previously.

The scene is always the same: following the copulation with Enki, the goddess has a nine-day pregnancy and then painlessly, 'as if oiled', gives birth to a daughter. Then we meet the same daughter, obviously nubile by now, by the riverbank, where Enki 'sticks out of the marshland'. Kramer was puzzled by what Enki could be 'stretching out', but I think that this is a rather obvious reference to an erection. The sight of the lovely young girl in the marshes has produced an immediate effect on the god. We hear him speak about it to his confidant and minister (Sumerian sukkal), Isimud. Isimud encourages Enki with a phrase full of double meanings and allusions,[13] impossible to translate in all its resonances. Literally, it means that 'alone he set foot in the boat. Then he lodged it on dry land'. Only Jacobsen (1987a: 192) noticed the proverbial usage – 'once one has taken a decisive step there is no turning back' – although he failed to spot the sexual metaphor. He translated:

> With a (favourable) downstream wind blowing for my master
> A downstream wind is blowing!
> He has put one foot in the boat,
> May he not stay the other on dry land.
>
> (94–6, 116–18)

Inanna elsewhere[14] compares her vulva to a boat, and the 'foot' is a likely euphemism for the penis. With one 'foot' in the 'boat', he will indeed not stay on 'dry' land for long! Then follows the full, if formulaic, description of their lovemaking:

> He embraced her, kissed her,
> Enki poured sperm into her womb,
> She received the sperm in (her) womb, the sperm of Enki.
>
> (99–101, 119–21)

In this manner Ninkurra, Ninimma[15] and Uttu are born.

The set pattern could continue, but now Nintur, one of the names of Enki's original partner, intervenes and speaks to the beautiful Uttu with motherly advice. Unfortunately, the passage is very damaged and the details of her speech are lost. However, there is a literary parallel in *Enlil and Ninlil*, where Nunšebargunu warns Ninlil to beware of the riverbank where the god (here Enlil) will see and desire her; he will make her pregnant and leave her. In this text, all that is preserved is Nintur telling Uttu that there is somebody in the marshes;[16] it is Enki (lines 131–2) who 'sticks out' in the marshes. The implications for a young girl are clear: she could use the situation of pre-marital sexual experiments to personal advantage, just as Ninlil does in the work mentioned above. After a gap in the text, somebody, probably Uttu, asks for gifts; they are highly symbolic ones; some fruits, especially apples, were appreciated for their aphrodisiac qualities.[17] Only then will he be able to take her 'on a lead', i.e. possess her. This is the first time that Enki's desire is frustrated. Instead of making love to Uttu straightaway, he has to bring her gifts.[18] Enki is set to work again:

> For the second time he fills the ditches with water, fills up
> The canals.
>
> (179–80)

Here the double meaning becomes comical indeed, as Enki had intended a different sort of 'watering'. An actual gardener is introduced at this point, who is delighted by Enki's efforts. Enki orders him to bring the fruit, which he lays in his 'lap',[19] and approaches the house of Uttu. He tells her that he is the gardener and has brought cucumbers, apples and grapes, 'for your "so be it"'. Uttu, 'full of joy', opens the door and Enki presents her with his gifts and pours out a 'large measure of beer' (line 177). At last he is able to take her in his arms:

> He embraced her, lying in her lap,
> Stroked her thighs, massaged her,

34

He embraced her (again), lying in her lap,
Copulated with the youngster and kissed her,
Enki ejaculated into Uttu's womb,
She received the sperm in (her) womb, the sperm of Enki.

(180–5)

The passage that describes their love-making is somewhat more elaborate than the terse stereotypical sequence of embrace, kiss, penetration found elsewhere in the text. But instead of ending in yet another pregnancy, Uttu, 'the seductive woman' calls out:

'Oh my thighs, oh my outsides, oh my insides!'

(186)

and Ninhursaga, her mother, promptly

'Wiped the sperm off her body'.[20]

A short gap in the text also prevents us from knowing what exactly Ninhursaga, did with Enki's seed. It somehow got into the ground, as eight plants, each one named separately, emerge (lines 188–95). The text is badly preserved, but no doubt the names have some bearing on the content. So although Uttu failed to become pregnant, Enki's sperm is still fertile. At the next scene, Enki is back in the marshes, 'sticking out'. He perceives the plants, which, like his daughters before, have now grown, and again he is overcome with desire and curiosity. He asks Isimud to name the plants and then proceeds to eat them one by one.[21] Having done that, he knows their 'hearts', (literally their 'insides', šà, synonymous with 'womb') and 'determines their fate'. This so enrages Ninhursaga that she curses Enki, threatening that she will 'not look on him with the eye of life' until he is dead. The gods are worried and it is only through the mediating offices of a fox that Ninhursaga is persuaded to cure Enki from his affliction. The details of the fox's mission and the possible rituals for removing the curse are missing. Ninhursaga then takes Enki, places him in her vagina and asks him where he hurts. For each affected limb she gives birth to a deity, four males and four females, and their names correspond phonetically to the different ailing parts of Enki's body.[22] This has the effect of restoring Enki's health. The text ends with a 'decreeing of fate' – each deity is assigned a function, the last one is Enzag, the Lord of Dilmun, and the final doxology is 'Praise to Father Enki'.

٭

The history of the interpretation of this composition reflects the prevailing modes of thought about ancient societies and the different theories about myth. It would go far beyond the scope of this study to enumerate all the propositions about Enki and Ninhursaga; I have selected those which regarded sexuality as its salient feature.

Witzel (1946: 245) considered the cause of Ninhursaga's outrage to have been Enki's homosexual intercourse with Uttu, whom he regarded as male, an assumption that has been proven untenable on philological grounds alone.

Kirk (1970: 97f.) referred to instances of sexual irregularity (repeated father–daughter incest, the removal of sperm from Uttu's womb by Ninhursaga), but linked it with a 'geographical or irrigation plane', saying that 'human fertility and natural fertility . . . are strictly interrelated' and that the 'irregular use of sex merely wastes the fertile potentialities of the water-god'. The scene with Uttu and the gardener, for instance, he relates to the extension of irrigation beyond the natural area of inundation into the desert fringes and he emphasizes the aetiological aspect of the text.

Alster (1978) took up the subject of irregular sexual behaviour and applied it to all the scenes of the text that describe intercourse. In this way he detected a series of 'unnatural' acts: first, Enki and Ninsikilla are not having any sex, as they are merely asleep; then Enki masturbates and Nintur picks up his sperm and impregnates herself; then multiple incest with Ninhursaga's daughters; and finally rape which did not lead to normal impregnation because the seed was removed from Uttu's womb and planted in the ground instead. He saw Enki's illness as a pregnancy from which he can only be successfully delivered by Ninhursaga placing him into her own womb. He concluded that 'only after the first male god became pregnant with himself and gave birth like a woman could other males come into being, and the continuous sequence of incest relations be broken'.

Attinger (1985: 52) singled out the importance of the father–daughter incest as the cause of Ninhursaga's curse. But like Alster he considered the establishment of exogamous marriage as the main theme of the composition.

Jacobsen in his last translation (1987a) refrained from any overall interpretation and remarked that the story was probably intended to entertain and flatter visiting dignitaries to Ur from Dilmun and emphasized their 'sailor's robust sense of humour'. He described the 'remarkable series of Enki's great-great-grandfatherly conquests [as] not without humour' and found in it echoes of 'an older cosmic genealogy' (ibid.: 184). Like Alster, he noticed the motif of male womb-envy and believed that Enki became pregnant and suffered because he was unable to give birth himself.

Even the measured approach of Kramer and Maier (1989), which underlines that Ninhursaga's anger was caused by the eating of the plants, contends that it was the series of sexual acts that 'wellnigh caused his death' (ibid.: 22).

I shall not try to formulate an 'interpretation' that accounts for all the motifs of this composition. There are still too many passages that remain beyond my comprehension linguistically or are just too damaged. But the observations by Jacobsen and Kramer and Maier, that it might in parts be satirical, seem worth pursuing. Jacobsen mentioned the 'sailors of Dilmun' and their hypothetically 'rough sense of humour'; he imagined the work to have been recited at the court of Ur. But it was fairly well distributed as a text, judging from the different versions and fragments that have come down to us, which proves that it was admired as a work of literature. We have now reached a stage in the study of Sumerian at which we are able to recognize a few puns (the names of the plants, for instance, or the eight deities born from them). But we lack knowledge about the so-called extra-textual framework, the social customs, the allusions to actual people and events, within which most humour operates. Faced with these limitations, I can only take stock of what *I* think is humorous, taking into account what we know about the literary protagonists. As this narrative is to a considerable extent concerned with sex, a prime target for humour (see also Lacan's phrase: 'L'amour est un sentiment comique' (1991: 46)), it creates an expectation of absurdity and exaggeration which then colours our whole understanding of the events unfolding. It might be useful here to refer to a short Sumerian tale, 'The Fowler and his Wife', recently re-edited by Alster (1993). One of the several preserved versions goes like this:

[A fowler] had some beer, and
Went to talk to his friend, but
Turned to a stranger instead.
His wife spoke to him at the door to the bed-room:
'The net was cast upon an **esig**-bird, the net was drawn up
  upon a raven.
The water has dried up in the little swamp,

37

So that your boat touches the ground.
A whirlwind blew.
Fowler, let your net be drawn up, let not your net . . ., let the
    raven rise!'

The *double entendre* permeating these lines was already perceived
by Diakonoff (private communication to Alster, quoted in Alster
1993) and Michalowski (1981). The wife complains that, owing to a
surfeit of beer, the fowler is unable to do his professional job
properly, but as she says it 'at the entrance to the bed-room', her
words take on another level meaning, which makes her criticism of
his performance as 'fowler' also hold good for his lack of success as
a lover – the little swamp drying up is an obvious reference to her
neglected vulva. The whirlwind is often invoked in potency incantation, and the 'rising' of the raven, a most useless bird to be caught,
points to the desired effect of the fowler's phallus and, at the same
time, the proper professional course of action to take. This composition is a good example of the witty anecdote, sometimes with a
moral warning (here probably against intoxication), that was so
popular in Sumer as to acquire proverbial status. As a work of
literature it obviously does not bear comparison with *Enki and
Ninhursaga*, but it reveals how much the Sumerian audience
appreciated cleverly camouflaged sexual innuendo and how much
the imagery of the swamp and its activities were associated with sex.

I have pointed out some of these absurdities in my synopsis, such
as the description of Dilmun lacking water, Enki's constant display
of his phallus, the significance of the fruit, the glut of sperm all over
Uttu, the lewd comments of Isimud, the appearance of the fox, well
known from popular proverbs and fables as a clever fixer etc. The
principle source of merriment is the priapic state of Enki, 'sticking
out of the marshes', as the text repeatedly puts it. Strong sexual urges
lead to excessive libido. This in itself is hilarious to observe, and
most antique (as well as modern) comedy is based on this principle.
In the grip of desire, the 'wise' Enki becomes a fool; he forgets to
provide 'water' for the city; he does not recognize his own offspring,
or the trap the mother-goddess sets for him when she frustrates his
immediate satisfaction; all he thinks about is sex – even the
consumption of the plants is a form of sexual greed. Inevitably, the
comic situation is heightened by the protagonist's discomfort; and
what could be more risible than a male made pregnant by his own
spilled seed? To say nothing of the humiliation of being at the mercy

of the Wife and having to borrow her sexual equipment to rid himself of this painful progeny. The successful delivery of the eight deities, and the various clever aetiologies they embody, is already the anticlimax, the restoration of 'normality' – the joke is over. Male gods are being born, normal marriage prevails, etc. This does all happen after the outrageously phallic (rather than amoral) activities of Enki. One reason why such a 'reading' is not improbable is a purely linguistic one that I have referred to several times, but which seems to me to be fundamental for the development of Enki's literary personality, the double meaning of the Sumerian sign a, denoting 'sperm' as well as 'water'. In this composition, the two levels of meaning constantly refer back to each other; the whole framework of the story is built on this ambiguous symbol. It takes place in Dilmun. Dilmun is famous for its abundant water. If Enki is also in Dilmun, he naturally is the source of all this bounty; his own 'springs' are full of fluid, hence the irrepressible urge to ejaculate. The debate whether he filled the 'ditches' with 'water' or a 'glut of semen' is rendered futile by this observation: one implies the other, but the sexual meaning makes it funny. It is not primarily a question of how important irrigation and water supply were for the Mesopotamians (that was all taken for granted), but how, given that there is this connection with seminal fluid and water, this can be funny, or problematic, or both. Another reason for adopting such a reading is the time of composition, the time of the Third Dynasty of Ur. Doubtless, the author made use of other sources, probably much older ones, but he turned them into a typical product of an age that admired wit, style and a certain 'raciness' in a literary composition (Rosengarten 1971; also Jacobsen 1987a). We do not get the impression of great religious intensity. A work such as *Enki and Ninhursaga* therefore makes no sense as a 'myth' or a deeply significant theological treatise. Kramer and Maier admitted that 'none of the currently known Sumerian theological credos or myths … shed any light on these questions' (1989: 23) and the highly theoretical, quasi proto-Platonic model of Rosengarten misses the mark.

Another point worth raising is Enki's 'trickster'-like personality that I have alluded to before. On the subject of the Huichol god Kauyumari, Barbara Myerhoff (1974: 85) writes that he appeared as a trickster 'engaging in extravagant sexual exploits "before he became sacred". He is an inexhaustible source of humour and entertainment and in his own way regarded responsible for several important Huichol characteristics and practices.' Since Enki, at least in some genres of Sumerian literature, displays other typical traits of a Trickster, such as being a mediator between mankind and the gods, featuring as a culture hero, and using his intelligence to solve problematic situations, his rather comical sexuality seems to fit in convincingly. There remains the dramatic climax of the story, the threat to Enki's existence. Are we to take this seriously? I have pointed out above that Enki's humiliation by Ninhursaga marks the high point of the comic situation that develops over many separate incidents. However, in these lines, when Enki's life is in serious danger, the gods, who have so far kept out of the story, make an appearance.[23] They are represented here by the Anunna, a collective term for the great gods in this context. They 'sit in the dust' (line 249), a well-known gesture of despair, until the Fox brings about the appeasement of Ninhursaga's anger. They are, then, instrumental in removing the curse by some ritual. This is the *deus ex machina* solution to Enki's threatened doom, and it occurs where comedy is on the verge of turning into tragedy. But because Enki is one of the major deities of the Sumerian pantheon, his disappearance cannot be condoned. It brings to mind another composition, which in many ways is not dissimilar to *Enki and Ninhursaga*, namely *The Descent of Inanna to the Underworld*, where the goddess of sexuality is resuscitated from death. If she were to remain in the Underworld, there would be no reproduction on earth, and likewise without Enki there would be no more a, the source of all life. It is no coincidence that it is Enki, alone among all major gods, who contrives to rescue Inanna! The reasons why Ninhursaga was in a position to threaten Enki are never clearly stated. Nowhere does she utter a reprimand or judgement on his actions towards his daughters; she only intervenes three times: to counsel Uttu, to wipe off the surplus semen and to utter her curse after Enki had eaten the plants and decreed their fate. I do not believe that incest or rape has anything to do with her anger; it is more likely his untoward assumption of responsibility regarding the plants – she (remember that she represents Earth) considers them as belonging to her domain.

So is there no hubris in Enki's behaviour apart from the comical exaggeration of his sex drive? If there is any warning, it may be that to give in too much to this urge makes a man vulnerable to the power of women. Enki allows himself to be manipulated by the young and voluptuous goddess, who uses his infatuation to her own ends – Uttu receives the fruit – and likewise Ninhursaga gains control over his life. After all, the game of love was usually played by the woman (see p. 56) as the active partner; again Enki comically and almost pathetically reverses the roles and almost comes to grief.

4

FROM ADOLESCENCE TO MATURITY
The myth of Enlil and Ninlil[1]

The male hero of this text is not Enki, but Enlil. But as it is primarily concerned with conception and fertility it fits in well with the narratives studied so far. It is set in the city of Nippur, the traditional seat of Enlil. There are various explicit references to actual localities in Nippur, such as canals, wells, parts of the temple area and especially gates. This makes it likely that it may have been used in some ritual procedures (Behrens 1978: 179).

The framework of the plot is to some extent a coming-of-age scenario, which describes the transition of the main characters from adolescence to full adulthood. The protagonists are introduced in the beginning of the text by age-classifications:

> Enlil (is) its adolescent boy (guruš. tur),
> Ninlil its adolescent girl (ki. sikil. tur),
> Nunbaršegunu was matriarch (um-ma).[2]

Nunbaršegunu is the mother of Ninlil and in a short speech she advises her daughter to beware of the 'holy canal' because there

> 'Bright-eyed' Enlil will see you.
> He will make love to you and when he has happily filled your
>   womb with fertile semen, he will leave you.[3]

Ninlil reacts like any curious adolescent: she puts her mother's words to the test. Enlil is her male counterpart, the prototypical guruš. tur, a young unmarried male. Like Enki in *Enki and Ninhur-saga* he lurks by the waterways, which in many places were grown with reeds and willows, providing some cover to spy on young girls at their ablutions. Like Enki he has a companion, Nusku, who echoes his master's wishes. When he first sets eyes on Ninlil by the canal, he makes no secret of his intentions:

> 'I want to make love to you
> I want to kiss you!'
>
> (28–9)

Ninlil replies that her parts are still young, her 'lips' little, and they 'know not how to kiss'.[4] Furthermore, she would get into trouble with her mother and father and she would have to tell her girlfriend. Enlil is not easily discouraged. He tells Nusku that he desires to make love to 'this beautiful and shapely girl', who has not yet had sex with anyone. The following passage also has a reference to a boat-like thing, 'a big one and a little one'. This is generally understood as Nusku providing Enlil with a raft or similar conveyance, which would allow him to achieve his aim.[5] At any rate, they find a suitable spot[6] and

> He followed the urge to make love,
> Followed the urge to kiss those lips,
> And at his first making love, at his first kiss,
> He poured into the womb for her the sperm, (germ) of Suen (the moon),
> The bright lone traveller.
>
> (50–3) (Jacobsen 1987a: 114)

Then the scene shifts abruptly to the Kiur, a forecourt of the great temple in Nippur, where the 'fifty great gods and the seven gods decide destinies' (lines 56–7). They seize Enlil, who is wandering about there, and tell him that he has to leave the city because he has become ú-zug, 'impure'.[7] Enlil leaves town but Ninlil follows; she probably remembers her mother's warnings and interprets Enlil's actions as those of an unfaithful lover. She is determined not to let him escape. Enlil is aware of her pursuit and tries to hide his whereabouts. His motives for doing so are less clear. Either he wants to avoid contaminating her, or is he just anxious to avoid another meeting, knowing what effect the 'beautiful and radiant' girl has on him. At any case, he instructs the man in charge of one of the city gates[8] not to disclose his presence to Ninlil. The goddess does indeed ask the man for Enlil but he gives an evasive answer. Then Ninlil draws herself up and speaks out:

> 'Having decided in my mind, I made my plans,
> And was filling from him my empty womb,

Enlil, king of all lands, made love with me.
As Enlil is your master, so am I also your mistress!'
(78–84; Jacobsen 1987a: 175–6)

If this interpretation is correct, it is indeed a bold statement and shows that Ninlil, on her way to becoming the future great queen of Ekur, is no foolish girl, but takes responsibility for the course of events. According to Jacobsen (1987a: 176), the gatekeeper swears an oath of allegiance by touching her genitals, and Ninlil confirms that the

'sperm of your Lord, the shining sperm is in my womb.'
(83)

From the ensuing retort

'My royal sperm may it go upwards, this sperm of mine may
it go downwards[9]!'
(84)

it is obvious that Enlil speaks these words. The following line makes the situation clear: Enlil

'lay down in the bed chamber in place of the man of the city-
gate'
(88)

and there makes love to Ninlil again,

ejaculating the semen of Nergal-Meslamta'ee into her womb.
(90)

The same sequence of events is repeated two more times. Enlil leaves, followed by Ninlil, and each time he makes love to her in the guise of an official in charge of a particular locality in and around Nippur.[10] In this manner the gods Ninazu and Enbilulu are engendered. The text then ends quite abruptly with a paean to the fertilizing powers of Enlil and praises Ninlil as the mother and nin ('queen') the female equivalent of Enlil.

Commentators on this work have mainly concentrated on the reasons for Enlil's banishment and the rationale behind the successive impregnations. Most influential was Jacobsen's view of Enlil as a 'sex offender', who was doomed to go to the Netherworld and therefore engendered several substitutes to take his place (see also

Cooper 1980: 180). Kirk (1970: 183) drew attention to the structural similarity of this text to *Enki and Ninhursaga*, especially with regard to the importance of fertility and the dangers of wasteful fertility in both texts. Behrens (1978: 184–9) rejected the theory of substitution on the grounds that there is no direct reference to such an intention in the narrative. Like Kirk, he linked the conception of several sons to fertility.

The goddess Ninlil has received considerably less attention, and then primarily as a passive character in Enlil's story, the recipient of male sexual violence. Cooper (1980: 169) even spoke of the 'typical ambivalence of the victim towards the oppressor', which make her not only follow Enlil after his banishment but also submit to further intercourse by trickery. For Jacobsen she is intrinsically bound to Enlil by virtue of sharing the same natural phenomenon, the wind (líl) on the basis of a doubtful etymology. He also mentions the 'all-engrossing craving for a child' as the motive for her actions. Behrens has drawn attention to the final doxology, which praises 'Father Enlil' and 'Mother Ninlil'.[11]

As in the texts we have studied so far, the concept of a is of paramount importance. In *Enki and the World Order* and *Enki and Ninhursaga* it was employed to make use of the full semantic possibilities of this sign, and, especially in the latter text, there is a persistent double meaning of 'water' and 'sperm'. *Enki and Ninmah* shifts the emphasis to the procreational aspect when it describes the role of the male in conception. The same happens in *Enlil and Ninlil*. However, the locale is not a mythical place, but the city of Nippur, and sexuality is seen in a social context. The characters are defined by age-categories. Enlil and Ninlil are both tur, 'under-age', 'imma-ture', at the beginning. With the onset of her menstruation, Ninlil needs to undergo purification in the 'pure canal'. Biologically she is now ready to bear children, although she is warned not to engage in intercourse without a formalization of her relationship with the man, as, so her mother tells her, he will leave her to fend for herself. Enlil's transition into manhood seems here to be achieved by his ability to impregnate. Having conceived his sperm, Ninlil will eventually give birth to the moon-god. This is the biological pattern of events that we found described in the cosmogonic sections of *Enki and Ninmah*. But as this narrative is set in a city, where social constraints operate against spontaneous procreation, the situation becomes complicated. Enlil's impetuous impregnation is punished by his temporary removal from the city. Ninlil is not to follow him.

However, she asserts herself by referring to her pregnancy, and each time she confronts Enlil he responds (though in disguise) by making love to her and engendering another son. On the surface, Ninlil pursues Enlil because she does not want him to escape, as her mother had predicted. She wants him to marry her. She is, one might say, after the Phallus – as the means to provide status and power. And she does indeed receive three more doses of Enlil's sperm. This allows her to prove her own capacity for conception – to be pregnant with four sons at the same time is a considerable achievement. The final result is described in the doxology: Enlil is hailed as 'lord' (en) and 'king' (lugal) of heaven and earth, who is almighty, whose word is unalterable and who produces abundance. He is confirmed as the supreme deity of Nippur. Ninlil, as we know, became his wife. At the end both are hailed as 'Father' and 'Mother'. They have achieved the transition from the socially powerless state of being tur to full adulthood and the top position in the city's hierarchy through their reproductive efficiency and tenacity.

It is instructive to set this text in relation to another composition known as *Enlil and Sud* (Civil 1983, Wilcke 1987). This also concerns Enlil and a young goddess.[12] Enlil meets Sud on the road and begins to talk to her, asking the girl for a kiss. But she does not allow him to engage in a conversation and goes straight back to her mother's house. Enlil then sends his envoy Nusku to her mother, with a proposal and the obligatory engagement presents, and thereby wins the hand of Sud in the most traditional manner. The young woman is escorted to Nippur with a huge caravan bearing her dowry and there consummates her wedding on the 'shining bed'. Afterwards Enlil assigns her divine functions.

This text portrays the girl as behaving in a restrained manner, winning Enlil's hand with her reticence, rather than her acquiescence. Ninlil's behaviour is different. She wins her man and her position because of her fertility and she offers Enlil a chance to prove his manhood. On the subject of eroticism, neither work has much to say. Ninlil speaks at first as a barely nubile girl who does not, as yet, exult in her sexuality. On the contrary, she is doubtful of her ability to have proper intercourse.

Enlil's reaction is described in the usual mechanical manner, as the result of seeing a beautiful and presumably naked woman. He follows the urge and makes love, ejaculating into her womb. The other acts of intercourse are preceded by the rather enigmatic argument about the future fate of the semen, but not by an erotic situation. The lovemaking is seen as an expedient to conceive further gods, rather than a situation of intimacy, although the fact that Ninlil has intercourse with apparently three different men adds a touch of frivolity. Sud and Ninlil both use their physical attraction to obtain their position. One behaves in the respectable manner and allows her mother to marry her off on advantageous terms, the other takes risks and shows herself worthy of her exalted position because of her intelligence and fertility, although Enlil's role as the provider of sperm is stressed. Enlil's behaviour in *Enlil and Sud* is more in keeping with his character as the supreme god of Sumer, whereas in the story of Ninlil he resembles licentious Enki. This may have been a deliberate parallel, especially with regard to the possible ritual background of the Tummal celebrations (Behrens 1978: 120–6). In this context Enlil is the local god of Nippur and thereby involved in local fertility rites, which seem to make use of the reed-bed symbolism. This may also explain the impetuous urge of Enlil, who thereby personifies the sexual ambience of the marshes.

Both stories, although *Enlil and Ninlil* more so, raise the question of virginity, or the value placed on virginity. It is said explicitly that Ninlil had not yet had sex with anyone, and she herself does not acknowledge the reality of her biological nubility. The legal texts show clearly that defloration, especially of a free girl, was a serious offence 'against the property of another person', specifically the girl's father or her betrothed future husband (Finkelstein 1966: 55). In Sumerian times it was sanctioned by forcing the man to marry the girl. But there is no actual word that denotes our concept of virginity; it could only be expressed negatively, as the absence of sexual experience.[13] There is no suggestion in the myth that Ninlil is devalued, or has brought shame upon her family, the common concept of Mediterranean sexual morality. Rather, she passes from immaturity (ki-sikil-tur) to sexual maturity, which is here achieved not only by the onset of her menarche but by her ability to conceive. In a singular, mythical compression, the goddess experiences the crossing of several biological as well as social boundaries. Significantly, this does not evolve any social ritualization for the divine protagonists, but it leaves open the possibility that the Tummal rituals may also have had some connection with rites of passage.

5

PHALLICISM IN
SUMERIAN LITERATURE

Jerrold Cooper (1989: 89) has characterized Enki's sexuality as 'raw, often violent, phallocentric and reproductive on both the meta-phoric and the concrete levels'. Is this statement applicable to the presentation of masculine sexuality in Sumerian literature in general?

Let us begin with the last item, reproduction. We have seen that the myth of *Enki and Ninmah* encapsulated the Mesopotamian theory of conception. But it was described in many other texts, as in this passage from a ritual for successful childbirth:

> (The woman) (. .) has the rightful human seed ejected in (her) insides, a semen ejected in (her) insides, contracted for (by marriage contract), giving the man off-spring.
>
> (Jacobsen 1973)

In other ritual texts the fertility of cattle or sheep becomes a metaphor for human procreation:

> The fine bull in the (pure) stall, in the pure fold, has mounted (this cow), has deposited in her womb the rightful seed of mankind.
>
> (van Dijk 1975)

Such references to animal reproduction are very common in Sumerian texts and point to the likely development of this theory as a result of selective breeding.[1] The cuneiform sign for 'pregnant' (peš$_4$) summarizes the concept very neatly, for it consists of the sign for 'womb', 'inside' (šà) plus a ('sperm', 'water'). The male is responsible for the fertilization, the woman provides the environ-ment for the foetus' growth and finally gives birth 'out of her womb'.

The fact that the primary impetus for the creation of a child came from the man is of great importance for the manner in which male sexuality is described. The fertilizing power of sperm is one of the key topics in *Enki and Ninhursaga* and *Enlil and Ninlil*. In both these myths, the male protagonists, typically young, vigorous gods, achieve impregnation with each orgasm. These acts prove their maleness and the biological, procreative function of copulation is thereby strongly emphasized. On a mythological level, the divine semen has generative or irrigational powers when the recipient happens not to be a woman: Enki's seed thrown on the ground produces plants; he fills the Tigris and Euphrates, as well as the springs of Dilmun with water. Enlil is lauded as the 'Lord Abundance', 'who lets the grain grow',[2] surely a reference to his fertilizing power. A hymn to Enlil also makes a connection between him and the fecundity of animals:

> Without Enlil, the Great Mountain (. . .) the beasts would not want to copulate
>
> (Kramer 1969: 51)

The phallocentrism of these texts can now be put in perspective: it demonstrates the unfailing efficiency of the male reproductive organ of Enki and Enlil respectively.

The description of the sexual acts which precede the successful impregnation is rather summarily treated with a typical sequence of events. The young male god sees a young female and desires to kiss her and copulate with her.[3] In the case of Enki and his various 'daughters', as well as with Enlil and Nannar when they first encounter their future spouses, the girl is presumably naked, as she is observed during a bath in the canal. Apart from the fact that the ambience of the reed-grown riverbanks or of the marshes is as such highly conducive to amorous adventure, it is the sight of female nudity which triggers the overwhelming sexual attraction. When Enlil meets Sud on the road, for instance, the situation is different, and Sud is safe from his ardour because it is a public space. In *Enlil and Ninlil* the subsequent series of impregnations with the disguised Enlil take place after he has been made to swear an oath, which seems to involve the touching of her genitals, an act he finds irresistibly arousing.[4]

But nowhere in our texts does the young god satisfy his lust immediately. He always begins by articulating his desire, either to his companion, Nusku, or to Isimud:

'This beautiful maid, is she not to be kissed?'

or directly to the girl:

'I want to kiss you, plant my penis'
(*Enlil and Ninlil* 28–9)

In comparison with the female voice, which exults in the verbalization of emotional and sensual desire, this is inarticulate, a command rather than a seduction. But as these texts are primarily concerned with the male perspective, the girl's tacit compliance is taken for granted. The urgency of the masculine desire to impregnate is in keeping with its biological function and the myths underline the basic justification of the physical need. *Enlil and Ninlil* also shows the constriction which society puts upon the procreative urge: to make an unmarried girl pregnant renders Enlil 'impure' and he suffers temporary banishment.

In keeping with the male god's laconic verbal approach is the minimal attention given to amatory technique: the stereotypical expression is 'he did indeed kiss her, he did indeed insert the penis',[5] while some passages also include the fondling of breasts,[6] and specify the position as lying down.[7] Then follows the intravaginal emission that leads to conception (except in the case of Uttu). The point of these myths is precisely *not* to dwell on erotic preliminaries and the enjoyment of the female partner, but to focus on the result, the impregnation.

There is a much older Sumerian text from the archives of Abu Salabikh, dating from about the middle of the third millennium (Jacobsen 1989). It concerns the love-affair between Lugalbanda and Ninsuna, who from later sources are known as the parents of Gilgameš.

The following is Jacobsen's provisional and very tentative translation:

Cherub Ninsuna was lifting out (baked) beer bread
  confections.
Cherub Ninsuna was very shrewd, she stayed awake
And lay down at his feet.
Wise Lugalbanda, passed his arm around Cherub Ninsuna
Could not resist kissing her on the eyes
Could not resist kissing (her) on the mouth
Also taught her much love-making.

Jacobsen points out that the text continues with a vision of Lugalbanda's mother, who appears to Ninsuna: 'The girl receives her civilly and asks to have plenty of offspring, five sons and five daughters. A happy ending is to be expected.' The text does not tell us about the circumstances of the couple's lovemaking, but as Ninsuna seems to ask for the blessing of the man's mother, one could assume that they were already married, or about to be married. Jacobsen's translation of the few lines suggests the loving relationship of the couple (her tentative advances and his tender response which leads to her initiation into lovemaking), but this may well be based on his own perception of an extremely difficult poetic text. On the other hand, considerate and loving treatment of the young bride, as being conducive to conjugal happiness, is often invoked in Sumerian Bridal Songs.

But the comparative brusqueness in the myths of Enki and Enlil should not be taken as typical. As pointed out above, it is strictly in keeping with the reproductive function of the male. The concept of rape is inappropriate here since these myths are not concerned with social customs and institutions but portray the activities of deities in a world largely devoid of human regulations. They should not be taken as a reflection of Sumerian attitudes generally. We have evidence from legal texts that forcible intercourse inflicted upon a free woman was a punishable offence. Already in the early, mid-third millennium version of a collection of admonitions and proverbs, known as the *Instructions of Šuruppak* we find a sentence which was interpreted as a reference to sexual assault:

> Do not commit rape upon the daughter of a man, she will announce it in the courtyard.
>
> (Alster 1974: 1, 67)[8]

The Code of Urnammu (twenty-first century) specifies that the fine for raping a servant girl was to pay 5 shekels of silver to her owner. Later the punishment was much higher: some hundred and fifty years later, according to the 'laws of Ešnunna', the fine was ⅔ of a mina of silver (Landsberger 1968: 7–49). The legal texts of later periods make it quite clear that the offence was not considered to be committed against the woman, but against whoever had a right to her and her body, although it is not certain that the same attitude was also current in the neo-Sumerian period. According to Babylonian and Assyrian laws, the girl remained under the authority of her father, who was to be compensated against any despoiling of his 'property'. Once the marriage was concluded, the woman belonged to her husband (Cassin 1987: 345).

It is important to note that in the Sumerian myths the male gods who seduce the young goddesses are not subjected to sanctions, nor is the girl 'dishonoured'. Elena Cassin wondered whether the fact that the women were 'taken in the open', in an uninstitutionalized context, did not make them more at the mercy of their partners than in a conventional marriage; probably it was assumed that they had to be grateful to the seducer for marrying them at all. But as pointed out above, the narratives in many myths do not need to operate in the familiar social atmosphere, as their purpose was often to demonstrate the difference between the way things were *then* and the present known to the writer (or indeed his audience), and we simply do not know yet what the social organizations at that time were like in respect to sexuality. All we can say is that in these works of literature the male gods incarnate the phallic sexual urge and the goddesses incite this urge by their sheer youthfulness and beauty. If there was an element of transgression in these myths, to which the audience was susceptible, it would have served to emphasize the divine force of sexual attraction and reproductive instinct.

There is also the myth of *Inanna and Šukalletuda* (Kramer 1949: 399ff.).[9] The male protagonist is Šukalletuda, a gardener's boy, who at the beginning of the story seems to have a problem in getting his plants to flourish. Inanna, the goddess, lies down in his now beautiful garden, and falls asleep, following her strenuous journeys to far-off lands. Šukalletuda takes advantage of her exhaustion and 'inserted his penis (and), kissed her'.

> The day broke, to the risen Utu, the [woman] in fear lifted her
> eyes.
> On that day, the woman, because of her pudenda,
> This is how she acted, this is how she destroyed.

Inanna is determined to punish the gardener:

> 'He who cohabited with me I shall find (even) in the foreign
> lands'

she vows, and when she fails to do so, since the man just 'disappeared' among the population, she sends a series of plagues over the whole country. Inanna, although she is the goddess of voluptuousness, is not to be taken advantage of. We shall see in a later chapter that it is always she who initiates lovemaking and that

Inanna's eroticism celebrates sensuality. But she is not to be used as an object of phallic impulse. Although the garden is a popular locale for amorous encounters, and a metaphor for the female genitals, the action of Šukalletuda constitutes a violation. But why? Does sexual intercourse without the consent of one partner make it an offence? We shall see from the love-songs that the sensual pleasure experienced by women during intercourse was much emphasized. Does it show a lack of respect for the goddess of love on the man's part not to do it properly, so to speak, rather than 'stealing' his satisfaction from the woman's body. The text itself does not elaborate, but I am not convinced by Alster's argument that we have here a defloration of the goddess (Alster 1973: 30) and that the rivers being filled with blood, one of the punishments she sends, represents her blood. When Gilgameš taunts Ištar in the sixth tablet of the Babylonian epic, he recounts the story of the gardener Išullānu (lines 64–79). This is interesting for the inversion of the Šukalletuda motif. Išullānu is said to have been an indefatigable gardener, who 'was always bringing you baskets of dates'. But here it is the goddess who desires him and expressively invites him to make love to her:

'let us enjoy your strength, put out your hand and touch our vulva!'

But the man rudely refuses:

'Me? What do you want from me? Did my mother not bake for me, and did I not eat?
What I eat (with you) would be loaves of dishonour and disgrace, Rushes would be my only covering against the cold.'

(Dalley 1989: 79)

Upon which Ištar hits him and turns him into a toad.

The structure of both stories is parallel. Šukalletuda desires her and satisfies his lust upon the sleeping goddess without her invitation, whereupon he is punished. With Išullānu it is the goddess who invites him to have sex with her, but he refuses to comply and also gets punished. As far as the goddess is concerned, it comes to the same thing, as intercourse during a deep sleep is not what she would call an erotic experience worth having. We would conclude that in both cases the hubris is his failure to give her pleasure.

One could say generally that in these Sumerian texts, which deal with the masculine perspective of sexuality, the phallus is not presented as an instrument which provides women with an orgasm. Even the physical experience of the male is not explicitly described as one of physical satisfaction or pleasure, as in the case of women in the love-songs, although this is obviously implied. Either the stress is on the inseminating function of ejaculation, or on the metaphorical irrigational function, or on the physiological and psychological satisfaction of the sexual urge. The man's desire is often provoked by the sight of a naked female body.

But whereas in the culture of ancient, post-Aryan India, where phallicism was predominant, we find the image of Lord Kṛṣṇa satisfying the thousand Gopis all at the same time, allowing each one to be possessed of his member, we have no parallel for such phallic feasts in the Sumerian literature.

The role of the phallus here belongs to reproductive sexuality and, by extension, to water-based fertility. It seems that from the latter stems the claim to authority, enshrined in political and economical power.

6

FEMININITY AND EROTICISM IN SUMERIAN LITERATURE

AMBIGUOUS FEMININITY: THE GODDESS INANNA

The sexuality of the youthful gods is wholly preoccupied with phallic displays and impregnation as proof of virility. We have seen Enki ever 'extending' himself in the marshes, lying in wait to spy on young women. Their lovemaking is spontaneous and usually takes place in the open air, among the reeds. The female partners are barely nubile, sexually inexperienced and often unwilling, but prove suitable receptacles for the 'fertilizing semen'. With the exception of the fragment from Abu Ṣalabikh, the gods do not speak of love or their emotions. They merely voice their desire to kiss and copulate as a prelude to the act and they do not verbalize their enjoyment. The texts instead emphasize that male orgasm is an act of creation. It is ideally situated within the context of marriage (*Enlil and Ninlil*). All the gods of the pantheon have their spouses. While Mesopotamian literature grants a certain licence to the adolescent gods, there is no philandering or adultery, as in Greek mythology. There is also no equivalent to the Hindu phallic deities, neither an 'erotic ascetic' such as Śiva, nor a promiscuous Kṛṣṇa. Male sexuality was not a popular subject in Sumerian texts. If an official ideological position could be gauged from the available material, the importance of the male's role in procreation contributed to his superior status. The 'lusty bull' is a favourite epithet to describe masculine strength. However, the texts that praise the great gods, or indeed kings, build up a much more complex and elaborate rationale for their pre-eminence and privilege, as we saw in *Enki and the World Order*. But while the notion of male fertility was important, it would be an over-

55

simplification to base the patriarchal organization of Sumerian society on this concept.

In a commentary on Plato's *Symposium*, Lacan commented that women in Greek society played their significant role in love, 'le rôle actif tout simplement' (Lacan 1991: 44). When Plato differentiates between the *erastes*, the active lover, and *eromenos*, the passive beloved, he applies it to the relationship between a boy and his adult male lover. In a heterosexual context, the woman was the lover and the man the object of her love (Lacan: 'elle exigeait son dû, elle attaquait l'homme'). This does not imply that women were free to choose husbands and indeed lovers. We know, on the contrary, that the social restrictions imposed on women limited their ability to make such decisions (Pomeroy 1975). But we also have to recognize that in many traditional societies there is a difference between public life and public utterance, often dominated by men, and private life and private discourse, dominated by women (Winkler 1990: 5ff.). Marital and sexual relationships are essentially private, and within the parameters of intimacy women may assert influence and power. The more women's access to public participation is restricted, the more intense is their focus on domestic life. The manipulation of sexual gratification, to grant and to withhold, to entice and reject, is a very widespread strategy for extending influence. This is where the woman can 'attack', it is her 'proper' sphere that she can control. In love literature, references to the world outside the home or the bedroom are avoided. In Mesopotamian literature, the woman's voice dominates the poetic discourse. She speaks of her desire and demands the gratification of her sexual needs, while the male voice is often an imagined response to her pleas.

The paradigmatic figure in the majority of these texts is the goddess Inanna. While there were a great number of female deities in Sumer, none could rival Inanna is a subject of literary composi-tions. The beginning of this poetic fascination was traditionally ascribed to the first author in history we know by name, the princely priestess Enheduanna, who lived during the twenty-third century (van Dijk and Hallo 1968: 189ff.). Most of her work is only known from much later editions, dating from the Old Babylonian period, and specialists are not unanimous in accepting a third-millennium origin (Civil 1980: 229). Before the Sargonic period Inanna had no literary personality that we know of. On the contrary, in the archaic texts the sign DINGIR. INANNA (MÙŠ) was used generically to designate GODDESS, or maybe a certain kind of goddess.[1] Although the royal inscriptions of Sargon do not make any special references to Inanna, later tradition has it that he was particularly devoted to the goddess and owed his spectacular rise to supreme power to her influence.[2] Sargon belonged to one of the Semitic groups which coexisted with the Sumerians, particularly in the more northern parts of the country. His goddess may have been an ancient Semitic deity, probably a form of Eštar or Ištar (Roberts 1972: 37–9), an astral goddess with a dual personality – male as Morning Star and feminine as Evening Star. The warlike features of the goddess were certainly stressed more during the Old Akkadian period than before, as can be seen in the divine epithets (Roberts 1972: 37; Ichiro 1979: 291). We know too little about the early DINGIR. INANNA, who was worshipped at Uruk and other places, to speculate on her specific function or character; many a local deity only developed a distinct mythical personality through the literary activity at the major temples. But by the Isin–Larsa period, Inanna has acquired a formidably complex character, extolled in lengthy hymns, myths, ritual invocations and courtly poetry. Her planetary aspect as Venus was one important element at a time when astronomical observations were gaining in accuracy[3] and great attention was paid to the cyclical appearance and disappearance of this planet and its relative position to other stars and constellations.[4] The syncretism with other city-goddesses, notably Ninisinna, the 'lady' of the capital Isin, made it politically advantageous to proclaim her superior status in the pantheon and emphasize her close links with the ruling Isin dynasty. It is difficult to evaluate when Inanna was first linked with sexuality; certainly by the Sargonic period she was invoked in love incantations, together with Išhara. In the literary texts this aspect became pre-eminent over any connection with reproductive fertility the goddess may have had before, and she became *the* woman among the gods, patron of eroticism and sensuality, of conjugal love as well as adultery, of brides and prostitutes, transvestites and pederasts. This separation of fertility and sexuality, however, was not as clear cut as this evidence suggests. According to incantations, which to some extent reflect the concerns and beliefs of the people better than the scholarly and priestly compositions, we have instances of Inanna/Ištar being invoked to assist in childbirth (Farber-Flügge 1984). The same view of the goddess as a helper of women is present in the Old Babylonian story of Etana, the man who ascended to heaven on the back of an eagle (Kinnier-Wilson 1985). He does so

57

on behalf of his wife, who has problems with giving birth, and who asks Etana to procure the 'plant of birth' (*šammu ša aladi*), which, as is eventually revealed to him, is in the possession of Ištar (Kinnier-Wilson 1974: 237). But on the whole the responsibility for childbirth in the official literature was given to one of the mother-goddesses, such as Ninhursaga or Nintur in Sumerian, Aruru, Mami, Belet-ilî, etc. in Akkadian texts.

We shall briefly examine two of the compositions that were ascribed to Enheduanna, in order to illustrate the theological components of Inanna's personality.

The poem known as *Nin-me-šar-ra* (van Dijk and Hallo 1968: 9–10) comprises some 150 lines and consists of a lengthy hymnic address to the goddess, followed by a narrative section in the first person singular which recounts the fate of the putative author ('I, Enheduanna'). She was driven from her priestly office and city, and suffered in exile, but by persisting in praising the goddess won back her favour and was restored to her previous position. The text is quite difficult and the two published translations differ in many respects. We shall concentrate on the epithets and statements concerning Inanna, rather than the fate of Enheduanna, which is outside the range of our enquiry. The hymnic tenor of the first 80 lines is like that of *Enki and the World Order*, which we discussed in a previous chapter. We have seen in the latter text how Enki's position in the pantheon was established by kinship with other great gods – he is the son of An and younger brother of Enlil. He was also said to have been nurtured by the mother-goddess and hailed by the Anunna. His administrative acumen, the established rites at his temple in Eridu, and his creative potential as a god of divine fluid a, were cited as proofs of his divine competence.

Inanna's genealogical position as the 'eldest daughter of Suen'[5] is not as important as that of Enki's, since the moon-god was not considered to be one of the major executive gods. The term used most frequently to describe her relationship with the senior gods is the comparatively vague 'beloved'.[6] Like Enki, she is also in possession of the me, the all-important prerogatives which define the areas of divine influence. As the distribution of the me was traditionally the sole right of An, Inanna (like Enki) receives them from him. She is also said to 'make decisions at the command of An' and carry out his instructions. Her most contentious epithet is nu-gig-an-na, a title often translated as 'Hierodule of Heaven'[7] but which remains obscure in its precise meaning. The exercise of her functions is described in the next passage. Unlike in Enki's paean, where his fertility and wisdom are emphasized, Inanna is associated with dangerous and destructive forces. She is likened to a dragon, thunder and rainstorms (lines 9–18), 'riding a beast' or 'flying on the wings of the storm':

> 'Mankind comes before you in fear and trembling at your
>   Tempestuous radiance'
>
> (21–2)

She punishes those who withhold homage by cursing their vegetation, leads away the troops into captivity, fills the rivers with blood (43–50). By removing herself from the unfaithful city she turned away from its 'womb':

> Its woman no longer speaks of love with her husband.
> At night they no longer have intercourse.
> She no longer reveals to him her inmost treasures.
>
> (55–7)[8]

This is the only reference to Inanna's aspect of a love-goddess. The litany-like recitation towards the end of the composition summarizes the terrible aspects of Inanna – they all end in the phrase hé-zu-àm, which could be rendered as 'that which you are known for' – she is

> high as heaven, wide as the earth, destructive of rebel lands
>   and their people,
> Devouring corpses like a dog, of fiery countenance,
> With a terrible glance, intolerant of disobedience, triumphant
>   in war.
>
> (122–32)

But once her rage is spent, through the continuing offerings of her devotee, she is 'clothed in womanly beauty', sumptuously dressed 'like the light of the new moon', and the poem ends with an invocation of her three most salient attributes: 'destroyer of the rebel lands, endowed with me by An and lady wrapped in beauty'.[9]

The other Enheduanna composition, known as in-nin šà-gur₄-ra (Sjöberg 1976), also emphasizes the destructive and aggressive character of this deity. In terms of the hierarchical positions, she seems to be contending for the place of Enlil, the storm god, rather than that of An, from whom she receives the me and whose commands she carries out. There are several other compositions about male deities which have a similar theme, such as the poems about the warrior-god Ninurta. This is in contrast to *Enki and the World Order*, where Enki assumes none of Enlil's functions or prerogatives but those more often associated with female deities, fertility and social order.[10] If Enki is trying to supplant a goddess he must necessarily prove competence in her traditional spheres of influence. In the case of Inanna the reverse is the case and her masculine qualities are emphasized, especially her role of kur-gul-gul ('destroyer of the (foreign) land'),[11] who suppresses insurrection and rebellion at the periphery of Sumer, which threatens the well-being of the country. Her frightening aspect must be understood to be directed against the enemy, even the enemy within, as is shown in lines 51–7 and 92–9, which are directed against Uruk because it rebelled against her father Nanna-Suen.

A very important feature of this composition is a long passage of some 60 lines which enumerates Inanna's prerogatives and spheres of activity. They are arranged in an antithetical combination of attributes, which contrast negative and positive effects, summarized in each line with ^dinanna za-a-kam ('Inanna they are yours'). These attributes are comparable to the list of me in the myth of *Inanna and Enki*; here, as in *Inanna's Descent*, they are called garza,[12] and, as Sjöberg said, represent 'Inanna's omnipresent and omnipotent role in human affairs' (Sjöberg 1976: 163). Here are some examples:

Neglect, careful preparation, 'to raise the head' and to subdue are yours, Inanna, (137)

To build a house, to build a woman's chamber, to have implements, to kiss the lips of a small child are yours, Inanna, (138)

Swiftness, foot race, to attain desire are yours, Inanna, (139)

To interchange the brute and strong and the weak and powerless is yours, Inanna, (140)

To reduce, to make great, to make low, to make broad, to . . (and) to give a lavish supply are yours, Inanna, (155)

To initiate a quarrel, to joke, to cause smiling, to be base and to be important are yours, Inanna, (159)

Misfortune, hardship, grief, to make happy and to elucidate are yours, Inanna. (160)

This ambivalence, which is here ascribed to Inanna, was perceived as a general condition of human life, as we can see from the so-called

Wisdom Literature. The theological interpretation linked the often-experienced reversals of fortunes to the will, or even the capriciousness of the gods. It cannot be said to be a specifically feminine trait, since male gods, especially Enlil, can also behave unpredictably, with devastating consequences. Inanna's influence in the texts above is perceived to be on a grand scale, while other texts concentrate on her aspect as love-goddess. The passage is taken from a bilingual Old Babylonian text, edited in 1927, which is too fragmentary to allow a definite connection with Inanna, but the general content makes it very likely (Scheil 1927):

> You search a house with a large family,
> You enter this house, like a good omen,
> You make the house prosper, purify it,
> Repair its walls.
> (Wife), house-keeper, young girl, daughter of the house,
> You widen their hearts,
> All good things you do not have a share in depress me, oh say:
> O you, you are the stability of the town.

This beneficial effect in the domain of women is contrasted with the following:

> The one who stands at the cross-roads and roams the streets,
> The one who sits in men's assemblies and finds out about the
>   man's house,
> The wife, the girl who stay in their women's quarters and do
>   not relax with you,
> You make friend quarrel with friend!
> Your ears are pricked, your eyes dart about,
> You let women live in their enclosures,
> And seed dispute amongst them!
> (. . .)
> O you, you are the woman.

In Innin šagurra, there are some damaged lines (75–8) which also allude to Inanna's influence on adolescent and mature women, as well as prostitutes:

> She dresses the adolescent girl in her chamber, . . canals and
>   dikes . . heart, desirability . . ,
> the woman she rejects, . . in an evil way,
> in the entire country . . . to her . . [. .]

She lets her run around the street, lets her stand on the b[road market'(?)]).[13]

She is also responsible for the reversal of traditional sex roles:

> To turn a man into a woman and a woman into a man are
> yours, Inanna. (120)

But the Enheduanna poems generally concentrate on the warlike and fear-inspiring personality of Inanna.[14] This is in keeping with the iconographical presentation of the goddess on cylinder seals from the Akkadian period onwards, a fully dressed female, standing on a large feline animal and bristling with weapons (Frankfort 1939).

Most Mesopotamian hymns addressed to a single deity are an exaltation – underlining the unique capacities and status of the god or goddess. There is always an element of judicious flattery involved when a divine being is singled out in this manner. One could call that the etiquette of addressing gods in a polytheistic system. He or she is the most powerful, the most indispensable, the most competent and the most awe-inspiring of all. The great emphasis on the terror some gods inspire may be attributable to the same submissive position assumed by the worshipper. Actual specific functions are naturally included in the enumeration of potential influence. We do not really know whether these texts were recited before the statues of gods or read to them, and what role they played in the cult, although some later, first-millennium rituals contain such references. They were certainly a very popular genre of text and it is difficult to imagine that they should have been composed only for the literate scholar.

In the case of the Inanna hymns quoted above, we can conclude that they address the goddess at the height of her power, probably in connection with the temporary astronomically exalted position of the planet Venus. The primarily masculine and martial characteristics of the mythological persona of Inanna are used to describe the far-reaching repercussions of this exaltation. It also means that the goddess is invested with phallic power. She was given her share by An and went on to accumulate more and more divine prerogatives, as the myth of *Enki and Inanna* describes. In fact, Inanna's bid for power is well documented by a variety of hymnic texts. Not surprisingly, this has led various male scholars to the conclusion that this drive was exaggerated, even a hubris. But although Inanna experiences the limits of her influence in the Underworld, where she is successively deprived of power and ends up as a 'shrivelled bag' hung on a nail, she does not permanently 'die', but like her planetary equivalent, Venus, rises from her periodical invisibility to a new ascent.

The second interesting point is that Inanna as a theological construct is just as contradictory as Enki. He is a male deity who subsumed a feminine element (Nammu, Tiāmat), and compensates by becoming the most overtly phallic among Mesopotamian gods. Inanna operates within the male domain of warfare and celestial rulership, and becomes identified with eroticism and sensuality, the most feminine of goddesses. It is this latter aspect which will concern us in the following chapters.

7

THE BRIDAL SONGS

The masculine and aggressive aspects of Inanna the Warrior (ur-sag) were particularly emphasized in texts with political undertones, such as royal inscriptions, or hymns that linked the deity with the ruling dynasty. The third millennium was an age characterized by frequent internal conflict between city-states, as well as by raids from abroad, and the dynastic and local deities were said to march at the head of the armed forces of their domains. On the famous Stela of Vultures, for instance, now in the Louvre, the god of Lagaš, Ningirsu, is depicted as holding a gigantic net filled with captured enemies. At some point, maybe in the Sargonic period, Inanna joined the ranks of the fighting gods, and we saw in Enheduanna's hymns that her fierceness was unrivalled. A text by Utuhegal, the king of Uruk who delivered Sumer from the foreign rule of the Guteans, illustrates how the goddess was invoked to participate in warfare:

(Utuhegal) went before Inanna and prayed:
My lady, lioness of battles, who challenges the foreign lands,
Enlil has charged me to bring back kingship to Sumer,
Be (you) my support!'

$$(16-24)^1$$

Like male martial gods, she lends her power to assist the king in his military aspirations, she punishes his enemies and generally functions in a masculine capacity. Her exaltation as Queen of Heaven, another popular theme in Mesopotamian poetry, may have had a primarily astronomical and ritual origin. However, unlike in the later Babylonian tradition, where her high status was linked to her marriage to the sky-god Anu (Lambert 1982: 173–218), her femininity was not emphasized in this context in the relevant Sumerian compositions.

While it is important to refer to the broad range of Inanna's functions in cuneiform literature, we shall, in the following chapters, concentrate on those texts which elaborate on her specifically female characteristics and her role as love-goddess.

The functions and personality of a deity are usually described by epithets and standard phrases (Seux 1967). They denote his or her city and temples, as well as particular qualities. Goddesses, like women generally, were defined by their kinship relations with other, particularly male, deities. However, some goddesses had a specific area of professional competence. Nidaba was a scribe, Ninisinna a healer and midwife, Nanše a dream interpreter, etc. Some were patron deities, in charge of certain cultural or natural phenomena: Ašnan of grain, Ninkasi of beer, Nintur of childbirth, Ninsun of cows, etc. Some epithets consist of titles of office (nin, sukkal, nu-gig), and these are more problematic. We cannot tell to what extent they were merely honorific or had a specific connotation. Like similar terminology in all languages, such titles can convey different meanings at different periods and contexts.

The choice of descriptive epithets depends to some extent on the purpose and nature of the composition; long, hymnic texts would deal with all aspects in turn; while shorter ones concentrate on a salient feature. In the literary texts, some deities came to epitomize a particular position of kinship, or profession. Geštinanna, for instance, figures predominantly as the loyal sister of Dumuzi, Ningal as Inanna's mother, Nunšebargunu as the Old Woman. Many other goddesses are primarily wives and in-laws, or even concubines (dam-banda), such as Šuziana, the secondary wife of Enlil. To some extent the descriptive epithets of Mesopotamian goddesses reveal the cultural perception of women and their role in ancient society.

To return to Inanna. It is remarkable that the texts are not at all consistent when it comes to her genealogy and kinship ties. However, in the texts describing her betrothal and wedding to Dumuzi, she is usually called the daughter of the moon-god Nannar-Suen and his wife Ningal, and the sister of Utu, the sun-god. Very rarely is Inanna addressed as 'mother'[2] and never, to my knowledge, as 'Old Woman'. Instead, the age-group designation most closely linked with Inanna is that of the ki-sikil, 'maiden'. In the myths described in previous chapters, as well as in non-literary texts, this term was applied to young girls between the onset of puberty and the consummation of marriage. Although Inanna is often described as having passionately consummated her wedding to Dumuzi, ki-sikil remained her standard epithet, sometimes with dam ('spouse') added on alongside. But like the Greek term *parthenos*, it may also denote independence from the authority of a husband (Devereux 1982: 81).

There are many Sumerian texts that dwell on Inanna's love-life. Until recently, all these texts were said to relate to a 'Sacred Marriage' ceremony, a symbolic union between king and goddess, such as was proposed by Sir James Frazer in his *Golden Bough*. The ramifications of this notion will be discussed in a later chapter. Here it suffices to point out that such a 'catch-all' category fails to do justice to the complexity of the original text material. Some texts are indeed concerned with Inanna's wedding, some speak of the king as her lover, others cast the goddess as a professional lover, others again speak of erotic love but do not mention Inanna. I shall deal with these various aspects in turn.

The group of texts that I propose to designate as Bridal Songs feature Inanna as a girl expecting to be married. They pertain to the period between the onset of puberty and the wedding rituals. We do not know very much about the social customs surrounding marriage and betrothal in neo-Sumerian times let alone earlier, but contracts and legal texts suggest that girls were married soon after the onset of their menarche, and could be betrothed or contractually married much earlier (Wilcke 1985: 244; 1967–8; 153–63; Greengus 1969: 529–53; Milroop 1992: 213–16). The prospective union and any financial settlements were agreed by the parents, and there seems to have been some transfer of gifts from the groom to the bride, while she was given a portion of her father's wealth as a dowry. There is even less evidence on actual wedding rites, and the literary texts, such as the songs under discussion here, form the basis of our present understanding. The problem is that we do not know whether these songs reflect or describe current and common practice, or whether they are special, as befitting a goddess. The basic procedure of the wedding-day rite, according to the bridal texts, is the following. The groom, accompanied by male friends, comes to the house of the bride's parents, bringing gifts. The bride meanwhile is dressed by her female friends and relatives, having bathed and scented herself beforehand. She puts on all her jewellery and awaits her groom. In the songs she welcomes him with phrases such as 'He is the man of my heart', which may constitute her official acceptance of his suit. There is no mention of veiling, or any further ritual. The bride-father gives a banquet, and eventually she follows the groom to the house of her in-laws. Patrilocality was common but not obligatory. The urban conditions especially allowed for more flexible arrangements, such as neo-locality, or even matrilocality. It is also quite clear that the Bridal Songs are primarily relevant for the socially and economically higher strata of society. Although the sexual union of the young couple is an important subject in the songs, it is not clear whether it was part of the wedding ritual, and indeed where it took place. The Bridal Songs are also not directly concerned with the period of integration into the new household, or even the socially important event of the birth of the first child, but primarily with the preparation for and the anticipation of the new status. They concern the liminal period, up to the point where groom and bride meet on the threshold of the bride's home. It is for this reason that the term Bridal Songs appears more appropriate than Wedding Songs.

As far as the social reality of this liminal stage is concerned, most of the legal evidence comes from much later (second- and first-millennium) sources. Finkelstein (1966: 363) pointed out that, although married women's movements in public were rather restricted, especially in Assyria, 'it was more or less expected that nubile young ladies would parade in public – with greater or lesser innocence of design, with or without their parents' approval'. According to the Bridal Songs, young persons of both sexes were able to meet in public and form romantic attachments, although there is an air of furtiveness to their meetings. The main figure of authority for the girl is her mother, but the brother also plays an important role. The emotional state of the girl is a major theme. She dreams of her lover, she longs to meet him again, in secret, and she looks forward to her wedding-day, primarily in anticipation or even reminiscence of sensual pleasure. It is doubtful whether such conditions reflect the real situation of Sumerian upper-class girls; we have no evidence that there was any institutionalized encouragement of 'experimental' pre-marital sex. But the poetic texts nevertheless formulate cultural ideals, even if they do not conform with prevalent social mores. A well-known study of Bedouin poetry, for instance, has shown that the medium of song and poetry allowed the expression of sentiments and emotions which a society with a very strict code of female modesty would not tolerate in real life (Abu Lughod 1986: 183ff.). I do not believe that we have such a pronounced dichotomy between poetic content and social restrictions in the Sumerian Bridal Songs. Rather they enforce the traditional values of harmonious marital relations, based on sexual fulfilment. By stressing the positive experience of conjugal happiness, the Bridal Songs may serve to alleviate feelings of ambivalence and anxiety on the part of the bride. I am inclined to relate these songs, like lullabies or laments over dead relatives, to the world of women, since the female perspective is dominant. Even if women had limited legal status and were not given much of a say in the choice of a husband, this does not preclude emotional involvement. Even a marriage arranged since childhood is an exciting and unique event in the life of the bride. Although the Sumerian Bridal Songs are all said to concern Inanna, a goddess, and are not 'folklore', but a literary product, they might well have an origin in traditional songs that accompanied the various stages of the *rite de passage* which a wedding entails. But the transition from folk-song to cult-song, or folk-song to literature, is not unique, but occurs in different cultures and different historical circumstances.

In the Sumerian material, as far as the Bridal Songs are concerned, we note the absence of any extraordinary events, of major transgressions leading to catharsis or tragedy. In *Enlil and Ninlil*, the goddess achieved royal status as Queen of Nippur and wife of Enlil after an illegitimate pregnancy. But the salient point of this myth was to prove that her fertility matched that of Enlil's and that her loyalty deserved his devotion. The pre-nuptial impregnation did contravene customary behaviour, but it was presented as a unique event of cosmic importance, leading to the birth of four important gods. Although the framework of the myth is also a rite of passage, it describes an extraordinary, mythical situation that only happened to Enlil and Ninlil. We have also seen that the situation was quite different in the text describing the wedding of Sud, where everything was done with impeccable propriety, and did not involve any transgression of normal behaviour. The courtship of Inanna and Dumuzi is essentially like that of Enlil and Sud. Inanna may be less demure than Sud, but in spite of her flirtatiousness, she never experiences Ninlil's dilemma. Even the choice of a 'shepherd' for a lover does not seem to cause much concern, and according to one text her brother positively urges her to accept his suit.

The temporal framework of the Bridal Songs is the period of time between the girl's first awareness of sexual desire and her wedding day, with transitional stages set by formal betrothal and the preparation for the ceremonies. The texts are often structured like libretti in which the girl, her beloved, members of their families, as well as guests and friends, speak their parts. But the emotional focus is the couple in love, or more accurately the girl in love, because the male's part in these scenarios is marked by stereotypical expressions that betray the projection of fantasy. The voice of the bride expresses desire; it is usually concentrated on her 'object of desire', Dumuzi, the shepherd, the 'man of her heart'.

As the songs were, as I have said, not folk-songs, but literary compositions with a view to cultic usage, little though we know about that, they had to conform to literary conventions and expectations. In the Song of Songs the lover is none other than Solomon, although the 'Shulamite' is less exalted. In the Sumerian texts, the protagonists are Inanna and Dumuzi. Her mother is Ningal, her brother is the sun-god, and her home is a temple. Dumuzi's mythological personality is more fluid, and his family is less well defined, apart from his sister Geštinanna. According to some texts his mother was Duttur and his father Enki (Kramer 1963: 439; Jacobsen 1987a: 3–7). In other sources his mother is Ninsun. Jacobsen pointed out that both goddesses have affinities with the herding environment. Dumuzi is always the 'shepherd', who lives and operates in the edin, the semi-desert beyond the cultivated land. Dumuzi represents pastoralism, and some texts are actually set in or near the sheep-folds.[3] The literary topic of the Sumerian woman marrying a pastoralist may reflect an actual practice of intermarriage between the two groups, the settled agrarians in and around cities, and the nomadic or semi-nomadic herders at the fringe of Meso-potamian urban civilization.[4]

Let us now look at some of the texts. The 'Wiles of Women' is how Jacobsen referred to a charming work of some fifty lines, in which a female and male voice alternate (Kramer 1963: 499–501; Jacobsen 1987a: 10–12). Somewhat breathlessly, the girl (Inanna) recounts that having spent her day dancing and singing,

> 'He came up to me, he came to me, the lord, companion of
> An,
> He came up to me, took my hand in his, Ušumgalanna
> embraced me.'[5]

But she wards off his advances:

'Where now, wild bull! Let me go, that I can go home!
What stories could I tell my mother Ningal?'

To which he retorts:

'I will teach you, I will teach you, Inanna, the wiles of women,
I will teach you:
I was out in the street, walking with my friend, making music,
She danced for me, we sang and time went by.[6]
Use this as an excuse with your mother, as for us, let us have
Fun in the moonlight!
Let me prepare you a pure, a sweet, a princely bed, let me
loosen
Your combs, let me have a sweet time with you, in joy and
plenty!'

(lines 13–22)

Inanna's reply is missing where the text is broken; only the first line
is partially preserved. She seems to say that she is not a girl of the
street. It is not quite certain whether the text on the reverse really is
a continuation of the same work; the house (of Ningal) will be
prepared with cedar oil to make it fragrant, and Ningal will accept
her prospective son-in-law with the following words:

'My Lord, you are indeed worthy of the holy lap;
Amaušumgalanna, son-in-law of Suen, lord Dumuzi, you are
indeed worthy of the holy lap.'[7]

and praise his riches and his 'sweet grass of the steppe'.

The first part reminds us of the initial meeting between Enlil and
Ninlil, but we are not told much about the circumstances or the
place of this encounter. In both cases the young man makes the first
move in addressing the girl. It is possible to take this too as a
description of a first encounter, but the immediate intimacy suggests
either that she had seen him before, or that her desire now finds an
object, a personal focus. Dumuzi himself suggests the fib Inanna is
to tell her parents to explain her staying out late, although he calls
it the 'wiles of women'. Dumuzi is much more loquacious than the
male gods in the myths. He seduces with words, evoking the shared
pleasures of lovemaking. According to Wilcke (1970: 86), the
missing part of the composition described the girl spending the night
with her lover. The second part certainly provides the setting of the
marriage ceremony and the official acceptance of Dumuzi as the

groom, Wilcke interpreted the activity of neighbours at an effort to pacify 'die erhitzten Gemüter der Eltern'. Alster (1933: 21) suggested that the whole scenario, including the dialogue, could be regarded as a fantasy on behalf of the girl. She dreams about the meeting with Dumuzi and imagines him talking to her. Even the 'happy end', the officially sanctioned marriage, may express the wishful thinking of a nubile girl. The strong erotic element in this text seems to substantiate the idea that the main voice here is female. The unusual eloquence of the male partner and the content of his seduction speech, which promises exactly what the girl expects, contradicts the customary brusqueness of the man in similar situations described in the myths. Maybe the 'Wiles of Women' do not merely refer to Inanna's rather feeble excuse, but the female preoccupation with love in general. Inanna's 'fantasy', according to Alster, concerns her desire to be married. In an earlier article Wilcke (1967–8: 154) surmised that this text may allude to a period of 'engagement', where the groom, sometimes accompanied by his ku-li ('friend'), moves into the house of his prospective father-in-law, having deposited his bridal gift, where he stays up to four months. Both the groom and the bride's father may revoke the marriage agreement during this time, and sexual intercourse (or full sexual intercourse) was not condoned during this experimental period. But whatever the supposed social background to this text, it does show quite clearly that the emotional attachment of the bride to her future husband is very important, and, furthermore, that sexual intimacy, spontaneously desired by both partners, is practically a prerequisite for the decision to marry. The flirtatious banter between the lovers introduces this intimacy and the sentence spoken by Inanna's mother, 'He is indeed worthy of the holy lap/embrace', seems to seal it. The latter phrase is very interesting in this context, for it could be taken either as formulaic, the official acceptance of the groom's request to marry the daughter, or as the recognition of sexual relations between the young people. It could also, of course, be specific with respect to Inanna, as the same phrase was used to describe the king's suitability, as we shall see later.

A similar text, which Kramer called the 'Sated Lover' (1963: 509–10) was given quite a different interpretion by Jacobsen (1973: 199; 1987a: 8–9). Again it is made up by speeches, some in the female 'dialect', the Emesal, some in standard Sumerian. Kramer considered it to contain a dialogue between the lovers, and a soliloquy by Inanna, 'in which she chants of meeting her beloved, designated here as "brother"'. Here is the latest translation by Alster (1993), who generally accepted Kramer's understanding of the text:

'The brother makes me enter his house:
He made me lie on a honey-smelling bed,
After my precious, dear one, had lain by my heart,
One-by-one, making "tongues", one-by-one,
My brother of the fairest face made fifty.
He became (?) like a silenced man,
With an 'earthquake' he was put to silence.
My brother, with a hand put on his waist,
My precious, sweet one, the time passes!
(Lover:) Set me free, my sister, set me free!
Come, my beloved sister, let us go to the palace (*var.* to our
    house)!
May you be a little daughter in my father's eyes!'

Jacobsen took the terms 'brother' and 'sister' at face value and interpreted the whole composition as a dialogue between Dumuzi and his sister Geštinanna, although neither of these is named in the text. He then took the passages where they go to Inanna's house and lie 'on a honey of a bed' to have occurred between Inanna and Geštinanna as her confidante, 'who loses no time in relaying the exciting news [of her love for Dumuzi] to her brother, and Dumuzi – pretending to have official business in the palace – is quick to be off to reassure the suffering Inanna that he loves her too'. Jacobsen's interpretation seems distinctly contrived, as if to avoid an erotic meaning at all costs in spite of the highly charged language. Furthermore, the terms 'brother' and 'sister' were standard expressions of endearment between lovers, not only in Mesopotamia, but also in ancient Egypt, the Song of Songs, Arab love poetry, etc.

Alster found that this was another example of a meeting that actually only takes place in the girl's mind. The most interesting line in this respect is line 29, which I quote in Sumerian for its delightful resonances:

dili-dili-ta eme-ak dili-dili-ta
One by one – making tongues – one by one

eme-ak ('tongue making') usually implies speaking, chatting (the proverbial 'sweet nothings'?). But it could also have, as Alster duly noted, a double meaning, and imply lovemaking.[8] The following lines speak in favour of a sexual meaning, as the 'brother' is silenced by an 'earthquake' – surely a reference to orgasm[9] – although Inanna is willing to continue this form of passing time. Again, the scenario is one of pre-marital lovemaking, with the man expressing his desire to formalize their sexual union, since the last line explicitly says that the girl should become the daughter-in-law of his father. The text is also imbued with a sense of irony, that the inexperienced ki-sikil is well able to exhaust the ardour of her lover, even rather overtaxing his virility.

The above text may form part of a longer composition, which strings together several separate items: dialogues, monologues, short descriptive passages, and chorus-like invocations. One such text has become known as the 'Manchester Tammuz' (Alster 1992), pre-served on several tablets from the Old Babylonian period. Again, the context is the prospective marriage of Inanna and Dumuzi. There is an interesting contrast of tone between the different voices, which are never directly identified in the text. The girl expresses longing for the company of her lover:

'[He] brought joy into the garden,
I am the girl, the lady, where are you, my man?
[The shepherd(?)] brought joy into the garden,
I am [the girl(?)], the lady, where are you, my man?
Into the garden of apple trees[10] he brought joy,
For the shepherd(?) the apples in the garden are loaded(?) with
    attractiveness (hi-li),
Into the garden of grapes he brought joy.

(1–7)

The garden is a universal metaphor in love poetry, well known from European folk verse, from Latin, Egyptian, Chinese and Sanskrit sources (Atkins 1978: 222ff.). Like all successful metaphors, it operates on several levels of meaning. The garden can be a real garden, a favourite place for amorous trysts. We must also bear in mind that the garden has a special significance in an arid country. In ancient Mesopotamia, as in the Middle East today, these enclaves of lush vegetation, profuse growth, coolness and shade form a tangible contrast to the heat and dust of city streets. There were groves of trees and shrubs attached to temples as well as private houses and palaces. The garden was a microcosmic model of civilization, the triumph of human control over a difficult environment. The domestic garden was, furthermore, an extension of the realm of women, and especially that of aristocratic ladies, who lived in considerable seclusion. We have to remember here that, according to Herodotus, one of the fabled Wonders of the World was a garden in Babylon built for the wife of a king! But in poetry the desire to enter the garden also means a desire for sensual pleasure. We have already noted how the langauge of love is deeply imbued with vegetal imagery. The fruits of the garden are full of voluptuousness. The lovers desire each others' 'fruit', and we shall see that the female genitals are likened to a garden, the male member to apple-trees. In Sumerian texts 'garden' and 'bed' are used in very similar contexts, and both are associated with the feminine, the artifice of eroticism, distinguished from the marshes of the phallic gods, or the furtive pleasure of the city street.

The important words here are me-me and hi-li. The former can mean both 'silence' and 'joy' (Alster 1993: 20); the latter has several connotations, but basically expresses the notion of something that is conducive to the inducement of sexual desire, similar to the Greek term *kharis*, and hence often translated as 'charm' or 'sex-appeal',[11] although neither of these lexemes are able to convey the semantic range of the Sumerian word. People possess hi-li, Inanna is its divine personification, the object of desire is also invested with hi-li. But it is also applied to jewellery, clothing, furniture, fruits and trees. To some extent hi-li is a concept that needs to be understood as part of 'magic' discourse. It is an inherent quality that can permeate objects and living beings alike, and produces an effect in other people, causes a distinct attitude, inspires love, admiration and, perhaps above all, sexual desire.

The lover is identified as the one who will bring sensual fulfilment 'to the garden'.

The 'chorus' affirms that Inanna needs to be united with her beloved (lines 16–18):

> 'Let her go to Amaušumgalanna,
> The bull, Dumuzi, provides happiness.
> Let her go to Amaušumgalanna!'

The ceremonial reception of the groom by the mother is, as we have seen, an integral part of the wedding ritual, and occurs in most Bridal Songs, as here in lines 20–4:

> 'In mother Ningal's gate he stands indeed.
> I, with joy, I, the lady, am coming.
> Let the man speak the word to my mother.

Let our neighbour sprinkle water on the ground for the lady!'

The groom arrived with the customary gifts:

> 'For you, maiden, when I put the gifts before you, I will add
>   more for you,
> Holy Inanna, let me bring them to you!'

He proceeds to enumerate the various items, such as differently dyed clothing, and so on, which go on for some length. The text is interrupted several times by the impatient exhortations of the girl (lines 44–53, quoted here lines 44–45, 47):

> 'Me, let me go, let me go, to the garden let me go!
> Me, the lady, let me go, let me go to the garden!
> In the garden dwells the man of my heart!'

Significant portions of the text are missing, but more lists of gifts are mentioned, and Inanna, now obviously not 'any' bride but goddess, is said to proceed to (the temples of) Abzu–Eridu (lines 108–13). She demands copious supplies of various commodities, such as flax, barley, wool and oil, the staple subsistence items of the Sumerian economy (lines 111–21). Dumuzi, and in a variant Inanna herself, supplies these provisions, and all is now set for the official proclamation of their wedding:

> 'When he brings her dates as (a gift of) flax, the luxuriant one
> (Will say): 'Let us be my spouse' (i.e. let us confirm our
>   marriage).
> And my mother shall belong to your mother,
> And my sister shall belong to your sister,
> Maiden Inanna, he shall be your 'only one!'

The groom then joins in, with a presumably customary phrase, referring to the consummation of the marriage and probably defloration and impregnation:

> 'Oh let me plough the field, let me plough the field!'
> (line 130)

The latter sections, the bringing of rich gifts and the newly established integration of the two households, is repeated several times. In lines 153–7 it is expressively stated that Inanna will join his family:

> 'Into my house, my great building, to my family, let me

75

THE THIRD AND EARLY SECOND MILLENNIA

introduce you.
Let me introduce my "vulva", the daughter-in-law, to my
family!'

(lines 154 and 157)

A last part contains the self-praise of Inanna, the Queen of Heaven
and Earth, which is clearly taken from religious hymns.

The various speech parts in this poem follow one another without
producing an internal dynamic through interactive dialogues. Inanna's impassioned longing serves to punctuate and interrupt the
rather mundane description of the preparation for the wedding
ritual. At times this reads like sheer impatience, at other times like
an attempt to escape her fate and retreat into the privacy of her
fantasy. But generally the work is less given over to the expression
of private emotion, and more concerned with actual ceremonial. As
such it may well reflect a ritual enactment of divine betrothal and
marriage (see chapter 12), incorporating elements of Bridal Songs in
a ritual framework.

The wedding itself seems to be the most important subject, and
Inanna's feelings are only quoted as it were in parenthesis. In the
more intimate Bridal Songs, Inanna's psychological state as bride is
the primary concern. This need not always take the form of erotic
day-dreaming, but can be more direct and humorous. One such
text[12] begins with Inanna taunting her lover that, without consulting
her family, 'he had come chasing after her', to which he replies, in a
conciliatory tone, that his family's status is equal to hers, and should
not provide material for a dispute (lines 7–22). Here are some
extracts from this passage, using Jacobsen's somewhat idiosyncratic
translation (1987a: 4):

'Girl, please don't, as it were, start a quarrel,
Inanna, let us, as it were, talk it over.
(. .) My father is, as it were, your father too.
Inanna, let us, as it were, talk it over.
My mother is, as it were, your mother too.
Ninegalla,[13] let us, as it were, wise you up.
(. .) I am also as were I Utu,
Ninegalla, let us, as it were, wise you up!'

Then the chorus adds the following comments (lines 23–5):

76

The words they spoke, the words of delight are thirty.
(He) with whom she quarrelled (became) the one dear to her
heart.

(Wilcke 1976: 296)

This leads directly to the rapturous and thrice-repeated exclamation:

He who made the šuba-stones, he who made the šuba-stones,
he shall plough the šuba-stones!
Inanna, stretching from the wall, stretching from the wall, his
spouse, the nu-gig, speaks to Amaušumgalanna:
Plough the šuba-stones, plough the šuba-stones, who will
plough the šuba-stones for me?
Amaušumgalanna answers the nu-gig:
She is the nu-gig, my spouse is the nu-gig!
He ploughs them for her, for holy Inanna, the priestess,
He of her šuba-stones, he of her šuba-stones, he ploughs the
šuba-stones indeed!

(lines 25, 30–2, following Alster 1993: 23)

The reference to šuba-stones occurs in several other texts, often in connection with the term of office nu-gig.[14] It probably denotes a specific ornament worn by women who bore this title (so Jacobsen 1987a: 6). The link with the verb 'to plough' suggests a sexual meaning, but the reason for this remains enigmatic (see Alster 1933: 18). But juxtaposition of the latter passage about Inanna receiving šuba-stones (we know that her statues were decorated with jewels and precious stones), to have them 'ploughed' by Dumuzi, and the preceding courtship scenario, may well fit an actual ritual investiture or initiation of a nu-gig, choreographed like a wedding.[15]

Other compositions, although they too emphasize the apparel of Inanna and the gifts brought to her, are comparatively mundane and closer to 'real' wedding celebrations. One poem from Nippur (Kramer 1963: 407–9; Jacobsen 1987a: 19–23) introduces the 'bridal-lers' of Inanna. Led by the groom Amaušumgalanna, Dumuzi's official name in such songs, they include the Farmer, the Fowler and the Fisherman, who all bring gifts pertinent to their profession: choice butter and milk from the Shepherd, honey and wine from the Farmer, birds and 'precious carp' from other two. They all arrive at Inanna's house and call to her mother Ningal to open the door. Ningal turns to her daughter:

'Verily, you are his spouse, he is your spouse (..)

Verily, your father is (now) a stranger only.
Verily, your mother is (now) a stranger only.
His mother you will (have to) respect as if she were your
     (own) mother,
his father you will (have to) respect as if he were your (own)
     father.'

(Jacobsen 1987a: 21)

Her words mark the transitional stage in the wedding ceremony, where her allegiance shifts from her father's family to that of her husband. Dumuzi, standing at the door – he himself occupies the same marginal position at this point – calls out impatiently:

> 'Make haste to open the door, my lady,
> make haste to open the door!'

Inanna is prepared:

(She had) bathed in water, anointed herself with sweet oil,
Put on for an outer garment the grand queenly robe,
Also took her 'man-beast' amulets,
Was straightening the lapis-lazuli stones on her neck,
And held her cylinder seal in her hand.
The young lady stood waiting, Dumuzi pushed open the door,
And like a moonbeam she came forth to him out of the house.
He looked at her, rejoiced in her, took her in arms [and kissed
     her.]

Then follows another ritual, involving prayers to the personal gods, but this passage is badly preserved. Finally Dumuzi speaks to his bride, and here we have again a note of private intimacy. He reassures her that he will keep his wife in the station to which she is accustomed: she will eat at a splendid table, while his brother and sister will eat elsewhere. Nor will she have to do any domestic chores, such as spinning, weaving and cooking. Obviously Inanna is exempt from the usual difficult position the new bride finds herself in her in-laws' household.

This last text seems the most genuinely traditional Bridal Song, in spite of the fact that Inanna the goddess is the main protagonist. It dwells on the psychologically difficult transition of the bride from her parents' home to that of her groom's family, but she is reassured that she will be treated well. The descriptions of the ceremonies do not seem to describe any special ritual to which the marriage symbolism was added.

It is clear that the category of Bridal Song can only be used as a provisional vantage point. The songs' actual purpose may vary considerably, and even the internal context is not totally coherent. Some texts dwell on the intimate longings of the young girl expecting marriage, but who chooses the 'man of her heart'.[16] Erotic fantasy plays an important part. To what extent this emphasis on sexual fulfilment in marriage is the result of Inanna being the epitome of the Bride is difficult to decide. But the fact that Inanna, 'goddess of voluptuousness', should provide the paradigm for the literary Bridal Songs, and hence be considered a suitable role model for the young girl awaiting marriage, indicates that the importance of erotic satisfaction within marriage (and before) was recognized. Inanna's wedding to Dumuzi may constitute a cultural ideal, in spite of the fact that (or indeed because) it was rarely achieved in real life.

8

INANNA AND HER BROTHER

Inanna's relationship with her brother has special importance in the context of Bridal Songs. He is closely involved in her nuptial arrangements and some texts are set in dialogue between brother and sister.

One such text concerns the making of the bridal sheets (Kramer 1963: 512; 1969: 68–73; Jacobsen 1987a: 13–15). The two initial lines establish that Utu and his 'young sister Inanna' are the speakers. He tells her of the flax that is luxuriantly growing in the field, which he will bring her.

> 'Brother, when you have brought me the green flax, who will ret it for me?
> Who will ret it for me?'

asks Inanna.

> 'Sister mine, I will bring it to you retted,
> I will bring it to you retted.'
> 'Brother, when you have brought it to me retted,
> Who will spin it for me, who will spin it for me?'

'Already spun I will bring it to you' replies Utu, and so the song continues in the same pattern of question and answer, throughout all the stages of spinning, dying, weaving and bleaching, until Inanna asks:

> 'Brother, when you have brought it to me already bleached,
> Who will lie down there with me?'

to which Utu replies that it is Amaušumgalanna ('Companion of Enlil, the offspring of a king'), who will lie down there with her. She is overjoyed:

'Is that true? He is the man of my heart.
The man my heart told me.'

Formally, the gradual progression from the living green plant to the woven and dyed sheet builds up a momentum of expectation and curiosity which culminates in the direct question 'and who shall lie there with me?'

The poem conveys the impatient curiosity of the bride and her exultation is won from the teasing delays of the long string of questions. The linen sheets can also be understood as a metaphor for the girl herself. She is transformed from 'a lovely young thing', the green shoot, to the bathed and anointed, beautifully bedecked bride, who, like the sheets, lies on the bed in expectation of her groom. The words describing the growing flax are exactly the same as those used for beautiful girls elsewhere. The final purpose of the sheets and all their elaborate stages of manufacture is the wedding bed and all the long and complicated pre-nuptial preparations have the same aim.[1] The teasing tone is also evident in the final question as to the identity of the groom, and the – surely feigned – surprise that it should indeed be the 'man of her heart'. The wishes of the brother, the male representative of her family, and those of the young girl coincide. One even feels a certain complicity between Inanna and her brother, based on an emotional intimacy.

Even when Utu is apparently hostile to his sister's wishes, as in the following text, it seems that by knowing her heart better than she does he brings her to realize her true desire. In this text Utu is the sponsor of Dumuzi's suit in the contest between the Farmer (Enkimdu) and the Shepherd (Dumuzi) (van Dijk 1953: 73ff.; Kramer 1969: 69f.). Sumerians were very fond of contests of wit, as numerous 'disputations' on cuneiform tablets testify. Bird argues with Fish, the Hoe with the Plough, the Crane with the Raven, one graduate of the tablets house with another, etc. The dialectic discourse was also an important part of the educational curriculum (Wilcke 1975: 250ff.). Here the representatives of the two basic modes of existence at the time, the pastoralist who lives in the uncultivated semi-desert and the settled farmer, are engaged in such an exercise.

Utu begins by praising the Shepherd:

'Sister mine, marry the shepherd; Maid Inanna, why be
    unwilling?
His cream is good, his milk is good,

81

The shepherd, whatsoever he touches is bright (. . .)'

To which Inanna retorts:

'The shepherd I will not marry,
I will not wear his coarse garments, I will not accept his coarse
  wool,
I, the maid, will marry the farmer,
The farmer who grows many plants, the farmer who grows
  much grain.'

Then Dumuzi himself speaks up and, in a manner typical for the adamin-duga dialogues, defends his case by matching the advantages and products the farmer can offer with those of his own, one by one:

'The farmer, what has he more than I?
If he gives me his black flour I give him my black ewe,
he gives me his white flour, I give him my white ewe'

This attitude is summarized by the question:

'How can the farmer have more to offer than me?'

Although it is not expressly stated here, Inanna seems to have been convinced as well. Enkimdu, the Farmer, admits the superiority of the Shepherd, who then magnanimously invites him to the forthcoming wedding feast, where the Farmer will arrive with some of his own produce:

'Why should I strive with you, O shepherd?
Why should I strive with you?
Let your sheep pasture, eat the plants along the (irrigation)
  canal,
Let your sheep graze on my (freshly) cultivated ground'

And Dumuzi replies:

'I, the shepherd, will count you as my friend at my wedding'

And Enkimdu promises to

'(. .) bring wheat, to bring you beans and (other) pulses,
Maid, whatever is fitting for you (. .) I will bring.'
                                        (Kramer 1969: 7)

The outcome of this contest provides social harmony all round; the Farmer becomes the friend and cognatic relative of the Shepherd.

The text has therefore direct relevance for the existence of exogamous marriage settlements. Although the strict tribal organization was to some extent loosened by the development of urbanism, it probably remained a cultural constant among the semi-nomadic pastoralists. But as in contemporary southern Iraq, there were close ties between herding shepherds and agriculturalists, who could have had the same tribal affiliations and exchange marriage partners (Fernea 1971: 176ff.). The disputation-dialogue confirms that it is more advantageous to Inanna (who represents a farming background) to wed a shepherd, because he can supply her with all the dairy products and meat that are unavailable to the farmer. The text is also an example of the traditional manner of arranging marriages within a patrilinear society, where economic and tribal politics are an important factor. Unlike the Bridal Songs discussed in the last chapter, this text does not represent the point of view of the girl. It is more in keeping with actual practices by making her an object of competitive rivalry. But since Dumuzi was known as the traditional lover of Inanna, he has to win the contest. Inanna rejects him. At first, because she finds his way of life uncongenial, her arguments are not based on an emotional preference. In fact, the erotic attraction emphasized in other texts is replaced here by the satisfaction of material needs. The compliance of the bride in following the wishes of family, here represented by her brother, assures social harmony; Enkimdu and Dumuzi reaffirm their collaboration and the whole community benefits.

Much more intimate, and seen from the perspective of the house (the realm of women), is another dialogue between brother and sister, which describes the final preparations of the wedding, just before the bride receives the groom in her mother's house (Kramer 1963: 407–9; Jacobsen 1987a: 16–18; Alster 1985: 146–52).

> 'My sister, what did you do in the house?
> Little one what did you do in the house?'

he asks her in the beginning. In reply the bride enumerates the various stages of her *toilette*:

> 'I washed myself, I rubbed myself with soap,
> I washed myself in the pure tub,
> I rubbed myself with soap in the white stone vessel,
> I pleased myself with the fine oil from the stone jar,
> I dressed in the gala robe, the robe of "queenship of heaven".

This is why I shut myself in the house,
I painted my eyes with kohl,
Straightened my hair (. .)
Took a golden ring on my finger
Put small beads around my neck.'

(Alster 1985: 151)[2]

Thus she presents herself to the brother and breaks out into a song of admiration for his 'most pleasing and radiant sister'.

'Bring in my bridegroom,
Let him come, let him come,
Let him bring fine butter and cream'

she urges the brother who escorts her into the chamber. Then follows a song which sounds like a quotation from a much older source, a traditional wedding song:

'Now my breasts stand up,
Now hair has grown on my vulva,
Going to the bridegroom's loins, let us rejoice!
O Baba, let us rejoice over my vulva!
Dance! Dance!
Afterwards they will please him, will please him!'

(Jacobsen 1987a: 18)[3]

The relationship between Inanna and Utu in these compositions is marked by a playful intimacy. He takes an interest in her affairs, seems to be anxious for her happiness, and he takes an active part in the preparations for the wedding. The father is practically never mentioned in these songs.[4] But as in traditional contemporary societies, such as Turkey for instance, where the role of the bride's brother closely resembles the one described in our texts, it is the brother who knows his peer group from which the sister, or the parents, choose a husband. He is the one who can vet eligible marriage partners and is able to advise her and the family on the candidate's suitability. The relative importance of the brother for his unmarried sister seems to be higher where young girls and boys have limited opportunity to get to know each other.

There is also a very interesting aetiological myth which explains Utu's link with beer-making and Inanna's expertise in erotic matters (Kramer 1985; Bruschweiler 1987: 58–61).

Inanna asks her brother to accompany her to the Mountain of Cedars (kur ᵍᶦˢerin), where aromatic tree oils, silver, salt and lapis lazuli are to be found. Because, she tells him,

> 'What concerns women, (namely) men, I do not know,
> What concerns women, (namely) love-making, I do not know,
> What concerns women, (namely) kissing, I do not know.'

But by eating 'what there is in the mountain', presumably some product of the cedar, she will gain the necessary expertise. Then Utu is to take her back to Zabalam, to her mother Ningal, her mother-in-law Ninsun and the sister-in-law Geštinanna. In the concluding lines she praises Utu:

> 'Whoever walks alone, whoever has left his house,
> whoever has left his house, whoever walks alone,
> You, Utu, are their mother, you Utu, are their father,
> Utu of orphans, Utu of widows, (. .)
> Utu you always support(?) the widows,
> There is joy in your company, joy for the one who journeys
>   with you.'

(Bruschweiler 1987: 59)

The references to Inanna's in-laws should be taken here as references to her prospective relatives, to indicate her status as a bride who has not yet consummated her marriage. The final praise of Utu is interesting in this context. We know from solar hymns that Utu was seen as a guide to travellers and a companion to the lonely (Castellino 1976: 71–4). In this passage he is accompanying the young girl to some rite of passage. As far as I am aware, there are no other references to such rites in other Bridal Songs, but, as Dowden has shown (Dowden 1989), evidence for such institutions is often extremely circumstantial, and it would be vain to speculate about specific forms it might have taken. But a temporary absence from familiar surroundings and the instruction in matters concerning this stage of life are general characteristics. The journey to the kur, and the explicit purpose to 'learn what concerns women', point strongly in this direction. Alster (1993: 17) noted that, in looking at the phrase 'let me ride with you to the mountain', 'one cannot possibly avoid the impression that she wants to have intercourse with him [i.e. her brother] herself', noting that the allusions to trees and their sap may also have a euphemistic meaning. The brother may have played an important role in such ceremonies, if only ritually.

As far as I am aware, only one text deals unambiguously with the subject of incest, including sibling incest (Alster 1975b: 216–9). Here we have Dumuzi leaving his wife Inanna in the city in order

> 'To go to the desert land,
> To look after the holy stall,
> To learn the ways of my holy sheepfold,
> To provide food for my sheep,
> To find fresh water for them to drink.'

Inanna's answer is too obscure for a translation. At any rate, Dumuzi is next found in his stall, in the company of his sister, presumably Geštinanna:

> 'The stall is filled with plenty,
> The sheepfold flows with abundance.
> They eat – pure food they eat,
> They pour honey and butter,
> They drink beer and wine,
> Dumuzi, to bring joy to his sister
> The shepherd Dumuzi takes it into his heart.
> He lined up [?] [sheep], brought them into the stall,
> The lamb, having jumped [on the back] of its mother,
> Mounted her . ., copulated with her,
> The shepherd says to his sister:
> "My sister, look! What is the lamb doing to its mother?"
> His sister answers him:
> "He having jumped on his mother's back, she (?) let out a
> shout of joy."
> "If, he having jumped on his mother's back, she (?) let out a
> shout of joy,
> Come now [?], this is because . . he has filled her with his
> semen.
> The kid having jumped [on the back of his sister],
> Mounted her . ., copulated with her."
> The shepherd says to his sister:
> "My sister, look! What is the kid doing to his sister?"
> His sister answers him innocently [?]:
> "He having jumped on his sister's back, she [?] let out a shout
> of joy."
> "If, he having jumped on his sister's back, she [?] let out a

shout of joy,
Come here now [?], [this is because] he has flooded her with
his fecundating semen. .."'

(Kramer 1969: 102–3)

Kramer found this dialogue an attempt by Dumuzi 'to amuse his sister'. The text could also be understood as contrasting the ways of the steppe, exemplified by the 'sheep-fold' and the ways of the city. Inanna is always associated with the latter; she stands for the urban, agrarian side of Sumerian civilization. Dumuzi, the pastoralist, represents the herding culture of the steppe, which, while coexisting with the settled farmers, was outside the control of urban institutions. The shepherds and nomads were considered to be outsiders with proverbially different cultural habits. But, as we have already pointed out, their mutual economic and social interdependence was substantiated by intermarriage. In Sumerian literature it is always the male nomad or pastoralist who marries into the urban community, never the other way round. In fact, as we see in the Dumuzi love texts, the shepherd becomes the archetypal lover of Inanna, the desired Other. Their essential difference provides the erotic attraction of the unfamiliar. Here it is sufficient to note that, by marrying Inanna, Dumuzi partakes of this notion. But now he leaves the city and returns to the steppe, alone, with the quite legitimate intention of looking after his flocks. There, he is surrounded by the wild, uncivilized antics of his livestock. Animal sexuality, quite obviously, is beyond social restrictions and entirely, instinctively lusty. Dumuzi himself is not only observing this sort of behaviour, but seems to be under its influence. Because by describing, quite explicitly, what the animals are doing, he also addresses his sister, and incites her to watch and even comment upon it. Now we know from the various potency incantations that to describe the copulation of animals was considered sexually stimulating (Biggs 1967: nos. 1–9). Hence the arousal of Dumuzi, and of Geštinanna, is implicit. The message is clear: out in the steppe anything goes and even Inanna's own husband is not immune to its temptation. It is interesting that while Inanna's range of erotic activity includes other, potentially disruptive and deviant forms of behaviour, such as homosexuality, adultery and prostitution, it does not seem to take in incest or rape. Both may therefore be taken to belong to the 'wild' and instinctual manifestation of animality. It is also interesting that they are associated with the male sexual perspective, as the recurrent references to the fertilizing semen imply.

Apart from this particular text, 'brother' and 'sister' were used as general terms of endearment between lovers. This has parallels in other cultures, perhaps most notably in the love poetry of ancient Egypt (Vernus 1992: 19). This accounts for a certain ambiguity in our understanding when the text does not supply the personal names or the setting.[5]

To summarize, we can state that the role of the brother in the love literature has more than one dimension. In the context of Bridal Songs, he is the one who mediates between the young girl and the world of men; he can advise her in choosing a suitor and takes an active part in the various preparations. He also acts as her friend and confidant, rather like a sister, who is emotionally close to the young bride-to-be. This intimacy between the siblings sometimes prevents a definite interpretation of the setting. The involvement of the brother in any rites of passage may be alluded to in the myth of Inanna's journey to the kur.

The strong bond between brother and sister in the love-songs has a counterpart in those pertaining to the death of the young god. Dumuzi as a dying god finds shelter and comfort in the arms of his sister Geštinanna, as does Damu, another doomed god, with Gunura. In fact, in the face of death, the sibling bond is stronger than that of sexual love, as the fate of Dumuzi proves. In one particular text it is the love of the sister which achieves a partial salvation by offering her life for his (Alster 1972), as in the myth of *Inanna's Descent to the Underworld*. Within the genre of the lament over the dead god, the sister's voice is heard more often than the lover/wife.[6]

We have seen how, through the prototype figure of the 'Maid' Inanna, the nubile girl proceeds to the most important event of her life: her sexual maturity and marriage. Our Western culture places a considerable distance of time between the two, but in many pre-industrial societies they roughly coincide, and it is not unreasonable to assume that girls in third-millennium Mesopotamia were married soon after their menarche. The texts, which may incorporate traditional songs, present a situation where the girl has some degree of freedom to meet young men. The Inanna texts seem to reflect the aristocratic social milieu, where adolescent girls were expected to behave with some decorum but were able to form attachments. The choice of the groom, however, rests with the elder members of the family, notably the mother and the older brother.

It is interesting that cuneiform literature has, as far as is presently known, not produced the romantic song of thwarted love and spurned affection, which is so richly represented in the Renaissance period and classical Arabic literature. The girl naturally rejoices when the young man whom she finds attractive becomes her groom. The brother of Inanna has a very close relationship with his younger sister, and one could surmise that such sibling attachments were encouraged by Sumerian society. The absence of the father in the majority of these texts is not unusual. He is a marginal figure in the process; female initiation in the widest sense of the word is a matter for women. The male authority is represented in these texts by the brother, who has free access to his sister and takes a prominent role in the actual arrangements of betrothal and the wedding feast. The emotional state of the girl is well observed: impatience, flirtatiousness, curiosity, deceit and excitement are conveyed in stylistically elaborate means of poetic artifice, which are only too often quite untranslatable. In this respect, the most skilful example is the composition known as 'The Bridal Sheets', where the slow and tedious process of turning the fresh green flax into a bleached and woven sheet is related to the girl's progress from puberty to marriage.

The erotic content of the bridal songs is generally limited to anticipation and longing for the absent lover. In many cultures the adolescent fantasy of as yet unfulfiled love is the mainstay of poetic inspiration, or the only socially condoned expression of erotic feeling. However, it also remarkable that while, say, Egyptian love-songs, Sapphic odes or Elizabethan lyrics frequently dwell on the painful symptoms of projected love, this topic of *chagrin d'amour* is virtually absent in Sumerian poetry. What it does convey, very skilfully, is the mounting impatience and restlessness of lovers: 'Oh let me go to the garden, to the man of my heart' – such exclamations punctuate the ponderous preparations leading to the wedding. If our interpretation of the texts is right, the girl also indulges in erotic fantasies about meetings with her lovers. But even when this imaginative dimension is absent in the text, she is said to have expectations of conjugal happiness based on sexual fulfilment. We shall see in the following chapters that the bridal prerogative was greatly expanded to accommodate even royal ideology.

9

INANNA REJOICING IN HER VULVA

In the Bridal Songs Inanna represents the voice of the adolescent girl. She expresses her longing to be in the presence of the beloved:

> 'I am the girl, the lady, where are you, my man?'

and

> 'Me, the lady, let me go, let me go to the garden! In the garden dwells the man of my heart.'
>
> (Alster 1992: lines 4, 46–7)

These romantic sentiments imply the temporary separation of the lovers before their wedding. We also found a certain amount of imaginary intimacy in anticipation of time spent together. The bride is shown as looking forward to her married state, not least because she will enjoy then full adult sexual relations:

> 'Going to the lap of the groom – let us rejoice,
> Let us dance, let us dance,
> O Bau, let us rejoice over my vulva!
> Let us dance, let us dance,
> (until) the end it will please him, it will please him!'
>
> (Alster 1985: 152)

Intercourse with full penetration was the traditional consummation of the marriage. It allowed the 'fertilising sperm to be deposited in the woman's womb'[1] and thus induce pregnancy. It seems that it was also the form of sexual act which was forbidden to the unmarried girl (Cassin 1987: 341).

Another poem focuses on Inanna's anticipation of sexual relations within marriage (Kramer 1963: 505–8). In preparation for the wedding bed Inanna bathes and dresses in her grand robe:

'The lady started to sing in praise of herself,[2]
The gala[3] will sing of it,
Inanna started to sing a song of praise of herself;
She sang a song of her vulva.'

(Alster 1993: 21)

In this song she implies that:

'My bridegroom will rejoice in me; the shepherd, Dumuzi,
   will rejoice in me.'

She then embarks on a highly evocative eulogy of her vulva (gal₄-la),
which is unfortunately obscure in some parts (lines 17–24, obv. col,
ii). She compares it among others to a horn:

'The heavenly barge of the moon (with its) mooring ropes,
The lovely crescent of the new moon,
A fallow plot in the desert, a field of ducks, full of ducks,[4]
Well-watered hilly land'

and asks rhetorically (lines 25–37):

'For me, open my vulva – for me!
For me, the maiden, who is its ploughman?
My vulva, a wet place, for me –
For me, the lady, who will provide the bull?'

(Alster 1993: 24)

To which the audience replies:

'Oh, lady, the king will plough it for you,'

and she urges him herself (line 40):

'Plough my vulva, man of my heart.'

The ploughing metaphor, which we often find in the Bridal Songs,
is then not just a general euphemism for sexual intercourse, but
applied more specifically to the first penetration of the vagina. The
young woman is compared to a field waiting to be rendered fertile,
by the plough (i.e. the penis) driven by the bull (i.e. the man). It is
in the context of marital intercourse that the male sexual role defines
itself as the provider of fertility. The woman joyfully participates
and declares her readiness 'to be ploughed'. It is hardly a coincidence
that the description of the vulva in the text above captures the stages
of sexual excitement in the woman. At the beginning her vulva

resembles the narrow curve of the new moon until it opens 'like a boat with its mooring ropes' (more likely to refer to the labia minora than pubic hair). Then there are several references to the transudation of the mucous membranes ('well-watered low land', 'my vulva, a wet place'), at which point she cries out for the 'plough'.

If one takes the setting of these lines within the context of a marriage ceremony into account, one could say that Inanna stands for the Bride, who rejoices in her vulva because it symbolizes and contains her new identity as a sexually active and hence reproductive woman. The transitional process is only completed when she gives birth to the first child (Cassin 1987: 356). The Sumerian songs are phrased in such a manner as to emphasize the sensual pleasure the bride is to experience. In contrast to contemporary Bedouin societies of the Middle East, there seems to have been little value put on reticence and modesty in sexual matters (Abu Lughod 1986: 107ff.). The bride flaunts the evidence of maturity ('our parts have grown hair', 'our breasts are now standing out') and take an interest in amatory arts (see the erotic fantasies in the Bridal Songs). She is portrayed as keenly anticipating the sensual experience of the marital bed. But we have to remember that Inanna's role as the goddess of sexual love might also have influenced the explicit nature of these references.

Not all songs or poems that mention the vulva, or the woman's delight in her organ, refer to the wedding night. One must remember that the ideogram for 'woman' in the earliest cuneiform texts consists of the sign depicting the public triangle – just as 'man'/ 'male' is represented by an ejaculating penis. This sign, SAL, could be read as munus, or mí ('woman'), or as the syllable gal in the word gal$_4$- la ('vulva'). This identification of the part with the whole is also reflected in the Sumerian idiom: somebody who chases women is someone after the vulva (Gordon 1959: 469, 512). Many other references to female sexuality concern the state of the vulva. In one song Inanna is introduced as the 'vulva, the daughter-in-law' (Alster 1992: 23, lines 154, 157), and in the as yet unpublished disputation between two women, one pours scorn on the other, saying she was

'A daughter of a poor man, no man appreciates her vulva'
(Alster 1975: 98)

One bilingual Sumerian–Babylonian proverb has an ageing woman protest that she is still sexually desirable:

'My vulva is (still) fine, although people say it's finished with
    you'
(Lambert 1960: 248)[5]

while in another, a calculating woman muses:

'Who is rich, who is wealthy, for whom shall I reserve my
    vulva?'
(Lambert 1960: 227)

A poor man's daughter who is unable to provide her with a dowry
cannot capitalize on her main asset:

'Her vulva is not valuable to her; she is a woman whom the
    man
With whom she lies down does not veil, who is not given as
    his wife'
(Gordon 1959: 482).

A proverbial blessing for a young man includes an invocation to
Inanna:

'To cause a wife with a hot "lap" to lie down with you'
(Gordon 1959: 115).

In the erotic love poetry the state of arousal is signalled by references
to the vulva's 'wetness', as we have seen in the bridal text quoted
above:

'My vulva is wet, [my vulva is wet],
I, the queen of heaven, [my vulva is wet],
Let the man on top [put his hand] on my vulva,
Let the potent man [put his] hand on my vulva.'
(Alster 1993: 20)

or, as in this balbal song to Nanaya, where she addresses her lover:

'Do not dig a [canal], let me be your canal,
Do not plough [a field], let me be your field,
Farmer, do not search for a wet place,
My precious sweet, let me be your wet place!'
(Alster 1975)

Alster proposed that 'beer is used as a metaphor for the moisture of
the woman's genitals' when it is said that 'like beer her vulva is
sweet' (Alster 1993: 19), although the references to sweetness may

refer more specifically to taste, as in this passage:

> 'Like her mouth, her vulva is sweet'
> (Alster 1985: 133)

or

> 'bereitest du mir doch deine süße Stelle,
> berührtest du mir doch deine Stelle, die süß wie Sirup ist'
> (Römer 1976: 373)

which raises the question whether these lines should be understood as references to cunnilingus. There is no conclusive evidence that such a practice was taboo.[6] It would appear that if female sexuality was taken seriously, as these texts certainly suggest, then oral sex could hardly have been excluded.[7]

Inanna's organ is often called úr-ku(g) ('the holy lap'), ku(g) is an adjective that is also applied to Inanna herself, as well as to numerous other deities, temples, places and artefacts, and it is usually translated as 'pure', 'holy'; the opposite of ku(g) is KUG-AN = azag ('taboo', '(ritually) unclean'; also 'demonic' and 'dangerous'). It is well known from anthropological literature that genitals are associated with power and are subject to all kinds of regulations and prescriptions, and it is curious that there is very little material on this subject in Sumerian sources. The notion had much greater currency in the later second and first millennia, especially in connection with magic. The apotropaic use of genitals or genital symbols is well documented from many parts of the world: one need only think of the Sicilian *fica* or the Celtic Sheilag-na-gig.

Inanna's vulva is a *pars pro toto* for the goddess herself as deity of sexuality. This is also borne out by the countless figurines and terracotta models of female nudes found all over the ancient Near East and the vulva-shaped votive offerings which were deposited in the temples of Ištar as the most appropriate ex-voto.

Finally, to conclude this chapter there is literary myth from the Isin–Larsa period, which has Inanna use her vulva, or rather the power associated with it, to further the prestige and divine status of her city Uruk (Farber-Flügge 1973). The very beginning is fragmentary, but it does state that 'her vulva was admirable' (gal₄-la-ni u₆-di-dam) and that 'she spoke confidently to herself, pleased with her vulva'. Then she plans her actions: she will bestow all manner of graces upon the en (or Uruk?) and then she will set foot in Eridu and speak words of flattery to Enki. Enki, however, in his 'wide understanding', is aware of Inanna's intentions. He instructs his minister Isimud to receive the Maid Inanna with customary welcome, offering her cakes, cool water and beer. Later he joins her himself, and they drink beer and wine together until Enki becomes quite intoxicated. Under the dual influence of drink and Inanna's charm, he begins to hand over to her one by one the me he has in his possession. These include a variety of trades and professions, cult offices and ritual implements, as well as aspects of human behaviour (disputes, lying, slander, peacemaking, reverence, hard work, but also kissing, copulating, prostitution, etc.). The list is enumerated several times in the text. When Enki recovers from the effects of the beer, he discovers that the me are missing. Isimud tells him how Inanna had loaded them all on to the 'boat of heaven' and is on the way to Uruk. Enki sends him out with the command to stop the 'boat of heaven' with the help of various demonic forces, but Inanna is able to repel them all and get the boat with the me safely to Uruk. The final part of the text is fragmentary; there is a confrontation between Inanna and Enki and some other god who probably mediates between them. In his commentary on this composition (Alster 1975), Alster concentrated on the sexual aspect. Crucial to his argument is his interpretation of Enki's relationship with Inanna. Since she persistently calls him 'a-a' ('father'), and he addresses her as 'dumu' ('child'), Alster concluded that Enki was 'presumably her father' and that 'the pattern of the myth is a violation of the sexual taboo', namely that of incestuous temptation: Inanna purposely set out to 'enchant Enki', being as she is 'endowed with enormous sexual attraction'. He also restored some of the fragmentary lines towards the end of the composition with a curse of Enki, in which 'the vulva of certain women shall be crushed'.

Inanna was, as we have seen, usually called the daughter of the moon-god Nannar. There are passages in other texts (notably *Inanna's Descent*), where she also speaks to Enki as her father. This could be a term of respect towards an older person, as Farber-Flügge pointed out. While we cannot be absolutely certain as to what the poet intended by this use of the kinship terminology, it is worth considering whether the subject of incest is necessary to the understanding of the work. Inanna sets out to get something belonging to another deity and another city. She trusts in her feminine charm, epitomized by her 'astonishing vulva', and travels to Eridu in her má-an-na, the 'boat of heaven', which is also sometimes used as a metaphor for her genitals. The alcohol Enki serves in the course of the banquet does the rest. (Inanna also has affinities with beer and the premises where it was consumed, as we shall see later.) She also uses a very efficient spell, which is repeated seven times to repel the demonic hosts of Enki, although the exact meaning is still unclear:

'Water did not touch your hand, water did not touch your foot.'

There may be a sort of magic contest going on between Enki and Inanna, between the power of the vulva and the power of the phallus, along the lines of the contest in the Enmerkar epics, but more subliminal. The final outcome is at present impossible to determine, although the stylistic closeness of the text to other compositions of the UrIII period (Farber-Flügge 1973: 20–34) seem to speak in favour of a positive outcome for Inanna.

Just as the cuneiform sign for 'vulva' could stand for 'woman', the vulva is the epitome of a woman's sexual identity. It seems to have predominantly positive associations; it is not feared or spoken of as shameful or contaminating. The nubile girl rejoices when her pubic hair appears. The bride can be introduced as the 'vulva' to her parents-in-law, Inanna lauds her genitals in a highly poetic style; indeed Inanna's vulva was 'holy', rather like the Baubo (Devereux 1981). In so far as Inanna stands for the power of sexuality, the vulva is sacred as such. Interestingly, the penis of Enki (or Enlil) is never called kug, quite unlike the lingam of Şiva. According to the later omen-texts, semen was a highly polluting substance, whereas female exudations are said to taste sweet. The vulva is the instrument, the prime tool, of female sexuality; its various stages of excitement are carefully observed. While the phallus represented fertility, the vulva represented sexual potency and became the primary focus of Mesopotamian eroticism.

10

'MY CONSORT, MAID INANNA, LADY, VOLUPTUOUSNESS OF HEAVEN AND EARTH'

The title of this chapter is a quotation from a royal hymn, in which Šulgi of Ur (c. 2094–2047) praises his physical prowess, his wisdom and his close relationship with the great gods of Sumer (Klein 1981: 198–9). He calls himself the 'child of Ninsun', 'the choice of holy An's heart', 'the man whose fate was decreed by Enlil', 'who was endowed with wisdom by Enki', 'the wise scribe of Nisaba', 'brother and companion of Utu', 'beloved by Ninlil', 'cherished by Nintu', etc. Such epithets are typical for this type of literary composition, which focuses on the function and personality of the king, often expressed in mythological terms. His most intimate connection, however, is with Inanna.

In the sentence above the king refers to her as 'my consort', although the next epithet declares Inanna (still) to be a ki-sikil, a title normally incompatible with that of a married woman. Even if one allows for the fact that ki-sikil was a standard appellative of the goddess, its juxtaposition with the title nitadam, 'spouse', affirms the position of independence, which the divine partner maintains vis-à-vis her mortal husband. The next apposition, nin ('lady', 'queen'), confirms Inanna's status. The last words, hi-li-an-ki-a, refer to Inanna's function as goddess of love on a cosmic scale. This one line neatly contains the tenets of the king's 'marriage' to Inanna: she chooses the 'husband', continues her independence and has the greater divine status. In fact, in most of the texts that refer to the relationship between king and goddess in marital terms, the king is said to be *her* 'consort' (dam), or her 'beloved husband' (dam-ki-agá), 'husband chosen by Inanna's heart' (dam-šà-ge pà-da-ᵈinanna), 'the selected husband' (dam-igi-íl-la) and 'husband, the ornament of the holy loins of Inanna' (dam-me-te-úr-kù-ᵈinanna) (Kienast 1990).

While there are quite a few of these short references to the king being Inanna's consort in the various royal hymns, there are only three texts which elaborate on this subject.

To my understanding, the Bridal Songs were not specifically concerned with the divinity of either protagonist, although the Bride was called Inanna. But in these three texts, where the king's intimate relation with Inanna is described, she is very much the goddess. Her divinity is of central importance, and is clearly emphasized by epithets and direct allusions to her power and influence on a cosmic and national scale. She is explicitly identified as the goddess who resides in the temple Eanna at Uruk (Šulgi X), the 'great heavenly lady' (nin-gal-an-na), who sits on a throne with An, and decides the fates of Sumer with Enlil, 'the mysterious star, star of Venus, who fills the sky with shining light' (Inanna-Dilibad), the 'queen who encompasses the universe, queen of heaven and earth' (Iddin-Dagan hymn). The 'bride' of these texts is no bashful maiden, but the goddess who invites the 'groom' to her 'sacred bed'; none other than the goddess of love, 'who looks to having nations multiply'.

The first king to be associated with Inanna in this manner was Šulgi, the second king of the Third Dynasty of Ur. One hymn describes him touring the major temples of this realm to offer sacrifices and receive the blessings of each deity in turn (van Dijk 1954: 83; Kramer 1967: 369ff.; Klein 1981: 135–66). His very first stop is Uruk, where he presents wild bulls and young kids and enters the shrine, bewigged and dressed in a special robe. When Inanna beholds him she breaks into a long chant, half of which consists of a 'decreeing of fate'. She assures him of her continuous support and confirms the king's suitability for his royal office. The first twenty-five lines of Inanna's song (lines 14–38) are taken up with the sensuous recollections of erotic encounters with 'the shepherd Dumuzi', i.e. Šulgi.[1] She received him in a state of ritual purity, having bathed and adorned herself with cosmetics. The following details of their lovemaking are difficult to translate because there are no known parallels for most of the expressions used. From the tentative version prepared by Klein it seems that Dumuzi's caresses are metaphorically described:

> 'Since by his fair hands, my loins were pressed,
> Since the lord, the one lying down by holy Inanna,
> The shepherd Dumuzi,
> In (his) lap smoothed me with milk

Since in my . . . pure arms . . he relaxed,
Since like choice . . . (and) choice beer,
. . . . he touched,
[since] the hair (of) my lap he [ruffled] for me,
Since with the hair (of) my . . he played,
Since on my pure vulva he laid his hands,
Since in the . . of my sweet womb he laid down,
Since like his "black boat" he . . .
Since like his "black barge", he . .
Since on the bed he spoke pleasant (words),
I (also) will speak pleasant (words) to my lord,
A good fate I will decree for him!'

The detailed description of caresses refers to the sensuality of
Inanna, who demands that the act of physical love be conducted
with the right attitude and dedication. The text also implies that
Šulgi was equal to this challenge, since she rewards his competent
lovemaking by decreeing a 'good fate' for him. In her account of
their intimacies she refers to the king as the 'shepherd Dumuzi', her
proverbial bridegroom and lover, but at the beginning of her
'blessing', she specifically identifies Šulgi himself as the 'righteous
shepherd'. But there is nothing to indicate that this was a wedding
ceremony as Klein and others suggested (van Dijk 1954: 84, 86; Klein
1981: 125). The gifts Šulgi brings to Inanna are not different from
those he offers other gods on his 'pilgrimage'. There are no
processions, no acclamations of the bride, no mention of Inanna's
parents, etc. Instead, we get the impression that the king comes to
the goddess as to a courtesan (the expression 'hierodule' would be
appropriate for once!). She receives him bathed and perfumed, with
rouged mouth and kohl on her eyes. Proving himself in bed, the king
gives her her dues; not just in gifts and sacrifices, but through service
to her sexuality. At the end of her long blessing, she declares him
suited not only for the 'brilliant crown' and the exercise of kingship
but

'To dance on my holy knees/breast like a tender calf
You are suited'

(Klein 1981: 153)

which in the present context is an unmistakable euphemism for
intercourse.

The other two compositions are set in the reign of Iddin-Dagan of Isin (*c.* 1953–1935), who was a great admirer of the UrIII kings, and especially of Šulgi. One text refers to the sanctuaries of Eridu but it is not certain whether the lovemaking between the king and Inanna was understood to have taken place there as well (Kramer 1963: 501ff.; Jacobsen 1973: 40–3). Inanna does not speak herself but her actions, as well as those of the king (again identified with Dumuzi), and to some degree her emotional state, are almost breathlessly commented on, in Emesal, by observers.

> 'The day is named, the day is fixed, the day the lord arouses
>   the woman.
> Give life to the lord! Give the lord the staff and crook!
> She demands it, she demands it, she demands the bed,
> The bed that rejoices the heart,
> She demands it, she demands the bed;
> The bed that makes the embrace delicious, she demands
> It, she demands the bed,
> She demands the bed of kingship, she demands it; she
> Demands the bed of queen-ship, she demands it;
> By him (making it) delicious, by him (making it)
> Delicious, by the delicious bed;
> By the bed that makes the embrace delicious, by him
> (making it delicious); by his delicious bed of the delicious
>   embrace'

and so on, in an incantatory manner, until Ninšubur, the minister of Eanna (Inanna's temple), leads the king, wearing his hi-li- wig, to the 'loins of Inanna' (úr-ga-ša-an-na-šè) and wishes that

> 'The lord whom you have called to (your) heart . . . enjoy long
>   days
> In your delicious, holy lap, grant him a pleasant reign to come'

as well as other blessings and finally

> 'The king goes with lifted head to the holy lap of Inanna and
> Embraces the holy one'.

The rest of the tablet is broken off but, as in the Šulgi text, there is no reason to see this encounter as the consummation of a marriage. The erotic urge of the goddess, however, is strongly emphasized and, again, the king is said to comply, although the broken state of the tablet precludes speculation on the outcome.

There is only one text which in some ways recalls the celebrations

of divine marriage in Babylon or India (see chapter 12). It describes
the rituals of the New Year festival in the capital, Isin, where Inanna
was identified with the city's local deity, Ninisinna (Römer 1965:
128–208; Reisman 1973: 185–202). The style of the composition is
that of a hymnic praise to Inanna.

The festival involved spectacular processions of her cult personnel, complete with ecstatic transvestites and much beating of drums,
special offerings of incense, food and beer, the recitation of songs,
etc. This was followed by a special ritual, the lovemaking of Inanna.
The 'sacred bed' was prepared with precious oils, sweet herbs and
the 'cover which rejoices the heart'. The text continues:

> 'My lady bathes (her) pure lap,
> She bathes for the lap of the king,
> She bathes for the lap of Iddin-Dagan,
> The pure Inanna washes with soap,
> She sprinkles cedar oil on the ground,
> The king approaches (her) pure lap proudly,
> He approaches the lap of Inanna proudly,
> Amaušumgalanna lies down beside her,
> He caresses her pure lap.
> When the lady has stretched out on the bed, in (his) pure lap,
> She makes love with him on her bed,
> (she says) to Iddin-Dagan: "You are surely my beloved."'
> (Reisman 1973: 191)[2]

The festival then continues with further offerings and the admission
of 'the people' to the great shrine, where the king is seated on a dais
next to the goddess. This is the beginning of a tremendous feast to
the accompaniment of music:

> 'The palace is festive, the king is joyous,
> the people spend the day in plenty'

while Inanna is praised as the 'hi-li (the embodiment of sex-appeal)
of the black-headed people'.

The description of the actual encounter between the king and
Inanna does not differ significantly from those of the two other
texts. The king is expected to provide sexual satisfaction for Inanna,
who has prepared for this encounter by bathing. Again, none of the
traditional wedding phrases used in the Bridal Songs are quoted
here, but the setting within the festival, and the descriptions of the
other rituals, especially the public admission to the banquet in which

the goddess sits next to the king, emphasizes the ceremonial role of the ruler and his intimate relationship with Inanna. Because of the wealth of ritual detail that this text provides, it has been taken as an actual description of the festival, interspersed with a hymnic section which could be quotations of songs used at the ceremonies (Reisman 1973: 185). However, Kramer's often-voiced idea that the ritual involved the king playing the role of Dumuzi, and consummating the marital union with a priestess representing the 'mother and fertility goddess' to ensure prosperity and fertility for the coming year (Kramer 1967a: 141; 1969: *passim*) is based on Frazer's interpretation of seasonal rites. Like Inanna's 'battles', her love-making may have been described in song, maybe with some mimic gestures. The later Babylonian 'divine marriage' texts clearly refer to the statues of the gods, and I do not know of an instance where a deity could be represented by a human actor in the manner of a passion-play. The highly stylized language of the composition, which fuses descriptive elements with metaphorical and hymnic passages, also does not allow us to read it as a factual observation.

While the post-Frazerian ideas of the 'sacred marriage' that pro-motes fertility are losing their currency among contemporary cuneiformists, it is nevertheless an interesting fact that the concept of a sexual relationship between king and goddess existed in the first place. I am inclined to see this as a development of royal ideology generally. In this respect it is useful to look briefly at another literary topic, that of the divine birth of kings.

We have seen that the motive of sexual reproduction was used in Sumerian literature to explain cosmogonic processes, the birth of deities and, to some degree, the fertilization of the land. From the Early Dynastic period on, some rulers claimed to have personal relations with the gods: they are 'beloved' by their city's chief deity and 'chosen' to lead and govern (Sollberger and Kupper 1971: No. 1A3b). In some inscriptions gods also appear as metaphorical parents and wet-nurses to the future kings. Eannatum of Lagaš, for instance, writes on his famous victory stele:

Ningirsu (the city-god of Lagaš) planted the seed of Eannatum in the womb of Ninhursaga (the mother-goddess), Ninhursaga gave birth to him. Ninhursaga rejoiced in Eannatum. Inanna held his arm and pronounced his name to be 'Eanna-Inanna-Ibgalkakatum'. She placed him on the holy knees of Ninhursaga. Ninhursaga fed him from her holy breast. In Eannatum, the seed implanted in the womb by Ningirsu, Ningirsu rejoiced.

(Sollberger and Kupper; 1971: 48)

The royal inscriptions of the Sargonic kings were notably more reticent about intimate relations with gods, but the tradition was kept alive at Lagaš, where all rulers, from Ur-bau onwards, claim divine descent and the love and friendship of the gods. Gudea, for instance, addresses the goddess Gatumdug, and holds her solely responsible for his birth:

'I have no mother – you are my mother. I have no father – you are my father, you implanted in the womb the germs of me, gave birth to me from out of the vulva, sweet, O Gatumdug, is your holy name!'

(Jacobsen 1987a: 391)

The long poetic compositions addressing the powerful kings of the Third Dynasty of Ur abound with descriptions about the intimacy between the gods and the king; divine parentage is naturally included, as in this hymn to Šulgi:

Shepherd Šulgi, when your seed was placed in the holy womb, your mother, Ninsun, gave birth to you, your personal god, pure Lugalbanda fashioned you, mother Nintu nurtured you, An gave you a good name, Enlil raised your head, Ninlil loved you.

(Klein 1981: 74–5)

The idea that human beings were children of gods was not restricted to kings, as a great number of personal names with the form 'God/ dess X is my father/mother' demonstrates. The nature of the relationship was one of dependence and trust. But with the development of a royal ideology which elevated the ruler to a position of physical closeness to the city-gods – not least because he had privileged access to the gods' temples and rituals – his parental connection to the city-gods was given great prominence. He was king by virtue of the gods' will, he was selected for this role and his very existence was the result of divine lovemaking. It justified his position of unparalleled centralized authority through divine approval, and established the motivation for the continuing help and support of the deities in their love and friendship for the person of the king.

This emphasis of an emotional bond between god and king is characteristic for the literary definition of Sumerian kingship. The texts of the third millennium refer to several different kinds of love, among which maternal love has a most prominent place. The maternal aspect need not be limited to one goddess, but can be shared among several female deities, who nurse the royal infant together. Fatherhood of gods is also well documented, and in Eannatum's inscription mentioned above, Ningirsu delights in his human offspring. While this relationship is one of love, it also acknowledges the difference in power and status.

Other forms of love, such as that between siblings and friends, are based on a position of equality, and such epithets are on the whole reserved for kings and rulers. All these forms of emotional attachment exclude the erotic. The phrase 'chosen in the heart of God/dess X', and the epithet 'beloved' (ki-agá), are also not used exclusively in a context where a goddess is involved, but are used with either male or female deities. So we can state that up to the Third Dynasty of Ur, and indeed after the Isin period, the emotional relationship between kings and the gods is characterized by a feeling of love and affection (quite apart from responsibility, trust, etc.), which is likened to that between parents and child, siblings or friends generally. The possibility of erotic love as part of the mythology of kingship was only pursued during these two hundred years.[3] The ideology of kingship was probably the most important literary topic of this period. This was approached from two angles, the religious and the pseudo-historical perspective.

First, a few notes on the deification of Sumerian rulers.[4] There is some evidence that the kings of the Third Dynasty of Ur introduced special royal festivals and employed priests to administer to the statues of their likeness (Wilcke 1974: 180). They also built temples for them, such as Šulgi's E. hursag in Ur or Šu-Suen's at Ešnunna. However, there is no information as to whether there was any direct ritual expression of divine status. It is unwarranted to assume that the statements contained in the literary products of the time should have a correlative in the actual life of the court and country. In the texts the divinity of the king is expressed primarily in relation to his subjects. From his position as the pinnacle of a very hierarchically structured society he is seen as 'the god of his land', 'true (zi) god', 'protective god of Sumer and Akkad', whose

word is the word of An, the determination of fate is given into
your hand as a god.

(Wilcke 1974: 179)

He can also be identified with the office of minor gods in a sort of
pragmatic syncretism, as the titles 'Enkimdu of the people' and
'Ištaran of the seed of Sumer' demonstrate. All this is far removed
from the fully developed theory of divine kingship of ancient Egypt,
where the Pharaoh was Horus incarnate, or the Japanese concept of
the *tenno*, the divine emperor. On the contrary, the texts make it
quite clear that the king owes not only his existence, but his office
and his persistence in that office, to the great gods and is only a 'god'
by virtue of his exalted position among other mortals.

To come back to the question of the king's relationship with
Inanna, we notice that he is addressed as 'Dumuzi'. We have
mentioned before that Dumuzi is a highly ambiguous figure in
Sumerian literature. According to the Sumerian King-list (Jacobsen
1939) there were two Dumuzis: one was called 'the Shepherd', and
was said to have ruled the antediluvian dynasty of Badtibira for
36,000 years; the other, known as 'the fisherman, whose city was
Kua(ra)', succeeded Lugalbanda as king of Uruk in the second
dynasty after the Flood. Then there is also a tradition of a divine
Dumuzi, who appears in early god-lists.[5] Amaušumgalanna, sometimes quoted as a sobriquet of Dumuzi, is also mentioned in god-
lists. In several texts Dumuzi gets killed by bandits in the steppe, or
is pursued by a host of demons (Alster 1972: 14), and this dead
Dumuzi is also the subject of lamentations. We have also seen that
Dumuzi was the proverbial lover of the Maid Inanna in the literary
Bridal Songs. The same doubt as to the primacy of their association
should be voiced in relation to those texts where Dumuzi is a victim
and calls himself her husband. The Dumuzi of the lamentations may
originally have been quite a separate personality from the lover of
Inanna. Equally confused are the statements in the texts about his
status. It is not clear who dies, the man, the 'Shepherd', the king of
Uruk, the husband of Inanna, or a god, as all these epithets can be
found in one and the same text. But in respect to our enquiry, it is
interesting what Dumuzi says when, pursued by demons, he tries to
take refuge in the house of the Old Woman Belili:

'Old woman! I am not (just) a man (lú), I am the husband of
   a goddess!'

(Alster 1972: 76f.)

105

And to Utu, the sun-god, he pleads;

'O Utu, you are my brother-in-law, I am your sister's
husband!
I am the one who carries food to Eanna,
I am the one who brought wedding gifts to Uruk,
I am the one who kisses the holy lips,
I am the one who dances on the holy knees, the knees of
Inanna!'

(Alster 1972: 78f.)

He obviously expects special consideration because of his relationship
with Inanna, but as the end of the story demonstrates, it does not
exempt him from the fate of mankind, and he must die. To what extent
Inanna is held responsible for this death will be examined later.
Naturally, when the royal hymns address the king as Dumuzi, the fateful aspects of this character, let alone his tragic end, were suppressed in
favour of that of the youthful and potent lover of Inanna.

The 'pseudo-historical' aspects of kingship were explored in narrative poems. The protagonists of these compositions are not gods, as
in the myths, but kings, specifically kings of the First Dynasty of
Uruk. The court of Ur was keen to promote the idea that Ur was a
legitimate successor to the illustrious house of Uruk (Hallo 1966:
137), and both Urnammu and Šulgi claim descent from Lugalbanda;
and in one text, Gilgameš is lauded as the 'brother and friend' of
Šulgi (Klein 1976: 271).

The notion that the intimate relationship with Inanna was of
fundamental importance to the king was a key element in the poems
about Enmerkar, the predecessor of Lugalbanda on the throne of
Uruk (Kramer 1952; Berlin 1979; Jacobsen 1987a: 275–319). All
three texts concern the land of Aratta, which is described as being
somewhere in the Eastern mountains. Most commentators have
referred the content of these narratives to the actual political and
economic relations between Mesopotamia and the East, especially
the trade in precious stones and metals for agricultural produce. In
Enmerkar and the Lord of Aratta we hear that skilled workmen
were sent from Aratta to build the shrines of Uruk. Very important
is the fact that the goddess Inanna was also associated with Aratta.
It is well known from Middle Elamite sources that female deities
were very prominent in the early Iranian, pre-Persian periods.[6] The
Mesopotamians may have considered this local goddess to be an

equivalent to their Inanna, unless one assumes that Inanna was herself an eastern import, a theory which can not be substantiated, unless Aratta and its archives should happen to be discovered. At any rate, all the texts concerning Aratta agree that Inanna is also at home there, and also loves the en ('lord') of Aratta. As the stories are all told from the perspective of Sumer, her presence in Uruk at the same time proves problematic, unless it can be shown that she abandons one for the other. The ens of the two cities are therefore engaged in competition with the purpose of deciding where Inanna's loyalty lies. The erotic relationship with the en is most clearly brought out in *Enmerkar and Enšuhkešdanna*. Enmerkar taunts his counterpart that he is only able to see Inanna in a dream, whilst he, Enmerkar, actually lies down with her 'in sweet slumber' on the 'adorned bed' (Berlin 1979: lines 62–3, 80–1). He is also able to describe the ornamentation of the bed, and boasts that

> 'The day did not dawn, the night did not pass,
> I myself, accompany Inanna for [15] double hours'
> (Berlin 1979: lines 87–90)

The translator, Adele Berlin, interpreted these words as an erotic metaphor. A magic contest between a sorcerer from Aratta and a witch, the Old Woman Sagburru from Uruk, eventually determines the outcome of this rivalry and the en admits that Enmerkar is 'the beloved lord of Inanna', who has truly chosen him for her holy lap' (Berlin 1979: lines 275–6).

A very similar line is pursued in *Enmerkar and the Lord of Aratta*, where the latter had made a bed for Inanna, as well as a house of lapis lazuli, set a golden crown on her head and yet

> Pleased her not as well as did the lord of Kullab

Although the lord of Aratta is at pains to dispute that, and asserts that she

> 'has not abandoned her home, Aratta,
> has not abandoned the ornate bed'

nor

> 'has she abandoned the lord, her one of the clean hands'
> (Jacobsen 1987a: 315, lines 558–64)

The closing passage of this composition does not specifically refer to a decision as to who should have undisputed access to Inanna, but the tenor of the whole implies that she has the interests of Uruk at heart. The erotic aspect is not stressed in this text, nor is it stressed in the Lugalbanda poems (Wilcke 1969). But it is made quite clear in the narratives about the ancient rulers of Uruk that they had a special relationship of intimacy with Inanna. This need not always be expressed in marital terms; Enmerkar in the Lugalbanda story is called the brother of Inanna (Wilcke 1969: 42).

In the context of the royal hymns of the UrIII/Isin period, where the affinity to the ancient lords of Uruk was a well-known topic, the kings of Ur might have been seen as continuing the privileged association which the kings of Uruk were having with Inanna.

There is also another element that is relevant here, the office of en as a priestly function, which the kings are said to fulfil.[7] According to the *Lamentation over the Destruction of Ur*, Nanna chooses the en priestess for šà-hi-li-a (variously rendered as 'voluptuously', 'in blissful delight', or 'for attractiveness', 'ardent heart' (Jacobsen 1987a: 471))', the same phrase that was used in a Šulgi hymn with reference to his selection by Inanna, which I paraphrased as 'for my sex-appeal'. These passages have been taken to refer to the assumed 'sacred marriage ceremony'. The office of en was traditionally always occupied by a person whose gender was complementary to that of the deity served, Inanna having a male en, the moon-god Nanna a female one (Akkadian *entu*). This has the possibility of an erotic dimension. The *entu* could be called the spouse of the deity, as in a text from Emar, which actually describes the dedication of an *entu* as a marriage ceremony (Dietrich 1989), although this may be a West Semitic tradition, as Emar lies in the Middle Euphrates region, well outside the Sumerian heartland.

The intimacy between Inanna and Enmerkar in the Ensuhkeš-danna epic may also derive from his function as en. He resided in a building called the Gipar, together with some other temple person-nel; but only of the en it said that Inanna 'had called him to her holy lap' (Berlin 1979: 58–9).[8] It is clear from some of the royal hymns that some UrIII kings, certainly Šulgi and Urnammu, were perform-ing what one might call priestly duties in the various temples of the realm, including that of the en. In fact, in the hymn known as Šulgi X, the king could be greeted by Inanna as ú-mu-un, which is the Emesal form of the word en, when she says 'Since for the king (lugal), the en, I bathed'. This implies that at least by the UrIII period there was a metaphorically erotic dimension in the priestly relationship with Inanna. It is possible that an ancient title was reinterpreted during this time to suit the royal ideology. We know nothing about the cultic function of the en in Early Dynastic Uruk, and the portrayal of the ancient Urukian kings in the heroic poems is clearly anachronistic, as well as idealized, to fit the tenor of the narratives.

In the royal hymns, the assumed erotic relationship that the en of Uruk had with the city-goddess Inanna became fused with her traditional association with Dumuzi, who in turn was known as a king of Uruk and the proverbial lover of the goddess.

The royal ideology of the time assured that the kings of Ur (and her successors at Isin) were closely associated with the national pantheon in terms of symbolic kinship, or related by 'descent' to the quasi-ancestral heroes of the ancient Urukian dynasty. They were further commissioned by the national gods to fulfil their royal functions and exercise divine control by proxy, hence their 'deification'. The revivalist interest in the Early Dynastic culture of Uruk may have led to the emphasis on the relationship between Inanna and the en of Uruk. But whether as en of Uruk, or as the 'shepherd Dumuzi', Inanna's lover in the Bridal Songs, or both, the important fact remains that the king is relating to Inanna in a way that is appropriate to the goddess, i.e. sexually. At the same time he comes into contact with her divine power. Symbolic intercourse is an important element in many initiation ceremonies (Parrinder 1980: 51), and it is conceivable that a ritual for the installation of the en, for instance, had such a component. I have mentioned that the female en-priestess was called the 'spouse' (dam) of the god she served.

The notion of eroticism as a display of power, as well as an aesthetic, seems to have been developed some time in the UrIII period. As we shall see, the love-life of king Šu-Suen became legendary, the topic of courtly literature. At the same time we find Inanna increasingly identified as the major deity of sexual energy, and becoming a dynastic goddess (she was later identified with Ninisinna of Isin, when this city became capital). The ideological connection with Early Dynastic Uruk revitalized the concept of the king being the en of Inanna. The royal hymns of the UrIII period continually stress that the kings made frequent visits to the temples of all the major deities, celebrated the traditional festivals and affirmed their personal relationship with the gods. They are full hyperbolic descriptions of the kings' superior abilities, whether at war, at sports, in the arts, in administrative acumen, or in piety. A symbolic relationship with Inanna, either by virtue of being successors of the kings of Uruk, or by virtue of being her en, was similarly exaggerated to demonstrate that the Sumerian rulers not only had access to this particularly powerful form of divine energy, but were suitable for their office because they were able to satisfy her erotic demands. As such, it was yet another proof of their extraordinary vigour and virility, one of the main topics of royal hymns.

11

'WORDS OF SEDUCTION'
Courtly love poetry

The Sumerian king's erotic relationship with Inanna can to some extent be understood as a product of royal ideology, which claimed that the sovereign had quasi-divine status and was integrated in the pantheon with symbolic kinship ties. His sexual union with Inanna has therefore been regarded as a marriage, not least because the texts identify the king as Dumuzi, who in the Bridal Songs always features as the goddess' groom. I have tried to show that there is no substantial evidence, within either the three key-texts or other contemporary sources, that would warrant the conclusion that the UrIII kings (or their successors at Isin) celebrated, let alone acted out, a divine-marriage rite. But if he did not 'marry' her, and if we discount the fertility-rite aspect, then why do they talk about their sexual union? In trying to answer this question we need to look at other literary sources of the period that deal with sexuality.

There are, in fact, a number of texts which have a decidedly erotic content. They are usually classified as 'love-songs' or 'royal love-songs'. These texts, along with the royal hymns, are a characteristic component of late Sumerian literature. Judging from the careful script and the number of extant copies, the love lyrics were valued and appreciated by a literate audience. We know from various hymns that the court at Ur actively promoted music and poetry. In fact, Šulgi prided himself on 'having learnt the art of the scribe' and having 'dedicated myself also to music'.[1] He even claims to value the songs composed in his honour as the worthy lasting achievements.[2] A number of erotic songs directly address Šu-Suen, the son of Šulgi, and although, as Alster (1993: 18) suggests, the name Šulgi could stand for 'any man', such a reference would be unthinkable without a precedent. The love-songs, even when they apparently refer to the 'low-life' milieu of the 'alehouse', have a decidedly courtly tone.

In his address to the Rencontre Assyriologique in 1974, Kraus had already formulated the question: 'Ist die "Heilige Hochzeit" eine literarische Angelegenheit? Verklärt die Hofdichtung ... etwa das Eheleben des Königs zeremoniell zur "Heiligen Hochzeit"?' (Kraus 1974: 249).

I fully agree that the erotic activities of the king in relation to Inanna are a literary topic, and Kraus's idea that one should look at the 'Eheleben' of the ruler is worth considering. In fact, we know nothing about the private life of Šulgi or Šu-Suen as such, except the names of their wives, of which they definitely had more than one (Michalowski 1976; 1979; 1982; Steinkellner 1981). The main wife seems to have borne the title nin ('queen'). Others were called lukur[3]; their personal relationship with the king is documented by inscribed items of jewellery that have been excavated at Ur (Sollberger and Kupper 1971: 150). Such a 'beloved' lukur could rise to the rank of first wife, as seems to have been the case with Kubātum, Šu-Suen's queen (Steinkellner 1981: 80). Royal wives, lukur and nin, were highly esteemed, since libation offerings were made for them after their deaths and occasionally during their lifetime (Frame 1984: 3–4). They obviously shared the quasi-divine status of the king.

The royal household, like that of more humble citizens of the period, was polygynous. It allowed the man to have more than one woman living in the same house, and to have sexual relations with them all. We know very little about actual practices in the neo-Sumerian period, to what extent that there was a difference of status between the women, how widespread the custom was, etc.[4] Intimate relations with female slaves were also fairly common, as some of the proverbs show. Polygyny fosters sexual competition to win the favours of the 'master', and expertise in erotic matters is an important factor. This can also include skills in music-making, recitation and dancing. The royal households of Ur comprised several 'wives', concubines and slaves, as well as singers, dancers and musicians. Some of the love-songs, especially when they are directed at the king, could be understood as a manifestation of seduction through poetic artifice. Others, such as those which are set in the form of a dialogue between lovers, are a stylistic variation of the same scenario. This raises the question of their authorship: could they have been composed by women? We know that royal wives 'composed', or at least commissioned, literary compositions (Kramer 1967: 104ff.). Are the versions we know originals or have they already passed through some stage of editing? Could it be that these texts were written by poets of a later date, who evoked an idealized or imaginary setting, like Byron does in his harem poetry? In the absence of reliably dated sources these questions are very difficult to answer with any certainty, although I would like to believe that they represent the 'true' voice of Sumerian women.

One very interesting text, which has been much commented upon, names three women, who all have some connection with king Šu-Suen (Falkenstein 1947: 43–50; Sollberger 1978: 99–100; Alster 1985: 140–6; Jacobsen 1987a: 57–60). This used to cause all manner of speculation, but we now know that Abi-simti, the first woman mentioned, was in fact his mother, while Kubātum was, as we have seen, his 'lady' and 'queen' (nin); she is not referred to as a lukur in this text, but she is hailed for having given birth to Šu-Suen's offspring. The third woman is called a sa-bi-tu-ma, an Akkadian loan-word, variously rendered as 'tapstress', 'ale-wife' or 'barmaid'; Jacobsen reads her name as Il-ummiya.[5] As far as I am aware this person does not appear in any other documents – here she is praised for her 'beer' and her 'vulva'.

The first part has a double reference to motherhood:

'The pure one gave birth, the pure one gave birth
The lady, the pure one, gave birth
Abi-simti, the pure gave birth
The queen, the pure one, gave birth
My loom(?) (Alster: cloth beam) of the cloth of pleasure, my
    Abi-simti
My warp beam on which the warp is placed, my lady
    Kubātum'.

(Alster 1985: 134)

Abi-simti, the king's mother, is likened to a cloth beam while his wife, Kubātum, has apparently just delivered a child, and is likened to the warp-beam.[6]

The text switches to Emesal, the 'dialect adopted for female voices in Sumerian literary works' (Schretter 1990):

'Because I sang it, because I sang it, the lord gave me a
    present!
Because I sang the a-al-la-ri-song, the lord gave me a
    present!

A gold pin and a cylinder seal of lapis-lazuli – the lord gave me
a present!
A gold ring and a ring of silver – the lord gave me a present!
O lord! Your present enhance the hi-li (sex-appeal) so that you
look at me!
O Šu-Suen, your things enhance the sex-appeal, so that you
look at me!'

(9–14)[7]

Still in Emesal, the text then talks about the 'tapstress', Il-ummiya:

'The beer of my . . . Il-ummiya, the tapstress, is sweet!
And her vulva is sweet like her beer – and her beer is sweet!
And her vulva is sweet like her mouth and her beer is sweet'

(18–22)

The concluding lines are in the main dialect again:

My Šu-Suen with whom I am pleased,
My one with whom I am pleased,
My one by whom I am made cheerful ever!
Šu-Suen, my one with whom I am pleased,
My Šu-Suen, beloved of Enlil, my king, god of his country.
(23–7)

(Jacobsen 1987b: 60)

The main problem with this text is to decide who is speaking at any
one time, as the first-person suffix is used throughout. There seems
to be an alternation of a female and a male voice, signalled by the
change of 'dialects'. All translators agree that the first six lines are
spoken by Šu-Suen, who exults his own birth and that of his son. It
is more difficult to allocate the speaker of the last five lines, which
contain the blessing. Alster (1985: 142) thought it was Kubātum,
although it is not in Emesal; Jacobsen (1987b: 60) suggested some
'Lord in Waiting', 'who kept Šu-Suen company on his lonely watch'.
Kubātum is generally taken to be the speaker of the Emesal lines
addressing Šu-Suen and also of those praising the 'tapstress'.[8]

My own interpretation of this curious text agrees with Falkenstein's idea that there is a single narrator (Falkenstein 1953:
119–20, 370). He thought this to be the 'tapstress', in whom he
divined a priestly lukur, who took the 'mother-goddess' part in the
Sacred Marriage rite. The latter suggestion is now unacceptable, and
there is not much reason for believing that the lukur had a priestly

function at that time. But Il-ummiya's presence in this text does not make sense unless one takes her to be the instigator, or even the author, of the text. However, if that were the case, she uses an interesting literary device, because she does not speak as herself, but assumes the voice of another personality. I propose that this is Inanna, or 'Baba', as the doxology here specifies.[9] The change of Emesal to Emegir (the 'normal' form of Sumerian) within one speech by the goddess is not unusual in such compositions – we also find it in Šulgi hymns (Klein 1981: 137). If the love-goddess provides the framework of the text, some of the problematic issues become clearer. She first speaks about Abi-simti and Kubātum, who are said to be 'kug' ('pure', 'holy'),[10] and this could conceivably apply to some ritual function, although the fact that their sexual activity resulted in childbirth, and thus consolidated their position in the royal household, would also merit the praise of the goddess.

The passage about receiving gifts is usually taken to be put in the mouth of Kubātum, mainly because of the archaeological evidence. But either woman could be the recipient of the king's largess. The reason for getting them is her 'having sung/uttered' the a-al-la-ri song. Jacobsen takes this to be 'the cry of exultation with which she greeted the newborn baby' (Jacobsen 1987b: 60). I take it as an interjection or self-quotation by the singer herself, who was rewarded for the performance which had attracted the king's attention. She is also confident that the gifts will increase her charm and sex-appeal further. But this quote is put in parenthesis, as the blessing for the king in the next two lines (17–19):

> May your city raise its hand in greeting like crab(?)
> May it lie down at your feet like a lion-cub, O son of Šulgi!

has the goddess speaking again.

Then comes the part where the *sabitum*'s erotic qualities are praised: her drink is as sweet as her vulva, which is as sweet as her mouth. The allusion to beer can be understood as having several levels of meaning. Beer is the intoxicating drink that the real *sabitum* dispenses, although the person addressed here, obviously part of the royal household, is hardly an ordinary innkeeper. Alster proposed seeing the references to beer, when linked as here with the vulva, as pointing to vaginal secretions;[11] presumably implying that her beer tastes as good. Jacobsen understood the 'mouth' to mean the utterance, as in a similar passage:

My beloved makes my fame appear in all mouths!
As sweet as her 'mouth' is her vulva, as sweet as her vulva is
   her 'mouth'.[12]

I think that here the singer speaks of herself, but as recommended
not by the king (Alster), or by Kubātum, but by the goddess, who
acknowledges the singer's erotic and artistic qualities.

The last lines of the text, spoken in the main dialect, are another
blessing addressed by Inanna to the king, a reference to the genre of
texts in which he is said to be her lover. Falkenstein's version is the
most convincing as it brings out the fact that the king is rewarded for
his sexual participation:

Šu-Suen, who has blessed me,
You who have touched me,
Šu-Suen, who has blessed me,
Beloved by Enlil, my Šu-Suen, my king, god of your country.
                                       (Falkenstein 1953: 120)

This text is a unique composition and may well have been inspired
by the event of Kubātum's delivery and subsequent promotion of
rank. It provided an opportunity for another woman to put herself
in the limelight with a very accomplished song.[13] Alternatively, one
could imagine Kubātum to be the 'author', as Falkenstein has
suggested, and take the 'tapstress' to be her *alter ego*, thereby
indicating that although she was unable to have intercourse while in
confinement, she reminds the king of their erotic bond.

The other texts addressed to Šu-Suen are formally much simpler, as
the main speaker is one woman. But the poetic artifices they use,
especially the allusion to Bridal Songs, are no less sophisticated.
Here is one in Jacobsen's translation (1987a: 88–9):

Man of my heart, my beloved one,
O! that to make your charms, which are sweetness, are honey,
   still more sweet –

Lad of my heart, my beloved one,
O! that to make your charms, which are sweetness, are honey,
   still more sweet,

You, my own lord and sergeant at arms would march against
   me!
Man, I would flee from you – into the bedroom.

116

O! that you would do, all the sweet things to me,
My sweet dear one you bring that which will be honey sweet!

In the bedroom's honey-sweet corner
Let us enjoy over and over your charms (hi-li) and sweetnesses!

Lad, O! that you would do all the sweet things to me,
My sweet dear one, you bring that which will be honey-sweet!

Man who has become attracted to me,
Speak to my mother, she would let you!
She has worn down my father.

She knows where you would be happy;
To sleep, man, in our house till morning,
She knows where your heart would rejoice;
To sleep, lad, in our house till morning!

When you fell in love with me,
Could you but have done, lad, your sweet thing to me!

O! my lord and good genius, my lord and guardian angel,
My Šhu-Suen, who does Enlil's heart good,

The place where, could you but do your sweet thing to me,
Where, could you but – like honey – put in your sweetness!

O squeeze it in there for me! as (one would) flour into the
measuring cup!

O pound and pound it in there for me! as (one would) flour
into the old dry measuring cup!

In his commentaries to this text, Alster (1985; 135; 1993: 22) wrote that, to his understanding, it was the voice of 'any girl singing to her lover' whom he hopes to marry. He was generally arguing against the common interpretation of such texts as referring to the king marrying a 'priestess' in a Sacred Marriage ceremony. While I agree with this, I would not class this composition as a Bridal Song. There are references to the formal proposal made to the mother, and the lover is called 'man of my heart', a phrase which, as Alster (1993: 18) suggested, may have been the bride's official acceptance of her groom. But I think that the crucial difference between this text and the Bridal Songs is in the treatment of sexuality. While the bride might engage in erotic day-dreaming, she does not take the initiative and invite her lover to make love to her. She might look forward to their intimacy, but the dialogues usually have 'Dumuzi' suggesting secret trysts. Here it is the woman who urges her man to 'do the sweet thing'; and her tone betrays erotic experience much more than the somewhat vague exhortations of the bride. This is a seduction scenario, an invitation to make love, 'over and over'. Furthermore, the traditional phraseology of the Bridal Songs is used in such a way that is subverts the original context. In normal circumstances it would be most unlikely that 'my mother would let you sleep in our house till morning'. We find a similar instance in another composition, where the parents of the bride apparently encourage the lover to come secretly at nightfall:

> O our son-in-law, as you let day slip by,
> O our son-in-law, as you let night fall,
> You (now) let the moonlight turn in, the stars all wane!

> O our son-in-law, as you let day slip by,
> O our son-in-law, as you let night fall,
> As you let the moonlight turn in, the stars all wane,
> I (now) unfasten for you bolt and pure lock from the door!
>   Run! Come quickly!

(Jacobsen 1987a: 90)

There are several possible reasons for these allusions to the nuptials. First of all, the Bridal Song was probably the older, more traditional form, which served as the established frame of reference (the development of the madrigal may serve as a comparison for this process). Second, the erotic associations of the wedding-night and the pre-marital period of expectation were to some extent already expressed in those songs. By incorporating the theme of transgression against social rules of conduct (not to sleep with the girl before the wedding-night and certainly not with the parents' conniving), the 'love-song' or (probably better) seduction song, distances itself from the more 'naïve' form of the Bridal Songs. Furthermore, the woman speaking, who is surely not an inexperienced adolescent, assumes the role of the ki-sikil, but subverts it by calling upon her lover to violate convention and thus bring immediate fulfilment to the proverbial erotic longing of the bride. Generally speaking, the 'voices' of the bride and the experienced woman often overlap in these texts. The bride aspires to the expertise of the seasoned lover in order to please her husband and herself, while the latter is fully aware of her own erotic capacities but assumes the pretence of innocence and the keenness of emotion felt by the young girl. As in Greece, where the Golden Aphrodite appealed to virgins and *hetairai* alike, Inanna's gift is sought by both.

The royal hymns, a very popular genre of court literature, also exercised some influence on the composition of love-songs:

> O my (beloved), fair of locks, my (beloved) fair of locks,
> My sweet one, tree well grown
> O my (beloved), fair of locks,
> O my (beloved) fair of locks, like a date-palm!
> O my (beloved) fair of shaggy neck – like date fibres!
> Man, who for your locks were acclaimed in the assembly,
> My sweet one, who kisses our bosom (in greeting),
> Lad who for your locks are honored in the assembly,
> My brother of fairest face, who kisses our bosom!
> My (beloved) with a lapis lazuli beard!
> My (beloved) with roped locks!
> My (beloved) with a beard mottled like a slab of lapis lazuli,
> My (beloved) with locks arranged ropewise!
> You are my turban pin, my gold I wear,
> My trinket fashioned by a cunning craftsman,'
> 'My beloved bride makes my fame appear in all mouths!
> As sweet as her mouth is her vulva
> And as sweet as her vulva is her mouth.'
> (gap)
> You are truly a sweet one to talk with!
> You are truly one producing a reign of pleasant days!
> You are truly one establishing prime counsel and honest judgement!
> You are truly one establishing (in the cult) purity and clean hands!
> Beloved of Enlil, may the heart of your personal god,
> Should it become embittered, again relax!
> Come with the sun!
> Go with the sun!
> May your personal god light the way for you,
> Have hod carriers and (pick)axe carriers even it for you!'
> (Jacobsen 1987a: 91–2)[14]

The phraseology of this text, especially the description of the man,

who is not actually identified by name, resembles that of another
Šulgi-hymn (Klein 1981: 72–3), where the king is also said to have
a lapis-lazuli beard (line 7) and trees (lines 32–5):

> 'You are strong as an ildag-tree planted by the water-course,
> You are a sweet sight, like fertile mes-tree, laden with colourful
>   fruit,
> You are cherished by Ninegal, like a date-palm (of) pure
>   Dilmun,
> You have a pleasant shade like a cedar, a seed, growing on the
>   Hasur mountain.'

The final blessing, too, with the invocation of the gods, has a very
official ring to it. But the allusions to the hair, though difficult to
understand, and the quotation of praise for 'the sweet vulva',
introduce a more intimate note.

The contrast between the 'private' and the 'official' tone is even
more pronounced in this text, again following Jacobsen's translation:

> My 'wool' being lettuce he will water it,
> It being box-(grown) lettuce he will water it
> and touch the dubdub bird in its hole!
>
> My nurse has worked at me mightily,
> Has done my 'wool' up in a 'stag' (arrangement),
> Has gently combed it,
> And is straightening my 'May He Come!' (breast-shields).[15]
>
> Let him come! Into my 'wool', it being the most pleasing of
>   lettuces,
> I shall with arousing glances induce the brother to enter.
> I shall make Šu-Suen – all ready – show himself a lusty man,
> Šu-Suen, to whom my [allure] be without end!
> [Šu-Suen, whose allure to me] will [never cha]nge!
> (gap)
> You are truly our lord! You are truly our lord!
> Silver wrought with lapis lazuli! You are truly our lord!
> You are truly our farmer bringing in much grain!
>
> He being the apple of my eye, being the lure of my heart,
> may days of life dawn for him! May Šu-Suen [live long
>   years!]

(Jacobsen 1987a: 93)

Jacobsen explained some of the more obscure metaphors: 'Wool and lettuce stand in these songs for pubic hair; watering the lettuce for sexual intercourse' while he assumes that the rather obscure dubdub bird 'serves apparently as a sobriquet of the clitoris'. I shall discuss the horticultural similies below; but this text is also interesting as it describes the woman's preparation for her *tête-à-tête*: the complex hair-do and jewellery, but also the psychological anticipation (again in analogy to the Bridal Songs?). The woman seems to engage in some form of internal monologue while she gets ready to receive him, thus revealing her true intention to seduce him, while the lines actually addressed to 'Šu-Suen' are almost overly polite and respectful. The combination of the two make it into an amusingly erotic piece.

Metaphors of fruit, lettuce and honey are ubiquitous in love poetry.[16] Here is another song from Jacobsen's collection:

> Vigorously he sprouted, vigorously he sprouted and sprouted, watered it – it being lettuce!
> In his black garden of the desert bearing much yield did my darling of his mother,
> My barley stalk full of allure in its furrow, water it – it being lettuce,
> Did my one – a very apple tree bearing fruit at the top – water it – it being a garden!
>
> The honey-sweet man, the honey-sweet man, was doing sweet (things) to me!
> My lord, the honey-sweet man, the godly one, my darling of his mother,
> His hands honey sweet, his feet honeying, was doing sweet (things) to me!
> His limbs being sweet, sweet honey, he was doing sweet things to me!
>
> O my one who of a sudden was doing sweet (things) to the whole (insides up) to the navel, my darling of his mother,
> My desert-honey loins, darling of his mother, you watered it – it being lettuce!'
>
> (Jacobsen 1987a: 94)

The translation quoted here suggests that this is phrased like a reminiscence; in Kramer's version (1963: 508, 521) the tense is left more fluid, more like a commentary on present, past and future activity, which to my mind is more fitting. Here, all formal references to either courtly phraseology, or Bridal Songs, are dropped.

I prefer to understand the whole as an erotic text that operates on double meaning, pushing the horticultural references to the limit, in order to convey a feminine perspective of sexuality. The first part in particular seems to refer to female genitals. This is conveyed better by Alster's recent translation (1993: 21):

> It sprouts, it sprouts, it is the lettuce he watered,
> In the garden of deep shade, bending down his neck, my
>   darling of his mother,
> My one who fills the grain in their furrows with beauty, he
>   watered,
> My apple tree bearing fruit at its top, it is the garden he
>   watered.

Even this version falls short of making the genital symbolism transparent. Subconscious androcentric perceptions often influence the understanding of such texts (see Winkler 1990: 180ff.). In this case, there seems to have been more emphasis on the action of the phallus than the original justifies (note how Jacobsen uses the third-person masculine in the first lines!). I think that 'it' is the vulva, here compared to a leafy, fast-growing vegetable, which does not exactly 'sprout' but 'swell'. The two translations differ in detail in line 2, but they also describe the vulva as a flourishing 'garden', 'bearing much yield'. I would, furthermore, suggests that sa₆-ga ama-na-mu, which Kramer paraphrased as 'my favoured of the womb', might be a reference to the clitoris in this context – literally 'my (one which is) good/delicious/(part) of its mother', namely the most important part of the whole.[17] The following two lines stand in apposition: Alster's 'the grain in the furrow' avoids the too phallic connotation conveyed by Jacobsen's 'barley stalk'. It is 'filled with' hi-li, also the source of sexual enjoyment – so I would read this line as:

> my barley-corn in the furrow, filled with sexual pleasure, he
>   waters it.

The last line summarizes the whole stanza, this time making the image clearly feminine in the context:

> A fruit tree bearing fruit at the top – such is the garden he
>   waters.[18]

At first glance, it is suggestive of a phallic metaphor, and indeed often can be in a different context, such as the royal hymn mentioned above; but here the 'garden' is more appropriately seen as the vulva, with its 'fruit' at the top. The second part then goes on to describe what the 'honey-sweet man' does: 'he sweetens me ever'. sa₆-ga-ama-na-mu is used here again in line 6, following epithets of the man, and it seems to apply here to him rather than the bodily part, another instance of the possibility of several meanings, which is such a typical feature of love poetry. In the last two lines the orgasmic conclusion is described, with a possible reference to penetration – the whole 'garden' having been watered.

I propose such a reading on the grounds that if one does assume a genital metaphor at all, it is much more in keeping with Sumerian attitudes to describe the vulva than the phallus. I have mentioned before that the latter was not significant as an erotic symbol, while the former is the subject of praise in various texts. Furthermore, the love poetry speaks particularly of woman's pleasure, her body is the centre of attention, her vulva 'astonishing'. This should be taken into account when this poetry is studied by a generation of scholars who might have heard of textual deconstruction.

The lettuce, mentioned in these texts (hi-is^sar *hassu*) is probably *Lactuta sativa*. In Egypt it was the attribute of the fertility god Min, and the plant was regarded as an aphrodisiac (Rundle-Clark 1959: 205; Lurker 1980: 76). In Greek mythology the lettuce stands for potency, but also for impotence.[19] In both instances the plant has phallic connotations, easily suggested by the elongated shape and the white sap. In the Sumerian texts it is generally associated with the female organ, and the metaphor is less obvious. Jacobsen thought it represented the pubic hair. Maybe the visual aspect is less important here, although the overlapping leaves and their texture, as well as the milky or clear sap, are quite evocative. Lettuces and similar fast-growing vegetables, like cucumbers and melons, all of which were grown in Mesopotamian gardens, require frequent watering. I imagine that this association with water might also have contributed to the metaphorical range: the vulva, like lettuce, is said to need the 'watering'.

We have seen above that làl ('honey') is frequently used to describe sensual pleasure. The expression 'to taste the honey-plant' was a common euphemism for intercourse. Here the lover is equated with the sensation he brings – his very limbs are 'honey', but they 'bring sweetness', orgasmic enjoyment. The metaphor extends from activity ('to do the sweet thing') and personal attributes ('whose limbs are honey') to the location:

> The brother makes me enter his house,
> He made me lie on the honey-scented (or 'flowing') bed'
> (Alster 1993: 22)

or

> In the house where we sleep, where honey is made to flow,
> Let us enjoy your sweet sex-appeal
> (Alster 1993: 22)

This 'honey' was date-syrup rather than the bees' product.

I have to concede that we know nothing about the circumstances which may have prompted the composition of these songs. But I do believe that the references to king Šu-Suen are not as fortuitous as Alster suggests. The refined language, with all the resonances of courtly poetry, locate these texts very much in the royal entourage. Even though we cannot be certain of the fact that these songs were actually composed for royal concubines or educated courtesans, their content suggests the psychological premiss of such an origin. Sexual competition fostered by a polygynous household induces women to be inventive and resourceful in sexual and erotic matters.[20] The courts at Ur and Isin were much given to flaunting their cultural sophistication, and in these circumstances it is not altogether surprising to find a highly developed aesthetics of eroticism, which is at odds with the straightforward treatment of sexuality in the myths. Lovemaking in these texts is not the spontaneous off-loading of libidinous urges. The young gods were said to copulate outdoors, wherever lust befell them, and they seemed to care little about their partners' consent or pleasure, as long as their keen desire to impregnate was fulfilled. Here, things are quite different, as the man is no longer the unwed guruš, who has no legitimate outlet for his sexual energy. On the contrary, the beloved of these texts is the 'husband', or indeed the royal husband, who by dint of his social position has access to several women. In this context, he is the object of his wives' rivalry. In practice, in truly polygamous marriages, where the wives have equal status, there is a rota-system, whereby the husband's nightly visits are regulated (Fainzang 1988: 91). In a more open system, where there are not only official first, second and third wives, etc., but also concubines and slaves, as for instance in imperial China, the choice of sexual partner was entirely the husband's (van Gulik 1951). The competition for his attention and lasting affection (after all the most important means to personal influence, power and wealth under the circumstances) was naturally much keener. This means that women had to make full use of their eroticism. Interestingly, the Sumerian texts always highlight the importance of women's pleasure. Men trying to please more than one of the ladies must have been able to exercise some control over their bodies, but also, more importantly, respond to the women's sexual signals. How does this manifest itself in our texts?

First of all, it is the woman who addresses the man (or, in the Lacanian sense 'attacks' him). She lets him know that she desires him to pleasure her. She also tells him that she knows he can do that; she suggests that he can fulfil her ('you will do the sweet thing to me'). This is, in fact, the psychological key to the love-songs, to reassure the male that his lovemaking succeeds in 'sweetening the lap', has done so before, and will do so now. The short phrases, the frequent commands, references to touching, smell and taste – all contribute to a verbalization of lovemaking, a virtual description of physical intimacy, where the man responds and the woman leads. Since the verbal forms in Sumerian do not have 'tenses' in the manner of Indo-European languages, translations sometimes suggest reminiscence or anticipation. I believe that the love-songs always depict the present, the immediacy of emotion.

Cooper (1989: 88) expressed surprise that there is never any mention of the penis, while the vulva is subject to elaborate praise. In fact, the male experience or pleasure is never directly alluded to. This is, I think, quite in keeping with the delicate task of getting the man to perform satisfactorily, as mutually enjoyable lovemaking was seen as the woman's responsibility. The manner in which this is expressed, the references to literary genres, the choice of metaphor, and no doubt the musical accompaniment, contributed to a total eroticization of the discourse, which we can only dimly perceive. The word is indeed in the service of desire.

The *mise-en-scène* of such lovemaking is secondary to this psychological dimension, but is also important as it clearly distances this level of sexuality from the 'wild' and the impetuous copulation depicted in other texts.

The woman always prepares by bathing and scenting her body,

dressing her hair, darkening her eyes. She also has a special room prepared: the bedroom with its aromatic oils and herbs, the bed covered with soft sheets, sprinkled with herbs (the only permissible manifestation of 'nature'!). The luxury of a bedroom was certainly only the privilege of the very wealthy; the privacy of a room to oneself must equally have been beyond the means of all but the very rich. The miniature beds found as votive offerings to Inanna/Ištar are probably symbols of such 'beds of delight'. These preparations are also mentioned in the bridal texts, and therefore the usual interpretation was to see all these references as pertaining to wedding ceremonies. In fact, we have a reciprocal relationship here, as in the poetic interplay between wedding-song and love-song. For the high-class courtesan, the aristocratic wife, the professional lover, such a setting was the normal sphere of operations; for the 'ordinary' girl, this only happened as a rite of passage on her wedding-day, on the occasion of her first introduction to adult sexual life.[21]

There is also a highly erotic dialogue which Jacobsen (1987a: 97) dubbed the 'Tavern Sketch'.[22] In deference to the notion of the Sacred Marriage, this was originally interpreted as a confrontation between Inanna and Dumuzi, where the latter is punished by death for the ensuing hubris (Falkenstein 1953: 61–2; Kramer 1969; Alster 1985: 159–60). Alster (1985: 3), while denying the explicit connection with Inanna and Dumuzi, saw the threat and death-penalty applying to the 'stranger' from out of town who visits the inn, Jacobsen (1987b: 50) called it a 'crude low-life piece' in which 'a stranger, after an evening in the ale-house, makes a play for the tapstress, a plea full of beery sentimentality'. In order to win her confidence, however, he must swear that he is not an enemy. 'The oath she proposes, the kind taken while touching the genitals of the person to whom one swears, is here clearly an erotic ploy' (ibid., 50). Sefati (1990) accepted the idea that an oath-taking is involved, but saw it as an oath of chastity that the lover is made to swear to the 'tapstress' not to have sex with other women. Alster's new translation (forthcoming) goes a step further in specifying that the lover's oath pertains to the period the man had spent away from the woman, in another town. The following translation is based on Alster's.

The first 11 lines are spoken by a man, who addresses his 'beloved sister'; there are numerous amorous endearments, which are awkward to translate – it helps to imagine them whispered, as the tone is one of extreme intimacy:

'O my *lubi*, my *lubi*, my *lubi*,
My *labi*, my *la[bi*, my *labi]*, my honey of the mother who gave
  birth to her[23]
My juicy grape, my honey sweet, my her-mother's honey-
  mouth,
The glance of your eye delights me, come, my beloved sister,
The words of your mouth delight me, come, my beloved
  sister,
Kissing your lips delights me, come, my beloved sister!
O my sister, the beer of your grain is delicious, my her-
  mother's honey-mouth,
The gumeze beer of your wort is delicious, come, my beloved
  sister,
In your house, your passion . . ., [come] my beloved sister,
Your house is . . . a storehouse, my her-mother's honey-mouth.'

The next 20 lines contain the woman's response, but as it is not
written in the Emesal dialect, opinions are divided as to where his
speech ends and hers begins.[24]

'You, prince, my [brother of fairest face(?)]
Swear to me, that when you dwelt, when you dwelt,
Brother, swear to me that, when you dwelt in the out-lying
  town,
Swear to me that a stranger did not touch (you) by the
  hand,
Swear to me that a stranger did not approach (?) (you) by
  mouth(?)!
My one who lifts the thin(?) gown off my vulva for me,
My beloved, man of my choice,
[for you(?)], let me prepare what belongs to the oath for you,
  my brother of fairest face.
My brother of fairest face, let me prepare what belongs to the
  oath for you:
May you put your right hand in my vulva,
With your left stretched towards my head,
When you have neared your mouth to my mouth,
When you have taken my lips into your mouth,
Thus you swear the oath to me,
So it is, dragon (?) of women, my brother of fairest face!
My blossom-bearer, my blossom-bearer, your charms are
  sweet!

My blossom-bearing garden of apple-trees, your charms are
  sweet!
My fruit-bearing garden of mes-trees, your charms are sweet,
Dumuzi-Abzu herself! Your charms are sweet,
My pure figurine, my pure figurine, your charms are sweet,
Alabaster figurine, tied with lapis-lazuli ornament, your
  charms are sweet.'

I have mentioned the different current interpretations of the oath-
taking above. I believe that Jacobsen's view of it as an 'erotic ploy',
as well as the desired confirmation of the temporarily absent lover's
faithfulness, are relevant here. Alster also noted that it 'remains
amazing that the oath is requested of the lover, and not of the girl'.
I would suggest that within the context of the man's departure, her
anxiety about his conduct is perfectly natural, and that secondly, the
theme of women competing for the sole attention of the man is
common in Sumerian poetry – as we shall see later, we have evidence
for the expression of female jealousy, but not of men doubting the
fidelity of their mistresses or wives.

The fact that the man has been away provides us with a scenario
for this dialogue: the intimate reunion of the couple, a form of poetic
pillow-talk. By referring to the formal gestures of oath-taking she
invites her beloved to touch and kiss her, to initiate their lovemaking,
to prove by his ardour that he still appreciates her after his absence.

Lines 27–32 have so far been taken as the woman's praise of his
manly charm ('my blossom-bearer'..., etc.). Jacobsen (1987b: 62)
took all the imagery here to refer to the male member. But I prefer
to read these lines as if they were spoken by the man, in praise of *her*
parts, a sort of eulogy of the vulva, and I would propose the
following reading:

'O my blossoming one, my blossoming one – your sex-appeal
  (or: voluptuousness) is sweet,
O my fruiting one in the orchard – your sex-appeal is sweet,
O Dumuzi-abzu, herself – your sex-appeal is sweet,
(it is) my pure "pin" (Sumerian dìm), my holy "pin" – your
  sex-appeal is sweet,
(it is) my shining 'ornament' set in lapis lazuli – your sex-
  appeal is sweet.'

Dumuzi-abzu cannot be taken to be an epithet for Dumuzi, as she
clearly was a female deity, part of the Lagaš pantheon. I would also see

the dìm and the 'fruiting of the orchard' as a clitorial metaphor, and the dìm giš-nu₁₁-gal suh za-gìn keš-da as an image for the vulva.[25] Although the choice of metaphors is to our sensibility more suggestive of phallic connotations, something which most of the (male) translators have been quick to perceive, the fact that Sumerian love poetry is almost wholly gynocentric, and that the references to male anatomy or enjoyment are almost totally absent (with the exception of the bridal context, where the role of the man as *deflorator* is given some prominence), we should be careful of assigning such meanings. If we accept that this fictional reunion eavesdrops on the lovers, it would also make better poetic sense to have the lover greet his woman-friend and affirm his continuing delight in her company. Then we have her response and the highly effective oath-ceremony which must have elicited appreciative applause from its audience, and finally his praise of her physical charms and sex-appeal, which was already indicated in his previous speech. As for the setting of the 'tavern', I would see that entirely as a figure of speech, with, as Alster again affirms, clear references to her state of arousal. It is certainly 'secular' as opposed to 'religious' in Falkenstein's or Kramer's understanding; and its setting is vague. However, imagery and content place it among the other courtly love-songs of the late UrIII period, and the 'low-life' aspect is quite inappropriate to do justice to the highly wrought artifice of seduction.

In these texts we have eroticism elevated to an art form, a divine and civilized mode of behaviour. And in this context only the female erotic experience counts. It is Inanna's and, through her, woman's general prerogative to demand 'the sweetening of the lap' and at the same time to be responsible for its procurement. The male voice, when quoted at all, speaks lines of intimate and sensual understanding, in response to the woman's emotion. Needless to say, reality may well have been quite different, even for the royal ladies at the court of Ur. But what counts here is the construct of an ideal. Like that of courtly chaste love in the High Middle Ages, courtly erotic love was a cultural ideal in the first two centuries of the second millennium. And the value placed on this expression of physical love then found its way into other areas of literature, especially the royal hymns. From this point of view, it makes sense to have the king make love to the goddess. But it is quite the opposite of the neo-primitive 'fertility rite' notion that the construct of the Sacred Marriage implies.

12

THE RITES OF DIVINE LOVE

The Sumerian songs concerned with the marriage of Inanna and Dumuzi may go back to traditional Bridal Songs. Sometimes Inanna is addressed as a goddess, but generally she appears like any human bride.

Other compositions refer specifically to the conjugal state of gods. We have already mentioned that most deities were said to be wedded, and we have looked at the myth of *Enlil and Ninlil*, which describes the unorthodox process of marrying a girl made pregnant.

Other texts concern various ritual practices that are associated with the wedding of a local deity to a national or cosmic god, or the union of the local divine couple.

An example of the survival of such rites into modern times is a festival of the Minaksi temple in the South Indian city of Madurai, described by the Cambridge anthropologist C. J. Fuller (1984).

In Madurai, the goddess Minaksi stands for the ancient autochthonous female deity, the focus of the Tamil village-based ritual, but she is also the consort of Śiva (here called Sundaresvara), who manifests himself not as the anti-social 'erotic ascetic' (O'Flaherty 1973) but as the fatherly, married god and monarch (Fuller 1984: 9; Shulman 1980: 4–5, 24ff.). However, Fuller notes that 'in ritual, a connection is postulated between a goddess' regular sexual relations with her husband and her relative passivity' (Fuller 1980: 327). An important part of the daily service to the gods is the *palliyarai pūjai*, the 'bedchamber worship', in which the 'portable image Sundaresvara is taken from the god's temple to the bedchamber in Minaksi's temple.... The divine couple are offered food and lamps are waved in front of them – ... and songs and music are performed, while a swing (a favourite repose of Hindu lovers) on which the images rest is gently rocked. Afterwards, the bedchamber doors are closed ... and the entire building is shut for the night' (Fuller 1984: 11). Apart from this daily conjugal union, there is also a special festival, the Cittirai, performed between April and May, which celebrates the mythological achievements of the goddess, enacted in a series of plays. On the tenth day her wedding is held, which constitutes the 'climax of the Temple's ritual year and attracts large crowds.... On the morning following the wedding day ... the images of the god and goddess are placed on two vast wooden carts ... and dragged around the streets by hundreds of men who volunteer for the task each year' (Fuller 1984: 20).

The symbolism of divine marriage is also of great importance in Hindu mythology. On a cosmological level, Viṣṇu and Lakṣmi represent the creator and creation, she being the Earth and he her support, while Rāma and Sita are the 'model couple', the exemplary king and blameless husband with his faithful wife. There are other such ideal prototypes for human marital relations, such as Śiva and Pārvati, Kṛṣṇa and Rādha.

We also have various references to the ritual of divine marriage from Bronze Age Greece. In Pylos the god Poseidon, represented by a painted and perfumed statue, was joined by his consort on a bed, while the community witnessed the proceedings (Bonnefoy 1981: II 296a). Another Mycenaean ritual concerned the wedding of the goddess Hellotis (later Europa) to Welkhanos (later assimilated to Zeus) under a perennial plane tree, said to be the site of the first amorous encounter between Zeus and Europa (ibid.).

We could look further for similar cases, notably in Shintoism and South East Asian and African tribal religion, but this brief excursion must suffice to show that marital relations between gods were not only of fundamental importance in the development of a poly-theistic pantheon, but that the celebration of the gods' nuptials also formed an integral part of the ritual year within the community. The type of marriage, and to some extent the actual ritual proceedings, are modelled on traditional customs.

To return to Mesopotamia: relevant information must be gleaned from passages in hymns, myths and ritual activities. So we hear, *en passant*, the following references to the marital life of gods:

My husband, lord Pabilsag, son of Enlil, lies in there ... with me, lying contentedly

(Falkenstein 1953: 190)

My mother Uraš, mistress of the gods, delights in An
on the holy bed, where he makes magnificent love to
her

(Sjöberg 1960: 71)

The young man makes love to his wife, Suen is well
pleased with fair Ningal

(Sjöberg 1960: 71)

Bau, the goddess of Lagaš, was married to Ningirsu, and there are
several passages which refer to their betrothal and marital state.
Falkenstein (1953: 364) remarked that the relationship between Bau
and her spouse resembles that between Inanna and Dumuzi in Uruk.
He regards the Bau as the local (original?) deity, who unites herself
with the 'well-built' 'king' Ningirsu, epithets also applied to
Dumuzi. She is described as

the august daughter-in-law of Enlil, who presents him with
offspring (. . .)

and states that it was An,

your father (. . .), highest of the gods, who clothed you in
divine raiment,
Gave you the hero of Enlil, Ningirsu, (to be your) husband,
Gave you the Eninnu, the 'Holy City', the sanctuary, which
'lets the seed emerge out'.

(Römer 1965: 238)

The texts above date from the Isin period, but Bau already featured
in Gudea's inscriptions, which describe in great detail the building
and solemn dedication of the Eninnu temple at Lagaš.

Only when all the other deities of Ningirsu's court have been
assigned their respective posts, and Gudea has presented offerings of
weapons and furniture and is finally fully confirmed in his office as
ruler, does the ritual union between Ningirsu and Bau take place:

Its bed, when it had been set up in the bedroom,
Was (like) a young cow kneeling down in the place where it
slept,
On its pure back, spread with fresh hay,
Mother Bau was lying down with lord Ningirsu.[1]

This was, as Falkenstein pointed out, 'das zentrale Geschehen im
kultischen Festkalender der Stadt'.[2] The festival coincided with the

high-water level of the Tigris, the period of greatest potential
agricultural success, and Bau herself, upon her entry into the temple,
is likened to a garden, providing 'abundance for Lagaš'.

It is not unlikely that divine marriage rites were more common in
Mesopotamia than the paucity of written evidence suggests. While
we have detailed accounts and timetables for minor and major
festivals, their function was probably much too common knowledge
to merit more detailed information (Sauren 1970: 11–29; Limet 1970:
59–74). Considering the fact that we have a myth of Enlil's wedding
to Ninlil, it seems not unreasonable to speculate that this event was
also celebrated at Nippur. According to an inscription by king
Šu-Suen, the gods embarked on a ritual boat-ride:

> Towards the cane-brake of Enlil's Tummal,
> Towards Ninlil's place of joy, Enlil, together with Ninlil,
>   sailed.
> He had sacred songs and incantations sung to him,
> For him he placed appropriately singers in the pleasing 'house
>   of the lyre'.
>
> (Civil 1967: 11f.)

The 'place of joy' might refer to the place where Enlil first
impregnated her. This boating expedition seems to have had a very
ancient tradition, and we do not know whether the myth describes
the original rationale of this trip of Tummal. But it appears that, by
the UrIII period, it was connected with divine nuptial celebrations.
There is more substantial information about divine marriage rites
from Akkadian texts, mainly dating from the first millennium. The
ceremonies are referred to as *hašadu* or the *parṣi hašadi* and take
place in the temples of the deities concerned. They involve the god
Nabû, who rose to great popularity at that period in both Babylon
and Assyria, as well as Šamaš, Marduk, Assur, Anu and other minor
gods.

Nabû was the son of Marduk. He was the patron deity of scribes,
but was also seen as an important official in the divine organization
of the world. His spectacular rise to the status of great god may have
been due partly to his mediating role: Nabû was probably the least
terrifying and formidable god of the Assyro-Babylonian pantheon,
he was thought to be open to supplication and generally well
disposed towards mankind (Pomponio 1978). His consort in the
South was Nanâ, the Ištar-like goddess of love. It is an interesting

development to have this quintessentially independent erotic goddess married to Nabû. In Assyria, his wife was Tašmētu, known since the Old Assyrian period. She was his more traditional marital partner, mentioned in the majority of texts. We have three letters by temple officials which refer to the nuptials of Nabû and Tašmetu in Assyria,[3] from which I shall quote the pertinent extracts, following Matsushima's translation (1987: 132).

> On the third day of Ayyaru, at Kalhu, will the bed of Nabû be set up.
> Nabû enters his bed-chamber.

The following morning Nabû leaves the *adru* precinct of the palace (literally the 'threshing ground', a suitable open space) and everybody is to go to the garden, where sacrifices are to be performed. There is mention of a chariot which is to take the god for a ride. Further sacrifices follow and bread is eaten in the temple.

Another letter is addressed directly to king Esarhaddon. Here both partners are mentioned:

> On the fourth day of Ayyaru will Nabû and Tašmētu enter the bed-chamber.
>
> (15–17)

There is to be a sacrifice in this room, before the statues of the gods, so that

> they will cause them to live for 100 years, their sons, and the sons of their sons will live for a long time
>
> (14–16)

In the third the king is informed that the following procedures are to take place:

> Tomorrow, the fourth day, towards evening, will Nabû and Tašmētu move into the bed-chamber. On the fifth day they will given food of (or: for) the king. The *hazannu*-official sits down. The (cup shaped like a) 'head of the lion' and the *tallakku*[4] will be brought to the palace. From the fifth to the tenth day, the gods (stay) in the bed-chamber, assisted by the *hazannu*. On the eleventh day Nabû will come out. He will 'free his foot'[5] go to the *ambassu*(-park) and kill some wild bulls. Then he will come up again and take his place again.
>
> (lines 6–17, rev. 1–5)

In view of the variations in procedure described in these letters, it is doubtful if they all refer to the same ceremonial. The actual ritual probably varied from temple to temple, and the mention of the king's sons in one letter points to the possibility that the exigencies of the court were also accommodated. What these texts do say is that there was a ritual where the Nabû and Tašmētu went into the bedchamber, and that this event was important enough to merit the attention of the king, if not his actual presence. The excursion into the park or garden is an interesting feature, but he seems to go there alone. It is not clear whether this was an integral part of the *hadašu* festival. In a letter-prayer addressed to Tašmētu, Ashurbanipal describes a procession of Nabû and his consort:

> On the fifth day of the month, the procession of Tašmētu.
> When she leaves from the *mummu* (and proceeds) towards
>   Nabû, . . .
> The son of Bēl (leaves) the Tablet-House to be a house-holder.
> (lines 9–10; Matsushima 1987: 152)

Then follows a brief dialogue, presumably between the divine couple, in which he calls her *hirti ina ra'amte atti* ('you are my beloved wife'; line 15), and the fragmentary enumeration of various gates, presumably of temples, and then they enter the sanctuary. The text ends with the king's supplication for her blessing. There is no indication in this text that it refers to the divine marriage ceremony, but it cannot be ruled out as a possibility.

From Babylon, we have a ritual calendar that also deals at some length with the festival of Nabû and Nanâ's wedding. For the month Ayyaru, we have the following entry:

> On the second day (the day of the Stable), when the shining
>   Sun is rising,
> Nabû, in his capacity as bridegroom (*hadaššutu*),
> Is clothed in a garment befitting his rank of supreme deity.
> From the Ezida (temple) he emerges at night-time, shining like
>   a star at night,
> Splendidly like Sîn, illuminating the darkness.
> Towards the inner quarters of Eharšuba he luminously directs
>   (his steps),
> He enters into the presence of the 'Lady'.
> All is prepared for the nuptials.
> The inner quarters of Eharšuba he illuminates as if it were

(broad) day.
On the bed of the 'sweet night' they lie down to sweet sleep.
On the 6th day he goes out into the garden
And he boards . . .
On the 7th day, he directs (his steps)
Towards the Emeurur, towards holy Eanna.
He emerges to (go into) the garden: he enters the garden of
    Anu and installs himself.
Since he has taken the heavenly kingship . . .
The incantation of the *ašipu*: 'He clothes himself in the
    himšatu of adate-palm and the crown of Anu.'
On the 17th Nanâ leaves the Eharšuba
                              (Matsushima 1987: 158–60)

Pomponio has drawn attention to the fact that the sojourn in the 'garden', which is also mentioned in another part of the text, was an important part of the ritual. He suspected that the 'garden must symbolise the relationship between the Divine Marriage ['iero-gamia'] and the rebirth of vegetation' (Pomponio 1978: 134). While the garden in the love-dialogues is a well-known locale for erotic encounters and also a metaphor for the act of love itself, there is no indication in these texts that what happens in the parks of the royal cities in Assyria (or indeed the garden of the Anu-temple at Uruk) primarily had something to do with fertility. Nabû goes there alone and seems symbolically to exercise functions of kingship: driving about in a chariot and hunting in Assyria, receiving a ritual connected with the sovereignty of Anu in Borsippa. It seems that the basic ceremony of celebrating the consummation of marriage by the gods in their bedchamber was extended to include rituals on behalf of the king.

Marduk, the great Babylonian national god, and his wife Ṣarpā-nitu, also had their rituals of divine marriage, although the evidence for these is at present rather indirect. The royal annals of Ashurbani-pal, for instance, have lists of temple furnishings that he dedicated to Marduk. Some of these had been removed from the Esagil temple in Babylon by Sennacherib when he sacked the city in 689. They include a bed of *musukkannu* wood,

'covered with gold and precious stones
for the delicious bed of my lord and the lady,
To consummate the marriage, to make love,
I artfully fashioned it.

In the KÁ. HI. LI. SÙ, the residence of Ṣarpānitu,
Filled with loving charm, I have installed it.
(Matsushima 1988: 100)

In a parallel text mentioning the marital bed, Ashurbanipal adds the reason for his gift of the bed:

[For] my own life and long duration of my days I have offered (it)
When the marriage takes place, they enter into the chamber of love (*bīt ru'ame*).
(Matsushima 1988: 103)

and he asks them to bless his kingship and bring low his enemies. He also adds a pertinent curse against whoever usurps his inscription and claims the rewards of Ashurbanipal's votive offerings:

May Marduk, king of the gods, take away his potency and destroy his seed,
May Ṣarpānitu pronounce evil against him, on (her) marital bed.

The marital bed may not just have been used on the occasion of a wedding-celebration, but served as a regular sleeping-place for the divine couple. It is possible that the actual marriage between Marduk and Ṣarpānitu took place on the occasion of the New Festival, probably some time between the eighth and the eleventh day, either in the 'festival house', the Bīt-Akītu, or the temple Esagila. Unfortunately, the relevant portions of the text that describe the events of the festival are too fragmentary to settle this point (Frankfort 1950). Texts from Uruk, however, specify that wedding rituals for Anu and his consort Antum did take place in the Akītu-house of Anu. One describes a nocturnal ceremony, where the god Anu is represented by his 'sandal' (*senu*). This is carried in procession, accompanied by the 'daughters of Anu and Uruk', to the Enir, the 'chamber of the golden bed of Antu', where it is put on a stool. The 'daughters of Anu and Uruk' sit down on chairs, while the priest mixes wine and oil for libation at the door of the sanctuary. Then a bull and sheep are sacrificed and meat, perfume, fruit, etc. are offered first to Anu and Antum, and then to all the other gods assembled in the courtyard (Thureau Dangin 1921; Matsushima 1988: 110–15).

This brief enumeration of the texts referring to a ritual union of a divine couple shows two things: first, that the great temples at least made provision for the conjugal state of its deities, just as they made provision for other bodily and social functions. The gods are envisaged as sexual beings who enjoy a blissful marital life. A special bed was set up in a specially designated part of the temple (in Akkadian the *bīt erši* or the KÁ. HI. LI. SÙ), which was defined as the 'house of love' (*bīt ru'āme*) or the 'marital quarters' (*bīt hammuti*). In the Sumerian texts, the bed is usually called the 'shining bed' (giš-ná-gi-rin-na), and was installed in the Gipar. This is where Inanna and Dumuzi are said to lie together; and in the poem of Enmerkar, the 'lord of Aratta' taunts his rival that he himself sleeps there with Inanna. Bau and Ningirsu also 'make it pleasant together' on their pure bed 'strewn with pure plants' (Gudea, Cyl, BXVII 1–3). Given the existence of the married quarters, one would expect a daily ritual that would unite the divine couple at night, just as there are daily rituals for meals, ablutions, audiences, etc. Again, the ethnographic study of the Minaksi temple, which I have quoted above, offers a useful comparison.

In addition to such daily rites, along the lines described for Minaksi in India, or Anu at Uruk, there were special feast days, involving processions outside the temple precinct. It is far from certain whether all married gods celebrated their marriage at a particular time in the ritual calendar. The information from the first millennium points to such events in Ayyaru (April–May) for Nabû and Tašmētu in Assyria and Nabû and Nanâ in Babylonia (probably Borsippa, the main site of Nabû's temple), and probably for Marduk and Ṣarpānitu. There is no direct information on this point from the Sumerian sources. Considering the scarcity of the evidence, actual wedding rituals between gods were probably a rare exception rather than the rule in Mesopotamia. I would also suggest that the word *hašādu/hadaššutu* does not denote specifically such hierogamy, as Matsushima (1988: 118) proposed, but refers more generally to the married state of gods and the ritual accommodation of this fact.[6] Within this general frame of reference it was possible to integrate other rituals and ceremonies, such as those relating to kingship, where the ruler or his descendants seek the blessing of the divine couple, public processions, etc. At any rate, the subject of divine marriage in Mesopotamia is far removed from the Frazerian idea of a peasant fertility rite, and the parallels from Archaic Greece are less helpful than those from Hindu India, with its comparable ritual and cultural complexity.

PLATES

Plate 1 Frit amulet in the shape of a penis, clearly uncircumcised. It was found in the Ištar temple at Assur. First millennium. Vorderasiatisches Museum, Berlin.

Plate 2 Stylized vulva made of frit from the Ištar temple at Assur. Various Akkadian incantations and prayers mention that such objects, ideally fashioned from gold or lapis lazuli, were dedicated to the goddess. Only the cheap versions have survived. First millennium. Vorderasiatisches Museum, Berlin.

Plate 3 Copper pin head in the shape of a house sheltering a couple. The woman on the right touches the man's shoulder, while they gaze into each other's eyes. S.W. Iran, second half of the third millennium. Louvre.

Plate 4 Alabaster plaque from Susa. Such plaques functioned like framed
pictures; they were attached to walls by means of a large metal nail through
the central hole. The lower register depicts a scene that is well known from
cylinder seals of the period, a naked hero slaying a large feline that had
attacked a bull. The upper register shows a banquet, also a common motif
in such votive plaques. But the details of this banquet are unusual. A person
seated on left seems to balance a woman on his knees who is holding some
cup. Before them kneels a nude man, apparently ithyphallic. On the left
side sits a man in the traditional fringed skirt, also raising a cup to another
nude, possibly female, who stands opposite him. Generally, nude and
totally depilated male figures appear in Sumerian iconography in ritual
contexts, performing libations, etc. It is not clear whether this scene should
also be taken as a ritual performance or a sort of 'symposium'. First half of
the second millennium. Louvre.

Plate 5 Examples of mass-produced terracotta figurines of nude women. Such figures were very widely distributed all over the Near East. Their purpose however, remains obscure. Early second millennium. Louvre.

Plate 6 Terracotta moulded relief of *coitus a tergo*, with the woman drinking beer through a long hollow tube. This might illustrate the connection frequently made in love-songs between sex and alcohol, maybe a scene from the *é-eš-dam*, or 'tavern'. Tello, early second millennium. Louvre.

Plate 7 Terracotta moulded relief, probably showing a lascivious dance rather than an act of copulation. The male figure on the left is playing some kind of stringed instrument, while the woman holds a small drum. She looks over one shoulder at her partner and suggestively displays her buttocks. From Larsa, early second millennium. Louvre.

Plate 8 Fragmentary terracotta moulded relief depicting a couple embracing on a bed. Interestingly, the draperies covering the bed are indicated by cross-hatchings. From Kiš, first half of the second millennium. Louvre.

Plate 9 Model bed made of white clay with a nude couple making love. The woman's leg is raised over the male's hip. First half of the second millennium. Louvre.

Plate 10 Terracotta moulded relief of embracing couple on a bed. From Susa, first half of the second millennium. Louvre.

Plate 11 Engraved shell, often thought to depict the love-goddess Ištar, wearing the horned crown with the star emblem of Venus and a transparent cloak. From Mari, first half of the third millennium. Louvre.

13

L'AMOUR LIBRE OR SACRED PROSTITUTION?

It is not always possible to locate an erotic cuneiform text in a particular social or ritual situation. The persistent obsession of Assyriologists with the Sacred Marriage meant that practically every text with a sexual content was considered to refer to the goddess' wedding. This overemphasis of a marital context needs to be redressed. I have tried to show that the key-texts concerning the Sumerian king's relationship with Inanna do not constitute a marriage ceremony. In fact, the marital paradigm is only partially relevant for the sexual affinities described in Mesopotamian literature. Bottéro (1992: 134) introduces the term 'amour libre' for sexuality outside marriage ('pratiqué librement par chacun pour son propre plaisir'), although he immediately qualifies this statement, saying that it was supplied 'par des "spécialistes" exerçant ce que nous appellerions la prostitution', who could be of either sex. Mesopotamian vocabulary lists provide us with a range of relevant terminology, although it is unclear what social status or specific services the various categories implied at any one time. The courtly love poems are predominantly set as seduction scenarios where the woman invites the man to make love to her. This may have been inspired by the polygynous nature of aristocratic households, where the concubines and wives vied for the attention of their 'master'. However, one could also ask whether the erotic poetry of the UrIII period could be connected to high-class courtesans. Unfortunately, while there is ample evidence for their existence and status from imperial China, Japan or classical Greece, we know little about such women in Mesopotamia.

However, as far as the court of Ur is concerned, the short inscriptions by, or for, women, with the title lukur-kaskal-la, are of relevance here. They appear on votive offerings, a materialized form of prayer, addressed to a god/dess with a wish for the 'life' of some person important to the dedicator. This was a practice well established since the Early Dynastic period. High-ranking officials at the court of Kiš dedicated luxury items, such as a silver vase, a lapis-lazuli bead or the like, in order to secure the gods' blessing for the king. The costly nature of such an offering reflects the prestige and wealth of the donor. Aristocratic women, judging from the seal-inscriptions, had access to both property and political influence, and so it does not surprise us to find them among those who presented personal votive gifts. Significantly, the title is usually followed by the epithet ki-aga ('beloved'). One lukur, called Eanita, dedicated an inscribed agate-pearl to Inanna, with a prayer for king Šulgi, and so did Kubātum (Sollberger and Kupper 1971: 143). A full dedicatory inscription addressed to Nanâ, for the life of Bur-Sîn of Isin and her (own) life, is found on an agate-plaque by Nanâ-ibsa, his lukur-kaskal-la (Sollberger and Kupper 1971: 178).

The latest example comes from the reign of the last king of Isin, Sînmagir (1827–1817). A woman called Nuṭṭuptum wrote on a clay-cone that she had a certain building (e-šutum) erected for the life of the king and her own life. She identifies herself as 'his beloved lukur-kaskal-la, mother of his heir' (Sollberger and Kupper 1971: 181).

There is at the moment no consensus about the exact meaning of this term. Falkenstein (1953: 370), typically for the time, saw the lukur as a priestess who represented the goddess in the ritual coitus with the king during the Sacred Marriage. Sollberger and Kupper translated 'concubine'; Renger (1967: 149) defined her as 'a much-beloved, non-cloistered courtesan'; Jacobsen (1987b: 57 note 2) identified the lukur-kaskal-la especially as concubines, on the strength of a lexical equivalent with Akkadian šugitum and suggested that she may have been 'a handmaiden who accompanied a man on his journeys (kaskal)'. Kang (1972: 261) saw them also as concubines and 'secondary wives of UrIII kings', while for Steinkellner (1981: 80) she is simply 'the king's wife'.

With regard to the lukur[1] women mentioned in the text samples above, several facts emerge: there could be more than one at the same court, they sometimes bore children to the king, they disposed of sufficient funds to make costly offerings on their own and their king's behalf, they are always called 'ki-aga' ('beloved').

The evidence of the bilingual lexical lists is, as often with titles, vague. In an Old Babylonian list[2] the term lukur is correlated with nadītum, qadištum, batultum, which are also ambiguous, denoting some function in the temple organization, of which nothing more definite can be said than that the women so designated were 'set apart for the service to a god' (Lambert 1991: 140). First millennium synonym lists, however, do equate these titles with words for 'prostitute',[3] although this does not necessarily help our under-standing of the term's relevance for the beginning of the second millennium. However, it does seem likely, considering the standard adjective 'beloved' and the references to the king, that the lukur-kaskal-la women of the UrIII and Isin period not only had sexual relations with the king, sometimes leading to the birth of an heir, in which case they could rise to the high status of royal wife/mother, but that they were given a prestigious title, which they liked to flaunt on their ex-votos. I propose, therefore, as a hypothesis, to regard these women as royal courtesans who had achieved a superior position and were distinguished from other women of the royal household. But the criteria for this distinction remain uncertain; it does not seem to depend on bearing the king's offspring.

Now to another exponent of *l'amour libre*, the so-called 'sacred prostitutes' (Greek: *hierodouloi*), whose existence in Mesopotamian temples has been postulated since the early days of Assyriology. Here is a short song dedicated to the goddess Nanâ, which consists of a short dialogue between a man and a woman:

> 'Come with me, my sister, come with me,
> Come with me from the entrance of the bed-room (or cella),
> When you talk to a man, what a woman (*lit*, it is a woman)!
> When you look at a man, what a woman!
> When you lean the side against the wall, your nakedness is
>   sweet.
> When (you) bow down, the hips are sweet.'
> 'When I am standing against the wall – that's one lamb,
> when I bow down it is one and a half shekel.'
> (Alster 1993: 19)

The related text, which almost repeats the above passage verbatim, has a longer list of prices, but the first part of the tablet is broken. The third passage has the woman speaking:

> 'Do not dig a [canal], let me be your canal,
> Do not plough [a field], let me be your field.
> Farmer, do not search for a wet place,

My precious sweet, let me be your wet place.
Let the ditch(?) be your farrow,
Let our little apples be your desire!'
(Alster 1993: 15, 20)

These texts, like many of the love and Bridal Songs, were designated as balbale of Nanâ. We have seen that they often allude to erotic situations in a more or less defined social setting. Here we have a case which seems devoid of romantic sentiment and passion, since the sexual act becomes a transaction to be paid for. It is interesting that, taken out of context, the second quotation would fit into a Bridal Song. It is a further instance of the blurring of specific contents in these poems.

The prices mentioned in the first texts seem rather substantial for a minimal coital engagement (standing intercourse *a tergo*), although it has been suggested that the lamb especially may constitute a 'traditional donation to the temple' (Alster 1993: 15f.) This interpretation hinges on the translation of pa-pah as 'cella' or 'cult-room', which, as Alster observed, can also denote 'any bedroom', and the mention of the goddess Nanâ's name. Alster pointed out that 'not a single detail in the Nanâ songs ... refers unambiguously to a temple or a ritual'. The woman is not designated here by any appellative or title. Yet it is so far the clearest case of a professional transaction of a sexual nature.

Terminology is a problem here, as modern languages lack a suitable vocabulary for such persons. 'Prostitute' evokes contemporary social conditions and morals; 'harlot' rings with biblical and ecclesiastical disapproval; '*hetaira*' has a specific socio-historical context; and 'courtesan' has (etymologically, at least) an aristocratic association (and I have used it for such women in this study). The word 'hierodule' was often used by classically educated Assyriologists familiar with Herodotus, to render Sumerian words (nugig, nu-bar and lukur) which were translated in the bilingual lexical and other texts by Akkadian expressions for 'common prostitute' (*kezertu, harimtu, šamhatu*) as well as on occasion by titles for temple employees (*naditu, kulmašitu, qadištu*). This apparent contradiction between the secular aspect and the religious association was solved by the invention, with a nod to cross-cultural parallels in ancient Greece or India, of the term 'sacred prostitute'.[4] Like the 'sacred marriage', the 'sacred prostitute', who engages in sex as a magical rite in the context of some fertility cult or officiates in the

150

rites of Inanna/Ištar, belongs to the 'Golden Bough' school of historical anthropology. In a recent survey of the evidence, Lambert noted that while 'most of these titles have etymologically some implication of religious office ... some [women bearing them] at least, and in some areas and period, served as common prostitutes' (Lambert 1991: 141).

Georges Bataille (1987: 133) remarked that

> prostitution seems to have been a complement to marriage in the first place. The prostitute was dedicated to a life of transgression. The sacred or forbidden aspect of sexual activity remained apparent in her, for her whole life was dedicated to violating the taboo. Religion, far from opposing prostitution, was able to control its modalities as it could with other sorts of transgression. The prostitutes in contact with sacred things, in surrounding themselves sacred, had a sacredness comparable with that of priests.

It seems that in Mesopotamia, where all sexual behaviour was under the auspices of Inanna/Ištar, sexual acts outside marriage could be condoned and to some extent institutionalized. The goddess is linked with prostitution in several compositions. The long list of Inanna's me, the divine prerogatives she obtained from Enki (Farber-Flügge 1973) includes the following which relate specifically to sexuality:

> The standard, the quiver, the wielding of the penis, the kissing of the penis, the art of prostitution, the art of speeding

as well as

> the art of forthright speech, the art of slanderous speech, the art of ornamental speech, – ? –, the cult prostitute, the holy tavern (I, v, 29–32)

The 'standard' and 'quiver' are obvious metaphors for penis and vagina; then follows the masculine sexual activity and possibly a reference to fellatio, nam-kar-kid is the standard term for prostitution. The second group has something to do with different kinds of utterances or discourse; 'scandalous speech' would fit better than 'slanderous'; amalu, here rendered as 'cult prostitute', is a component sign consisting of ama + ᵈInanna; its proximity to the next term (dam) suggested the translation. We shall come back to the éš-dam below. Some of the items of this list seem to belong to the more controversial aspects of sexuality, which will be discussed in a separate chapter.

Inanna is identified with libido:

You are Inanna (who) in the streets of Kullab make (people) copulate.

(Benito 1969: line 364)

As a ki-sikil, Inanna lent her name to adolescent sentiments, and the bride was encouraged to identify with this particular aspect of the goddess's 'sexual persona', as the inspiration for conjugal happiness. But the texts also demonstrate that, ultimately, though such an archetypal bride, Inanna was not a 'proper' wife:

When the cattle has been set loose on the hills,
When the cows and sheep are returned to the pen and fold,
My queen, you disguise yourself, you put on your neck the
    pearls of the harlot.
From the éš-dam you fetch men.
From the lap of Dumuzi, your husband, you sneak away, to
    make love to your seven nimgir.

(Alster 1974: 84)

or

You are the one who picks up a man in the éš-dam, from the lap of your spouse Dumuzi you sneak away

(Ibid.: 84)

and generally she is called

The prostitute (kar-kid), setting out for the éš-dam, who makes the bed delicious

(Volk 1989: 219)

who says of herself:

When I sit by the gate of an inn (éš-dam),
I am indeed a prostitute who makes love

(Ibid.)

Lambert suggested that the term kar-kid might be understood to mean 'she who works the quay' (Lambert 1991: 138, 157), the ancient equivalent of roadsides, as the rivers and canals provided the main means of transport between cities. The word is already attested in Early Dynastic sources and has no religious connotations. This secular aspect of the profession is also born out by the Akkadian equivalents (*šamhatu, harimtu, kezertu*). kar-kid is not one of Inanna's official titles, unlike the more ambiguous term nu-gig, which was used by royal wives in the Early Dynastic period and may originally have been the title of a high office.

When Inanna abandons the lap of her husband for sexual adventures she goes to the classic locale, the éš-dam, the 'tavern', where barley beer was offered. This is described as 'a place of relaxation, (for) the joy of drinking' which makes 'the heart happy again' (Civil 1976: 89). Inanna is the one 'who frequents the éš-dam'[5] to pick up customers. There was also an éš-dam-kù, 'the holy éš-dam', which seems to refer to one of Inanna's sanctuaries in Girsu.[6] Hallo and van Dijk (1968: 74) surmised that the term originally referred to a temple of Inanna, but that it later came to signify a 'brothel'.

In the absence of relevant earlier, third-millennium texts that substantiate whether or not the éš-dam had anything to do with sexual activity, such pronouncements remain speculative. All we can say is that at the period these texts were written, (during the Old Babylonian period), the éš-dam was associated with alcohol and sex.

One very interesting poem, from the Old Babylonian period, is the so-called 'Message of Lú-dingir-ra to his Mother' (Civil 1964; Cooper 1971). I believe that there is more to this 'mother' than first meets the eye. The form of the text is that of a letter entrusted to a messenger to take to the 'mother' in Nippur. She is described by cryptic clues or 'signs':

> My mother is a very cheerful person, she is covered with
>   ornaments.
> If you do not know my mother, I shall give you some signs:
> The name is Šat-Ištar, go to (her) with these instructions.
> (Her) body, face (and) limbs are smooth)?).
> The gracious goddess of her (city) quarter,
> since her childhood, had decreed her fate.
> She went directly (and) with reverence(?) to the house of her
>   father-in-law.
> She stands humbly before the goddess, her lady,
> Knows how to look after Inanna's place,
> Does not disobey the orders of the king,
> She is energetic, makes her affairs prosper.
> Is loving, gentle (and) lively.

A lamb, good cream (and) sweet butter flow from her. I shall
   give you a second sign about my mother:
My mother is like a bright light on the horizon, a doe in the
   mountains,
A morning star (shining even) at noon.
A precious carnelian stone, a topaz from Marhaši.
A treasure for the brother of the king, full of charm (hi-li).
A seal of nir-stone, an ornament like a sun,
A tin bracelet, a ring of antasurra,
bright gold and silver
(but) she is alive, a breathing thing.
(She is) an alabaster statuette, placed on a pedestal of lapis
   lazuli –
A living figurine, (her) limbs are full of charm. I shall give
You a third sign about my mother:
My mother is a heavenly rain, water for the best seeds.
A bountiful harvest, which grows a second crop:
A garden of delight, full of joy,
An irrigated fir-tree, covered with fir-cones:
An early fruit, the yield of the first month;
A canal which brings luxuriant water to the irrigation ditches,
A sweet Dilmun date, sought in its prime.
I shall give you a fourth sign about my mother:
My mother fills songs (and) prayers with joy,
Her glance is sparkling(?) in the Akitum-festival.
. . ., daughter of a king, a song of abundance.
She brings joy to the dancing places,
A lover, a loving heart of inexhaustible delight,
Food for the captive(?), who returns to his mother. I shall give
You a fifth sign about my mother:
My mother is a palm-tree, with a very sweet smell.
A chariot of pine-wood, a litter of box-wood.
A good . . . giving perfumed oil.
A bunch of fruits, a garland growing luxuriantly(?).
A phial of ostrich shell, overflowing with perfumed oil. When
   you stand in her radiant presence, (thanks to) the signs I
   gave you, say to her: 'your beloved son Lú-dingir-ra greets
   you!'

(Civil 1964)

The question arises whether this rather extravagant praise of a 'mother' should be taken as a sign of special filial devotion, perhaps written by a literate son, who had heard too much love poetry. Cooper (1971: 90) suggested that maybe this 'mother' was not meant to refer to a natural mother, 'but to the goddess Inanna in motherly guise', and he pointed to the erotic metaphors of the texts.

The text has also been connected with the so-called Wisdom Literature, partly because that was how it survived in different translations into the middle of the second millennium (Hallo 1974: 196). Wisdom Literature is composed of popular epigrammatic sayings, proverbs, riddles, fables and the like, and played an important part in scribal education. The posing of rhetorical questions or the setting up of a problem is a common device in this genre.[7]

I believe that this poem is a complex riddle that makes the reader guess the identity of the 'mother'. The author provides five descriptive clues which should allow the messenger, i.e. the reader, to figure out the answer. The first sign (gizkim: a term taken from omen literature) gives the name of the woman as Šat-Ištar, 'She of Ištar' (Stamm 1968: 263) – the first important clue; then follow further biographical details: she was singled out from childhood for a special fate, married early and developed a devotion for Inanna, while keeping to the expected standards of behaviour. Because of her ability, her 'affairs prospered', so that now she is a source of well-being and wealth (expressed by the butter/cream metaphor). The second sign makes almost exclusive use of the symbolism of artifice, comparing the 'mother' to an alabaster statuette, precious stones, items of jewellery, etc., yet stresses the fact that we are dealing with a living and not inanimate being. The jewellery metaphors are very similar to those used in courtly love poetry. The reference to the king's brother may signal that the woman has achieved a high position at court and is treasured there like a work of art. The third sign, in contrast, is given over to horticultural allegory, centred around the familiar simile of the kiri la-la, 'the garden of delight', with its first fruit, fir-trees and the well-watered canal, summarized by the reference to the 'sweet Dilmun date'. By now, things are becoming clear. The fourth sign tells us of the 'mother''s activities: she sings and prays joyfully, takes part in the festivals, dances, and is 'a lover, a loving heart (or womb!) of inexhaustible delight'. The last clue rather mixes the metaphors of artifice, but concentrates on the sensual impression her presence conveys, which is expressed by references to the fragrant smell surrounding her, caused by the scented oils she uses. It is obvious by now that the answer to this riddle cannot be Inanna herself, as the service to Inanna is explicitly mentioned. I can only see this as a description of what we called a 'professional lover' or courtesan. Treasured by the king's brother, she makes public appearances in all her finery, a devotée of Inanna, and in turn is supported by the goddess, as the name implies. The reference to 'mother' (ama) might be a pun on AMA.ᵈINANNA, which we found listed among persons connected with sexuality in a list of Inanna's me. If my interpretation of Lú-dingir-ra's letter is correct, then we have lavish praise indeed for her cultural influence.

14

LIMINAL SEXUALITY
Eunuchs, homosexuals and the common prostitute

We have seen that the personality of Inanna/Ištar had a male component, an aspect of martial power. To some extent, the goddess unites gender roles, although she is never bisexual or androgynous. Her sexual identity is always that of a woman, even when her cult statue wears a beard to emphasize her special function in the sphere of warfare (Groneberg 1985).

But just as the goddess could not be envisaged as an adolescent bride or a prostitute, so she can also be associated with persons of doubtful sexual identity. A comparatively early example is the famous 'Inanna-Dilibad' hymn which dates from the reign of Iddin-Dagan (1984–1954) (Römer 1965: 128–31, 137–9; Reisman 1973)). It includes a description of the procession taking place on the New Year festival. People are playing lutes, harps and drums, and acclaim the goddess with shouts of 'hail!' (silim). Then comes a contingent of sag-ur-sag, with their typical hair-style, colourful ribbons and the 'physical characteristics of divinity on their bodies'.[1] I think that the following 18 lines all refer to sag-ur-ra. They are also called lú-zi, 'real/veritable men', who approach the goddess. They hold the balag instrument (probably a drum: Black 1991: 28f.), are girded with the sword belt,

> the spear, 'the arm of battle' they grasp in their hand.
> They walk before the holy Inanna,
> Their right side they dress with men's clothes,
> They walk before the holy Inanna,
> Their left side they cover with women's clothes.
> They walk before the holy Inanna,
> To the great Lady of Heaven, Inanna, I would say: 'Hail!'
> With jump ropes and coloured cords they compete before her.
> (Sjöberg 1976: 224)

157

The sag-ur-sag are followed by the guruš, young men, 'carrying hoops', and the ki-sikil, maidens, including šugia women[2] with their special hair-do, who bring a sword and a double-edged axe before Inanna. Finally, the kurgarra seem to grasp this (or another sword) and pour out blood before Inanna, while the various drums 'make a loud noise'.

The striking thing about such passages is the inversion of traditional gender roles. Let us first look at the sag-ur-sag. Römer and Reisman translate this as 'male homosexual', mainly on the strength of Akkadian lexical equations with *assinnu*. The Sumerian word is composed of the generic term sag + ur-sag ('warrior'), which could mean, as Lambert (1991: 150) suggested, a companion or batman of a warrior. However, from the Middle Assyrian period onwards, LÚ sag was also used to write the Akkadian *ša reši*, which denoted a castrated person, and later also an official in the neo-Assyrian imperial administration. The sag-ur-sag are described here as being conspicuous by their apparel, their hair-style and their weapons. The interpretation of kuš-nam-dingir-ra is of crucial importance for the understanding of this term. kuš means 'body, skin'. nam-dingir expresses the abstract concept of divinity. I believe that it refers here to the physical distinction, divinely bestowed on these individuals, which I propose to see as a genital malformation, hermaphroditism, or absence of external genitals. Such congenital aberrations are statistically not infrequent. In modern societies they are generally detected at birth, and treated with either surgery or hormone therapy, to develop a fully sexed male or female (Jones and Scott 1971). In antiquity, as today in countries where modern medicine is not generally available, people lived into adulthood with these deformities, and were more or less marginalized as a result. The Indian Hijras or Hijaras, who have been the subject of several ethnographic studies, provide a useful example of a cross-cultural comparison (Sharma 1989; Nanda 1986, 1990). It was found that a significant number have congenital sexual defects, while some are homosexual transvestites and some castrated, originally normal, males. Contemporary Indian Hijras do not seem to be attached to a particular temple, although they do mythologize their condition by reference to the temporary sex-change undergone by Arjuna, one of the Pandava, in the Mahabharata (Sharma 1989: 134). However, they have achieved a kind of institutionalization by appearing, in female garb, at rites of passage, especially weddings and births, where they bless the couple and the child. The fact that their own sexual identity deviates from the culturally acceptable norm, enhances the magic potential of the Hijra, whose curse is feared as transferring their affliction to normal families.

The Mesopotamian sag-ur-sag, as well as the pilpili, the kurgarra and the *assinnu*, may well have been the Ancient Near Eastern equivalents to the Hijra. If that was the case, they were more fully integrated into the Mesopotamian public ritual by virtue of Inanna's inclusive sexual competence. After all, one of her oft-quoted epithets was 'the one who can change man into woman and woman into man'. It is in Inanna's power to assign sexual identity; the statement should not be taken as a reference to some vague ritual gender swapping, as Sjöberg (1976: 226) suggested, but as an acceptance of asexuality or hermaphroditism as divinely decreed. There are other instances of this attitude. In the myth *Enki and Ninmah*, which describes the invention of the human reproductive system, there were some individuals, fashioned by Ninmah, who had genital deformities. One was a woman who was unable to give birth, the other a man who suffered from some urinary problem, and one was called 'lú-su-ba-giš-nu-gar-gal-la-nu-gar', 'a person on whose body was neither a penis nor a vulva'. Enki, probably sarcastically, calls him a courtier and assigns him a place in the king's entourage (Jacobsen 1987a: 161). None of these deformities were eradicated; on the contrary, the myth makes it quite clear that such people had to be accommodated by society.

In the Inanna hymn quoted above, the sag-ur-sag emphasize their ambiguous gender by wearing male and female clothing and ribbons. They carry harps, probably signifying the musical feminine arts, and weapons. However, their performance before the goddess is done with harmless skipping-ropes and ribbons. Then we have a *defilé* of seemingly 'ordinary' young men and young women, who, in honour of the sag-ur-sag, or indeed of Inanna's own inherent sexual duality, parade with emblems of the opposite sex, the boys carrying hoops and the girls swords. The climax of the show is the appearance of the kurgarra, who lacerate themselves in an ecstatic frenzy to the accompaniment of drums. This text describes the ritual acceptance of liminal sexuality under the aegis of the goddess.[3]

In the myths about the Descent to the Underworld, the dead goddess was brought to life through the intervention of asexual begins, the galaturra and the kurgarra in the Sumerian version, and the *assinnu* in the Akkadian (Jacobsen 1987a: 220f.; Dalley 1989: 158f.).

In the cult, the galaturra was a chief chanter of lamentations and other ritual dirges (Lambert 1991). The kur-garra, who appeared in the hymn above as wielding swords and performing some ecstatic dance, is synonymous with the Akkadian *assinnu*, also known as *kulu'u*. The available evidence suggests that the people so designated fall into the same category as the sag-ur-sag.[4] The lexical definition of the *assinnu*, apart from sag-ur-sag, is ur-SAL, which means 'feminine man'. Another Akkadian synonym, *sinnišanu*, literally 'the womanlike one', also emphasizes the deviation from normal masculinity. In the omen-collection *šumma alu*, the *assinnu* is mentioned several times. First, his inability to achieve orgasm is described:

> If a man starts trembling while . . . for sexual potency, and like an *assinnu* fails to achieve a sexual climax.
>
> (Lambert 1991: 151)

And further on, in a section that deals with homosexuality and anal penetration:

> If a man engage in coitus *per anum* with his (male) equal.
> If a man has intercourse with an *assinnu*.
>
> (Lambert 1991: 145)

There is also a proverb from a Late Assyrian collection, which is relevant in this context (Lambert 1960: 218, 339). It quotes the remark of a *sinnišanu*, who enters a *bīt aštammi* (the equivalent of the Sumerian éš-dam). He raises his hand and says:

> My hire goes to my *anzinnu*.
> You (woman) are wealth (*mešru*), I am half (*mešlu*).

It is not certain who the *anzinnu* is here, he uses it like a reference to a pimp. His pun is interesting, for he seems to be addressing a female prostitute, telling her that she can command more for her services as a real woman, while he has to be content with half the price, as he himself is only 'half' male or female.

The example of the Hijra is again illuminating in this respect. They all eschew male behaviour, and always appear in female clothes. Apart from their singing, dancing and drumming (with tambourines) at weddings and birthdays, they also engage in passive homosexual prostitution, mainly to otherwise heterosexual men. Their services are significantly cheaper than that of even older women, precisely because they are only 'half' (Sharma 1989: 100).

He asked his informants about their own sexual satisfaction and found that most were unable to relieve their frustration genitally. He observed that their tendency to use obscene language may offer them deferred 'oral sexual satisfaction'. The Mesopotamian descriptions of the *assinnu* are remarkably similar; their female attire, their prostitution, even their obscenity is documented: see Inanna's swearing in the éš-dam and the exaggerated sexual language used in some Ištar-rituals (Lambert 1975a). The problematic social integration of these people is vividly recounted in *Ištar's Descent*, where they are cursed to 'eat from the gutter, drink from the sewer' and lurk about 'the shade of the city-wall', only rest briefly in some doorway, 'where the drunk and the thirsty shall slap your cheek' (Dalley 1989: 159). Yet in contrast to the Indian Hijra, who at least within the last few generations have not been affiliated to a temple, but form independent groups, the *assinnu* do have a place in the religious system. We do not know to what extent their affiliation to a temple guaranteed housing and subsistence. One could expect that some individuals who had some training in the performance of lamentations, who had secured an official position by virtue of their singing talents or other professional means, made a fairly good living, while others were reduced to fending for themselves. The *assinnu* also took part in ritual incantations of Ištar, another possible source of revenue. But it is striking that there are a number of rituals where the roles of the kurgarra have a destructive or dangerous aspect. In tablet 18 of Uru-amairabi, the hapless maidservant Amanamtagga is killed by the stick of the gala and the 'sword and club' of the kurgarra (lines 17, 19) (Volk 1989: 90). They are described as threatening in the Erra-epic (see below), and in a Sumerian text identified as a myth by Kramer (1990b: 143–9), but reads more like an expiating ritual against seizure, Dumuzi is trying to defend his sheep-fold and the fertility of his herding animals against the 'treacherous kurgarra' (kur-gar-ra-lul-la-ra).

But in spite of the dangerous and negative aspects of the kurgarra and similar people, they did seem to have definite roles in Mesopotamian society. One factor which speaks in favour of the social integration of asexuals, homosexuals, etc. is the very range of terminology to describe them. In India, they are all subsumed by the collective word 'Hijra', but both Sumerian and Akkadian vocabularies show much greater differentiation. There is, of course, the possibility that the original Sumerian terms referred to various official functions which might have nothing to do with sexual orientation. But at a later date, when such terms of office had become obsolete, they were used summarily for persons with a liminal status. The bilingual lexical lists of the late second and first millennium do not adequately define the terms, but present them as synonyms. Some were certainly still titles of temple or secular offices (both temple and court employed castrated men as well as asexuals), while others (such as *sinnišanu*) seem more descriptive, although 'like a woman' has a rather broad semantic range (effeminate, dressed or behaving like woman, etc.).

One might wonder whether the comparatively high profile of these people in Mesopotamian literature could be taken as a sign that they could have an influence on the composition of such texts. Kluckhorn, investigating Navaho ritual songs, was able to show that the personality of individual singers exercised considerable influence over the content of traditional narratives (Kluckhorn 1988). Interesting in our context was his observation that

> a transvestite called 'Left Handed' . . . enjoyed a tremendous reputation as a singer . . . he restructured a number of myths as he told them to his apprentices in a way which tended to make the hermaphrodite be'gôîdí a kind of supreme Navaho deity, a position which he perhaps never held in general tradition up to this point.

Inanna/Ištar may have been claimed as the patron deity of such groups in a secondary development.

The kurgarra, *sinnišanu* and similar people are often mentioned in connection with female prostitutes. There is likewise a considerable vocabulary to describe them.[5] Some terms are again titles of office (*qadištu, kulmašitu, ugbabtu, ištaritu*, etc.) (Lambert 1991: 138), while others are more unofficial, such as *šamhatu* (literally 'voluptuous one') and *kezertu* ('curly haired(?)'), both also used as actual names (Stamm 1968: 249). The equivalent for the kar-kid, the Sumerian 'common prostitute', is *harīmtum*. There is no general agreement among Assyriologists as to what extent the titles implied professional sexual activity, and this is not the place to assemble the arguments. I shall instead concentrate on the role of the prostitute in Babylonian literature, where there is no doubt as to the nature of their profession.

First, some epigrammatic proverbial observations:

A prudent *kezertu* slanders the . . . woman
At Ištar's command the potentate's wife gets a bad reputation.
(Lambert 1960: 219)

Here the prostitute (*kezertu*) is said to have an interest in casting doubts on the conduct of other women; even 'pillars of society' are not safe from rumour, but ultimately all private conduct and its evaluation is in the hands of Ištar.

In the following quote the wise man offers this counsel:

Do not marry a prostitute (*harīmtu*), whose husbands are
    legion.
A harlot (*ištaritu*) who is dedicated to a god,
A courtesan (*kulmašitu*) whose favours are many.
In your trouble she will not support you,
In your dispute she will mock you;
There is no reverence or submissiveness with her.
Should she dominate your house, get her out,
For she has directed her attention elsewhere.
(Lambert 1960: 103)

In another version of the text the following lines are added:

She will disrupt the house she enters, and her partner will not assert himself.
(Lambert 1960: 103)

This spells out the reasons why, from a man's point of view, an independent, female professional is not a good choice; but there is no general condemnation of her activities. In fact, we know from legal records that many prostitutes did in fact marry, and were encouraged or even forced by their future husbands to do so.[6] On the other hand, if a woman engaged in prostitution without his consent and knowledge, he could divorce her or, in some places and times, put her to death (Drive and Miles 1935: 44–5). Theoretically and legally, the control over a woman's sexual activity was in the hands of men, who, in their capacity as fathers, brothers or husbands, had responsibility for her conduct. But while adultery and rape constituted *de facto* a crime against a man's property (his wife, daughter), and was therefore punishable in accordance with other property offences, prostitution was a professional activity not without a certain status. Although it is most unlikely that intercourse was part of the religious ceremonies performed at the temple, payment for sexual services may well have constituted some of its revenue, as was the case in Corinth or Cyprus.

As mentioned before, the tavern or éš-dam was a place for relaxation and drinking, as well as for erotic adventure. One Akkadian ritual was meant to secure brisk trade for the tavern-keeper:

> Incantation: Ištar of the lands, most heroic of goddesses, this is your priestly residence: exult and rejoice! Come, enter our house! With you may your sweet bed-fellow enter, your lover and your cult-actor (=kurgarra)! 'May my lips be honey, my hands "charm"! May the lip(s) of my vulva be lip(s) of honey! As the birds twitter over a snake which comes out of its hole, may these people fight over me! From the priestly residence of Ištar, from the temple residence of Ninlil, from among the possessions of Ningizzida, seize him, bring him here, be gracious to him! May the distant one return to me, may the angry one come back to me! Like smoke may his heart return to me! As the rain fructifies the earth, so that vegetation is abundant, may the greetings addressed to me be abundant'. End-formula of the incantation.

> (Caplice 1974)

It is worth noting that the spell appeals to Ištar's sexual attraction and that the customers are supposed to come from various sacred places and processions.

The other proverbial place for the *harīmtu* is the street, the public place. While the average married woman restricted her public appearances (see Falkenstein 1966: 363f.), the prostitute 'went out'. This dichotomy between the woman who stays at home and the one who frequents the street is already apparent in the Old Babylonian lexical texts.[7] An Old Babylonian omen warms a man that

> if the (sacrificial) sheep grinds his teeth the wife of the man will commit fornication, she will go out of the house.

> (Falkenstein 1966: 362)

The most complex literary reflection on the Mesopotamian prostitute occurs in the Gilgameš epic.[8] She has the typical professional name of Šamhat, the Voluptuous One, and her function in the story is to seduce the 'wild man' Enkidu, whom the gods created as a companion to Gilgameš. As a result of their lovemaking, Enkidu is alienated from the animals of the desert and is taken to the city of Uruk,

Where young men wear sashes, where there is a feast every
    day, and where
The courtesans, impeccable in their beauty, lascivious, full of
    love-cries,
See the notables leave their bed at night (to join them).
(I, 200–5) (Bottéro 1992: 77)

Enkidu meets Gilgameš, who has been having dreams about his
arrival, and they become inseparable friends. Eventually, Enkidu
attracts the anger of the gods and is destined to die. On his death-
bed, he looks back on his life and curses the huntsman, who first saw
him in the wilderness. Then he turns to Šamhat and curses her with
'a mighty curse':

'May you not build a house for your pleasure
May you not dwell in the banqueting house of maidens
May beer dregs soil (?) your charming bosom,
May the drunk spatter your festive attire with vomit(?),
[3 lines very fragmentary]
. . . may the table, people's delight, a thing of pride, not be laid
    in [your house].
May the . . . of your pleasure be a . . . [. . .] abode.
May the potter's crossroads (quarters) be your sitting place.
May ruins be the place where you lie,
May the shade of the city wall be your standing place.
May briars and thorns skin your feet,
May drunk and sober strike your cheek.
. . . may they frequent your bordello (*altammaki* = éš-dam).
. . . may there be quarrels.
May [. . . of the] reliable . . . shout at you.
May the builder [not plaster the roof of your house],
[May] owls roost [in your . . .]
. . may] there be [no banquet]
[gap of three lines]
May the purple [. . .] become a dedicated thing,
May the soiled loin-cloth be a . . gift,
Because you have humiliated me, the innocent,
[Yes] me, the innocent, you have humiliated me in my
    wilderness.'
(Lambert 1991: 130)

The whole tenor of this passage is very similar to the curse Ereškigal utters against Asušunamir, the *assinnu* in the *Descent of Ištar* (Dalley 1989: 159). Both describe the negative aspects of their marginal existence. It is not clear to what extent this passage contrasts the prostitute's lifestyle with that of respectable citizens, or is confined to the expectations within that profession. Bottéro (1992: 140) reads '[Jamais] tu ne (t')é]diferas de foyer heureux! (…) [(Jamais) tu n'en]treras [au harem] des jeunes femmes!', while Lambert's translations suggests that the *bīt lalu* and *bīt qerit ardati* may be establishments connected with the services of Šamhat. The 'table, people's delight', is equally ambiguous. Does it refer to a wedding banquet or a sort of 'symposium' where courtesans entertained? It is of course possible that both meanings are intended, as the whole epic is pervaded by literary puns. The prostitute is clearly related to the tavern. Several lines describe other places she will haunt, and again they can be understood as referring both to her trade and to her personal life. They are certainly peripheral and uninhabitable for anyone but the most destitute. The potter's quarters were close to the clay-pits and kilns at the outskirts of the town, and the city-walls with their projections and recesses provided shade and shelter for the homeless. The ruins of old buildings that were scattered throughout the city had a similar function; her 'lying down' in them could also refer to her trade. Further down, her house, should she have one, is described as a near-ruin itself. The 'purple' garment that is contrasted here with the soiled and intimate lap-cover (*ulāp sūni*) takes up the theme of the initial lines. Either it symbolizes the prostitute's separation from respectable people, who would be privileged to wear the *takiltu*, or it denies her the rewards of her profession, the expensive dress that the successful courtesan might wear. The reason for Enkidu's bitterness is stated explicitly: through his congress with Šamhatu he has lost his *ellutu*, his purity, he has been literally destroyed by her; the verb *šamaṭu* ('to deflate, deplete'), is used in a punning contrast with *šamahu* ('to flourish'), from which the name Šamhatu is derived. It is remarkable that there is no reference to Ištar in this passage, although in Tablet VI, 165, she calls the *kezreti šamhati u harimāti* to mourn the destruction of the Bull of Heaven. Instead, the text concentrates on the secular aspects of the *harīmtu*'s calling. It also emphasizes the social marginality of the prostitute, who is seen here not as a 'holy' devotée of the goddess, but as an object of contempt. This negative view, which is characteristic of the Gilgameš epic, especially the Ninevite version, reflects a new attitude to sexuality, which will be discussed in chapter 21.

When Enkidu has uttered his curse, the sun-god Šamaš, whom he invokes, intercedes on behalf of Šamhat, calling down from heaven (VII, 35–9):

> 'Why do you curse, O Enkidu, my harlot Šamhat,
> She has fed you food for gods,
> Gave you beer, drink of kings,
> Clothed you with a great robe,
> And presented you with a perfect partner, Gilgameš.'

Like a brother, Gilgameš will now look after Enkidu, put him in a big bed, have the people of Uruk mourn him and 'roam the steppe, clothed only in a lion-skin' after his death. This speech by Šamaš calms the heart of Enkidu and he now adds blessings to complement the 'bad fate', which once uttered, is irreversible, like the curse of the bad fairy in folk-tales:

> 'Come Šamhat, I shall decree (another) fate for you.
> My mouth which [cursed you] shall now bless you.
> May governors and princes fall in love with you,
> At one league's distance slap one's thighs (in exasperation),
> at two league's distance tear (*lit.* shake) one's hair (in
>   frustration).
> May the soldier not refuse you, but unbuckle his belt for you.
> May he give you 'claw'-pins(?) and necklace(s)
> Earring(s) of . . may he have made for you.
> May a man whose storehouses are sealed up and whose goods
>   are piled up
> [. .]. .[. .] take you in to the . . of the gods.
> May the first wife, (though) a mother of seven, be divorced on
>   your account.'
>
> (Lambert 1991: 131)

This blessing highlights the economic advantages of a successful courtesan who wins the affection of princes, making them pine in her absence. She will be given presents and jewellery, and replace the legitimate wife not only in the husband's affection but also in his household. Line 57 is unfortunately damaged, so we do not know with what purpose the wealthy man is to take Šamhat to the temple(?) of the gods.

In the various incantation series against the influence of malevolent magic, prostitutes and *assinnus*, together with foreigners, are named as persons who are likely to engage in witchcraft and sorcery.[9] Their marginal social position, as well as their irregular sexual identity, quite apart from the inherent power of sexuality with its potentially disruptive influence, put the erotic specialists in the category of people to be feared, like demons and spirits. This demonic aspect of sexuality will be discussed in a separate chapter. However, much as the collective or the individual might be mistrusted for their possible evil influence, the fact remains that they were to some extent integrated into the socio-religious system. The disruption of these institutionalized services is described in the so-called Erra-epic (Cagni 1977; Dalley 1989: 282–316), which dates from the late second millennium. Erra, another name for the Underworld god Nergal, is raised from his sleep and the amorous embrace of his spouse by the demonic Seven. In the temporary absence of Marduk, he takes over the rule of the world, with catastrophic results, as the established order of things is totally upset. The cult in the major cities is disrupted, including that of the Uruk:

'In Uruk, seat of Anu and Ištar, city of *kezretus*, *šamhatus* and *harīmtus*,
Whom (or which, said of the city) Ištar deprived of husbands and handed over to you (Erra),
Sutean men and women scream their abuse;
They rouse Eanna, the *kurgarrus* and *assinnus*
Whose masculinity Ištar has turned to femininity to make the people reverend,
The carriers of dagger, razor, scalpel and flint blades,
Who regularly do [forbidden things] to delight the heart of Ištar:
You set over them an insolent governor who will not treat them kindly,
(But) persecuted them and violated their rights.
(With the effect) that Ištar became enraged and angry with Uruk,
summoned an enemy who despoiled the land like grain before (flood) water.'

(IV, 52–62) (Dalley 1989: 304f.)

This states quite clearly that the female and male devotées of Ištar enjoyed her special protection, and that they carried out their practices on her behalf. Even if the ordinary citizen was wary of these people and the 'forbidden things' they did, they were still part

of the divinely sanctioned world order. To persecute and deprive
them of the ability to carry out their 'rites' was a violation of that
order which provoked the anger of the goddess. This passage
underlines the ambiguous attitude of Mesopotamian civilization
towards marginal sexuality: feared, tolerated and institutionalized.

Part II

SOURCES FROM THE LATER SECOND AND FIRST MILLENNIA

15

EROTICISM IN
AKKADIAN LITERATURE

The composite ethnic nature of Mesopotamian civilization, since its very beginnings in the late fourth millennium, is by now a generally accepted notion. The phenomenal success at exploiting the potentially super-fertile countryside by means of irrigation attracted people from all corners of the Middle East to the alluvial plain.

Since the middle of the third millennium, cuneiform was used not only for Sumerian but also to render the Semitic language. Groups of Semitic peoples, who were indigenous to the desert fringes of the so-called Fertile Crescent, settled in Mesopotamia and eventually became the numerically and culturally dominant ethnic group. There was also close contact with the plains of southern Iran, where the cultural development was very similar to that of Sumer and where the system of cuneiform was used to render the local language, known as Elamite.

The written forms of Semitic during the third millennium are the Old Akkadian dialect of the Sargonic period and the so-called Eblaite, spoken by the inhabitants of the North Syrian town of Ebla, which, together with its well-stocked archive, was discovered in 1964. Another Semitic dialect, Amorite, is known mainly from personal names. Neither of these early attempts resulted in an adequate representation of the actual languages, since the great majority of signs in any given text were written as Sumerian logographs. We can understand the general meaning of such texts without knowing how they were pronounced. Eighty per cent of Eblaite tablets are administrative in nature, and the few literary works are either copies of Sumerian texts or so obscure as to make translations highly problematic.

The Old Akkadian texts include a number of fine royal inscriptions, hymns and prayers. One of the most important scribal centres for the written development of the Semitic languages was Kiš, where the oldest love incantation so far known has been discovered (Westenholz and Westenholz 1977). After the collapse of the Sargonic empire and the subsequent invasion by the peoples from the East, collectively known as the Gutians, the Sumerian system of interdependent city-states was revived towards the end of the third millennium. Ur, under the energetic leadership of Urnammu, achieved political hegemony over the other states, and assumed the rulership over Sumer and Akkad. The ensuing Third Dynasty of Ur achieved an unprecedented degree of economic and administrative centralization, and built on extensive trade connections, from the Indus valley to Baluchistan. Although the ethnic and linguistic composition of the population remained as heterogeneous as before, the main language used for written communication was Sumerian. Scribal training centres proliferated, due to the increased demand for secretaries to man the offices of the empire. The court itself greatly appreciated and encouraged the production of literary works. The dynasties of Isin and Larsa, which took over after the demise of Ur's supremacy, maintained the existing systems of administration and commerce, and continued to use written Sumerian, although bilingual and Akkadian texts began to disseminate the language (Hallo 1974: 199f.; Gelb and Kienast 1990: 339–54).

The first centuries of the second millennium saw the influx of great waves of immigrants from western Semitic groups into the Mesopotamian heartland. The vernacular language became almost exclusively Semitic. The fragmentation into smaller political units, and the ensuing intensity of military rivalry for control over larger areas, caused an increasing demand for intelligence and communication services which had to be able to reflect the spoken word with reliable precision. So, while for commercial and ritual purposes Sumerian could be maintained as a form of technical written language, it no longer met the demands of communication. The archives of Mari (nineteenth–eighteenth centuries) are a prime example of this development. The spelling of these texts is to a large extent syllabic, and tries to accommodate the phonetic properties of the Semitic languages.

After 1763, when Hammurabi took control over the whole country, written Sumerian ceased to be in use except for highly specialized quasi-scientific subjects such as omens, astronomy and certain ritual text categories. This transition from one form of literacy to another was made possible by the active co-operation of the scribal training centres, the so-called *bīt ṭuppim* (é-dub-ba-a), the 'tablet houses'. Students were taught by means of the traditional sign-lists and textbooks, which were translated into Akkadian. They were also obliged to copy works of Sumerian literature, especially proverb collections, royal hymns, legal compendia, etc., and encouraged either to make translations or to compose new works in the so-called Old Babylonian dialect of Akkadian. The rapid growth of literary development in this period is one of its major cultural achievements.

This pioneer stage was followed by one of consolidation during the reign of the Kassite Dynasty and the Second Dynasty of Isin. The task of collecting, editing and copying texts resulted in a fairly homogeneous corpus of literary material, which also comprised scholarly works, such as omen collections, incantation series, legal compilations, etc. During the second half of the second millennium, Babylonian became the language of international communication as the archives of Tell el Amarna in Egypt, Hattusa in Anatolia and other places in the Levant testify. The training of scribes in these far-off cities, which still made use of standard lists and exemplary texts in prose and poetry, contributed incidentally to the dissemination of Mesopotamian literature.

When the Assyrian kings of the first millennium tried to emulate the intellectual preoccupations of their southern neighbours, they sent out envoys to amass any texts that could be found, and had them carefully copied in the neat calligraphy of the time, indexed and shelved in the libraries.

Comparatively few texts have survived from the fabled city of Babylon itself, but the great temples of Sippar, Borsippa and Nippur had important collections of first-millennium and earlier compositions. Literary creativity at that time, during the so-called Neo-Babylonian period, was concentrated in chronicling the stupendous political events of the day; but prayers, hymns and speculative texts, full of acrostics and other proofs of scribal sophistication, were also much admired. According to Livingstone (1989: XII), even at this late period there were attempts 'to escape from the tradition and produce new material', especially in the court poetry of the Sargonic period.

If one looks for sexuality and eroticism among the texts written in the various literary forms of Akkadian, at first glance there appears to be less relevant material than in Sumerian. However, an Assyrian tablet, a sort of library catalogue, listed the titles, or rather incipits, of some 400 songs. Two hundred and seventy-five such titles are preserved, of which two-fifths are in Sumerian, the rest in Akkadian. As we only have the first few words of each song, it is difficult to decide what their contents were, but there are sections which seem to have been decidedly erotic in tone and content, as these examples show: 'O young man loving me', 'Come in, shepherd, Ištar's lover', 'I smile at the lusty shepherd', 'I'll let you stay the night, young man', 'Tonight, this evening', etc. (Black 1983; Finkel 1988). Only one of these Akkadian songs has so far been recovered (Black 1983: 30f.). This may be due partly to the nature of the existing tablet collections; another archive, not yet discovered, may one day fill this gap and restore the balance.

An important new genre, which made use of traditional elements of the Bridal Songs and courtly love poetry, were the ritual descriptions of divine lovemaking. This ritual use of erotic dialogue seems to have replaced the private and secular Sumerian love-songs. In fact, Akkadian erotic poetry rarely addresses personal, human emotions.

On the other hand, and this is a genuinely original contribution of Akkadian scribes, we have a number of love incantations, which aim to win the affection of the beloved by means of magic, and potency incantations to strengthen the male's capacity for sexual performance. But this must be seen in connection with a general proliferation in the official use of magic in all areas of life, which is typical for the second and first millennia. This preoccupation with magic reveals many of the neurotic dispositions of the time. The spells and rituals reflect anxieties and paranoid tendencies. Love and sexual obsession were sometimes regarded as an affliction caused by witchcraft and demons.

As far as narrative literature is concerned, the most outstanding work is the Epic of Gilgameš, in its various stages of redaction. There are two important episodes for our enquiry, the story of Enkidu and Šamhat, 'the Voluptuous One', in the Old Babylonian version, and the confrontation between the hero and the goddess Ištar in Tablet VI, as preserved in the Ninevite edition. The development of the text reflects the important changes in attitude towards the role of women generally, and feminine sexuality in particular. Other mythical texts touch upon the subject more obliquely, notably the story of *Nergal and Ereškigal* and the *Descent of Ištar*. The latest erotic texts in Akkadian are the still enigmatic and inappropriately dubbed 'love-lyrics', which dramatize female jealously (Lambert 1975b).

Akkadian literature must to some extent reflect the cultural norms of the second and first millennia. While the essential continuity of Mesopotamian civilization is often stressed, and indeed borne out by the longevity of its religious and political institutions, and the persistent use of cuneiform writing for 3000 years, there were also great upheavals in all important sectors of public and private life. The prolonged influx of tribally structured Semitic peoples from the west, and the waves of very heterogeneous ethnic groups from the north-east, could not have been assimilated without affecting the existing social fabric. The rise to political power of foreign elements, such as the Amorites, the Kassites, or the Aramaeans, inevitably meant that some traditional institutions and customs were reinterpreted by the new ruling élite, and that some of their own cultural traits were adopted by the natives. But one cannot blame any one of these groups for all the sweeping changes that transformed Mesopotamian society during the Old Babylonian period – the reorganization of legal and marriage practices are only two cases in point. The influence of the Hurrians on the formation of Assyria is still unclear, as is the impact of Indo-European culture. The reorientation of religious alliances and the emergence of new gods, are also sometimes related to immigration. But the ever-widening network of direct international communication, following the domestication of the horse and the camel, also had far-reaching consequences for the dissemination of ideas. At the same time, we have more evidence than before for cultural particularism, for relatively small communities having their own idiosyncratic social and legal practices, as the archives of Hurrian Nuzi, for instance, clearly demonstrate. Unfortunately, the textual sources are for many areas and long historical periods virtually non-existent. We are particularly ill-informed about marginal groups around the larger commercial centres or on the periphery of the various empires. Even within the heartland of the old Sumer, where the great temple estates managed to weather most political upheavals, there are large gaps in the written tradition, the so-called 'Dark Age' periods, when no scribal production was sustainable. In view of the increasing complexity of Mesopotamian culture during the second and first millennia on the one hand, and the great gaps in the textual documentation on the other, it is virtually impossible to ascribe the changes in attitude to sexuality, which we find in the Akkadian literature, to specific historical circumstances. To use contemporary Semitic cultural traits, e.g. those of Bedouin societies, as a model for comparison, is not without its pitfalls, because it is quite impossible to isolate centuries of Islamic influence, let alone that of Western civilization, and assume cultural continuity and stasis over millennia. I shall, therefore, present the relevant texts without undue speculation as to their specific cultural background.

When I presented the Sumerian sources, I divided the material into several categories, often guided by the fictional 'voices' or main viewpoint. With the Akkadian texts, this division into specific roles is inappropriate, because the whole subject of sexuality is not personified in this sense. With the exception of a few love-songs, which clearly follow the Sumerian prototype, we do not have spontaneous poetic expression of emotion. Instead, the subject is presented obliquely, less as the result of personal experience than as an issue to be reflected upon. The love incantations do sometimes insert quotations of the afflicted or frustrated lover, and the expected positive outcome is also 'voiced'; but these phrases cannot be taken as evidence for either a poetic effort or a reflection of contemporary language: they are part of the ritual.

The same applies to the Lamentations. They contain many mythological and literary references, sometimes actual quotations from other texts, and they are highly formalized in view of their use in the cult (Cohen 1988; Black 1991). But because of these stylistic peculiarities – the collage-like assembly of utterances, mainly of grief and despair, occasionally of triumph and joy – they have no appreciable connection with a particular social or personal context. References to sexuality are rare in these works, since the most often-quoted voice is that of the grieving mother or sister. Only when Inanna/Ištar speaks are there allusions to the bride deprived of her husband and lover, and her function as goddess of sexual attraction warranted the digressions into her love-life. In fact, some of these episodes are only known from the Lamentations.

In Sumerian, the most suitable medium for the articulation of physical love was lyric poetry, and we found that the woman's voice was its most vociferous exponent. In Akkadian, the tone of poetry is more solemn and official, 'hymnic-epic', as von Soden has dubbed it, which makes the intimate revelation of feeling more difficult. However, the Old Babylonian dialogues do betray a new delicacy and sensitivity. But as we have so few love-songs in Akkadian, we have to beware of jumping to conclusions.

If we look at the narrative compositions, the comparatively unadorned style allowed the psychological development of main characters to be recorded, and it is in this genre that the subject of love is treated in some depth, although one has to emphasize that it did not constitute a major theme: we do not have a single 'love-story' comparable, say, to Cupid and Psyche, or Leila and Mashnun. On the contrary, we get a critical appraisal of the different kinds of human love, especially in the Gilgammeš epic. But the scepticism articulated there heralds a new consciousness and a range of abstraction that Greek will bring to fruition.

16

BALLADS, HYMNS AND DIALOGUES
Akkadian love poetry

The prayers and hymns that were written to Inanna, or rather Ištar in the Akkadian language, often follow Sumerian prototypes. Ištar is still the 'lady of heaven', according to the Sumerian interpretation of her name,[1] she is exalted as the 'greatest of the Igigi', and she is still in charge of love and sexual attraction, as in this Old Babylonian hymn, composed for king Amiditana (c. 1683–1647):

> She of joy, clothed with love,
> Adorned with seduction, grace, and sex-appeal.
> Ištar is clothed in joy and love,
> She is seduction, grace and sex-appeal.[2]
> Honey-sweet are her lips, life is her mouth;
> Adorned in laughing femininity.[3]
> She is magnificent, (. . . .) is put on her head,
> Her colouring is beautiful, her eyes are shining and bright.
> Wherever she looks, there is gaiety,
> Life, power, protection.
> The young women she calls, finds a mother (in her)
> She (whom she) calls among people, she gives her a name.
> She, who is exulted among the gods, her word has weight,
>   (Yet)
> She is more amenable than them.
> She is their queen, they receive her commands,
> They all bend their knees before her.
> In their assembly, her pronouncement has exceeding power,
> Equal to Anum, their king, she sits amongst them.
> Through insight, deep wisdom and intelligence she is wise.
> They confer among each other, she and her husband.
> They occupy the throne dais together,

On the high temple, the abode of exultation;
The gods stand before them both, taking heed of their
  pronouncements.
The king, their favorite, the beloved of their hearts,
Keeps offering them splendid sacrifices.
Amiditana prepares for their fulfilment, the pure sacrifice of
His hands, bulls and sheep, only fattened ones.
Thereupon, she asks her Anum, her husband, for enduring,
  long life for him,
Many years of life, did Ištar give Amiditana, and kept on
  giving him.
Through her command, she subdued the four corners of the
  world for him,
Put the totality of settlements under his yoke.
What her heart desires, the song of her grace, is right for his
  mouth,
He fulfils thereby the command of Ea for her.
He heard how he praised her, rejoiced over him:
'May the king live!' – for ever may she love him!
May Ištar grant Amiditana, the king who loves you,
long enduring life! May he live!

The first passage reiterates the standard Sumerian epithets of the goddess' beauty and seductiveness. She is love and charm personified. The salient words here are: *inbu*, taken from horticultural terminology, literally 'fruit', in the context of love poetry it is 'ce qui donne la jouissance sexuelle' – as Thureau-Dangin explained (1925: 174).[4] *kuzbu*, according to the lexical lists and other textual passages, is the closest Akkadian equivalent to hi-li; and we encounter the same difficulties in finding an adequate translation in English – 'seductiveness', 'sex-appeal', irresistible attraction', 'voluptuousness' are some of the common renditions, although the word could also stand for 'orgasm.'[5] Ištar's epithet as *belet kuzbim* summarizes her sexual potential, *lalû* is a similar concept; often used synonymously, it is usually translated as 'lust'.[6]

Ištar also has authority among the gods, 'who bend their knees before her'. So far, all this is familiar. But the remainder of this hymn introduces different perspectives. Rather than being the sovereign goddess in her own right, she is said to share the throne with Anu, while some Sumerian texts on occasion called her 'superior to An'. But not only that; she is now made the wife of the divine patriarch, and derives her status through her association with him, sharing the throne-dais and conferring with him on divine matters. The same idea is also expressed in a somewhat later bilingual text, where 'Ištar the Star' is put in the same category as the astral deities, her brother the Sun (Šamaš) and her father the Moon (Sîn) (Hruška 1969: 473). But she is not only a connubial co-regent; like any king's wife, she uses her personal influence to further the fortunes of her favourites: she has to ask Anu to grant a long life to Amiditana. The pairing of Ištar with Anu can be understood as part of a general theological attempt to allocate spouses to hitherto unmarried deities.[7] Ištar's marriage to Anu remained a literary topic confined to hymns.[8] The liminal personality of this goddess, who derived her widespread popularity precisely through her association with sexuality that went beyond social constraints, was fundamentally incompatible with such channelling of her energy.

Amiditana is said to love the goddess, but she does not talk about his sex-appeal. The king's praise endeared him to her, and he thereby fulfils a pious command. The tone is altogether formal, polite and distanced. He demonstrates his love for the goddess by sacrifice and prayer, and is rewarded with military success (dominion over the four corners of the world) and a long life.

The relationship between the ruler and the gods is described in a manner quite different from the royal hymns of the UrIII/Isin–Larsa period. Old Babylonian royal inscriptions generally emphasized the humanity of the king, rather than making claims as to his divine status. The gods did indeed choose him, but as an able administrator and purveyor of justice.[9] Rather than blurring the distinctions between king and gods, as in the UrIII royal hymns, the Babylonian royal ideology underlines the gulf between them. All the mythological trappings of kinship between ruler and the national gods now disappear from the texts. We hear no more of the king's divine birth, of him being suckled by the mother-goddesses and being matey with the younger male gods. The symbolic sexual union between ruler and the goddess also lost currency, because, like the metaphors of divine kinship, it contradicted the spirit of this separation, the sense of propriety *vis-à-vis* the gods (Kienast 1990: 100).

Ištar is not the only goddess associated with sexuality. We know little about the origins of Nanâ (or Nanaya), who appears in Sumerian texts from the UrIII period onwards. She received offerings 'at the portals of the Giparu at Uruk during the Neo-

Sumerian period' (Sauren 1970: 24). She was a daughter of An, and like Inanna, a sister of Utu; she was also a manifestation of the planet Venus. There is a royal hymn to Išbi-Erra of Isin, which describes the relationship between Inanna and Nanâ, with the latter being 'educated' and 'available at the command of Inanna' (von Soden 1953: 237). In an Old Babylonian royal hymn composed for Samsu-iluna (c. 1749–1712), the son and successor of Hammurabi, Nanâ is described in terms that could equally apply to Ištar:

> The goddess, sun of her people,
> Implore, laud(?) her approach!
> She – moon-like to look at,
> Her shadow (. .), filled with splendour.
> In richness are stored up for her
> Fertility, glory, sweetness and sex-appeal;
> With joy, laughter and love she is richly endowed.
> (Hallo 1966: 243)

The text goes on to say that 'health, vitality and beauty' walk by her side, and that her father had given her a friendly disposition and allotted to her 'voluptuousness' (*našmahu*) and jubilation. She even, like Inanna, has her dark and masculine side as 'Irnina, the ferocious (*gaṣṣatu*)'.[10] The reverse side of the tablet, where she is asked to bless her 'favourite', her 'beloved', the king Samsu-iluna, is partly damaged, but she is made responsible for his successful rulership. In comparison with the Ištar hymn quoted above, this text seems to have a closer affinity with the Sumerian hymns of the Isin–Larsa period, where a goddess is invoked to secure the life and kingship of the sovereign on her own behalf.[11]

Nanâ is also the goddess invoked in a curious text where she is associated with a male god called Muati, probably another name for Nabû (Lambert 1966).

The beginning and end are missing. Somebody says:

> 'I will speak of her lover, she will joyfully fill his heart with
>   happiness.
> [Muati, I] will speak of her lover, she will joyfully fill his heart
>   with happiness.'

Then follows a passage in which the goddess addresses her lover:

> '. . . your love-making is sweet,
> The appeal (*ku-uz-ub*) of your love is sated with honey;

Muati, your love-making is sweet,
The appeal of your love is sated with honey.'

This is a literary quotation from Sumerian love-songs, where the woman praises her lover's erotic abilities before the act. But then we have a reference to a statue, followed by a wish for the king:

'The statue which you saw . . . constantly it is not . . .
I will complete you who have such a form filled with happiness
[. .]
Let the king live for ever at your (*fem.*) command!
Let Abi-šuh live forever [at your command].
Today our sensuous Muati . . . .[. .]. .'

Whoever commissioned the statue of Muati, and this is very likely to have been the king himself, puts himself at the continuous disposal of the goddess. The reverse of the tablet is damaged at the top, and the text takes up with:

'She looked on Babylon with her kindly eyes,
She blessed [it], she decreed its prosperity [. .]
Every day [. .] health [for] the king Abi-ešuh [. .]
She made him live in a . . abode . .[. .].
Lust, lust . . .
. . . of happiness . . .
She establishes sensuous Muati for us, makes him dwell . . .[. .]
Jewels rain down like dew.
[. . . .] he ever took pleasure in her, thirsting for her as for
     water,
. .]. . . . . is sweet
. . .]. . here is my sex-appeal, stir yourself that I may make love
     to you!'[12]
. .]. . . let me sate myself with your (*fem.*) lust.
. .]. . whatever [. .] . . he will bring . . with her . .'

(Lambert 1966: 53–6)

As Lambert pointed out in his edition (1966: 43), the text abounds with literary clichés that also appear in Ištar hymns and other love poetry. In contrast to the Sumerian love-dialogues, where the king is himself the lover, and where the lovers are in 'close-up', this is a composite text, where the king is clearly dissociated from the amorous preoccupation of the couple, who are identified as the deities Nanâ and Muati. Their dialogue is a collage of hackneyed

184

erotic phrases, a rather formal recitation, which is interspersed with
references to the king seeking the blessings of the goddess. This is
not a 'love-poem' in its own right, but probably a specially
commissioned text, maybe for the occasion of the statue's dedication. Considering that, at least during the first millennium, divine
marriage ceremonies between Nabû and Nanâ were celebrated in
Babylonia, this may have been a reason for including passionate
exchanges between the gods. On the other hand, Nanâ being an
Ištar-type goddess,'[13] it was seen as appropriate to allude to her
sexual relationships, and the statue may have been of Muati, thus
providing her with a consort. Unlike the Sumerian ruler, who vaunts
himself to satisfy the erotic demands of his goddess, the Babylonian
king abnegates this office to a god, but the goddess must not be
deprived of her sensual enjoyment. The text makes it quite clear that
the 'robust' (šamha, actually 'voluptuous', 'potent') Muati will be
equal to the task. The king, however, still expects the blessings that
the goddess usually bestows on her lover; but now her new husband,
Muati, intercedes for him and asks his spouse 'to let him live forever
at your command' (line 14). This is an interesting example of the
reversal of roles: Muati asks for favours that Nanâ alone can grant.

The framework for passion among the immortals is now en-
dogamy within the pantheon, so to speak, and ideally within the
context of divine marriage. I have referred to the rituals in a previous
chapter, and I have mentioned the attempts by Babylonian scholars
to match each deity with a spouse.

In the same article Lambert (1966: 52f.) published another, fragmentary text, probably part of a Lamentation. Of a god, whose name
does not occur in the preserved text, it is said that

> ... he was not sated with her charms (la-la-ša)
> He ... was disturbed and wept night and day.
> He wept, continuing by night,
> He was disturbed, he could not relax in the day time.
> In his [. .] his heart was burning,
> His lusty [soul] was crying out in agitation.

The text continues, but it is only partially legible. The motif of grief
is maintained. The last 10 lines on the reverse are better preserved
(12–21):

> The shrine laments, the bedroom weeps,

Wherein we used to perform the wedding rites.
The courtyard is in grief, the storehouses sob,
Wherein we used to perform the rites of mutual love.'[14]
Now the chamber I exalted is filled with punishment,
In which we used to sit joyfully.
The gate is [broken], its jambs (?) are destroyed,
[Where] you met and spoke with me.
[...].......
[...].. we used to perform .. [..]

As Lambert pointed out, the lovers 'reminisce on their former bliss' and refer to 'the marriage they had experienced in the now ruined temple'. It is interesting that the text specifically talks about the *šipir kalluti*, the 'bridal rites' and the *šipir tartami*, literally 'the rites of (intimate) concourse' within the temple. But, as in the compositions above, short utterances by the gods, which reveal the passionate nature of their union, are inserted in a text which as such has nothing to do with love.

Owing to the incomplete state of the tablet which de Genouillac found in 1912 at Kiš, it is impossible to say whether the surviving Old Babylonian text is a rare example of an independent love poem, or whether it too formed part of a composition that only quotes passionate speech (Goodnick-Westenholz 1987). The second column, although fragmentary, seems to continue the address to the male lover, but implies leave-taking, since the messages are mentioned:

'...I...
The beating of your heart is joyful music,
Rise (*te-bi-ma*) and let me make love to you!
In your delicious lap,
The one for love-making,[15]
Your passion is sweet,
Growing luxuriantly is your 'fruit'.
My bed of incense is *ballukku* perfumed.
O by the crown of our head, the rings of our ears,
The hills of our shoulders, the voluptuousness of our breast,
The bracelet of our wrists
The belt of our waist –
Reach out (and) with your left hand touch our vulva,
Fondle our breasts,

Enter, I have opened (my) thighs,
[. . .]'

The similarity in tone and imagery with the Sumerian love-songs is striking, including the use of the first-person plural suffix 'our' for the women's parts (Goodnick-Westenholz suggested that this may imply her sharing them with her lover). This is the female voice of seduction again, calling from her perfumed bed. The noticeable difference from the Sumerian poems lies in the directness of her address, especially the last two lines. Only in Bridal Songs does the young woman speak of her own genitals, as for instance in *SRT* 5, where she points out the visible signs of nubility ('now our vulva has grown hair . . . now our breasts stand up') (Jacobsen 1987a: 18). In the love-songs, the male lover sometimes describes the vulva as being as sweet as honey or beer, but even in the most intimate situation the woman does not talk of her bodily parts other than in poetic allusions. The whole tenor of this fragment has none of the intense intimacy of the Sumerian courtly love poem. Moreover, what do all the references to the woman's decoration, her crown, earrings, bracelets and belt mean here, unless they too are being put in the mouth of a cult-image who is about to celebrate the 'rites of intimacy'? When the setting is no longer a *tête-à-tête* between human lovers, but a symbolic act of a divine couple, the nuances and subtleties are uncalled for and the language becomes correspondingly stronger. The word magically creates and activates the love-making of cult images.

But even if one rejects this hypothesis – for there is no rubric which tells us the purpose of this text – it is an interesting example of the type of discourse that is considered erotic in Akkadian. The tablet came from the old scribal centre of Kiš, which was active throughout the preceding Isin–Larsa period, when courtly love poetry was much admired, and could be considered as an attempt to compose within the genre. Early Troubadour poetry, for instance, especially that of Guillem IX, Duke of Aquitaine, is also rather direct and 'earthy' in comparison to Ovid. However, unlike in Provence, we do not find a great development of courtly poetry in post-Old Babylonian poetry, although the tendency to write Akkadian love-songs, to some extent imitating Sumerian court poetry, was probably more popular than the few surviving texts suggest.

The catalogue of song titles mentioned above points in this direction. Several of these refer to shepherds, a perennial mainstay of the pastoral, but here the shepherd is Dumuzi, 'Ištar's lover'. Only one such song has so far been discovered:

> 'Come in, Shepherd, Ištar's lover,
> Spend the night here, Shepherd, Ištar's lover,
> At your entering, my father is delighted with you,
> My mother Ningal invites you to recline.
> She offered you oil in a bowl.
> When you enter, may the bolts rejoice over you,
> May the door open of its own accord.
> You, bolt, and wood – what do you [know?]
> What do you know – ..
> Yes indeed! I love him, I love him! The lusty ..
> He has left his dogs ..
> "Show me into the presence of Ningal!"
> When he had entered into the presence of Ningal ..
> The women divided the *mirsu*-cake in a bowl.'

Then follows a passage presumably describing the activities of the other shepherds during Dumuzi's absence – they seem to grumble about their extra workload, and in a rather broken section an invitation to eat is issued, maybe al fresco, as the 'noise of the flocks' (*ri-gim ṣe-ni-ka*) is mentioned.

> Ištar went to his sheepfold,
> She opened her mouth and said to him,
> 'How pleasant are the waters, the waters of your sheep-fold,
> Your waters are burbling, the waters of the cattle-pen.'
>
> (Black 1983)

The first part is reminiscent of the Sumerian Bridal Songs, where the young girl wishfully thinks about her betrothed and imagines him spending the night with the approval of her parents, even addressing the very door. Black also detected 'her lively fantasy' in the subsequent, partly broken lines, 'how she would intimately, perhaps even lasciviously, address him, encouraging him to relax, take off his sandals, eat and forget his shepherdly tasks for the moment' (Black 1983: 30). He contrasts this erotic day-dreaming with the feebleness of her words when she actually finds Dumuzi at his sheep-fold: 'All she can say is ... "How pleasant it is here"', although he admits that the 'watery reference' may have a sensual 'undercurrent'.[16]

As Black pointed out, there is an 'unstudied vernacular note' in these verses, which seems to be at odds with the literary references one can detect. As the written examples are limited to this text, we have no way of verifying to what extent Inanna and Dumuzi as pastoral lovers had become part of a 'folk'-tradition. It is more likely that this and similar works, whose titles alone remain, formed part of the scribal repertoire which built on Sumerian prototypes. This particular 'ballad' is preserved on a very carefully fashioned tablet with a beautiful archaizing script, with, as noticed by Black, 'a general air of painstaking artificiality'. The colophon identifies it as a 'library tablet of Taqīšum son of Meme-Enlil, *šāpiru* of the temple of Ištar'. This is interesting. Although it does not automatically imply that the song was used in the cult of the goddess, this is a possibility. It also seems to demonstrate that there was an abiding interest in the genre of the love-song at the scribal centres attached to temples, even though the courts apparently no longer sponsored their production. It certainly suggests a different context for the collection and composition of erotic poetry if the love-life of gods was subject to a ritual celebration.

I have quoted above an Old Babylonian dialogue between Nanâ and Muati. Here is another, considerably later text, from the Neo-Assyrian period, of an encounter between Nabû and Tašmetu (Matsushima 1987: 143–54; Livingstone 1989: 35f.). It begins with a prayer to both gods, assuring them of the audience's devotion (expressed by the first-person plural), concluding:

'May anyone trust in whomever he trust;
As for us, we trust in Nabû, we are devoted to Tašmetu!
What is ours is ours; Nabû is our lord,
Tašmetu the mountain of our trust! Ditto.
Say to her, to her of the Wall, the One of the Wall, to Tašmetu:
"Save (us?), and take (your) place in the sanctuary!
Let the scent of holy juniper fill the sanctuary! Ditto.
The shade of cedar, the shade of cedar, the shade of cedar, the
    king's shelter!
The shade of the cypress (is for) the dignitaries". The shade of
A sprig of juniper is shelter for my Nabû and my games
    (*mi-lul-a*)'. Ditto. (lines 4–10)
'Tašmetu, fondles(?) . . . gold(?) in the lap of Nabû'. Ditto.
"[Nabû], my lord, put earrings on me!
Let me make you happy [in the Edu]bba!" (the last sentence is
    repeated; lines 12–16)
"[My Tašmetu] I will put bracelets of carnelian on you!

. . . . your bracelets of carnelian!' (17–18; the next 8 lines are
  fragmentary)
"[Let me provi]de a new chariot for you [. . . .]!
Ditto . . [whose] thighs are like a gazelle in the plain!
[Refrain].
Ditto, [whose] ankle bones are an apple of Siman! [Refrain]
Ditto, whose heels are obsidian! [Refrain]
Ditto, whose whole being is a tablet of lapis-lazuli! [Refrain]
Tašmetu, looking luxuriant, entered the bedroom, [Refrain]
She closed her door, [putting in place] the bolt of lapis-lazuli.
Refrain.
She rinsed herself, climbed up, got on to the bed. Refrain.
Into a bowl of lapis-lazuli, into a bowl of lapis-lazuli, her tears
  flow. Refrain.
With a piece of red wool he(?) wipes away her tears. Refrain.
Thither, ask, ask, question, question! Refrain.
For what, for what, are you adorned, my(?) Tašmetu? Refrain.
So that I may [go] to the garden with you, my Nabû. [Refrain]
Let me go to the garden, to the garden and [to the Lord(?)
Refrain]
Let me go alone to the beautiful garden! Refrain.
They did not place my throne among the counsellors. Refrain.
May my eyes see the plucking of your (*masc.*) fruit. Refrain.
May my eyes hear the twittering of your (*masc.*) birds!
  Refrain.
Bind and harness (yourself) thither! Refrain.
Bind your days to the garden and to the Lord! Refrain.
Bind your nights to the beautiful garden! Refrain.
Let my Tašmetu come with me to the garden. Refrain.
Among the counsellors, her throne is foremost! Refrain.
(Break of 4 lines)
May her eyes behold the plucking of my fruit! [Refrain]
May her ears listen to the twittering of my birds! [Refrain]
May her eyes behold, her ears listen! [Refrain]
[. . .] 12. Tablet of Budilu, the scribe . .'

(Livingstone 1989: 35ff.)

In comparison with the older dialogue between Muati and Nanâ this
text employs a more flowery language, abounding in metaphorical
descriptions that are not always obvious. An important motif is the
'going to the garden', which we often found in the Bridal Songs. On

the strength of the imperatives in lines 22–3, Matsushima proposed to see this as a reference to the transport of the statues in some chariot to take them to the garden, where a divine marriage ceremony is to take place (Matsushima 1987: 147f.). There is certainly a cultic context for this composition, with its prayer-like introduction, the mention of the incense burning in the sanctuary, etc. However, there is little to suggest that this was a wedding rite. The gods come together at some place, although it is not clear where. Tašmetu begins the dialogue by inviting Nabû to put on her earrings, and he reciprocates with a poetic description of the lower parts of her body, without becoming too intimate. Interestingly, Nabû compares the beauty of Tašmetu to a lapis-lazuli tablet.[17] Then they enter the bedchamber, where she begins to weep and Nabû comforts her. It is not clear to me what this means in the given context. Is this an expression of extreme emotion or a metaphorical reference to her physical excitement? The passage is certainly rather oblique and open to several interpretations, as is line 14, which is rendered here as 'ask, ask, question, question!' The invitation to go to the 'garden' and the whole passage is, I think, largely euphemistic. From a ritual point of view it would make little sense to take the gods first to their bedchamber and then drive them to the garden for some amatory scene. By expressing her wish to go to the garden, Tašmetu may well signal her readiness to make love and to witness the 'plucking of his fruit', amid the cries of passion, which the 'bird' most likely signifies. The 'binding' and 'harnessing', again spoken in the imperative, can be taken as a sexual metaphor. Nabû, in a single line (25), affirms that she will indeed 'go to the garden' with him. While the general setting of this text may well be the kind of marital chamber ritual we have described above, it is a great deal more subtle than the Old Babylonian version, and the scribes use the literary repertoire of pastoral love poetry to express the conjugal lovemaking of the gods.

Finally, I would like to quote an Assyrian poem (Reiner 1985: 86ff.; Livingstone 1989: 37–9), which strikes a very personal note, and in spite of literary references to the Lamentation genre is a poetic documentation of deeply felt emotion for a human being. Again, as often, we have a dialogue form, with the bereaved husband addressing his wife, who had died in childbirth and who now answers him one more time, in a final love-song:

'Why are you (*fem.*) cast adrift like a boat in midstream? Your crossbars broken, your tows cut; your face veiled, you cross the river to the Inner City?'

'How could I not be cast adrift, how could my tows not be cut!

On the day I bore fruit, how happy I was!

Happy was I, happy my husband.

On the day of my labour pains, my face was overcast; on the day I gave birth, my eyes were clouded.

My hands were opened (in supplication), as I prayed to Belet-ili:

"You are the mother of those who give birth, save my life!"

When Belet-ili heard this, she veiled her face: "You [. . .], why do you keep praying to me?"

[My husband(?) who . .] cried out: ['(Do not). .] me, my charming wife!'

[. . .] over years

[. . . .] of earth (full) of misdeeds

[. . .] you used to go to the Inner City, you screamed in woe.

[Ever since] those days, (when) I was with my husband, (as) I lived with him, who was my beloved,

Death slunk stealthily into my bedroom.

It brought me out of my house,

It separated me from my lover

And set my feet towards a land from which I shall not return.'

(Livingstone 1989: 37–9)

17

LOVE MAGIC AND POTENCY INCANTATIONS

Magic permeated all aspects of Mesopotamian life. All kinds of misfortune, disease and even psychological problems were attributed to malevolent influences. The hymns and prayers, addressing the great gods, stress that they alone were responsible for the good or bad 'fate' of the country and its inhabitants, but an even greater number of texts, especially from the mid-second millennium onwards, blame demons, witches and evil spirits for bad luck and illness.

In monotheistic religions, the belief in demonic influences and magic activity is not commensurate with the idea of an all-powerful single deity and standardized ritual. The suppression of magic meant that it became marginalized into a 'folk religion' and survived in the form of superstition (Neusner and Frerichs 1989). Polytheistic systems, being more elastic in their accommodation of religious notions, do not exclude magic but incorporate it within the official cultic practice. In Mesopotamia, the temple organizations provided a range of services, from divination to incantations, to satisfy the demand. In fact, the correct procedures to be taken in identifying the sources of evil intent and counteracting it were the prerogative of specialists who had to undergo a lengthy training. Some aspects of sympathetic and analogic magic became a monopoly of the professional classes, who had a vast literature of omens, rituals and incantations at their disposal. This was complemented, on a more mundane level, by folk-magic, such as the wearing of amulets, habitual gestures for warding off evil influence, etc. While such private apotropaic measures, on a fairly elementary level, were accepted as common practice, any individual engagement in more elaborate forms invited the suspicion of witchcraft, which was severely punished (Abusch 1989). The sorcerer or the witch

(Akkadian *kaššapu* and *kaššaptu* respectively) were defined as illegitimate practitioners of destructive magic whose purpose was antisocial and malevolent. The licensed magician, the *āšipu*, on the other hand, was in league with the gods, employed by the temple, and generally represented the 'good' or 'white' aspect of magic. Generally speaking, any directed and formalized manipulation or invocation of demons and deities, as a professional service, had to be performed by an official practitioner, rather like the regulation of medical treatment in modern societies. Love magic, however, is a special case. It is not directly apotropaic or therapeutic, in the sense of cleansing the afflicted from a demonic influence. Its purpose is, on the contrary, more like that of 'black magic', to gain power over another person, to force him, or her, to do what one desired. Again, there is a wide range of practices, from folk superstitions, to sympathetic magic, spells, the use of aphrodisiac potions, to full-blown rituals administered by the specialist. We only have examples of such official, 'scientific' love magic from Mesopotamia, as only those which formed part of an *āšipu*'s repertoire were collected and written down (Biggs 1967: 6).[1] Within the category of mantic literature, these texts are sometimes distinguished by their poetic references; some were copied as part of scribal education. No doubt the existing love poetry, with its established themes (such as the affairs of Inanna and Dumuzi), provided a frame of reference which the magician alluded to. Inanna/Ištar was, furthermore, a powerful deity whose collaboration in the matter was of vital importance.

This can be seen clearly in a Sumerian incantation, which invokes the love of Inanna and Dumuzi, in order to overcome the reticence of a proud girl:

> who girdles herself. A woman who girdles herself is unheard of. The fair maid raises her head (proud) like a mountain bull.[2]

To remedy this situation, some honey or syrup is needed and probably some soil from the street (where the girl usually walks?), which had to be rubbed on the face. The intended outcome is described:

> Me, the fair youth, the fair maid, at the pure command of An and Enlil and Enki,
> Will follow behind me. Obeying this word Inanna gave me my beloved one.

The oldest extant love incantation was written in Akkadian and dates from the Sargonic period, around the twenty-fourth century (Westenholz 1977; Lambert 1987a: 37 note 6). It consists of passages of direct speech, although it is not entirely clear who speaks and to whom.

> Ea loves *irêmum*,
> Ir'emum, offspring of Ištar,
> Dwelling in you/her lap, in the 'spittle' of the *kanaktu* tree.
> You . . . , beautiful maidens,
> Blooming you are, to the garden you go down,
> To the garden you go down, you scraped off the gum of the
>   *kanaktu* tree.
> I have seized your spittle-laden mouth,
> I have seized your colorful eyes
> I have seized your urine-yielding vulva,
> I have vaulted into the garden of Sîn,
> I cut off branches for her day(?).
> You (*fem.*) shall go around me among the boxwoods(?)
> As the shepherd walks around his flock,
> The goat around her kid,
> The ewe around her lamb,
> The jenny around her foal.
> Arrayed with jewels are his arms,
> Oil and *tibbuttum*-plants are his lips;
> A cruse of oil is in his hand,
> A cruse of oil is on his shoulder.
> The *ir'êmu* have confounded her
> And even made her love-sick.
> I have seized your mouth, so fit for love–
> By Ištar and Išhara, I conjure you:
> So long as his neck and your neck are not entwined
> You shall not find peace.
>   (Westenholz and Westenholz 1977: 202–3)

The text has its obscurities and problems, but its basic features are typical for magic rituals. There is an evocation of divine precedent, rather enigmatically involving Ea and *ir'êmum*, which A. and J. Westenholz explained as 'partly a personification of love and sexual desire, akin to the Greek Eros' (Westenholz and Westenholz 1977: 205), but which could also stand as the equivalent of the Sumerian hi-li ('irresistible sex-appeal'). It is linked here with Ea, the master-magician, Inanna, and – the magically vital ingredient – the 'spittle of the *kunuktu* tree, no doubt some resin to be used as incense, balm or oil. The latter is mentioned again, this time more specifically in connection with the two beautiful young women, presumably Ištar and Išhara, 'who go to the garden', a well-known metaphor for lovemaking. Then the 'I' of the conjurer is introduced, speaking on behalf of his client, who is mentioned indirectly only in the last line ('*his* neck'). The vocabulary is technical here: *ahāzum*, 'to seize', is a technical term frequently used in spells. To be 'seized' are parts of the body that exude substances which may be magically manipulated, such as saliva, tears and urine; and openings which can be penetrated by the spell. This in itself is preceded by the procuring of some efficacious medium, here branches from Sîn's garden. The spell typically involves metaphorical descriptions of the desired behaviour; the girl should be made 'to turn around and around', i.e. be totally absorbed in the object of her love, like a shepherd or a mother animal with her young. It is possible that the next few lines describe her object of desire, as J. and A. Westenholz suggested (Westenholz and Westenholz 1977: 212), 'as beautiful and sweet as oil, and wealthy too'. On the other hand, it might be part of the ritual, describing a figurine of the lover, who is thereby to be imbued with sexual attraction. The spell also anticipates the outcome – the girl is indeed confounded by *ir'êmu* and is now 'sick' with love, the contagion having done its work, her 'mouth' (*pars pro toto*) being 'seized'. Finally, the magician again invokes the two goddesses not to let her have rest before 'their necks are (amorously) entwined'.

Sumerian love incantations are much rarer than Akkadian ones, but apart from the text quoted above, we have another curious example of an Old Babylonian incantation which has the formal characteristics of an exorcistic invocation (Falkenstein 1964: 113–29). However, its purpose is not to repel the advances of some evil spirit, but to gain control over the heart of a young and beautiful woman. A further twist to this inversion is the fact that the woman is a kar-kid, a prostitute.

> The beautiful maid (ki-sikil), who stands on the street,
> The maid, the prostitute, daughter of Inanna,
> The maid, daughter of Inanna, who frequents the tavern (é-éš-
>   dam),
> (She is) like rich cream, rich butter(?)
> A cow, the Great Woman of Inanna's
> The store-house of Enki.

Sitting down, she is an orchard of apple trees, bringing
    delight,[3]
Lying down (she?) . . . pleasure,
She is a sprig of cedar giving shade.[4]
I reach out for . . . . , ... loving of the heart (šà-ki-ága-kam),
I reach (my) hand, the hand of loving of the heart,
I direct (my) eye towards it, the eye of loving of the heart,
I direct (my foot) towards it, the foot of loving of the heart.
When it comes from the threshold, the shining. .
. . . . down from the threshold(?)
To spread loving of the heart,
To. .loving of the heart. . . .
. . . loving of the heart from above like. . .
It struck the chest of the young man like with a reed.
Asarluhi saw that,
Entered the house of his father Enki and said:
'My father! (Concerning) the beautiful maid who stands on
    the road–'
When he said it again, (he continued):
'I do not know what to do in such a case? What will calm him
    down?'
Enki answered his son Asarluhi:
'My son! What you do not know, how could I add (anything
    useful) for you?
Asarluhi! What you do not know, how could I add (anything
    useful) for you?
What I know, you know too.
Butter of a holy cow, milk of a šila cow,
Butter of a cow, butter of a white cow,
Pour it into a bowl, that belongs to the green šakan-vessel,
And sprinkle it on the breast of the maid!
Then the maid will not lock the open door,
Will not push away her crying child,
(but) will run after you.'
Incantation of the series of the é-nu-ri.

(Falkenstein 1964)

Here we have first a description of the situation, or rather a
description of the object of the young man's desire, a young
prostitute, a 'daughter of Inanna', who is compared to bovine
abundance. Her physical charms are referred to in the usual

horticultural metaphors that evoke sensual experience. But the young man seems to want more than her professional services; he wants to induce the 'loving of the heart', the emotion that he himself is feeling. This is interesting, because it seems to distinguish between sexual access, which, as a professional, she is wont to bestow on any partner who chooses her, and love, as affecting the heart.

The format of this text resembles the type of the so-called Ea–Marduk incantations, where the younger god, Marduk, asks his experienced father Ea for instructions. It is worth noting too that Asarluhi was a sobriquet for Marduk. Enki's solution, phrased in the manner of what he would do in such a case, is to use special milk and cream, and sprinkle some on the girl's breast. We are not told whether this would work for the young man, but the last line of his speech sums up the whole intention of the incantation: the maid will (henceforth) run after the person who thus gained control over her.

Excavations in the city of Isin brought to light an interesting tablet find (Wilcke 1985). It was inside a jar, which had been carefully buried near the great wall and filled up with sand. The colophon marked it as 'an incantation of a sherd from the cross-roads'. The tablet comprised 120 lines of text, divided into rubrics of different length. As Scurlock (1989–90) demonstrated in her review of Wilcke's edition, it is a collection of Old Babylonian spells, with abbreviated hints on accompanying rituals, of a possibly sorcerous nature,

> designed to give someone control over other person whether by forcing them to love him . . . or by forcing them to be generous with him . . . or by preventing them from being angry with him . . . or by otherwise making him able to be victorious over them. (ibid., 112)

Among the six love spells is one that is clearly destined to be used by a woman (lines 9–29):

> With the saliva of a dog . . .[ ]
> With a slap in the face, with rolling of eyes,
> I hit you on the head, disturbed your understanding.
> Give your understanding to me (lit. my understanding),
> Give your advice to me (lit. my advice),
> I hold you like Ištar held Dumuzi,
> (And) Zeraš binds her drinker.

I have bound you with my breathing (*lit.* breath-laden)
    mouth,
I have bound you with my urinating (*lit.* urine-yielding)
    genitals,
With my salivating (*lit.* spittle-laden) mouth,
With my urinating genitals.[5]
The (female) rival shall not go near you,
The dog is lying down,
The boar is lying down.
You, lie down again and again on my thighs!
Whatever is on the green fish, is to be added to the oil, it will
    be rubbed on.
Look at me and rejoice like a (bow)-string!
May your heart grow light as (inspired by) Zeraš
Keep shining upon me like the Šamaš!
Renew yourself to me like Sîn!
[. .]. . . and may your love renew itself!
[. . . . .] anointing with oil.
                    (Wilcke 1985: 199; Scurlock 1989–90: 108)

There is no direct invocation of deities in this spell, although Ištar,
Zeraš, the beer-goddess, the Sun and Moon are mentioned; the
targeted person is directly addressed throughout. Just as Ištar binds
Dumuzi, her lover, so the beer-goddess binds the drunkard, and
although the phrasing is very similar to the one in the Old Akkadian
incantation, here it is the mouth and the vulva of the lovelorn
woman that are instrumental in effecting control over him. Maybe
the female secretions were thought to be powerful magic substances
in their own right! The reason for the recourse to magic is obviously
jealousy: a rival has turned away his affection. In fact, this rival is
also involved in the spell; it is directed equally against her. Allusions
to dogs and boars are frequent in love magic, as their mating
behaviour was apparently found to be arousing. Like a dog or a boar,
the lover should continue to lie on her. Then follows a brief
instruction over a concoction with oil and a green fish, which is
presumably to be rubbed on the practitioner or the beloved. The
final lines describe the desired objective: his love will return.

The next spell (lines 30–6) is less straightforward, as the masculine
personal suffix is used at the beginning, and the female suffix in the
rest:

May your (*masc.*) thighs be moving, Erra-bani.

May your (*masc.*) hips be in motion.
May your (*masc.*) sinews be following.
May your (*fem.*) heart rejoice.
May your (*fem.*) liver be joyful.
Let me swell up like a dog.
Like a rope? are your (*fem.*) . . . may you (*fem.*) not pour it out
for me.

(Wilcke 1985: 201; Scurlock 1989–90: 110)

Wilcke explained this as a dialogue, since he considered all the spells to be on behalf of an *entu*-priestess in love with a man called Erra-bani. Scurlock (1989–90: 111) suggested that it is more likely to be self-referential ('the man talking to himself to raise his confidence before addressing the desired woman'). It could, of course, also be the magician speaking, who first addresses his (male) client. The first three lines are all about movement, which could in this context be euphemistic for the motions of intercourse. The next two lines state the purpose, to make the woman happy (the liver was linked with psychological moods and emotions). The last two lines may well have been meant to be spoken by the client himself, like a potency incantation addressing the state of his member, wishing it to become erect like a dog's, taut like rope[6] that will remain inside the woman in spite of her (over)-abundant lubrication.

While this spell seems to be concerned mainly with the actual physical act of lovemaking, and reassures the man about his performance, the next two are more generally applicable to inducing a state of infatuation, to inflicting love 'sickness' upon somebody:

> Be restless at night,
> Find not peace during the day,
> Do not sit (peacefully) at night.
> (lines 38–40; Wilcke 1985: 201)

Darling! Darling!
You (*masc.*) whom Ea and Enlil set up,
Like Ištar sits on her throne,
Like Narâ sits in her sanctuary,
(So) I have surrounded you. *Entum*-priestesses love burning
And married women hate their husbands.
Cut off for me her high-held nose.
(And) put her nose for me under my foot.
Just as her love has become higher than me,

So may my love become higher than her love.

(lines 42–51; ibid.: 201)

The magician sets up his client in the domain of love, like Ištar and Nanâ. The reference to the *entu*-women's 'burning' may have an erotic aspect here. As Scurlock (1989–90: 111) puts it, they '(who can't get married) want sex all the time'; they would burn with (unfulfiled) loving, while the married women hate the husbands (who fail to satisfy them). The rest of the spell is clearly addressed to a woman who has rejected a man's advances. She is now to be punished for her haughtiness, by submitting in her turn to an unrequited passion.

Finally, a short and incomplete spell, which seems to be addressed to a man, judging from the restoration of the personal suffix in Wilcke's edition. All his attention is directed towards the woman who loves him:

> Where does your (*masc.*) heart go?
> What do your eyes look at?
> To me shall [your hea]rt . . .
> To me shall [your eyes . . .].
> . .to me. .
> Look at me . . .[. . .]
> Like bread [you sh]all. . .
> Like beer [you shall. .]. .

(Wilcke 1985: 203)

The repeated entreaty to look at the lover echoes a thought common to most erotic poetry. It rests on the belief that if the beloved were only to set eyes on the person who adores him, he would be swept away by reciprocal emotion.

This short collection of spells deals with a whole range of amatory subjects that were not usually expressed in Akkadian (or Sumerian) love poetry. They reveal anxieties about potency, jealousy, loss of love, feelings of revenge, and address the psychological state of the 'patient' and his or her individual needs. We do not know whether the Isin texts were a compilation of spells that had been composed for particular people, as the occurrence of the name Erra-bani suggests, or whether they were excerpts from existing incantation series from which the *ašipu* drew his material (Biggs 1967: 5f.). I have the impression that these spells, although they follow the formal characteristics of magical texts, are quite original.

After all, the literate incantation specialist was presumably familiar with the general literary tradition, as certain standard phrases and metaphors suggest. The love incantations, despite their practical mantic purpose, are in part of the literature of love. They have the advantage that here a much wider emotional perspective could be used, dictated by the real individual necessity. The psychological insight of the love incantations has, to my knowledge, no parallels in either the divine love-songs, the ballads, or the narratives.

An Assyrian collection, first published by Ebeling in 1925, brings together love incantations that are much more formalized, with great attention paid to the accompanying ritual. I shall only quote some here, taken from Biggs (1967: 70ff.). The language of these texts is the 'scientific' mixture of Sumerian and Akkadian.

> Incantation. The beautiful woman has brought forth love.
> Inanna, who loves 'apples' and pomegranates,
> Has brought forth potency.
> Rise! Fall! Love-stone (na₄-ag), prove effective for me! Rise!
> .. Inanna ..
> She has presided over love.
> Incantation: For a woman to look upon the penis of a man.
> The ritual: either <to> an apple or a pomegranate.
> You recite the incantation three times.
> You give (the fruit) to the woman (and) have her suck their
>   juices.
> That woman will come to you; you can make love to her.
> If ditto. If that woman (still) does not come, take *tappinnu*
>   flour
> (and) throw (it) into the river to king Ea;
> You take clay from(?) both river (banks),
> From the far side (of the Tigris) and the far side (of the
>   Euphrates);
> You make a figurine of that woman, you write her name on its
>   left hip;
> Facing Šamaš you recite the incantation 'the beautiful woman'
> [Over] it. At the outer gate
> Of the West Gate you bury it. .
> During the hot part of the day(?) or during the evening(?) she
>   will walk over it.
> The incantation 'The beautiful woman' you recite three times;
> That woman will come to you (and) you can make love to her.

To make a woman 'talk', *mesu*-wood, boxwood,
. . .-stone, *sahlû*(?), the tongue of a partridge(?)
You wind up in sheep's(?) wool; you put it at the head of your
   bed, then
That woman, wherever she may go, cannot refrain from her
   'talking'. You can make love to her.

One spell, invoking Ištar, 'the Beautiful Woman', as the specialist
goddess of love, is used here with two different rituals. The aim is
to induce a desired woman to reciprocate the passion. In some cases,
a fairly simple ritual involving fruit is sufficient to procure it. Similar
love magic is well known from folk customs around the world.
Should this elementary procedure fail, another, more complex one,
using sympathetic magic, is called for (Biggs 1967: 74–7). Finally,
there is an interesting spell to 'make a woman talk' (*šudbubu*). The
precise meaning of this expression is unclear, but it probably implies
an emotional disposition that will make her willing to be seduced. A
similar text invokes the Pleiades. For the ritual a piece of cloth,
which had the spell spoken over it seven times, is also tied at the foot
of the bed; juniper has to be burned, beer libated, 'and she will come'
(Biggs 1967: 76). Another, with the same type of ritual, begins:

> Incantation. I have seized you! I have seized you and will not
>   let you go!
> Just as bitumen clings to the boat,
> Just as Sîn took over Ur, as Šamaš took over Larsa,
> As Ištar took over Ekur,
> I have taken hold of you and will not let you go!
> (Biggs 1967: 77)

It ends with an indication of the most auspicious day for the
performance of the ritual:

> You perform [this(?)] on the twenty-first day and (all) will be
>   well.

This is probably a reference to astrology. Planetary constellations
and zodiacal signs were considered to have an influence over all
aspects of life, including sexuality:

> Virgo: Generally favorable. Before Sîn and Šamaš he should
>   prostrate himself. He should make love to his wife (to
>   generate) joy of heart.
> Pisces: Joy of heart; he should make love to his wife, eat fruit,

his garden he . . .[7]
Love of a man for a woman: Libra.
Love of a woman for a man: Pisces.
Love of a man for a man: Scorpio.
To make a woman 'come': . . . .

(Ungnad 1941–4: 262)

Most of the love incantations address a woman; the male as a target is comparatively rare. This situation contrasts with the courtly love-songs, where the woman addresses the man and invites him to make love to her. The magical texts never refer to the social context of the protagonists. They seem to operate in an undefined 'realm of passion', a social vacuum, where only love and desire count. The explicit aim is physical and emotional satisfaction, not marriage or betrothal, not even any form of material reward. Nor is there any hint of social disapproval, secrecy, or the very real dangers resulting from adulterous affairs. The force of erotic attraction makes these considerations irrelevant for the lover, and the power of his magic compels his 'victim' to do likewise. The terminology of the spell is often the same as that addressing witches or spirits, the 'beloved' is 'seized' and 'held'. In this context, passion results from magic enchantment. Ultimately, if the belief in magical manipulation of emotions is widespread, then one can never be certain whether a sudden infatuation might not be caused this way. Love and sexual desire become symptoms of a 'possession' imposed by an outside agent, the individual can do nothing but submit. This idea became an important motif in love poetry from Ovid to the modern popular song. In Mesopotamia, with its institutionalized magic, such metaphors are absent from the literary treatment of love. It is worth considering to what extent love magic contributed to the general demonization of sexual love in Mesopotamian literature (see chapter 18).

There is another very interesting category of incantations which deals specifically with male potency. Some of the texts just quoted above had rubrics to identify their purpose, such as KA. INIM. MA KI. ÁG. GÁ. KAM 'Love incantation', (Wilcke 1987), or INIM. INIM. MA DIŠ. SAL IGI *ana* GIŠ. NA *ini-ši*, 'Incantation. For a woman to look upon the penis of a man' (Biggs 1967: 70), otherwise the desired outcome is summarized by the phrase 'that woman will come, you can make love to her'. The potency incantations have either the designation INIM. INIM. MA ŠÀ. ZI. GA, 'incantation for potency', or

INIM. INIM. MA DIŠ NA *ana* SAL GIN-*ka* LÁ, 'Incantation. If a man is not able to have intercourse with a woman' (Biggs 1967: 26) or a summary to the aim of spell and ritual, such as 'then they will find satisfaction together' (Biggs 1967: 40). The target of the spells is not a third person who is to be compelled to reciprocate the passion of the lover but the lover himself, who for one reason or another is unable to perform properly. Here are some examples from Biggs' collection (1967: 17):

> Incantation. Wild ass who had an erection for mating, who
>   had dampened your ardour?
> Violent stallion whose sexual excitement is a devastating
>   flood,
> [w]ho has bound your limbs?
> Who has slackened your muscles? Mankind has . . . your(?). .
> Your goddess has turned to you. May Asalluhi, [g]od of
>   magic,
> Absolve you by means of the plants of the mountain and the
>   plants of the deep and
> May he make your limbs attractive through the charms
>   (*r[u]-[a]-mu*) of Ištar! Incantation.
> Incantation for potency. Its ritual: you crush magnetic iron
>   ore, pit (it) into oil;
> He should rub his penis, <his> chest, his waist, and then he
>   will recover.

The man is not able to achieve and/or sustain an erection due to some bewitchment from which he can be 'absolved' (*pašāru*) by Asalluhi. The ritual prescribes practical treatment of the affected parts. Certain animals like the wild ass, the onager, the buffalo, the stag, the stallion, etc., whose ardour in copulation was much admired, often figure in these texts. They are evoked in order to connect their vigour with that of the sufferer by magical analogy:

> . . with the love-making of a mountain goat(?) six times, with
>   the love-making of a stag seven times . .
> with the love-making of a partridge twelve times make [love
>   to me]!
>
> > (Biggs 1967: 24, 21)

or more directly:

> Get excited like a stag! Get an erection like a wild bull!

Let a li[on] get an erection along with you!

(Ibid.: 22, 23)

Some rituals even specify that an actual animal be tied to the bed:

> At my head a buck is tied.
> At my feet [a ram is tied]!
> Buck caress me!
> [Ram], copulate with me!
> [. . .] Prance about, wild bull!
> Let your strength rise for you!
>
> (Ibid.: 31)

Apart from the magical transference of sexual power, the copulation of animals, imagined or actually observed, was certainly considered arousing:[8]

> Incantation: Let the wind blow! Let the mountains quake!
> Let the clouds gather! Let the moisture fall!
> Let the ass swell up! Let him mount the jenny!
> Let the buck get an erection! Let him again and again mount the. .young she-goat!
> At the head of my bed is tied (*var.* I have indeed tied) a buck!
> At the foot of my bed is tied (*var.* I have indeed tied) a ram!
> The one at the head of my bed, get an erection, make love to me!
> The one at the foot of my bed, get an erection, make love to me!
> My vagina is the vagina of a bitch! His penis is the penis of a dog!
> As the vagina of a bitch holds fast the penis of a dog, (so may My vagina hold fast his penis)!
>
> (Ibid.: 33)

Here a woman's voice is speaking. This does not mean that she wants the spell to work for herself. Rather, she is used here to dramatize the erotic fantasy element of the spell. She speaks to the famously excitable male animals to arouse their ardour, first suggesting that they mount each other, the ass the jenny, etc. then, building up the sexual tension, the male animals are 'tied to the bed', and now she invites them to copulate with her. She identifies her vagina as that of a bitch, firmly grasping the penis, and then proceeds:

> May your penis become as long as a *mašgašu* weapon!

206

> I am set in a net of love-making!
> May I not miss the quarry!

This spell does not invoke a deity, it works like a fantasy, to stimulate the mind rather than the member, although the second part of the text just quoted involves the treatment of the latter for good measure:

> Its ritual: pulverized magnetic iron ore, pulverized iron
> You put [into] *pūru*-oil; you recite the incantation over (it)
>   seven times; the man rubs his penis,
> The woman her vulva (with the oil); then he can have
>   inter[course].

It is interesting that the sexual power of the woman is here at once the cure and the problem. She can incite lust in animals, she would bring them to task. The reference to the vagina of the bitch is interesting here, as it could apply to female amatory technique, such as it is often mentioned in Arab and other erotological works (Burton 1989: 77).

The treatment with iron in oil occurs in a number of ŠÀ. ZI. GA rituals (Biggs 1967: 18, 22, 23, 32). The metal was presumably chosen because of its hardness. But in keeping with the motive of transferring the sexual potency of animals to the man, treatment can also consist of using some substance obtained from the animal itself:

> Its [ritual]; the hair(?) of a sexually excited buck, the 'little
>   thing'(?) of his penis,
> [Wool(?) of a] sexually excited ram, red wool . . .
> [You bind about his waist], you libate pure [water]; you recite
>   the incantation seven times.
>
> (Biggs 1967: 38)

> The penis of a male partridge(?),
> The saliva of a bull with an erection,
> The saliva of a sheep with an erection, [the saliva of a goat with
>   an erection]
> You give him to drink in water, then wrap him up in ha[ir
>   from the tail]
> And wool from the perineum of a sheep [and]
> Put at his(?) thigh(?) <and then> he will get potency.
>
> (Ibid.: 56f.)

The therapeutic rituals, a collection of potency rituals without spells, recommend a variety of concoctions, composed of animal, vegetable, mineral and metal origin, sometimes very complicated (see ibid., 57), which are either drunk in water, beer or wine, or applied as salves and poultices.

The symptoms of impotence are described in various ways. They can be described metaphorically, as in the first example quoted, where the complaint is referred to indirectly, asking the 'wild ass' who had 'dampened your ardour', and as here:

> . . Hunted wild ass! . .onager!
> Who has dammed you up like an opening in a *dilûtu*-canal
> (and) who has made you fall limply like taut cords (when they
>   are loosened)?
> Who has blocked your ways like (those of) a traveller
> (And) like the son of Gubala has burned your forest?
>
> (ibid., 17f.)
>
> Who has poured cold water of your 'heart'?
> (ibid., 19)

In other cases, such literary similies are replaced by a more technical use of language:

> [If a man]'s potency is taken away and his 'heart' does not rise
>   for his own woman or for another woman
>
> (ibid., 27)
>
> [If a man] has semen that will not flow and his 'heart' does not
>   rise to his woman
>
> (ibid., 7)

the cause of which, as of any other physical and mental complaint, was some evil intent. The treatment is therefore essentially the same as for other bewitchments, with an even more powerful spell and an appropriate ritual to alleviate physical symptoms (cf. ibid., 28, line 7: 'dispel my enchantment', *liṭ-ru-du ru-ḫe-e-a*). An additional feature of the potency rituals is the psychological dimension, the build-up of sexual stimulation through the verbal evocation of intercourse, including a good dose of bestiality.

The aim is obviously to cure the symptoms, but it is interesting how this is started. The simplest form is just ŠÀ. ZI. GA, translated by Biggs as 'he will recover potency', or *ana* NA ŠÀ. ZI. GA TUKU-*e*, 'to restore a man's potency' (ibid., 13, line 23). More specific is 'the risen condition of your "heart" (here as elsewhere in this context a

euphemism for penis) will not get tired' (ibid., 48, line 61), referring
to the ability to sustain an erection, so that 'he can have intercourse'
(ibid., 33, line 17 and 42, line 16). Other instances also mention the
woman, and this makes me wonder whether they were meant to
counteract premature ejaculation:

> The man and woman [will find satisfaction] together (SAL UR,
> BI [*i-nu-uh-hu*).

(ibid., 21, line 17; 23)

One incantation addresses this problem specifically:

> Incantation. I am clothed with copulation, I am enveloped
>   with interco[urse]!
> At the command of wise Ištar,
> Šamaš, Ea, (and) Asarluhi. Incantation formula.
> You recite three times: (if) the man's and the woman's hearts
> both wish, (but) they (still) [cannot] find satisfaction–
> The alleviating ritual: take .. flour(?), [put (it)] into *kasû*-
> water,
> you mix [. . .], keep ready,
> The sexual parts (?) of the man and the woman you stroke,
>   then they will find satisfaction together.

(ibid., 40)[9]

As a literary genre, the love and potency incantations are of
interest because they give expression to subjects which are not
generally voiced in either Mesopotamian love poetry or narratives.
The pathological aspects of being in love, the theme of enchantment,
the stratagems for being united with the object of desire, jealousy,
etc. are a mainstay of most love poetry from Ovid to the Romantic
Age, but in cuneiform literature these topics were only treated
obliquely, in incantations, omens and to some extent the Lamentations. The language itself betrays a familiarity with the 'courtly'
tradition of love poetry, in the choice of metaphors, poetic structure,
standard phraseology, etc. (Biggs 1967: 5 note 29). Love incantations
avoid references to social relationships, and they may be used for
legitimate or adulterous purposes. The potency texts sometimes
speak of the 'wife' as the interested party.

It has long been recognized that legitimate magic was a form of
therapy.[10] This is particularly evident in the ŠÀ. ZI. GA texts. The
delicate task of sexual counselling was performed in a ritualistic

manner that also addressed the psychological state of the subject. The spell could contain the invocation of specialist deities such as Ištar and a brief description of the symptoms, but then quickly proceeded to stimulate interest in sex by use of suggestive and often obscene language. Interestingly, this does not involve pornographic language, in the sense of describing intercourse between people. Instead, there are primarily evocations of animal sexuality. I do not think that Mesopotamians were only 'turned on' by bestiality.[11] Rather, such images were used because the sex-drive of human beings was comparatively unreliable in comparison with that of dogs, bulls, rams, goats and even partridges. Within the framework of magic analogy, the man derives additional strength from the invocation of copulating animals, and indeed this can be taken a step further, when some of their bodily substances are used for the ritual. The spell aims to stimulate sexual images and to reassure the patient that he partakes of the 'stallion's' potency. The ritual is usually fairly simple and involves the manual stimulation of the genitals with a ritually empowered substance such as an embrocation or salve. For more persistent complaints the ritual is more complicated, involving the preparation of multifarious concoctions and sympathetic magic performed on figurines. No doubt they were more costly.

So far, we have not found a love manual among the Mesopotamian texts. The potency incantations show that there was a demand for such a service, that men were acutely aware of their sexual performance. If one takes the tone of the love lyrics at face value, women expected to be physically satisfied (this is stated explicitly in some of the texts quoted above). The services of the āšipu were only available for those who could afford to pay. It is highly likely that ordinary people resorted to traditional practices, such as the wearing of 'love-stones' and similar talismans,[12] the use of aphrodisiacs, etc. Amatory technique must have played an important part and it is probably only a matter of time and chance until a relevant cuneiform text is found.

18

PROBLEMATIC ASPECTS
OF SEXUALITY
Sin and pollution

The recitation of sacred texts was an integral part of Mesopotamian liturgy. Apart from prayers and hymns, which praised the deity and confirmed his or her power and benevolence, there were special categories of texts that may somewhat summarily be designated as Lamentations. I have mentioned those that mourn the death of Dumuzi, or similar deities. These texts seem most closely related to the traditional dirge, an important constituent of funerary rites. The dominant sentiment in these laments is private grief, expressed by the mother, the sister, or the wife of the deceased.[1]

This female voice also dominates a different genre, the so-called Lamentations over Destroyed Cities, where the goddess, deprived of her sacred residence, deplores the death of her city (Michalowski 1989; Jacobsen 1987a: 359–76, 447–77). These extraordinary examples of collective grief were inspired by the accumulated experience of warfare, invasion and pillage. They movingly document the fragility of Sumerian urban civilization. The liturgical occasion for the recitation of such compositions was often, but probably not exclusively, the restoration of temples, when parts of the architectural structure had to be pulled down.

During the Old Babylonian period, and thereafter, various genres of liturgical texts developed, which incorporated different aspects of laments (the expression of grief), hymnic addresses to the power of deities and to some extent narrative, mythological material. The colophons designate such texts as a balag, and eršemma, etc. balag designates a musical instrument, probably a drum (see Cohen 1974; Black 1991). These compositions, which could be addressed to any of the gods or goddesses, were chanted by kalûs, the ritual performers, in the Emesal dialect. The formula of invocation to the god, confirmation of his power and descriptions of the devastating

211

effects of his fury, concluded by pleas to relent, was so successful that many different balag lamentations were composed and sung on a variety of occasions, even periodically once a month. They were in fact the only surviving genre of Sumerian literature that continued to be composed right into the first millennium. Each lamentation consists of a series of independent subsections, called kirugu, which do not need to have any formal or narrative connection with each other. One of the longest known Lamentation-series is Uru-Amirabi, directed to Inanna, with over 1000 lines preserved. The mythological background of the deity addressed is often quite secondary. This provides some interpretational problems when the texts concern deities that are well known to us from other, earlier or later, literary texts. This is particularly so in respect to Inanna and Dumuzi. Kutscher (1990: 42) believes that the emphasis on Inanna's amorous relationship with Dumuzi, and especially its ritual celebrations in a Sacred Marriage, was discontinued in the Old Babylonian period, in spite of the scribes 'at Nippur still busy copying sacred marriage texts'. Instead, the seasonal mourning, performed in the fourth and fifth months, the onset of summer, became increasingly popular. The decline of Dumuzi's status as a fully 'paid-up' member of the official pantheon, with maintained temples and regular offerings, declined at the same time. This is an interesting religious phenomenon, the reintegration of a god into the unofficial realm of popular religion, and especially relevant to women.[2]

In the balag texts, Inanna's predominant association with Dumuzi is that of a mourner, but the 'bridal' connection is not altogether lost. All these different components, snatches of narratives of disparate origin and context, were incorporated into these compilations of liturgical texts. Cohen and Volk have both pointed out that there is an additive structure in the balag texts, provided by the stringing together of separate kirugus, and that this limits or even eliminates any coherence in a narrative sense. In some Lamentations, the kirugus are like quotations from other, not always identifiable text genres.

This is especially the case with Uri-Amirabi, 'The City that has been pillaged' (Cohen 1988; Volk 1989), which addresses Inanna. Some kirugus exalt Inanna's superiority in battle and the power of her divine command, expressed in a self-laudatory style as in the Innin-šagurra or similar hymns. Others are more conventional dirges of the mother-goddess type (as in the Ur lamentation), others describe her suffering and distress. There are passages that refer to rituals in connection with the 'sheep-fold', for which she prepares by washing and anointing herself. She also speaks of 'going to the steppe', and we hear of a Dumuzi festival in the month of Abu. But the most idiosyncratic narrative in Uri-Amirabi concerns Inanna punishing a maidservant, (*amtu*) for having sex. Here is Cohen's translation:

> She goes wild. Ecstasy! She goes wild! Ecstasy! She has
>   intercourse.
> The young girl, the maidservant, has done the forbidden.
> The maidservant, Ama-nam-tag-ga (the 'Mother-of-Sin'), has
>   done the forbidden (nam-tag).
> The 'Mother-of-Sin', she of a bitter fate,
> She of a bitter fate, eyes blurred with tears,
> She who sat upon the holy throne,
> Who has lain upon the holy bed, the resting place.
> Has experienced both intercourse and fellatio.
> To the Lady of Heaven in Zabalam has been brought
> An account (of what had occurred), the like of which has
>   never been been uttered before.
> Her cries reach to the heavens.
> (The cries) cover (the horizon) like a garment, spread across
>   like linen.
> ... because of the young girl she is distressed.
> [The Lady of Heaven] is distressed because of the young girl.
> [...] is distressed because of the young girl.
> (Inanna) calls out to her [vizier]:
> My [vizier] with the lapis-lazuli shoes!
> My [vizier] with favorable words!
> My messenger with reliable words!
> My messenger with understanding, one of Akkil!
> The wench! The wench has behaved abominably!
> The wench! The wench has behaved abominably!
> The 'Mother-of-Sin' has behaved abominably!
> The 'Mother-of-Sin', she with a bitter fate,
> She with a bitter fate riddles (her) face with tears!
> She was the one who sat on the holy throne.
> Who lay on the holy bed, the resting place!
> She experiences both intercourse and fellatio!
> 'Come! Let's go! Let's go!
> As for us, let's go to the city!
> Let's go to the city and see!
> Let's go to the city, to Kullaba!

Let's go to the Hursagkalama!
Let's go to Eturkalama!
To the city! To the city! (Let's go) to the brickwork of
   Babylon.'
At the command of the Lady of Heaven,
The girl, the 'Mother-of-Sin', is set on a dust heap.
(Inanna) looks at her with death (in her) eye.
The lady shouts; it is a cry of sin.
She grabs her by her forelocks.
And the girl, the 'Mother-of-Sin', is thrown from the wall,
Let the shepherd kill her with his staff!
Let the gala-priest kill her with his drum!
Let the potter kill her with his pitcher!
Let the kurgarru kill her with his dagger and knife.
(lines 210–58; Cohen 1988: 592)

This is a very unusual text for several reasons, and its interpretation is difficult in the absence of any parallels. The exhortation by the choir, or the 'audience', to go to the various temples connected with Inanna, suggest that some ritual is being alluded to. The punishment effected by a shepherd, two officiants of Inanna's cult and, rather enigmatically here, the potter, also point in the direction of an expiation ritual. Inanna looks upon the girl 'with death in her eye' and 'utters the cry of sin'. The hapless girl has to pay the price for her transgression. But what was the nature of her sin? Cohen and Jacobsen, following the suggestion made by Falkenstein in 1952, assume that, in keeping with the traditional theme of Inanna's love-affair with Dumuzi, alluded to in other kirugus, the girl's 'sin' was to have committed adultery with Dumuzi. Inanna acts out of sheer jealousy. In Jacobsen's 1987 collection of Sumerian literary works, he inserted this text after 'Dumuzi's Wedding' and before 'Dumuzi's Dream', the story of his death. He assumes a connection between Dumuzi's act of unfaithfulness and Inanna's wrath towards him in other compositions, especially *Inanna's Descent*.

However, in this kirugu Dumuzi's name is never mentioned. Volk, in his discussion of the text (1989: 48, 52f.), warns against such 'eclectic' interpretation. We should not automatically link the girl's sexual activity with Dumuzi. What does it say about her nam-tág, her sin? There are three components: she sat on the holy throne, lay on the holy bed, and had come 'to know the penis' in intercourse[3] and

214

kissing. Jacobsen and Cohen take the second part of the sentence to refer to the penis, and hence opt for fellatio. I cannot see any reason for taking this phrase as substantially different from the usual sequence of intercourse and kissing that occurs in other texts, in spite of the late Emesal orthography, and Volk (1989: 61) also puts just 'Beischlaf' and 'Küssen'. In such works as *Enlil and Ninlil* or *Enki and Ninhursaga*, this phrase always described an act of full, penetrative intercourse.

Let us briefly look at the meaning of nam-tág ('sin') in other texts. There were special rituals against the effects of an oath, even one taken generations previously, as well as sins (Akkadian *arnu*[4]). Some of these sins are also crimes, such as murder, swearing a false oath, adultery, and intercourse with a priestess, others are involuntary contact with polluted people, etc. The connotation with adultery is also documented in a bilingual proverb: 'A man who has intercourse with (another) man's wife, his sin is heavy' (Lambert 1960: 119; 3–4). Note that the man's sin is 'heavy'.

Personally, I do not believe that we have an adulterous situation involving Dumuzi in Uru-Amirabi. Rather than looking for a (as yet at least) non-existent, mythologically narrative background, one might see whether the information supplied might not furnish a key to the understanding of this difficult text. To begin with, no particular sexual partner is mentioned, and as I pointed out before, the connection with Dumuzi is not supported by the text but inferred from the general background of Inanna's association with him. Nor do we hear that the maidservant was a priestess. If that had been the case, another term than the socially inferior gi$_4$-in (Emesal for geme, Akkadian *amtu*) would have been used. It appears that we have a series of transgressions here. The first 'sin' was to sit on the 'holy' throne, the second to lie on the 'holy' bed.[5] These items of furniture belonged to Inanna, the goddess, and were thus sacred, imbued with divine power.[6] The handling of cult objects and temple furniture was no doubt circumscribed by strict regulations in order to avoid incurring the wrath of the gods. I have just mentioned that elaborate liturgies were necessary to circumvent their anger when structural repairs were carried out; broken cult-statues and other inventory no doubt received similar special attention. Even within the private sphere, to eat something set aside as the portion of the god was a 'sin'.[7] The sin is an infringement into the sphere of the divine. As Oberhuber pointed out, nam-tag also means 'transgression into what should be untouchable', 'loosened'. It would therefore make sense to interpret the ritual described in Uru-Amirabi as a pacification for any involuntary trespassing against the rules concerning Inanna's cult furniture.[8] But this does not account for the sexual activities, the third 'sin'. However in the given context, the ritual of punishment could also atone for any transgressions against the regulation of sexual services incurred by the female personnel. If the phrase *'išari rehâ iltamad, našaqam iltamad'* is unequivocally connected with impregnation, as in the Sumerian myths for instance, then the 'sin' could be a form of intercourse that could result in pregnancy .We know that certain cult functionaries, such as the *entu*, *ugbābtu*, *igisitu*, were not allowed to become pregnant,[9] which on the whole curtailed sexual activity. The question here is to what extent the *amtu* is meant to represent all women servants of the goddess, and whether they were all under an injunction to avoid the 'fertilizing penis'. To this we have no answer at present.

Although balag-poems do make use of literary allusions and standard epithets, their purpose is not primarily narrative but theological, which includes an awareness of the correct ritual procedure. To interpret passages such as the one discussed here purely on the basis of literary and mythological material can be very misleading. Volk's translation of the first line, which I render here in English, brings out the possible ecstatic nature of the ritual:

> She fell into a trance! She [fell into trance. Wo]e! He copulated
> with her.
>
> (Volk 1989: 60)

In the lexical texts he quotes,[10] Amanamtagga corresponds to a masculine lú-nam-tar-gig-ga ('He whose fate is bitter'). He too may represent a scapegoat, who bears the 'sin, the bitter fate' on behalf of an institution, and may be punished metaphorically or even *in effigie*.[11]

But this does not address the question of what kind of sexual behaviour was considered taboo. I have discussed some aspects of this before, in connection with prostitution. We know from legal texts and proverbs that adultery and the rape of young girls was a serious crime. By the late second millennium and in the first millennium, and certainly in Assyria, they were not considered to be sexual offenses as much as assaults on somebody's property, daughters being their fathers' and wives their husbands' legal chattels.

More to the point are the omen-collections (Lambert 1991: 137).

These are portents that, provided they were interpreted correctly, according to a long and learned tradition, were considered helpful in determining the connection between cause and effect on an individual, collective and even cosmic level. Some omens were invoked in order to elicit an answer to a specific question, such as auspicious dates for important undertakings, the appointment of high officials, etc. Divination was a very important part of Mesopotamian 'science' and many different approaches and techniques were developed. The diviners inspected the intestines of sacrificial animals, the formation of incense smoke, oil on wine, etc. In addition, a wide range of data were collected, all of which recorded deviations from the normal state of affairs. The theory was that the gods were indicating future events in some code which could, given the right methods and proper diligence, be deciphered correctly. We have collections of physiological omens that list physical malformations, abnormal births, aborted foetuses (both animal and human), historical omens and also, and this is of interest here, omens based on the observation of animal and human behaviour. All these collected data were correlated with a meaning, or likely consequence, of the phenomenon observed. The guiding principles of these correlations are still largely impenetrable to our understanding.

One of the largest omen series was called *šumma alu*, 'If the City', after its inital section that deals with the location of cities and the idiosyncracies of their inhabitants. it originally comprised several hundred tablets, but only portions have survived. One section is concerned specifically with human sexual behaviour.[12]

It is often difficult to find any 'rational' link between the 'if' clause (the protasis) and its consequences (the apodosis), but in some cases, especially when the man has difficulties in his performance, the psychological stress could render him ill. For instance:

If a man has intercourse with a woman, he will have trouble every day.

If a man has intercourse with a woman standing up, he will get cramp(?) and fall ill.

If a man starts trembling while .. for sexual potency, and like an *assinnu*, fails to achieve a sexual climax during intercourse, that man will experience evil in circumstances of stress.[13]

Similar problems are described in the following clauses:

217

If a man has intercourse with a woman but has a premature ejaculation, so that he squirted sperm over himself . .

If a man has an ejaculation every time he comes near a woman . .

If a man has intercourse at night and then has an ejaculation in his dream . .

If a man talks to a woman in bed, and has an erection when he gets up . . .

By far the longest entries list the different circumstrances under which sexual encounters take place:

If a man grabs a woman on a cross-roads and rapes her . . .

If a man regularly goes to a prostitute at the cross-roads . .

If a man has intercourse with a woman on the stairs . .

If a man has intercourse in a cul-de-sac . . .

If a man keeps saying to his wife: offer me your anus.

It was also important to know which activities would render a person ritually impure (NU SIKIL) and a number of clauses dealt with such cases, although it is unlikely that they are an exhaustive list:

If a man has a woman keep taking hold of his penis, he is ritually unclean.

However, there were also cases when certain forms of behaviour, which one would expect to be either polluting or open to censure, were given an auspicious meaning (*CAD*, p. 95).

If a man has sexual intercourse with a *giršequ* for a whole year, the deprivations which beset him will disappear.

In some cases, an action will have bad effects for apparently trivial resons, but such evil consequences can be averted by the right ritual, so here the text offers the contra-indication as well:

If a man urinates in the tavern in presence of(?) his wife, he will not prosper, in order that (the evil) not affect him, he should sprinkle his urine to the right and left of the door jambs of the tavern and he will prosper.[14]

The eating of pork and beef rendered a person unfit to go into the temple. Blood, and also menstrual blood, were contaminating and had to be ritually washed off. Another polluting substance was male semen. If a man dreamed the night prior to his visit to the temple that he was making love to a woman but did not ejaculate, this did not constitute a cultic sin: he may go into the temple but must not stand before his god'.[15]

The behaviour of temple personnel, especially the female *entum*, whose sexuality was apparently strictly controlled as she was obliged to remain childless, also comes under scrutiny:

> If an *entu* priestess has anal intercourse to avoid pregnancy.
> The *entu* will contract a venereal disease.
> The *entu* shall have repeatedly intercourse with the *enu*.
> The *entu* will be faithless towards her lover.[16]

Unfortunately, before we have a careful and complete edition of the sexual omens, it is impossible to come to any conclusion as to the inner logic or conceptual framework of the texts. To begin with, one might emphasize a remarkable lack of what we would call 'moral judgements'. The various forms of behaviour are not 'good' or 'evil'; but they have either physiognomic or psychological effects. The rationale for the link between the observed (or assumed) behaviour and its consequence is only occasionally 'rational' for our understanding.

All in all, the evidence for the assumption that intercourse, or even certain forms of intercourse, were considered taboo in Mesopotamia is very scant. In Western, Christian, civilization, the concept of sexuality is intrinsically associated with 'sin', but it is entirely inappropriate to assume that this should also be the case for an entirely different and much older civilization.

19

WITCHES, DEMONS AND THE AMBIVALENCE OF LOVE

Mantic texts cannot be separated from the corpus of cuneiform literature as 'non-fiction'. Although we know little about the actual training process of incantation priests, diviners, exorcists and other professionals who aspired to the higher levels of their craft that were only accessible to the fully literate, it is unlikely that it excluded the study of a wide range of texts, as recurring literary clichés, for instance, demonstrate. We have so far only looked at incantations and rituals directly concerned with love and potency. We have seen that the context of love-magic allowed a much wider range of emotions to be expressed, such as envy, jealousy and possessiveness, whereas the traditional poetic medium only celebrated the joyful and positive aspects of love. If one looks at mantic texts generally, the subject of love and sexuality is treated from several perspectives and betrays considerable ambiguity.

Love incantations operate on the principle that emotions and behaviour can be magically manipulated. The right spell, the properly executed ritual, induce the desired person to come and surrender to the wishes of the magician's client. But if the psychological state of amorous infatuation can be provoked by the enchantment of the 'good' magician, it can equally be inspired by evil forces. Love can be a symptom of possession, as we find in a passage of Maqlû, the Assyrian anti-witchcraft incantation series (Meier 1967):[1]

> Witchcraft, sorcery, bewitchment, evil machinations,
> Sinister deeds, rebellion, slander, love, hatred,
> Mental instability (*lit.* changing from sympathy to hatred),
> Persecution mania, suicidal tendencies,
> Speech disorders, changing temper,

'Changing the heart', vertigo, madness. .[2]

(I, 88–91)

In the first line we have several terms that are synonyms for sorcery. Then follow other antisocial activities, including love and hate. There follows an enumeration of symptoms, all concerning the mental state of the afflicted. In this respect the person bewitched, or the person who hates or loves, is equally liable to suffer these conditions. Love in this context is not only the result of enchantment, it is an ambivalent force itself.

But the machinations of witches can also affect the sexual health of individuals, causing loss of libido, inability to achieve satisfactory intercourse, veneral disease, etc.:[3]

> The witch who crosses the road,
> Enters houses,
> Runs through the lanes,
> Races across the square
> She twists and turns,
> Stops in the street and steps out (again)
> Blocks the way.
> She robs the handsome man of his vitality,
> She takes the pretty girl's 'fruit' (*inibša*),
> With her glance she steals her sex-appeal (*kuzubša*).
> She looks at the young man, robs his vitality,
> She looks at the girl, she takes away her 'fruit'.

(III, 1–12)

The witch here destroys the basis of her victim's sexual capacities; merely by looking at people she can extract their vitality, *kuzbu* and *inbu* are seen here not just as personal qualities, but as substances that can be taken away. It is also worth noting that the witch is portrayed here as a female who frequents public places, who does not, like respectable married women, stay at home. The prostitute, on the other hand, in order to carry out her trade, is a *waṣitum*, 'one who goes out'.[4]

The disruption of sexuality is a theme we also find in other literary texts. In one of the Sumerian hymns ascribed to Enheduanna, Inanna's anger against her city has catastrophic effects for the people of Uruk:

'Its rivers run with blood because of you,

221

Its troops were led off willingly (into captivity) before you.
Its woman spoke not of love with her husband,
In the deep night she whispered not (tenderly) with him,
Revealed not to him the innermost treasures.'
(Kramer in Pritchard 1975: 126)

In the lamentation of Ibbi-Sîn, the divine ordinances (me) of Sumer
are under attack:

That the canals may bring bitter water,
That the good corn fields only yield grass
That the steppe only produce the herb of woe
That the mother neglect the child,
That the father not call his spouse by her name.
That the concubine not rejoice in the lap (of the master),
Children not grow up on her knees
The nurse not sing a lullaby.
(Falkenstein 1953: 189)

Gula, driven from her temple, deplores her loneliness:

My house, where no happy husband lives with me,
My house where no sweet child lives with me,
My house, through which I, its mistress, never grandly pass,
Never grandly pass, I which I dwell no more.
(Jacobsen 1987a: 62)

The untimely death of Dumuzi is lamented particularly because he
did not live to experience the joys of marital life:

My one who will never bring [betrothal gifts],
My one who [will never] carry [a wedding gift],
My one who [will never] make [love] [to a young wife],
My one who [will never] beget [children].
(Jacobsen 1987a: 36)

The galla-demons of the Underworld, who seek a substitute for
Inanna after her Descent, are described as totally unlike human
beings or gods:

They eat no food, know no water,
Eat no flour sprinkled (as offering)
Drink no water libated (as offering)
Accept no pleasant greeting gifts
Fill not with pleasure the wife's lap,

Kiss not the child, the sweet thing.
(Falkenstein 1953: 214)

These examples are sufficient to illustrate that a happy family life, defined by sexual fulfilment and the raising of children, was seen to be of fundamental importance. The young man, or in the other examples, the young girl, who dies before marriage, is mourned the more for never having achieved the full potential of human happiness. Siduri's advice to Gilgameš defines it as the divinely decreed good fate allotted to mankind. Anything that threatens this ideal state of affairs is feared. In the religious texts this is interpreted as a punishment decreed by the gods for some sin or sacrilege. In mantic texts it is the work of malevolent spirits, demons or witches. In the omen texts a variety of random causes are held responsible. The disruption of harmonious family relationships also includes the lack of respect for parents, or their neglect towards young children, mutual mistrust, and even the selling, exposure and eating of children in times of severe stress and famine. Such subjects were systematically enumerated as symptoms of social disintegration.

Erotic fulfilment within marriage and the procreation of children were only part of sexuality. When Ištar disappeared in the Underworld

No bull mounted a cow, no donkey impregnated a jenny,
No young man made love to a girl in the street,
The young man slept (alone) in his private room,
The young woman slept in the company of her (girl)friends.
(lines 76–80; Dalley 1989: 158)

This passage does not refer to married couples specifically; in fact the wording suggests sexual activity in any context. A Sumerian incantation against the demon Samana is even more to the point:

As he blocked the menstruation of the young girl,
As he blocked the potency of the young man,
As he blocked the hierodule in (the performance of) her office,
As he blocked the prostitute in her services,
Asarluhi sent a messenger to his father Enki.[5]
(Falkenstein 1953: 214–15)

In an Akkadian incantation against Šimmatu, the demon is described as a snake and scorpion, who bites and stings his victims:

You push the young man from the lap of the young woman,

223

You push the young woman from the lap of the man.

(Von Soden 1974)

The long litany of afflictions that befall the 'Righteous Sufferer' in the Babylonian text include his loss of potency (Lambert 1960: 34, 42–3).

All these examples, to which many more could be added, show that sexual life *per se*, of the individual and of society at large, was under a potential threat from the wrath of vengeful gods or the malice of demonic forces.

In the hymns and prayers it is Inanna/Ištar who represents and controls the me and garza of sexuality. She is in charge of sexual attraction (hi-li, la-la, *kuzbu*), of intercourse and kissing, she is the patron of brides, married woman and prostitutes, as well as of eunuchs and homosexuals. Her personality, which spans the roles of both genders, provides a unique frame of reference for all aspects of sexual behaviour. But whereas in other cultures the male and female elements complement and balance each other in symbolic union (e.g. Śiva and Śakti in Hinduism, or Yin and Yang in Taoism), Inanna/Ištar has no male counterpart, and we have seen that sexuality was generally considered the 'art/work of women'. This fundamental lack of balance, expressed by the mythic persons of the goddess, entails a functional instability. I have mentioned that unpredictability was a divine prerogative generally, but the hymns extolling Inanna make this into a fundamental aspect of her character. She can switch from benignity to malevolence in an instant, regardless of whether the punishment was deserved or not (Sjöberg 1976: 163; Hallo and van Dijk 1968). She can turn love to hatred and hatred to love, and, famously, 'women into men, men into women'. As Brigitte Groneberg once noted, this capacity for gender-metamorphosis may have originally been symbolic, 'um die Kluft der Polaritäten zu überbrücken' (Groneberg 1985: 44). The Sumerian sources (e.g. Inninšagurra or the Iddin-Dagan New Year Festival text) stress the ritual context of gender-role changes among normal people, as well as the possible integration of persons with some real genital malformations. These relevant passages all show a symmetrical or reciprocal gender-change:

> She (Ištar) [changes] the right side into the left side,
> She [changes] the left side into the right side,
> She [turns] a man into a woman,

She [turns] a woman into a man,
She ador[ns] a man as a woman,
She ador[ns] a woman as a man.

(Sjöberg 1976: 225)

However, in some of the Akkadian texts from the late second and first millennia, as well as from areas at the periphery of Mesopotamian culture, only the topos 'who changes men into women' remains. And in the context of the curse it no longer has anything to do with rituals, here it unequivocally means emasculation or castration:

Whoever shall change the settlement that Abdael made and will do evil against Yarimlim and his descendants – may the god Hadad dash him to pieces with the weapon which is in his hand. May Hebat-Ištar shatter his spear; may Ištar deliver him into the hands of those who pursue him; may Ištar . . impress feminine parts into his male parts.[6]

The same motive is found in the Hittite military oaths, also as a punishment (Oettinger 1976: 11). The Assyrian king Esarhaddon asks Ištar to punish his enemy and 'change his manhood into a feminine (state)' (Borger 1965: 99).

During the Neo-Assyrian empire castration was practised routinely to provide personnel for the upper-class women's quarters, as well as for civil servants whose sole loyalty was to the king, as they did not marry.[7] Although we know that kurgarrûs and assinnu formed part of Ištar's entourage, the concept of a castrating goddess is rare in Babylonian texts. In fact, it is alien to the Mesopotamian religious system and was probably an import from western Syria and the Levant, where, at least in Hellenistic times, the cult of the Dea Syria involved the self-inflicted removal of genitals in ecstatic rituals (Attridge 1976).

However, it is quite clear from the Assyrian mantic literature that Ištar and other deities associated with sexuality, as well as some of their cult personnel, prostitutes, and to some extent women in general, were seen to have an affinity with malevolent forces and evil magic.[8] We have seen before that Ištar, with her unpredictable nature, could bless and curse with equal measure. Significantly, she became one of the major deities invoked in incantations against all manner of enchantment during the first millennium. There is a whole series of magical texts that feature both Ištar and Dumuzi.[9] They were scheduled to take place in the month of Du'ūzu,

> When Ištar causes the people of the land to weep for her lover Dumuzi. (Every) man's family is assembled at an appropriate place (when) Ištar appears and deals with the affairs of people. She takes away disease and she causes disease. On the 28th, the day of the byre, you dedicate to Ištar a vulva of lapis lazuli with a little gold star. You pronounce the name of the diseased.
> (AIIa, 3–10)

The other ritual offerings are described in great detail. Then Ištar is asked to intercede with Dumuzi that he may take away the affliction; and then Dumuzi is addressed, and finally Ištar herself again, in an exulting passage that describes her authority over the demons:

> Without your permission the *gallû* demon cannot approach the patient (*lit.* the diseased),
> your envoy, the 'binder', cannot 'bind' the young man nor the young woman. (ibid.: 102–3)

These texts continually emphasize the erotic relationship between Ištar and Dumuzi. Although her masculine qualities are included in the 'litany' of praise (e.g. 101: 'the heroic one (. . .) who continually throws (enemies) down in the midst of battle'), her 'love' aspects are of great importance. The rituals also employ *assinnus*.[10] But most significant for the topic under discussion is her intimate association with demons. They obey her command, to attack whomsoever she chooses, to be restrained by her word. She is a mistress over demonic beings, and this brings her very close to being one herself. There is, at least since the Old Babylonian period (see *Inanna's Descent*), a definite link with the Underworld and its denizens. As she emerges from her captivity, she is accompanied by a host of demons who are under her control, and who eventually carry off Dumuzi. Dumuzi himself, by virtue of his temporary sojourn in the Netherworld, has connections with the realm of the dead. Now these rituals are said to take place exactly during the month when Dumuzi's death was mourned. The mythological background of Ištar's victory over death, her power over the Underworld demons and her erotic relationship with Dumuzi are particularly pertinent here. In the context of these rituals Ištar is the type of the dangerous, independent and ambivalent goddess, who is also the leader of a host of evil spirits, who slays and sends disease and suffering, but who, addressed properly and mollified by the 'right' kind of incantation, will use her supreme power to ward off her minions. The standard symbolic offering was a stylized, lozenge-shaped vulva,[11] which illustrates the connection between sexuality and magic.

Other Ištar-like goddesses also had demonic aspects. In a bilingual hymn from the first millennium, Nanâ speaks of herself as having 'heavy breasts in Daduni, a beard in Babylon'.

> They call me the Daughter of Ur, the Queen of Ur, the
>   daughter of the princely Sîn, she who goes round and
>   enters every house,
> a *qadištum* who holds the ordinances, she takes away the
>   young man in his prime,
> she removes the young girl from her bedroom – still I am
>   Nanâ.
>
> (Reiner 1974: 224)

These actions, 'going round the houses' (*muterribat bitāti*) and causing the premature death of men and women, was typical for malevolent demons. Yet she asserts that she is nevertheless a goddess with a cult in several temples. The real evil demons, unlike types of guardian spirits, were not part of the official religion and did not receive any regular ritual offerings. Like the evil spirits, the tormented souls of the unburied, they are marginal supernatural beings, although they were recognized as part of the pantheon, and in fact some of the most fearsome demons were created by Anu or said to be his daughters.[12] There was a certain fluidity in the malevolence of certain demons: some could be good or bad, and some obtained notoriety at a later historical period. Sickness demons, however, whose very names denote specific physical symptoms (*ahhazu*, 'the grasper' – jaundice; *namtar*, 'the fateful one' – epidemics; *bennu* – 'fits', 'epilepsy'; *unna*, 'fever' etc.) were always evil.[13] Especially feared was Lamaštu, a female demon, 'Anu's young daughter', who was held responsible for the death of mothers in childbirth, as well as illnesses of babies, which reflects the very real dangers of post-partum infections and infant mortality. A number of texts with incantations and appropriate rituals formed part of the professional responses to this problem. there were also amulets, and some of them depict Lamaštu as a fearful female, with the head of a lion, the body of a donkey and pendulous breasts, suckling a pig and a dog.[14] Other female demons were specifically associated with the night, the Lilītu and Ardat-lilî.[15] Another interesting example is

Kilili, 'who sits by the window' (*ša apata ušarru*). She 'drags the young man from the marriage chamber, makes the young woman leave the bedroom', the standard expression of sexual envy (Farber 1977: 79). One bilingual text, published by Landsberger (1968: 44–5), actually characterizes the Ardat-lilî as a virgin:

> Maid who (un)like other women no man impregnated,
> Maid, who (un)like other women no man deflorated,
> Maid, who in the lap of a husband had not had her sexuality touched,
> Maid, who in the lap of the husband did not remove her clothes,
> Maid, whose pin was never loosened by a handsome man,
> Maid in whose breasts was never (any) milk.

This passage is eloquent testimony that the social value of the state of chastity was just as ambiguous as that of its opposite, uncontrolled, 'free-lance' sexual activity. The virginal demon, deprived of an outlet for her *kuzbu*, steals the sexual attraction of others. These beings, like succubi, are the demonic personifications of sexual predatoriness. When they have no mate, they chose one among human men. When they have intercourse with their victim he can become infected with a dangerous or fatal illness. Some prey on couples who make love on the flat roof on a hot summer's night. They cannot have offspring, so they snatch the foetus and the new-born child. All evil demons are hostile to health and vitality, they will try and sap the manifestations of life. The demons of the night specifically subvert reproductive sexuality and destroy its fruit, the unborn child. Some late Mandaic texts from Syria, where the concept of demonic sexuality was developed much further, also envisage a sort of inverted or demonic form of impregnation which ensures the continued existence of Lilû-like demons. In these texts, the old West Semitic love-goddess Astarte seems to have fused with the Mesopotamian Lilû to personify the predatory, aggressive female sexuality (Fauth 1985). We have seen that Ištar too has affinities with demons: she is sometimes described as Kilili, or even Lamaštu. In these late texts the independent, female and erotic deities are dangerous, unpredictable and able to promote, as well as harm, human sexuality and fertility. The behaviour of parasitic demons, who attack the reproductive functions and kill small children, is structurally similar, although an exaggeration of its negative effects. If the love-goddesses can operate like evil demons, evil demons can also avail themselves of sexuality by seducing their victims or draining their sexual energy.

Another infernal aspect of erotic possession was the so-called betrothal or marriage with a dead person. Sometimes this was believed to have been ritually engineered by a witch who would make a figurine of her victim and place this effigy in the lap of a corpse in a symbolic sexual union (Abusch 1989: 31). As a result, the bewitched person was united with the *etemmu*, the spirit of this dead man and woman, a union which would eventually end in her or his own death. There are rituals to deal with some situations, involving a kind of (wedding) banquet for the spirit and his family (Oberhuber 1972: 81).

Ištar, in spite of her unpredictability and her dark side, was still one of the cosmic deities, decidedly one of the 'great gods', and she could be appealed to turn her force against the enemy, against evil, against malicious spirits unequal to her power. On a more mundane level, her human followers, the prostitutes and devotées, the asexuals and transvestites, commanded rather less awe. We have found the *assinnu* officiating in magic rituals, but it is hard to say to what extent this was due to his sexual status. The ethnographic data on the Indian Hijra included the widespread view that their curses were feared and their blessings sought, especially in respect to the hope for healthy and normal offspring. But we find the *ku'lu*, the *assinnu*, the *qadištu*, the *ištaritu* and the *kulmašitu*, as well as the *harimtu*, among the persons likely to engage in sorcery and witchcraft (Maqlû III, 40–61). I think this was not only because their behaviour was generally 'considered deviant' (Rollin 1983: 39), but because their livelihood depended to some extent on their sexual services, or their sexual status.

It has been pointed out before that women in general were considered more likely to engage in unlawful, private and therefore 'evil' magic than men. Although both the male and the female witch are addressed in the anti-witchcraft incantations, the lists describing likely suspects consist predominantly of women, and the verb-forms are usually feminine. The general explanation is the social inequality between the sexes, which marginalized women, and a patrilocal system of marriage, whereby wives had to integrate in the husband's or his father's household where she was essentially an outsider (Rollin 1983: 44). The custom of polygyny and the segregation of females in the 'women's quarter' of the house also fostered tension, jealousy and rivalry. Any domestic problem, such as the inability to conceive and particularly stillbirths, were routinely attributed to evil intent by other women or even witchcraft. Present-day ethnographies about Middle Eastern societies provide ample material for the existence of similar beliefs (Fernea 1965). We have seen that the legal sanctions against officially lodged and unproven accusations were severe, deserving the death of the accuser (CH § 2) and this may have curbed any tendency towards witch-hunts. We have as yet no proof of any actual court-cases against witches or sorcerers from Mesopotamia. The royal annals of the Hittite empire, on the other hand, are not without references to witchcraft being practised at court. The superior political position of the king's mother was a source of considerable tension; the mothers of Hattušili I and Muršilis II were accused of bringing witches into the palace, who cursed people or prompted, including the king, his children and wives (Bin Nun 1975). But the role of magic in the Hurrian- and Hattic-influenced Hittite empire is a subject beyond the scope of this book.[16]

It is important to put the textual evidence for sexuality in magic in perspective. Although love-goddesses could behave like demons, the same was said of male gods, especially if they had any connections with the Underworld, such as Nergal and Erra. Deities always transcended established categories and their benevolence could not automatically be relied upon. A famous Babylonian text from the first millennium addresses the philosophical and religious connotations of this problem, how the 'just man' is brought low by all sorts of calamities and disease and how all traditional methods, including magic rituals, fail to heal him. Then, suddenly, he finds himself restored to health and sanity; his god having decided to turn his favour towards him again (Lambert 1966: 63–91). Unpredictability, then, is typical not just for Ištar but for all deities. The behaviour of evil demons is also not circumscribed by gender-roles. They are characteristically composite, their bodies an assembly of animal or 'human' parts, sometimes male, sometimes female, but always able to de-materialize. The professional incantation priests and magicians attempted to systematize the essentially vague and formless demonic manifestations. The descriptions of demons in the relevant texts reflects the literary training of the scribes. Hence the similarities between hymns, Lamentations and the mantic literature. Certain stereotypical descriptions are found in all these genres, e.g. Ištar's wilfulness, the passivity of Dumuzi, the terror of darkness, etc.

The story of Šamhat in the Gilgameš epic dramatized the

ambivalent attitude to sexuality. On the one hand, there was the positive cultural aspect, the 'woman's art' that civilizes the wild man, on the other hand it was seen as weakening, alienating, and unworthy of heroes. Mantic texts express the same ambiguity. Demons attack peoples' sexuality, the major source of human happiness and fulfilment. But love itself can be magically inspired, and the witch can send erotic dreams to insinuate herself in the victim's psyche, come at night and lie with him. Sex manipulated by evil is destructive and leads to death.

20

THE ARTICULATION OF SEXUAL JEALOUSY

We have seen that most Mesopotamian erotic literature constructs an ideal of free choice and monogamous bonding. In the Sumerian Bridal Songs the young bride chooses her groom, or at least approves of her family's choice by admitting that he is indeed 'the man of her heart'. Yet we know from legal contracts that marriages were arranged at an early age and that parental control was absolute. One could argue that Inanna is no ordinary bride and that we simply lack the 'real' folklore that may have given voice to thwarted affection.

In courtly love-songs, these intense and intimate addresses to the lover can be appreciated against the institution of polygynous households, but this is decidedly only a subject, never a topic of the text. The young gods, with their phallic impetuosity, are interested in one girl only; even Enki, although he enjoys what is nowadays known as serial monogamy.

Only in the context of professional sexuality is promiscuity a subject, typified by Inanna the Whore (kar-kid), 'who fetches men'. But there is no descriptive elaboration of betrayal or jealousy. In Sumerian love poetry the woman is free to choose her spouse, to seduce her lover, to exult in her orgasmic eroticism. The man is portrayed as the ardent youthful lover, who might get the girl pregnant but always ends up marrying her, or as the skilled paramour who 'makes the bed sweet'. There is no room for negative emotions, no disappointment, no jealousy, no hatred of a spurned lover; only the impatience of the bride and her youthful longing are sometimes given vent.

In the Akkadian poetic texts, especially those that we can identify as being spoken by a divine couple, the situation is very similar. However, we have noted that in the medium of the love incantations this limited range was inappropriate. Here the 'patient' could declare his/her feelings of frustration, jealousy, or anxiety about his libido. After all, the incantations address real problems faced by human beings, they respond to a psychological contingency, and are not primarily concerned with cultural, or even theological, idealism. I believe that the literary love incantation came to exercise considerable influence on the discourse on love in Akkadian literature as a whole because it addressed human emotional needs. This interest in individual responses, this focus on 'humanity' rather than divine order, is generally characteristic of Akkadian literature, where the main characters are often mortal beings rather than great gods. I would even suggest that as far as the subject of love was concerned, incantation texts paved the way for this shift of emphasis; after all, they had a long tradition, going back to the third millennium. They allowed love to be regarded as an abstract concept, a commodity that could be (magically) manipulated. It was also an affliction, it could cause suffering. This admission of *chagrin d'amour* was only possible in the incantation literature and the Lamentation, but there the cause was already lost, as the lover was inevitably dead.

When somebody suffered from love the only cure was the presence of the beloved.[1] We have seen that erotic fantasies played a role in the Bridal Songs, where the young girl imagines that her lover is with her. The love incantations likewise build heavily on imagined scenarios. They often conclude different voices: that of the lover; the beloved responding accordingly; and the magician. We have also seen that the language of these texts is poetic and full of literary clichés. One could say that any love poem could be turned into an incantation by adding a suitable ritual and stating the present inability to achieve happiness. But the spoken, and even more the written, word had considerable power in itself. We have seen that in the cult, it made the lovemaking of gods a 'real' happening. The incantation-based love literature not only invokes a desired situation (e.g. to make the lover come and reciprocate the passion felt), it also provides the means to remove any existing obstacles, especially by eliminating any rivals.

An interesting text that testifies to the blurring of distinctions between incantation and love poetry is the following composition. In its present state it has no rubric declaring it as the former, and there is no ritual. It dates from the Old Babylonian period, and was most recently published by Held (1961–2). The same text had been edited before (von Soden 1950: 151–94), when it was understood as a discussion between Hammurabi and a young woman whom the king wants to marry to one of his sons. Von Soden saw the king manipulating the woman's compliance by introducing a rival. Held's reading disagreed with this interpretation. He showed convincingly that Hammurabi's name is only invoked in an oath-formula and that no priestly *nadītum* women are involved. Instead, he concluded that 'it is a dialogue between a young man and a young woman about love' (Held 1961–2: 1f.) and that it 'belongs to the category of love-lyrics'. He also found that 'a remarkable feature of our composition is its chastity and innocence. There are never any allusions to sex or sexual relations, no reference to the bed-chamber, no description of the human body' (ibid., 4). He declared that 'the modern reader is moved by the grace of the poem, its warmth of feeling and its high regard for love and faithfulness' (ibid., 3).

The tablet consists of four columns of text which are divided by horizontal rulings into passages. On the basis of the suffixes which alternate between masculine and feminine from one passage to the next. Held concluded that in the first case the woman is speaking to the man, whereupon he replies, etc. As a matter of fact, the suffixes can only tell us whether a male or female is addressed, but not what gender the speaker is, as Akkadian does not differentiate gender for the first person. Nor is the content of the respective passages indicative of a real dialogue. Somebody begins, rather abruptly, telling a woman to stop talking, because:

> 'What I say stands,
> I have not altered any argument in your favour,
> Or what is on my mind.
> He who clings to a woman
> Is like one who hoards the wind.'
>
> (I, 6–7)

This opening statement could be taken to be said by a reluctant male who resists love. The next passage is not a direct answer to the sentiments expressed here, nor does it address the man, but seems to give utterance to an inward prayer:

> 'May my loyalty remain constant
> Before Ištar, the queen.
> May my love prevail (and) shame (be upon) her
> Who slanders me.
> Give me devotion, passion,

234

The constant attention of my darling!
At the command of Nanâ [. .] forever!
Where is my rival?'

(I, 9–16)

The speaker, most likely to be identified as a woman in love,
confirms her emotional attachment and constancy, she prays to have
her love returned, and in the last line directs attention to the woman
who is her rival. According to the pattern he detected in the text,
Held took the following passage (lines 17–21) to be the words of the
lover. But it makes better sense to see them as directed against the
rival, spoken maybe by the goddess or by the woman in love as a sort
of spell, as the phraseology is similar to that of incantations against
evil influence:[2]

'I am more mindful than you
Of your tricks of days gone by.
Give in! Go!
Report to your (*fem.*) adviser
That we are wide awake!'

The woman speaks up again and makes her intentions clear. This
time she speaks to the object of her infatuation:

'I seize you[3] and this day
I will make your love and my love coincide!
By constantly praying to Nanâ
I shall win your affection, o my master, forever,
As a gift.

(I, 22–6)

The next passage is again addressed to a woman, but it can hardly be
the reluctant lover. I think that the rival is the target here again, and
the person saying the words, using the imperative forms to give
emphasis to the command – a typical incantatory trait – is again
either the infatuated woman herself or somebody on her behalf.

'I besiege you
I will make you (*fem.*) surrender.
Let your (*fem.*) supporter take possession of your
Charm. Get rid of your loose tongue!
Learn the truth.'

(I, 27–31)

It is interesting that the rival seems to be in league with another hostile female. The next passage is fragmentary, then the invocations against the opponent continue:

> 'On her (so that) she does not love you,[4]
> May Ištar, the queen, s[trike] with blindness;
> May she, like me, be afflicted with a sleeplessness;[5]
> May she be weary, [toss around] all night!'
>
> (II, 6–9)

Lines 10–19 are heavily restored, which makes their translation doubtful. In the following passage, the woman is joyfully confident that she will obtain her desire:

> 'I shall embrace him, I shall kiss [him]!
> I shall look and look [at him];
> I shall attain victory. .
> Over my go[ssiping women],
> And I shall [return] happily to my l[over],'
>
> (II, 23–7)

There is a large gap between the second and third column, and some fragmentary lines.

> 'As to the (women) repeatedly telling you:
> "Y[ou] are not the only one."
> Stop! I have taken my love away, I shall not . . [ ]
> Removed (it) from you,
> Put my "fruit" a thousand miles (*lit.* 3600) away!'
>
> (III, 6–10)

Here the beloved man is to be put totally outside the rival's reach. I do not believe, like Held, that the lover speaks of his own love here. The following is the woman speaking to the man, increasingly impatient:

> 'I see [your] 'fruit'
> O my lord, I long for your love!
> . . your laughter . . . [. .]
> Let it be hidden; God forbid that I should fail,
> Day and night I shall talk to you.'
>
> (III, 11–15)

The other woman is enjoined to take her place at the window and is taunted to 'catch my love' (III, 17–18). However, our lover feels restless:

> 'My eyes are very tired,
> I am weary of looking out for him;
> To me, it is as if he were passing by my quarter,
> The day has gone, (but) where is [my darling]?'

There is another break between columns III and IV, then somebody swears by Nanâ and Hammurabi that

> 'Your (*fem.*) love means no more to me than
> trouble and vexation.'
>
> (IV, 8–0)

Now another enemy is revealed, this time not a rival, but the gossips:

> 'They come down on me because I trust my lover.
> My gossipy women,
> More numerous than the stars of heaven.
> Let them hide! Let them be scarce!
> Let (all the) thousands (*lit.* 3600) of them go into hiding!
> I stay and
> Keep on listening to the words of my lord.'
>
> (IV, 10–16)

Finally, the male lover speaks out and confirms his love. This is, to my mind, the only case where it makes sense for him to talk, and even then he joins in the – now shared – task of banishing the rival:

> 'My only one, undisgraced,
> As before. .
> (When) I stood by you,
> And you leaned your shoulder (against me)
> "[Agr]eeable One" is your name,
> "[La]dy-of-Good-Sense" is your title;
> May the other woman be our enemy!
> Ištar being witness.'
>
> (IV, 17–24)

It seems to me that there is little reason to consider the whole composition as a dialogue between lovers. The main objective is the frustration of a rival's efforts to secure the lover's affection, interspersed with wishful thinking and expressions of the state of being in love by the afflicted woman. The language is often reminiscent of incantations banning hostile persons and forces. If we take it as whole composition, which begins with the male's refusal of love and ends with his final acceptance,[6] we would have another example of the woman's voice dominating the discourse on love. The man's lines seem like the quotations or imagined replies that we found in some of the Bridal Songs; they are part of the artifice and do not constitute a genuine dialogue. Rather than speaking directly to the lover, as is the case in most Sumerian love poetry, the woman voices her anxieties and frustrations and tries to better her chances by eliminating rivals or other women, who spoil her chances, like the gossipers. I suspect that the poetic admission of emotional insecurity was made possible by the format of the incantation, which caters for any number of psychological difficulties. Owing to the incomplete state of the tablet, we cannot with any certainty declare that this is indeed a love poem. If it were, the emotional volatility would give it more thematic affinity with the Egyptian love lyrics and the Song of Solomon (especially III, 1–3; V, 6–8; VIII, 6–7), where the beloved is away and the woman looks for him in vain, dwelling on the pain of absence. As for chastity, the text is clearly not as explicit as the Isin incantations (Wilcke 1985) or some of the divine love-dialogues (e.g. Lambert 1966), but the love the woman wishes to inspire is clearly not 'chaste' (see I, 14); the whole notion is profoundly misplaced in the context of Mesopotamian love literature.

The obstacles to happiness are threefold in this text. First, the indifference of the beloved. In this case he does not 'believe in love' and sees time spent in 'living with women' as time wasted. This sentiment is in line with the scepticism expressed in some Wisdom texts. Second, there are other women who might attract his attention, or try to seduce him. The third obstacle involves a larger social group: the collective of other women who pry into peoples' affairs and spread rumours. Their influence can make or break a love-affair as we also hear from Latin, Provençal, or medieval love-songs. The lover of this text addresses all these impediments, and in the end succeeds. The ultimate message, then, is not fidelity, but perseverance.

No other poetic text addresses the subject of erotic rivalry as clearly as the one just discussed. This is quite remarkable when one considers the social and legal dependence of women on men:

Adultery was then an offence not against a man's own wife but against the husband of the guilty woman, and he could condone it and accept compensation; but mere fornication was no offence in a man, whether unmarried or married. There was then almost absolute liberty for the husband but not for the wife.

(Driver and Miles 1935: 38)

Although a woman who had borne children enjoyed a certain protection against divorce, and the official acceptance of concubines was, at least in some periods, a matter of regulation,[7] it was of vital importance for the woman to secure and maintain her husband's affection and loyalty. As Abu Lughod argued, in her study of Bedouin love poetry, the majority of songs focus on courtship, or adolescent love, where the realities of adult married relations are as yet irrelevant. However, she also demonstrated that 'poems about rage, despair in respect of emotional hurt over the husband marrying another woman' (Abu Lughod 1986: 192–3) can be detected in the use of pain-metaphors, and the frequent allusion to weeping. The songs were part of an oral repertoire, allowed to be heard although they voiced sentiments that violated the existing moral code (Abu Lughod 1986: 221). The cuneiform poetry apparently lacks this subversive element; after all, only an educated minority was literate. In spite of all the artifice that suggests intimacy and emotion, the poems do represent the ideologically dominant voice. Female jealousy does not feature in the narrative literature (Enkidu can hardly be seen as Ištar's rival!). I have pointed out in the previous chapter that the so-called Amanamtaga-text should probably not be seen as an elaboration of Ištar's jealousy for some hapless servant who slept with Dumuzi, as some Assyriologists have suggested.

But there is a remarkable group of texts, from the first millennium (some copies were found in the Nineveh library), which allow the expression of extreme emotional disturbance, in the context of a public ritual, to be performed at Ištar's temple Eturkalamma and other locations in Babylon (Lambert 1975b).

These compositions, which Lambert originally dubbed 'Divine Love Lyrics' belong to the most difficult texts in cuneiform literature (see Edzard 1987: 57). It is not certain whether the various fragments form part of a series, or indeed what their textual relationship is. Also, the texts present considerable problems in terms of vocabulary and grammar. I shall only quote some relevant passages here.

Lambert concluded that the 'main actors are named occasionally as Marduk, his consort Šarpānîtu, and Ištar of Babylon, here referred to as his "girl-friend" (*tappattu*) or "concubine" (*qinītu*)', (Lambert 1975b: 99). He also stated that 'imagery of the boldest kind is commonplace, and the eroticism is the most explicit for ancient Mesopotamia'.

In comparison to Ištar, Marduk was a newcomer to the Babylonian official pantheon. Promoted as a national god by Hammurabi in the eighteenth century, he became increasingly popular in the whole of Mesopotamia and beyond. With the rise of the second dynasty of Isin he was declared 'lord of the gods' and took over from the ancient, but by then otiose, sky-god Anu and replaced Enlil as the executive god as well. The most splendid temples in Babylon were built for him and the important New Year festival included the recitation of a long text, the so-called *Enuma eliš*, a theological justification of Marduk's cosmic pre-eminence. He was integrated into the pantheon as the son of Ea/Enki and Damkina. His wife was always Šarpānîtu, his son Marduk. Ištar is often called his sister, although this did not conform with the tradition of her being the daughter of the moon-god Nannar (Babylonian Sîn), or with the alternative version of Anu being her father (as in Gilgameš). At any rate, Marduk's relationship with Ištar was not clearly defined. We have also seen that Anu too had ambiguous relations with the goddess. In some Old Babylonian hymns she appears as his official consort (Thureau-Dangin 1925), and in one Late Babylonian text he elevates her from a state of divine concubinage to his official wife (Hruška 1969).

We know from Ashurbanipal's inscriptions that he had a wooden bed made for Marduk, 'covered with gold and precious stones',

> For the delicious bed of my Lord and Lady,
> To perform the marital task, to make love
> (Matsushima 1988: 100)

The same text specifies that this bed was to be installed in the temple of Šarpānîtu, the KÁ. HI. LI. SÙ, or the 'House of Passion'. So Marduk, like other Babylonian and Assyrian gods, enjoyed an active love-life with his consort. However, according to these ritual texts, he also carried on an affair with Ištar. But unlike Anu, Marduk does not make Ištar his official wife; she remains the concubine. The ritual seems to be built around a triangular affair, with Šarpānîtu playing the role of the wronged wife who insults her rival, while Ištar is the seductive woman flaunting her sexual attraction. Edzard (1987: 50–70) has suggested that the texts may represent a dramatized ritual against a sexual rival. Ištar represents, as often in the late texts, the marginal part, the socially inferior position of the legally underprivileged concubine. But at the same time she stands again for the irresistible power of sex-appeal (*kuzbu*), which no social sanctions can ultimately constrict. Ṣarpānîtu takes on the role Hera plays in the Homeric tales, that of the legal wife who resents incursions into her domain. Between the two women, or goddesses, Marduk's role is limited, and his voice seems mainly addressed to Ištar, like an echo or refrain. But he is the object of their quarrel.

Much of the text is taken up with references to the ritual, which involves *assinnus* and *kurgarrûs*, part of Ištar's cult personnel, who apparently were to chant the dialogues, but who are also responsible for the ritual performance.

The ritual itself is called a 'ritual of lament' (*riksu ša sipitti*). Unlike the balag lamentations, which were recited in Sumerian, these are in Akkadian and there is no indication that the *kurgarrûs* were using Sumerian either. As Edzard points out, there is a refrain that poignantly contrasts the *riksi ša Ṣarpānîtu*, the 'lament of Ṣarpānîtu', with the *mîlulāti ša Marduk*, the 'pleasures of Marduk'.

'[The ritual], the ritual of lament. She is totally dejected (so
    Edzard 1987: 60). She was preferred to me, so I heard, to
    make love with'.
'[I bemoaned] Ṣarpānîtu, does she sleep in (her) cella (while)
Bel (Marduk) is on the roof?
of Bel. . .[ ]
". . . . . you are for me a little thing one can have for money. [8]
    My
. . . Together with the pleasant breeze. "You, whoever you are,
You, whatever be your name, you kept going to my husband's
Place; So it is (none other than) [you] the 'mother', Ištar of
    Babylon,
The pretty one, queen of the Babylonians,
So you are (then) the (good) mother, the palmtree, a carneol,
The most beautiful among the most beautiful,
Whose appearance is just so alluring,
Who is quite used up – and is still supposed to be beautiful?"'
                                    (IV, 18–22; Edzard 1987: 62)

[. .] as in the month of D'uzu, the . . . th day.'

(*BM* 41107 obv. 1–6)

This is the beginning of a large ritual tablet. It may set out the position of the main characters in a ritual that takes place at night or the evening, with Ṣarpānîtu being asleep inside the temple and Marduk going to the roof, where he meets Ištar, while Ṣarpānîtu gives vent to her feelings of betrayal and hatred for her rival. There is a large gap in the text, then the second column takes up with many succinct and often incomprehensible instructions for the priests.

'Give the concubine (*qinītum*) water [to drink . .'

Edzard suggested that, given we take Ṣarpānîtu again to be the main speaker, her demand for a drink for her rival may well contain a wish for her to be poisoned (Edzard 1987: 63). At any rate the phrase occurs throughout the text. There seems to be a fair amount of movement from one temple to the other, e.g.

'I will arise and take the road to Cutha. Babylon, seal . . .[ ]
"You are the mother, Ištar of Babylon", "To the garden of
    your lover when . ."
"When Ṣarpānîtu, full of jealousy, climbs up to the ziggurat".
Past the dais of the Anunnaki, (along) to the street of
    Eturkalamma up to the (. . .-) garden [ ]
The Lady (= Ṣarpānîtu) passes through the 'Gate of My Lady'
    and will . .[ ]
Ṣarpānîtu goes down to the garden and keeps calling for the
    gardener,
"Gardener, gardener, . .[ ]
what is the plant you have for my (female) friend Ṣarpānîtu to
    the garden . .[ ]"

(obv.Bii, 2–16; Edzard 1987: 64)

Maybe the gardener knows the right plant for the wronged wife; on the other hand, she may try to find an aphrodisiac for her own use. The text remains ambiguous. We have also seen that the garden is often no real garden, but a metaphor for the body, or sexual congress.

The 'pleasant breeze' comes up again and there is mention of 'the wifehood of sinful and despicable women' (Edzard 1987: 65) and the rubric says

That this is (what takes place) on the 4th day at noon and in the evening in the street of Eturkalamma at the river.

After more instructions, interspersed with short quotations, or probably only the opening words of a song or speech to be performed, we come to the following section:

> '... Facing the Akîtu of Šarrat-Nippuri she will stand and
> .... from the Akîtu to the city gate of Uraš.
> "Into your vulva, in which you set such great store, I shall make
> a (guard-)dog enter and will tie shut the door."
> "Into your vulva, in which you set such great store, instead precious stones before your face(?)."
> "O vulva of my girl-friend, why do you keep doing that?"
> "O vulva of my girl-friend, the whole district of Babylon is seeking a rag."[9]
> "Two-finger genitals,[10] why do you keep making trouble?" He/She
> will. .
> and will depart from the city gate and facing Hursagkalamma the
> kurgarrû will kneel and
> recite prayers and utter his chants. He will arise and sing,
> 'let me see great Kish, let me look on lofty Babylon', (etc.)
>
> (obv.iii, 5–14)

To us it seems incredible that such words should be said in a public religious ceremony, but the specific instructions on the tablet leave no doubt that this was indeed the case. They appear to be spoken on behalf of the aggrieved wife, Ṣarpānîtu. As in the 'love-song' quoted above, Ṣarpānîtu addresses her rival, here sarcastically called 'girl-friend', to revile her as whore. I leave it to the reader's imagination to 'translate' the passage into suitably offensive idioms:

> 'O vulva of my girl-friend, the whole district of Babylon is seeking a rag
> [To] wipe your vulva, to wipe your vagina.
> [Now] let him/her say to the women of Babylon: "The women will
> not give her a rag
> to wipe her vulva, to wipe her vagina."
> [Into] your vulva, in which you set such great store, instead
> of .... before your face,

Set you [ ] before you, sniff the smell of cattle.
Like something not mended by the tailor, like something not
soaked by the laundrymen.
Into your vulva into which you set such great store, I will
make a guard-dog enter and will tie shut the door.
I will make a dog enter and will tie shut the door, I will
    make a
hahhuru-bird enter it and it will nest.
Whenever I leave or enter
I will give order to my (*fem.*) *hahhuru*-birds,
"Please, my dear *hahhuru*-bird,
Do not approach the . . . .
Ditto. the reek of armpits.'

(LKA 92, 4–17)

This particular passage is followed by one addressing Ištar as the
'beautiful one, the queen of Babylon, a palm of carnelian'.

Elsewhere in the text we hear that these are indeed the rituals of
Ṣarpānîtu:

'Pleasure of Marduk,
Laments of Ṣarpānîtu,
In the ritual of Ṣarpānîtu
By night there is not a good housewife,
By night there is not a good housewife,
By night a married woman creates no difficulty.[11]
I am a . . . for Ṣarpānîtu,
My hair is flowing and my hands . . .
In my hostility(?) to Ištar of Babylon
For shade or open air I have covered my side.
These women – so long as he does wrong
My hair is flowing and my hands . . .
These women – so long as he is despised–
For shade and open air you have covered my side.
She who is present . . . a doll,
You (*masc.sg.*) hold back in everything that is not sound.
You are the good housewife – create a family;
You (*fem.*) are the fool – process wool.'

(Lambert 1975b: 109, lines 3–20)

It is not clear who is speaking here, but both Marduk and Ṣarpānîtu
are named at the beginning. Is the goddess here trying to assert her

marital rights? The passage is generally obscure, although the line about the hostile attitude to Ištar is typical of Ṣarpānîtu. Does Ištar utter the last two lines, sarcastically telling the wife to be content within the confines of family life?

There is also a curious fragment that concerns a vulva, probably Ištar's:

> 'Together with the pleasant breeze . . .
> It is cut off . . .
> In your vulva is hon[ey(?)]
> In its recesses . .
> Rub my seeder plough with oil . .
> That which is not pleasant of [your] vulva . . .
> The sailor of [your] vulva . .
> The cook of [your] vulva . .
> The basket-maker of [your] vulva . .
> The lizard of [your] vulva . .
> The gecko of your vulva . .
> The cat of your vulva . .
> The mouse of your vulva . .
> (Lambert 1975b: 113, lines 1–13)

In another tablet a 'boat of pleasure' (ᵍⁱˢ*maqurri ṣi-ha-at*) is described in highly technical but possibly ambiguous language, after all the vulva of Inanna was also compared to a boat.

So far I have not attempted to piece together all these fragments into a sequence of events, and until other texts with more substantial information are found the rituals of Ṣarpānîtu will remain enigmatic.

However, it is clear that the rivalry between the official wife and the lover constitute a ritual theme. This is interesting in itself as it poses the question: what could have been the purpose of a ritual that addresses the sexual jealousy of the spouse? Did it appeal to the *emuqti*, the good housekeeper who sees her husband's attention diverted to other women? Was Ṣarpānîtu a sort of patron deity of spurned wives? Does the ritual in fact succeed in banishing the extraordinary sexual attractiveness of Ištar? Or does it rather reflect on Marduk's erotic prowess, who reduces the great Ištar to a mere 'girlfriend' and concubine? Another possibility is the exaltation of Ištar as the Concubine, intrinsically related to Ištar the Harlot. There is an interesting Late Babylonian legal document that records the hire of a 'slave of Ištar' for the purpose of becoming the concubine of some man (Dandamaev 1984). It is possible that the huge growth of the city during the neo-Babylonian period, together with economic instability, produced a social climate which fostered the commercialization of sexual services. Ištar's 'image' or sexual persona might serve as an indicator of socio-economic circumstances, an idea which I cannot substantiate with any data.

Another possible explanation for these rites might be to see them as travesties of the 'straight' *haddašutu*, the ritual of harmonious conjugal love that we know was celebrated for Nabû and Tašmetu, and also for Maduk and Ṣarpānîtu. A possible clue for this hypothesis is the prominent role of the *assinnus* and *kurgarrûs*, who represent deviance and liminality in sexual matters and social norms. Here they seem to have been given free rein to stage an elaborate charade, involving the great Bel himself, his august wife and of course their patron deity Ištar. One could imagine that such a wild spectacle had a certain cathartic social function, allowing an outlet for represssed frustration and rage. It seems a characteristic trait of Mesopotamian civilization to cater for deviance, even institutionalize it to some degree, as the role of the *kurgarrûs* etc. suggests. There is an interesting text from the very late, Arsacid period, an administrative temple document, which could possibly refer to the 'jealousy' rituals (Hibbert 1985). It mentions the 'restless pacing to and fro before my lord' and a 'juniper garden' around Eturkalama, Ištar's temple in Babylon; the *kurgarrûs* and *assinnus* are equally involved here.

The misnamed 'love-lyrics' remain at present enigmatic, but they point to a polarization of interest between the claims of legitimate relationships and anarchic passion. They also show that *chagrin d'amour* now affects the gods as well. The love incantation has, at this stage, reached the realm of mythology. Now the great gods need them too.

21

LOVE AND EROS IN
AKKADIAN NARRATIVE
LITERATURE

The intense scribal training in the Old Babylonian period, brought about by the administration's need for clerks with a written command of the vernacular Akkadian, sparked off an interest in all aspects of the existing Sumerian literary heritage. It was as if the intelligentsia had to prove their mettle by being able to cope with all levels of literacy. Poetry, as ever, was one measure of their success. Owing to the high esteem the genre of courtly erotic poetry enjoyed during the Isin–Larsa period and before, the subject could hardly be neglected, although, maybe due to a change of attitudes, royal patronage declined and love poetry became associated with religious rituals.

As far as narratives are concerned, there seems to have been a greater general interest, and judging from the number of compositions for which there is no extant Sumerian counterpart, many of them appear to be original. Even when traditional material was used, the Akkadian version often differs significantly. It is not impossible that the many different cultural groups which settled in Mesopotamia during and after the Old Babylonian period contributed to the narrative repertoire of the period.[1] The foreign origin of such contributions is often obscured in the written forms, as they were integrated into the culturally dominant mythological framework; the gods who appear are practically always the well-established deities of the Mesopotamian pantheon.

An interesting question is to what extent narratives about gods were used for ritual purposes. I have tried to show that love-songs ascribed to deities were integrated in the routine of temple services that catered for the life of the gods; their lovemaking was obviously as important as their meals and regular outings.

*

247

One composition from the late Old Babylonian period concerns the acceptance of a new deity within the established pantheon through a ritual of aggregation, or adoption (Römer 1966).[2] It is of special interest in relation to those Sumerian myths that describe the phallic antics of young gods. The text refers to the birth of the Sîn (the Akkadian form of Nannar, the moon-god) and a minor god called Išum, whose cult was relatively new. As the beginning is broken, it is uncertain whether the relationship between Enlil and Ninlil was the same as that described in the Sumerian text, where Enlil impregnated her at their first meeting by the canal. However, the mention of the bed at the beginning of column II, the iterative verbal form of *itulum* ('to lie down', 'to have sex') and the reference to Sîn as 'legitimate child' suggest a more conventional situation. The childhood of Sîn is passed over quickly. We next find him as a young man who enjoys hunting and fowling in the marshes. In keeping with the traditional erotic connotations of this environment, he behaves very much like Enki, or Enlil; 'he directed his attention to Ningal':

> Sîn called her, approached (with the intent) to marry her,
> He kissed her but did not ask her father.

This means that, just like the Sumerian gods, he engages in pre-marital sex. As the tablet is damaged at this place we do not know how this is described. But that all is not well is clear from column III, where a distraught Sîn talks to Ninlil, his mother, and asks her to intervene for him. Her answer is not preserved, nor is there much left of columns IV and VI. A libation is mentioned, and the god Pabilsag also makes an appearance. When the text resumes, we are in Enlil's 'house', the Ekur in Nippur, and Ištar is on the scene:

> walking up and down like nurse, saying:
> 'I am looking after my brother, my brother who was born to my brother'

This rightly confuses Enlil, and he asks the 'lioness Ištar':

> 'What brother of yours are you looking after, your brother born to your brother?'
> She answered him:
> 'Ninlil has born Išum to Šamaš and when she got married, she left him on the street.

We have two examples of irregular sexual conduct here. First, the well-known pre-marital impregnation of Ningal by Sîn, and then an act of adultery by Sîn's mother Ninlil with Šamaš, who subsequently gave birth to Išum, Ištar, here affiliated to the Nippur pantheon as a daughter of Enlil, makes a comic appearance; although she is addressed as *labatum* 'lioness', she is left holding the baby.[3] Since we know that Išum was one of the Nippur gods, it seems likely that the text has Enlil accepting the child as his own. There is a Sumerian antecedent to this lenient attitude to female adultery, in an as yet untranslated text, where Pabilsag, whose birth was also the result of unusual circumstances, is recognized as Enlil's own son.[4]

A detailed analysis of this text is impossible, as large chunks are missing. But judging from the existing material, it seems less concerned with the procreative potential of the young god than with the problem of integrating marginalized offspring; the social consequences of irregular sexual behaviour are more important than the display of fertility we detected in *Enlil and Ninlil* or *Enki and Ninhursaga*. This is an instance of the de-mythification of the gods, since they behave like human beings rather than powerful and awe-inspiring deities and are even subjected to ridicule. It is difficult to judge whether such texts were primarily satirical, or whether they could provide a 'serious' aetiology for the integration of gods, but couched in a style that was suitable for 'fringe' cultic performances.

Elements of satire are also evident in a composition that describes how the god Nergal became the Lord of the Underworld. Two versions of the story survive. The older one dates from the middle of the second millennium and was actually found among the cuneiform records at Amarna in Egypt, the short-lived capital of Ekhnaton (Knudtzon 1915: 968–74; Dalley 1989: 178–81).

Ereškigal was the queen of the Underworld, defined as the domain of the dead, demons and evil spirits. Access to her realm was restricted to such denizens, and as the myth of *Inanna's Descent* demonstrates (Sladek 1974; Jacobsen 1987a: 205–32), the celestial gods were also in danger of losing their life should they venture there. However, there are some intermediaries who are allowed to cross these boundaries and in this case it is Namtar, Ereškigal's minister, who goes 'up' to the gods to receive his mistress's share of a banquet organized by the gods of heaven. He is civilly received by all gods save one who did 'not rise to his feet'. Ereškigal summons this god; it is Nergal. In order to punish him for this lack of respect, she intends to kill him. But Ea, the master magician of the gods, equips Nergal with powerful magic, and thus armed, he presents himself at the gate of the Underworld. He is able to overcome Namtar and turn the tables on his adversary:

> Inside the house, he seized Ereškigal
> By her hair, pulled her from her throne
> To the ground, intending to cut off her head.
> 'Don't kill me, my brother! Let me tell you something.'
> Nergal listened to her and relaxed his grip, he wept and
> Was overcome (when she said),
> 'You can be my husband and I can be your wife.
> I will let you seize Kingship over the wide earth! I will put the tablet
> Of wisdom in your hand! You can be master,
> I can be mistress,' Nergal listened to this speech of hers
> And seized her and kissed her. He wiped away her tears.
> 'What have you asked of me? After so many months, it shall certainly be so!'

With this Petruchio-like bravado he subdues the terrifying mistress of the Underworld to a docile wife, who is ready to hand over her divine prerogatives. Ereškigal's loneliness and misery is also a feature in other works, notably those connected with Inanna/Ištar's Descent to the Underworld. Here we have a solution for her problem; she gains one of the apparently celestial gods as a husband but loses her status as sole ruler of the Underworld. In fact, Nergal was well known as a chthonian god; his ancient cult site was Cutha, but he did not play an important role in the literary texts.

The later version, reconstructed from tablets found at Sultantepe and Uruk (Gurney 1960; Hunger 1976; Dalley 1989: 165–77), is considerably longer, and here the erotic relationship between Nergal and Ereškigal is much expanded. It is in fact the only Mesopotamian text that could be described as a love-story (Hutter 1985: 84–100). The narrative framework is the same. When Ereškigal's envoy Namtar goes up to heaven to receive her share of the banquet, Nergal is the only god who fails to kneel before him. The text is damaged at this point. It probably contained a passage about Nergal's intention of going to the Underworld, because when the text resumes, Ea gives him a special chair and detailed instruction as how to behave in the Underworld. He is not to sit on the chair they will provide, or eat the bread and the meat, or drink the beer. And when Ereškigal bathes and puts on her transparent garment 'allowing a glimpse of her body', 'you must not do that which men and women do'.

Nergal descends and Namtar identifies him as the god who would not kneel in his presence. Ereškigal has him admitted, and he passes through the seven gates. Once in her presence, he states the purpose of his visit:

> 'Anu, your father sent me [to see you],
> Saying "Sit down on that throne,
> Judge the cases of the great gods."'

There is no reaction by Ereškigal to this speech, but her servants present him with the various items mentioned above, all of which he refuses. Even when she bathes, the usual prelude to sexual activity, he resists. There is another gap in the text here, after which she has another bath, and this time she succeeds:

> He gave in to his heart's desire to do what men and women do.
> The two embraced each other
> And went passionately to bed

where they remain for six days and nights. On the seventh day Nergal arises, and pretending that Ereškigal had sent him to heaven, he tricks Namtar into letting him leave the Underworld. The gods cheer him at his arrival as the 'son of Ištar', in view of his amorous exploits. Ea predicts that Ereškigal will come and look for him, as now, having transgressed against the rules that would have protected him, the Underworld has a claim. Ea therefore resorts to magic and transforms Nergal into an old man, 'blinking and bald'.

Back in the Underworld, Ereškigal seems unaware of his departure. She calls the servants to sprinkle the room with water. When Namtar informs her that Nergal had left, she cries out aloud, and weeps:

> 'Erra (another name for Nergal), the lover of my delight –
> I did not have enough delight with him before he went!'

Her vizier, disturbed by her grief, offers to go up to heaven again in order to 'arrest that god':

> 'let me take him to you, that he may kiss you again!'

Ereškigal gives him an emotionally charged message to take to the great gods:

'To say, ever since I was a child and a daughter,
I have not known the playing of other girls,
I have not known the romping of children.
the god whom you sent to me and who has impregnated me –
    let him sleep with me again!
Send that god to us, and let him spend the night with me as my
    lover!
I am unclean, and I am not pure enough to perform the
    judging of the great gods.'

To underline the seriousness of her demand she utters the threat of raising the dead to outnumber the living.

Ereškigal's speech is a carefully worked progression from her personal predicament, especially the loneliness of her youth and her present love for Nergal, to the political implications of her situation – pregnancy would not allow her to continue in her office. She does not mention that Nergal had offered to perform the judging of the great gods himself. Namtar repeats her message, and cunning Ea invites him to pick out the offending god, whom he promptly fails to recognize. When he reports these events to his mistress she immediately sees through Ea's trick and instructs Namtar to go for the 'bald, blinking and cringing god'. Ea, of course, had meanwhile changed Nergal's appearance a second time, and Namtar is unable to identify him. But then something happens – the details are lost owing to a break in the text – and Nergal is once more resolved to go to the Underworld. This time Namtar advises him on how to assert his authority over the doormen of the seven gates. When Nergal has successfully accomplished that and stands in the court-yard of Ereškigal,

> He went up to her and laughed,
> He seized her by the hair
> And pulled her from her throne
> By her tresses.
> The two embraced each other
> And went passionately to bed

for another six days of lovemaking. Now Anu intervenes and sends down his messenger to confirm that Nergal is to remain forever in the Underworld.

As mentioned before, this is essentially a love-story. The setting in the Underworld does not distract from this theme but enhances the poignancy of the drama. Even in the *Descent of Ištar*, where Ereškigal was portrayed as the opposite of Ištar, the Underworld was not immune to love and sexual desire. But while there it is associated with the marginal sexuality represented by the *assinnu*, probably due to the context of Ištar's cult, the love between Ereškigal and Nergal conforms to the heterosexual norm, as Ereškigal assumes that she is pregnant and other texts describe her as a mother. Here, love extends to the Underworld.

In the Amarna version, Nergal, initially reluctantly, takes over the Underworld by sheer force and magic power, and Ereškigal, taken by surprise, offers herself in marriage. But there is no erotic tension in the text. The later version has Nergal intending to take up the office of judging in the Underworld, probably on Anu's command, and is then seduced by Ereškigal, who acts like Ištar, or one of her devotées. Although Ea had warned Nergal not to give into his urge to respond to her signals (letting him see a glimpse of her body). He cannot resist. As Hutter 1985 rightly notes, there is no justification for the assumption that Nergal raped her. Ereškigal gains control over him by the force of her erotic attraction. She thus represents the power of feminine sexuality, which is stronger than Ea's 'wisdom'. The poem also dramatizes yet again the traditional masculine reaction to female erotic provocation that we saw in the 'young men' myths. Nergal at first escapes, when he realizes after their six days of passion, what this entails. But Ereškigal's appeal to the celestial gods, that she has a woman's right to be sexually satisfied, is ultimately heeded, in spite of Ea's magic tricks at camouflaging the god. Nergal, his status in the Underworld assured by the divine sanction, joins Ereškigal. In his second encounter he takes the initiative, and his display of force here takes on an erotic dimension, signalled by the verb ṣiāhu ('to laugh'), which is conceptually linked with lovemaking in the Akkadian texts (Hirsch 1982: 117). It signals his readiness to respond to Ereškigal's demands to be loved, and duly leads to the next bout of intimate congress. His assertive, 'phallic' behaviour also highlights the fact that he is now the ruler of the Underworld and that Ereškigal had traded in her position as main authority to Nergal. So much for a 'happy end'; but there remain some ambiguities: both gods have lost something in exchange for sexual activity – Ereškigal her queenship and Nergal his place among the celestial gods. In this respect he has 'died' to his previous self.

The heroes of Akkadian narratives are not always deities. They can be human, or at least partially human; but their powers are ultimately limited, and they are mortal. Like the heroic characters of Homer, they interact with the gods, but depend on their support. The fundamental problem that all these 'epics' address is the 'fate of mankind', death. Etana flies to heaven on the back of an eagle, in order to find the plant of birth for his barren wife; he looks for immortality through his descendants (Kinnier-Wilson 1985). Atrahasis, the flood-hero, ensured the survival of mankind when it was faced with the threat of extinction, and was exempted from death as a reminder of the gods' promise (Lambert and Millard 1969). Adapa was given the opportunity to win godlike immortality, but missed his chance because he was not able to interpret the will of the gods (Picchioni 1981; Dalley 1989: 182–8). The central issue of the story of Gilgameš, which was not developed in the Sumerian forerunners, is likewise a quest for immortality. And like all the other heroes, except the survivors of the Flood, he fails.

Gilgameš, like Lugalbanda and Enmerkar, was one of the 'historical' rulers of the legendary First Dynasty of the Uruk who became the subject of heroic poems. Gilgameš and Lugalbanda even acquired divine status. The stories of their deeds were no doubt handed on orally through the generations, although their literary transmission seems to go back to the Early Dynastic period (Biggs 1977). While the exploits of Enmerkar, Ensuhkešdanna and Lugalbanda were written down in Sumerian only, and failed to enter the literary Akkadian tradition, some of the Sumerian stories about Gilgameš formed the basis of a new literary work, which was composed, in Akkadian, during the Old Babylonian period. The work enjoyed great popularity in the peripheral areas of Mesopotamian civilization, copies were found as far afield as Anatolia and Palestine. The most comprehensive, and to some extent substantially reworked, edition dates from the seventh century. It was found in Ashurbanipal's library in Nineveh.[5]

Sexuality and love are maybe not the single most important theme of the Gilgameš epic (Foster 1987: 21–42). But both the Old Babylonian and the Ninevite version have important things to say on the subject. Unusually for Mesopotamian literature, they present more than one viewpoint, allowing several voices to be heard.

I have already quoted substantially from the Old Babylonian version, in respect of Enkidu's initiation into society by Šamhat, the courtesan. Enkidu, a savage who, like the Wild Boy of Aveyron (Shattuck 1980), lived entirely deprived of human company, and fed and drank like the herbivorous beasts of the steppe, became the peer and companion of Gilgameš, the king, the pinnacle of urban society. His acculturation was achieved by a series of initiations, of which sexuality was the first, followed by the consumption of bread and beer (the culturally most important foods of Sumerian civilization), the wearing of clothes, and a haircut.[6] The story tells us that the gods had created Enkidu as a counterpart to Gilgameš, his equal. In the Sumerian stories there was no indication that Enkidu was not Sumerian, and his function is that of a social inferior, a servant of slave of his master.

Enkidu's function is very different in the Akkadian text. He offers a new perspective, from which the traditional values associated with the Sumerian city, as the embodiment of civilization, could be re-examined. One is very much aware, in the Gilgameš epic, that this is a critical, even an outsider's perspective. The Sumerian tales of Enmerkar, Lugalbanda, etc. describe confrontations with a foreign power, far-off Aratta, but they can only conceive of Aratta in the same terms as Sumer itself. Both the en of Aratta and the en of Uruk vie for the favour of Inanna, and although Uruk comes out as 'superior' to Arratta, it is not seen as fundamentally different.

But the collapse of the Ur empire at the beginning of the second millennium, and the gradual socio-cultural transformation of the country that finally resulted in the establishment of the Amorite Dynasty, had changed this ethnocentric view of the world. The Other had come to stay, and although the continuity of Meso-potamian civilization, especially in terms of institutions and religion, had become practically a cliché, there were important changes of cultural values, and I believe that the Gilgameš epic is probably the only major literary work that gives expression to that experience. This critical view might well have contributed to the popularity of the work outside the old heartland of Mesopotamian culture.

The probing antithesis between city and desert, tradition and individual responsibility, is especially noticeable in episodes that concern the function of the erotic. In this context, Enkidu is indeed the equal of Gilgameš, but significantly not as a *social* equal, as, say, another Sumerian king or prince would be (and unlike Achilles and Patroclus, or even Arthur and Lancelot). The gods placed him in the steppe, the archetypal wild place, which was always regarded as outside the bounds of Sumerian statehood, a place where ghosts lurked and lawless nomads who 'knew no grain'. Enkidu is neither a ghost nor a pastoralist, initially he is one of the truly wild creatures, but magnificently so, as the texts repeatedly emphasize. The huntsman is too frightened to approach this formidable creature, whose very existence threatens his livelihood. So the elders send Šamhat to tame him, a woman alone. But nowhere is any astonishment expressed at this fact. Instead, it is clear that only the sexual capacity of a well-versed professional is a match for the wild man's power. More than a match, because after six days and seven nights of having been treated to 'woman's work', he was not only weakened physically but also fundamentally changed. In this story, sexual intercourse has a double significance. On the one hand, it is an activity that animals also engage in, and Enkidu responds like any male beast to the female on heat. (He also responds like the 'young gods' in the Sumerian myths to the mere sight of a naked woman. The strength of his passion is commensurate with his superior, godlike strength, which Šamhat remarks upon. But as it is performed by a knowledgeable courtesan (and not a mere nubile girl as in the 'phallic' myths), this lovemaking is also his introduction to human intercourse as such, with its reciprocity and mutual consideration. After this, Enkidu is unable to resume his former life, his intimacy with the woman cancels his intimacy with nature: he has been transformed. All further action now moves towards Gilgameš, towards the city. Step by step Enkidu becomes further initiated: first by meeting other human beings, the shepherds in their stall, still out in the steppe, but with human aims and preoccupations. From now on, Enkidu will be on their side and do what the legendary chiefs of old had to do: fight the predatory lions and wolves that threaten their herds. He shares the shepherds' food, and drinks seven jars of beer. He is anointed with oil (the steppe equivalent of having a bath), and once dressed 'he became like any (civilized) man (Akkadian *awîlum*)'. But this does not mean that Enkidu unreservedly accepts the customs of this civilization. Though distanced from the pure state of the savage, and indeed a true human being, he is not a city dweller. His values are not those of the city. This is made clear in both the second- and the first-millennium edition of the epic. Let us first carry on with the Old Babylonian version. On their way to Uruk, Šamhat and Enkidu see a festively attired man hurrying along the road, carrying a tray or basket of food. Asked where he is going, the young man answers:

> 'They have invited me to a wedding (*lit.* the houses of fathers-in-law)
> This is the custom of the people (here)

To choose (thus) the future spouses (*lit.* daughters-in-law).
I am in charge of the victuals, delightful food in the place
    (*lit.* city) of the in-laws.
For the king of Uruk of the Cross-roads,
The curtain (*lit.* net) is opened,
(that) keeps back the others,
To the advantage of the bridegroom.
The legitimate wife he will impregnate,
He first,
And then the husband.
Thus it was ordered by the counsel of Anum
And since his birth (*lit.* when his umbilical cord was cut)
It was destined for him (as his privilege).'
                          (IV, 144–59; Bottéro 1992: 226–7)

Gilgameš apparently makes use of the *droit de cuissage*, the right
to deflower the bride before her husband.[7] There is no evidence for
such a custom from Mesopotamian legal records, but the familiarity
with the concept at least proves that the author knew it to have been
practised somewhere and at sometime. In the text it is made out to
be a divinely decreed royal privilege. After a gap in the text of some
12 lines, Enkidu and Šamhat arrive at Uruk, where the people marvel
at the sight of him. They compare him to their king and agree that
he is indeed a match for godlike Gilgameš. The ensuing fight
between Enkidu and Gilgameš is set in the context of a wedding,
where the 'bed for Išhara was set up', a phrase that indicates the nine
days that elapse after the initial bridal ceremonies, which are held
under the auspices of the love-goddess Išhara. Enkidu bars the way
to Gilgameš, 'blocked the door with his foot, did not let Gilgameš
enter', apparently to prevent him from claiming his right to the first
night. Enkidu weeps, but owing to a break in the Ninevite tablet,
where the episode is described, we do not know why. But outrage
at Gilgameš' abuse of royal power is the only plausible motivation
for Enkidu's behaviour. Bottéro suggested that Enkidu represents
here a different ethnic culture, 'plus primitive et plus frustes, mais
aux mœurs plus strictes que celles des citadins' (Bottéro 1992: 227).
But there the matter rests, because in the midst of their struggle, they
recognize each other (the text is broken here). Gilgameš and Enkidu
become friends and decide to embark on the dangerous expedition
to the Cedar Forest, which is guarded by the demonic Humbaba.
Before their departure, Ninsun, the mother of Gilgameš, conducts a

ritual for the safe return of her son, and in a rather enigmatic passage asks Enkidu to guard her son:

> 'Mighty Enkidu, you are no issue of my womb,
> But now I implore you
> With the devotées (*ši-ir-gi*) of Gilgameš,
> The priestesses (*ugbābati*), *qadištu* and *kulmašitu* women,
> Thus she charged Enkidu with the mission (*lit.* put an
>   obligation on his shoulder).'
> (III, 17–21; Bottéro 1992: 96–7)

The female personnel of the temple are involved in the ceremony, and they are all described as being devotées of Gilgameš, but the meaning of this reference remains unclear. Lambert (1991: 49) and Foster (1987: 33) suggested that Enkidu was thereby accepted or adopted into Gilgameš' household. It may signify the final and ceremonial integration of Enkidu, not only into urban culture, but also into the kin group of Gilgameš.

The two heroes set off with their mighty weapons and achieve their aim, having slain Humbaba and felled the trees of the forest. When they return, Gilgameš, like the Homeric heroes, has a bath and presents himself in all his royal glory. This sets the scene for the remarkable encounter between Gilgameš and the goddess Ištar, which only occurs in the Ninevite version of the epic (Tablet VI). The whole episode is imbued with a strong dose of satire, and Ištar is treated to the most abusive and irreverent discourse of Mesopotamian literature.

> Ištar, the princess, raised her eyes to the beauty of Gilgameš,
> 'Come to me, Gilgameš, be my bridegroom.[8]
> Give me the gift of your "fruit" (*inbika*),
> You will be my husband and I will be your wife.'
> (VI: 6–8)

The goddess, who in this passage is always addressed by the title *rubûtu*, 'princess', rather than by any of her standard divine epithets, addresses Gilgameš abruptly. Her speech is an odd mixture of a harlot's proposition and an actual marriage proposal. She clearly desires Gilgameš sexually, but she does not invite him just to make love to her; she wants him as a bridegroom, but takes on the traditional masculine role in this exchange; Ištar is here very clearly the 'phallic' partner, who makes the first move.[9] This is made even more obvious in the following lines, where she enumerates the advantages this union will bring to Gilgameš:

> 'I shall have a chariot of lapis lazuli and gold harnessed for
>   you.
> With golden wheels and horns of amber(?),
> You shall harness *ūmu*-demons as big mules,
> To enter our house through the fragrance of cedar!
> (And) when you enter our house the highest functionaries of
>   the clergy will kiss your feet,
> Kings, nobles, princes shall bow low before you,
> They will bring you tribute,
> All the products of the mountains and the country.
> Your goats shall bear triplets, your ewes twins.
> Your loaded donkeys shall go faster than the mules,
> Your horses shall run proud at the chariot,
> (and your oxen) shall be without equal at the yoke.'
>
> (VI: 10–20)

She offers him the accoutrements of royal wealth and supreme
power, as well as fertility of herds and fields. Superficially, this looks
like the traditional divine blessings bestowed on the kings, and one
is reminded of Inanna's blessings in the UrIII royal hymns, although
that old Sumerian topos of the goddess's marriage to the king no
longer had currency when the epic was written. Instead, as Tzvi
Abusch has convincingly shown, the literary works of the first
millennium, especially the incantations, were more relevant here
(Abusch 1989b). He also points out that Gilgameš was by this time
known as one of the judges of the Underworld, and he concludes
that

> Ištar's marriage proposal constitutes an offer to Gilgameš to
> become a functionary of the netherworld. The details of her
> offer may be understood as referring to funeral rites and to
> activities that Gilgameš will perform in the netherworld. The
> order in which the items are cited may even represent a
> continuous progression: Gilgameš the king will wed Ištar and
> go to his new home, the tomb, the netherworld; there he will
> be accorded the rites of the dead and exercise his infernal
> powers. Our text describes a funeral ritual. Obviously our text
> makes use of figures and forms drawn from the realms and
> rituals of marriage, food and fertility, and perhaps even
> political activity. But the unifying and dominant image remains

that of the grave and Ištar as its symbolic representation.

(Ibid.: 367)

The most striking literary parallel is *Nergal and Ereškigal*, where Ereškigal makes the almost identical marriage proposal to Nergal. This interpretation may well account for Gilgameš' subsequent rejection of Ištar's offer, and one could also detect here the irony that Gilgameš so violently rejects a fate he cannot avoid, since everybody knows that he did die and did become a functionary of the Underworld, although not by marrying Ištar. But should Ištar's offer be seen as a snare? Does she see herself as a 'symbolic representation of death'? Her proposal of marriage is indeed uncharacteristic for a woman, but then with respect to the two-thirds mortal that Gilgameš is, she is his superior. And her promises can be taken as pertaining to the real world, they merely reiterate the gods' blessing for the ruler and his superiority in all spheres of life. The Sargon legend, which was still current at the time, showed how the goddess had helped the young man, who worked as a cupbearer to the Sumerian king, to achieve his ambition and found an empire (Lewis 1980). Gilgameš, the 'modern' king, proves sceptical. First, he ironically asks her what he would have to give as a bride-price, and goes on to question his ability to keep her in the way she is accustomed to. For him, the union with a goddess is clearly absurd:

> 'What would I have to pay if I married you?
> Would I give you, (fragrant) oil and clothes for your body,
> Would I give you food and provisions,
> Would I provide you with bread fit for gods,
> Would I provide you with beer fit for kings?'
> [. . .]
> would I [. . .]
> [N]o, I do not want you [for a wife].' (24–33)

Then he launches into a series of metaphorical insults, which are still obscure in places. He compares Ištar to 'a fireplace that goes out in the cold weather, a draughty door that cannot keep the wind out, a palace that collapses on the warriors within(?), an elephant that throws off his harness(?), (a piece of) bitumen that stains whoever touches it, a waterskin that [soaks] its carrier, an ill-fitting shoe, etc.' (lines 33–42; Foster 1987: 34–5). Ištar brings only discomfort, unease and danger, even death. He then elaborates on her love-life:

> 'Not one of [your] lovers [have you loved] forever!

Not one of your favourites escaped [your snares]!
Come here, that I recite(?) your lovers' (fate) to you!
[...]
Tammuz, lover of your youth
You decreed annual mourning for him.
You loved the colourful *allallu* bird,
But you hit him and broke his wing.
(Now) he stays in the woods crying "My wings".[10]
You loved the lion of unmatched strength,
(Then suddenly) you dug seven and seven pits for him.
You loved the horse, reliable in battle,
You decreed the pointed whip and reins for him,
You decreed that he should run endless courses,
You decreed that he should be exhausted and thirsty,
You decreed weeping for his mother Silili.
You loved the shepherd, the herdsman,
Who prepared flat bread for you on the cinders,
Who cooked ewe-lambs for you every day.
(Then suddenly), you struck him and turned him into a wolf,
So that his own boys pursued him
And his dogs snapped at his hind quarters.
You loved Išullanu, your father's gardener,
Who kept bringing you baskets of dates,
(And) provided you with lavish dishes every day.
You lifted your eyes to him and went to him:
"My (very) own Išullanu, let us enjoy your vigour,
Let your hand be stretched out to me and touch our vulva!"
(But) Išullanu said to you:
"What do you want from me?
Has my mother not cooked and have I not (already) eaten?
What I would eat (with you) are the bread of obscenities and
    curses.
And [my] covering against the cold (would only be) rushes."
(And) you, when you heard him saying this,
You struck him and tur[ned] him into a toad(?),
You made him live in the place (of his work),
Where . .[ ] he can neither get up or down.
As for me, you will love me and then treat me just like them!.'
                              (VI, 46–79; Bottéro 1992: 126–7)

This passage includes some aetiological tales which are only known from this one text. Ištar's affairs with animals especially are without parallels. Harris (1990: 226, note 39) took them as subtle 'allusions to the boundlessness of Ishtar in the range of her lovers: bird, wild animal, domestic animal, and human'. The only well-known episode is that of Tammuz (Dumuzi), Išullanu brings to mind another gardener, Šukalletuda in the Sumerian tale, who raped the sleeping goddess (Lambert 1991: 140), Gilgameš remonstrates that Ištar is destructive in her affection, unpredictable and inconsistent. Her actions are often those of a witch who turns those that offend her into animals. The implication is that sexuality itself is dangerous and can be the downfall of people who give in to the seductive urgings of Ištar. This Ištar is not the Lady of Heaven but the Harlot, never constant, fickle in her affection, impossible to please, with one disastrous affair after the other. But she is powerful, she can affect her lover's life permanently, decree an evil fate, curse the kill. To give in to her demands is to take an incredible risk. Female sexuality, represented by Ištar, is dangerous, and Gilgameš rejects it and her. Foster (1987: 36) remarked that while the human *harīmtu*, Šamhat, succeeds and indeed makes Enkidu into a man, Ištar's appeal fails. Gilgameš' behaviour contrasts with his previously described sensual indulgence. It signals a change in his character.

Ištar is furious, and now she does assert her divinity. She goes straight to heaven and demands from Anu, here called her father, that he send down the Bull of Heaven to avenge the insults and curses against her. This mythical beast is the personification of divine wrath, and as Anu says, his appearance implies a seven-year period of famine. As he does not wish the country to be punished, he demands that Ištar provides contingency supplies to meet the food shortage, which she promises to do. As she leads the Bull into the centre of Uruk, he kills two hundred with a snort of his nostrils. But Enkidu grabs hold of his tail, and Gilgameš thrusts his sword into the Bull's neck. As a final taunt, Enkidu tears off part of the carcass and throws it at Ištar, who has watched the scene from the city walls, shouting:

> 'If only I could get you,
> I would do the same to you,
> I would hang its entrails from your arms.'
> Then Ištar assembled *kezertus*, *šamhatus* and *harīmtus*,
> To set lamentation over the Bull of Heaven's shoulder.
> (VI, 162–6; Bottéro 1992: 132)

This may well be a reference to some of Ištar's rites. It is interesting that the women classified here all have connections with prostitution, while the women officials enumerated by Ninsun (*ugbatus*, *qadištus*, *kulmašitus*) have more general connections with her mainstream cult (Lambert 1960: 121).

Foster declares that 'this final act consigns her (Ištar's) majesty to the domain of whoredom, where the poet wold have her remain' (Foster 1987: 36). For Foster, Ištar personifies here the unproductive side of sexuality, 'the lowest common level of human experience' (ibid., 22), and its rejection is a necessary step in Gilgameš' 'ascent of knowledge'. I would take issue with his emphasis on reproduction, or its lack. This is one aspect of sexuality that is not relevant to the epic. There is no mention, in the whole composition, of any sexual act resulting in pregnancy. Unlike the Sumerian 'young gods', neither Enkidu nor Gilgameš proves his manhood by impregnating. To introduce the Aristotelian, and in the wake of it, Christian dichotomy between lawful reproductive sex, and sinful (=wasteful) non-reproductive sex is a serious anachronism. By rejecting Ištar, his city-goddess, as if she were an ageing prostitute, Gilgameš turns his back on the city values that she represents. His previous attitude, before the arrival of Enkidu, was to embrace wholeheartedly the 'feminine' character of Sumerian city life. This is clear in the passage of the first tablet where Šamhat praises the city to Enkidu:

'Come, let me take you to the enclosure of Uruk.
Where the young men wear sashes.
Where every day there is a feast,
Where the drums do not cease,
Where voluptuous ones (*[šam]-ḫa-ti*), of unsurpassing beauty,
Full of sex-appeal (*kuzbu*) and pleasure
(See) the great dignitaries lea[ve] their beds at [night].
You Eniku, [you who does not know] how to live,
Let me show you Gilgameš, a man of joy and woe!'

(I, 6–14)

Indeed, he is a man full of charm and sex-appeal (*zu-'u-na ku-uz-ba ka-lu zumrī-šu*, line 17), whose energy is such that he does not sleep by day and night, which fact had wearied his citizens beyond endurance. In fact, Gilgameš identified with the powers of Ištar only too much, and his subsequent development is a corrective to this over-active sensuality.[11] Ištar is not condemned here, she is treated with irony (as in the Agušaya-hymn), but so is Gilgameš, who is always given to quite staggering exaggeration. His rudeness to the goddess after all costs him dearly, as the killing of the Bull of Heaven, added to the previous transgression, the slaying of Humbaba, makes his action irredeemable. Enkidu, by the will of the gods, has to die. Gilgameš is distraught at his loss, deranged by grief and disgusted by the physical reality of death, 'the worm that fell from the nose' of his friend. He decides to leave the city and the boundaries of civilized life altogether, and roams the wilderness dressed only in lion-skins. His aim is to reach the End of the World, where the antediluvian couple, Utnapištim and his wife, dwell for eternity, and to ask them for immortal life. From this perspective, Gilgameš rejected Ištar, the local city-goddess, and also urban civilization. The hubris of concentrating too much on her erotic aspect was his, but it is not as such 'low' or even 'unproductive'. Such simple structuralist opposites are not particularly helpful in this complex literary work. The change of perspective, from the local and particular to the universal, is also signalled by the choice of Gilgameš' personal god, the solar deity Šamaš, who guided his expedition against Humbaba and who intervenes several times in the story. This is unusual for a king of Uruk. In the Sumerian story *Gilgameš, Enkidu and the Netherworld*, the situation is quite different; there is no question about his allegiance to Inanna, the goddess of Uruk. When she finds her sacred *halub* tree invaded by demonic creatures, Gilgameš cuts it down for her; indeed Utu, the sun-god, advises her to go to Gilgameš. A scene like the one described in the sixth tablet of the Ninevite epic would have been unthinkable in the Sumerian ideology. The change in religious attitudes that occurred gradually during the Old Babylonian period resulted in an increased veneration of supranational, cosmic gods, rather than allegiance to local city-deities. Indeed, Šamaš rose to great popularity during this time, and long hymns emphasize his function as a supreme and impartial judge who watches over all people, regardless of their social status and ethnic allegiance. He is also the patron of travellers and of people away from the relative safety of their cities. Both Gilgameš and Enkidu seek the assistance of Šamaš on their journey to Humbaba, and he remains their guiding god for the rest of the epic.

Although the text does not say it in these terms, his conversion to heroic life, and later the quest for eternal life, has a strong element of masculine asceticism. This is a new idea in Mesopotamian thought, one that is more familiar from Indian religion. It may be significant that the only visual representation of Gilgameš and Enkidu occurs on a Mitanni cylinder seal (Lambert 1987b). It is possible that ideologies similar to those that shaped the Vedas were communicated to Mesopotamia via such peoples as the Hurrians. But this is impossible to prove in the absence of suitable written evidence.

Let us now turn to the nature of Gilgameš' relationship with Enkidu. If we regard his previous identification with Sumerian urban values as an expression of 'feminine' sensuality, which he rejects, does his love for Enkidu represent an alternative? The text is ambiguous on this point, and interpretations vary from affirmations of a homosexual, or at least homoerotic context, to its strict denial.[12] The terminology of the text is interesting in this respect. Before Enkidu is 'discovered', Gilgameš has two dreams that he recounts to his mother Ninsun, who interprets them. Both dream accounts use puns that rely on the double meaning of the key-words. In the first dream, he sees a block fall from the night sky, which proves too heavy for him to lift. He tried to move it over but it would not budge:

'The people of Uruk were gathering around it,
The men crowded over it,
The young men massed over (to see it)
And kissed its feet like small children.
For myself, I loved it as a wife.
I put it at your feet,
(And) you treated it equal to me.'

(I, 26–39)

The second dream is very similar, this time the object is an axe, and again Gilgameš is unable to lift it, and feels a strong emotional and sexual attraction towards it. Ninsun interprets the dreams as being favourable:

'A mighty companion will come to you,
Who can save his friend's life,
He will be the most powerful [in the land],
The most vigorous,
His strength like that of the block (fallen) from heaven.'

(I, 21–4)

As Draffkorn-Kilmer has shown, the 'block' (*kiṣru*) sounds very much like *kezru*, the male equivalent of *kezertu*, literally 'the curly haired' one, a male prostitute, while the 'axe' (*ḫaṣṣinnu*) could be taken as a pun on the familiar *assinnu*, the potentially sexless, often passive homosexual. This may be fortuitous, but both dreams emphasize the strong erotic feelings the strange objects arouse in the hero. Both dreams are recounted to Enkidu by Šamhat, after she had made love to him, when she tries to persuade him to accompany her to Uruk. She also tells something about mutual love, although the exact wording can only be guessed at, due to a gap in the text. When the two men eventually meet, Enkidu challenges Gilgameš to a fight, preventing him from entering the house where the wedding-party was going on. Instead they embrace and wrestle, and the whole populace watches the mighty impact of their struggle, which in itself could be seen as a euphemistic description of a different sort of wrestling. The reference to the 'foot' and sudden 'weakness' that gives way to tenderness is quite revealing in that sense, but is still presented in such a way that a 'straight' reading is possible! At any rate, the two are now friends. However, even if there is a physical side to their friendship, Enkidu is no mere passive paramour, their friendship means the sharing of adventures, and they depart together to slay the dreaded Humbaba and kill the Bull of Heaven. The latter exploit marks the high point of their association. They are triumphant, riding together through the streets of Uruk in their chariot, admired by the populace, boastingly asking 'who is the most beautiful among the young men, the most glorious of males?' To which they answer that it was Gilgameš, but also Enkidu, who dared to throw the bull's thigh at Ištar's face. They have a tremendous feast at the palace, and eventually lie down to sleep. From now on, from this climactic celebration, the downfall begins, for this very night Enkidu has an ominous dream that reveals to him his approaching death. Gilgameš is distraught at his friend's demise and 'mourns him bitterly like a wailing woman' (VIII, 4–6), which anticipates the grief of Achilles for Patroclus. He orders a statue to be made of his likeness (as Hadrian would do of Antinous!), and after the funeral rites, the description of which is mainly missing due to gaps in the texts, forsakes his city. For he is now afraid of death and looks for external life. He traverses the Mashu-mountains, where the frightful scorpion-people live, and eventually comes to Siduri, the Alewife who lives by the Sea. She is afraid, for his appearance is wretched and emaciated. But he replies that it could not be otherwise now that his friend

'[Whom I loved so much, who experienced every hardship
   with me,
Enkidu, my friend whom I loved so much]'
                                        (VI, ii, 1–2)

has died. In the Nineveh version she then sends him on his way to
Uršanabi, the ferryman, who takes him across the Waters of Death,
to where Ut-napištim, the Mesopotamian flood-hero, is living.
Gilgameš repeats the same message to them and adds that he is afraid
of having to share the fate of his friend. He does not want to rot like
Enkidu, whom he refused to bury for seven days (X, 16):

'Am I like him? Must I lie down too, never to get up again?'
                                        (X, 13–14)

Ut-napištim rebukes Gilgameš for exaggerating his grief and rebel-
ling against the common fate of mankind. He then tells him the story
of the flood and that his own gift of eternal life was a unique event
granted by the gods. Gilgameš would have to overcome sleep before
he could even begin to find eternal life, a test that the hero fails. But
as a consolation, Ut-napištim gives him a robe that will not soil on
the journey – he also makes Gilgameš cast off his mourning attire
and have a ritual bath – and tells him of a plant that will rejuvenate
the old. The latter he promptly loses to the serpent. Then he returns
once more to Uruk accompanied by Uršanabi, who is barred from
his previous occupation. Here, with Gilgameš back at Uruk, the old
story probably ended. However, the Nineveh version added another
tablet, a modified translation of the Sumerian tale about the
Underworld, which fits rather uneasily into the story as Enkidu is
still alive at the beginning of the tablet. But it contains the famous
dialogue between Gilgameš and the spirit of Enkidu, who tells him
what the Underworld is like and thereby reminds the audience that
Gilgameš' destiny, like that of all mankind, is death. It also prolongs
the relationship with Enkidu beyond death, in a communion of
spirits.

It is the first time in literary history that male friendship became
the dominant theme. There is no Mesopotamian parallel, as in the
Sumerian tales, where their relationship is one of master and servant.
Enkidu's role is complex. It is important to our subject, as love and
erotic attraction play a significant part here. Enkidu, specially
created by the gods, is a match for Gilgameš; he is his equal in
strength and beauty; both are extraordinary characters. Their mutual

and also predestined attraction is the dynamic force that propels the story. Enkidu is the Other for Gilgameš, as Dumuzi was for Inanna. He is associated with the wild country outside the boundaries of the city. He is outside urban hierarchical structures and his eminence is based entirely on physical strength. He is weaned from the wilderness by the courtesan and their lovemaking marks the transition to his life with Gilgameš. It also proves Enkidu's virility. Although the dreams use a language that has possible homosexual undertones, Enkidu is no *assinnu*, no sexless creature. Of Gilgameš we hear that he never sleeps and that his vigour is unabated in spite of constant partying and the services of all the courtesans. He even takes on the virgin brides. In this respect Gilgameš' libido is as boundless as that of a woman; he identifies with Inanna's insatiable appetite. I have remarked before that the goddess personifies the city, and that the city takes on a feminine persona. Here this is extended to Gilgameš, who behaves like the goddess. It would therefore be illogical for him to seek a feminine counterpart; his real Other is Enkidu, the Wild Man, the totally unfeminized one. Enkidu's aggression, his nomad-like puritanism towards women, which comes across clearly in his curse of the courtesan, are proofs of his phallic masculinity. But as his destiny is to complement Gilgameš, it is not directed towards procreation or even sensual fulfilment in the arms of his friend, but towards adventure and the winning of fame. This is a new idea, the heroic ideal which supersedes the common notion that Man can only partake of eternity through his offspring. The hero wins 'a name' by performing extraordinary deeds of valour. This entails a sublimation of erotic energy, a dissociation from the confines of the known world and an exploration of the wilderness. It is also characterized by the confrontation with fear and how to overcome it. At this stage, the heroes become 'one', their differences in opinion, sexual preference and social status blur, and the common quest unites them. Together they transcend sensuality. It is only as an aftermath of the successfully completed adventure, when they return to the city, that their union is broken. For now, after Gilgameš has left the city and become more like Enkidu, slain a mighty demon and thereby proved his manliness, he has become the Other and is in turn desired by Ištar. He rejects her, with somewhat feeble arguments; but essentially because he is not able to fulfil this role, he cannot be her partner as he has become identified with Enkidu. This marks the crucial stage of fundamental confusion and arrogance. Enkidu's reaction, when confronted with the Bull of Heaven, summarizes their joint defiance and insults the goddess further. The gods' plan has clearly misfired, because now the individual vigour of Gilgameš and Enki is doubled by their mutual identification, and there are two bullies instead of one. One last night of triumph, and possibly sexual passion, and then fate intervenes. Enkidu has fulfiled his destiny and is, like Dumuzi, sacrificed so that Gilgameš can continue to fulfil his. This similarity with Inanna's hapless lover is emphasized by the long description of mourning, where Gilgameš weeps like a woman, and actually speaks like the bereaved goddesses in the Lamentations. The extremes of his grief over his friend and lover finally push him to abandon his previous life completely and to become like Enkidu. The quest for eternal life is motivated partly by fear of death and partly by the fact that he now lives out the heroic mode to the full, having internalized Enkidu to such an extent that his friend's physical presence is obsolete. The advice of Siduri in the Old Babylonian version, to seek happiness in marriage, can no longer reach him. It only sounds banal in the circumstances. His love propels him towards eternity, but not his 'seed', his children. However, eternal life eludes him. The final evocation of his friend's spirit foreshadows his own death, where ultimately he will find Enkidu again. It is remarkable that, like the only other love-story of the Ancient Near East, *Nergal and Ereškigal*, the epic locates the fulfilment of love in the Underworld.

GLOSSARY

Akkad (Agade) A city in northern Babylonia, as yet undis-
covered, the capital of the first Mesopotamian
empire, founded by Sargon (2334–2279). As a
geographical term, it denoted the northern
region of the country, as opposed to 'Sumer'
which designated the south.

Akkadian A linguistic term, derived from the ancient
designation *akkadû*, which is used to differentiate the various, related East-Semitic dialects,
such as Old Babyonian, Assyrian, etc., from the
Sumerian language.

Amarna Ancient Egyptian city, founded by Ekhnaton
(1369–1353), where a number of Babylonian
documents were discovered. The so-called
Amarna Period (fourteenth century), is marked
by international communication, conducted in
Babylonian as a *lingua franca*, between Mesopotamia, Syria, the Mitanni kingdom, Anatolia
and Egypt.

Amorites Semitic-speaking, mainly pastoralist tribes living
to the west of Mesopotamia. During the
second millennium, they constituted politically
organized units, and large numbers became
integrated into the native Mesopotamian population. One of their tribal leaders, Hammurabi
(1794–1750), founded the Amorite or First
Babylonian Dynasty.

An (Akkadian Sumerian *an* means 'heaven', as well as 'god'; he
Anû) is the sky-god and supreme patriarch of the

270

	Mesopotamian pantheon; his main sanctuary was at Uruk.
Annunaki	A collective term for deities in a position of authority, serving, for instance, as judges in the Underworld.
Aratta	A city and region somewhere beyond the Zagros mountains in Iran, trading partners with Early Dynastic Sumerian cities.
Aruru	A Babylonian mother-goddess.
Asarluhi	Ancient Sumerian god, a son of Enki; since the Old Babylonian period identified with Marduk, especially in magic texts.
Ashurbanipal	Assyrian king (668–627), whose lasting achievements, other than successful military campaigns, were the building and decoration of his palace in Nineveh, and the foundation of his collection of literary works in the famous 'tablet library', the remains of which are housed in the British Museum.
Assyrian	The Semitic dialects spoken in the region of Assyria, to the north of Mesopotamia, during the second and first millennia.
Atra-hasis	Eponymous hero of an Old Babylonian flood-epic.
Babylon	City on the Euphrates, capital of Babylonia since the eighteenth century. It was famously extended by Nebukadnezzar II and remained a metropolis long after Babylon had ceased to be politically independent, until its destruction by Alexander the Great. The name also refers to the kingdom of southern Mesopotamia, as opposed to Assyria in the North.
Babylonian	The Semitic dialects spoken in southern Mesopotamia during the second and first millennia.
Bel	Literally 'Lord', an appellative and sobriquet of Marduk.
Eanna	Temple in Uruk, cult centre of Inanna and An (later Ištar and Anû).
Ekur	Temple in Nippur, sanctuary of Enlil.
Elam	Country in southern Iran (Susiana), with a close cultural connection with Mesopotamia.

Emesal	Literally 'tongue of woman', a Sumerian dialect characteristic for certain texts, often spoken by female protagonists, also used in Lamentations. The so-called 'main dialect' is known as emegir.
Enheduanna	Daughter of Sargon of Akkad, en-priestess of Nanna-Suen at Ur, reputed author of several literary works in praise of Inanna and editor of a collection of temple hymns.
Enmerkar	Legendary Sumerian king of the First Dynasty of Uruk, hero of two epic poems.
Erra	Babylonian chthonian god, identified with Nergal.
Esagila	Temple in Babylon, main sanctuary of Marduk.
Fara	Modern name for the Sumerian city of Šuruppak, near Nippur, important for its archives of Early Dynastic texts.
Geštinanna	Sumerian goddess, originally part of the Lagaš pantheon. As the sister of Dumuzi, she plays an important role in Sumerian literary texts.
Gudea	Sumerian ruler of Lagaš (2141–2111), immortalized on numerous basalt statues (now mainly in the Louvre); commissioned lengthy inscriptions on cylinder-shaped stones.
Hittites	A people of Indo-European origin who settled in Anatolia. By the middle of the second millennium they had established an empire that comprised Anatolia and northern Syria.
Hurrians	Formed part of the population of northern Mesopotamia. Their language, which does not belong to any known linguistic group, was written in cuneiform, but few texts are preserved. The Hurrians formed a kingdom in the middle of the second millennium (see **Mitanni**).
Isin	Ancient city in Babylonia, seat of a dynasty (c.2017–1924) founded by Išbi-Erra. The rulers of Isin strongly identified with their Sumerian predecessors at Ur.
Kassites	Like the Hurrians, the Kassites spoke a unique language, and were thought to have come from the north-east. A Kassite dynasty ruled Babylonia between 1740 and 1158.

Kiš	City near Babylon, seat of several dynasties during the third millennium; also a well-known scribal centre.
Kullab	A district in the city of Uruk.
Lagaš	Sumerian city of some importance during the third millennium, that yielded a vast amount of texts, from Early Dynastic times down to the beginning of the UrIII period.
Larsa	City in southern Babylon, temporarily seat of a dynasty, though it had to contend with Isin for political supremacy.
Lugalbanda	Legendary king of Uruk, son of Enmerkar, father of Gilgameš; one of the deified heroes of the First Dynasty of Uruk, which in turn is only known from a work of Sumerian literature, the so-called Sumerian King-List (see Jacobsen 1939) which cannot be considered as a historical document.
Maqlû	Title of a collection of incantations and rituals against witchcraft and demonic possession.
Marduk	City-god of Babylon and national deity, especially during the first millennium. The son of Eâ, husband of Ṣarpānîtu. His main temple was the Esagil.
Mari	Ancient city of the middle Euphrates (now in Syrian Tell Hariri) on a crossing of important trade routes, reached greatest political importance at the beginning of the second millennium, when its ruler Zimrilim built an extensive palace. The archives of Mari, written in Akkadian, are an invaluable source on the economy, history and social organization of the period.
Mitanni	Name of the Hurrian kingdom in Northern Syria and Upper Mesopotamia, which from the sixteenth to the fourteenth century was an important political power.
Nabû	Babylonian god, son of Marduk, husband of Tašmetu (or Nanâ, in Babylon). Patron deity of scribes.
Nanâ (Nanaya)	Sumerian goddess with close syncretistic affinities to Inanna. Also worshipped at Uruk and

	identified with the planet Venus. She shares Inanna's association with sexuality and warfare.
Nanna(r)-Suen	Sumerian moon-god, worshipped at Ur; in Akkadian Sîn. His wife is Ningal.
Nanše	Sumerian goddess associated with the pantheon of Lagaš; patroness of fishing and oracular divination.
Nergal	Babylonian god; ruler of the Underworld, his main sanctuary was Cutha.
Nineveh	Assyrian city with a long history of occupation; one of the capital cities of the Assyrian empire; cult centre of Ištar.
Ningal	Sumerian goddess, wife of the moon-god Nanna(r).
Ninhursaga	Sumerian mother-goddess, main sanctuary at the (as yet undiscovered) city of Keš.
Ninisina	Patron goddess of Isin; daughter of An and wife of Pabilsag. Healing goddess. Identified with Inanna in some literary texts of the Isin–Larsa period.
Ninlil	Sumerian goddess, wife of Enlil, worshipped in Nippur.
Ninmah	Sumerian mother-goddess.
Ninšubur	Originally a deity of Lagaš. In mythological texts, always a messenger, or sukkal, as for Inanna in *Inanna's Descent*.
Ninsun	Sumerian goddess, worshipped in Kullab. Associated with cow-herding. Mother of Dumuzi, also mother of Gilgameš in the Epic.
Nintu	Sumerian birth-goddess; often identified with Ninhursaga.
Nippur	City in central Babylonia, where Enlil's main sanctuary, the Ekur, was located. Also important scribal centre, where many Sumerian literary texts were discovered.
Nisaba (Nidaba)	Sumerian goddess, patron deity of scribes.
Nuzi (Modern Yorgan Tepe)	A city in eastern Upper Mesopotamia, centre of an area with a culturally and ethnically mixed population, where an archive, dating from the middle of the second millennium, was discovered.

Pabilsag	Sumerian god, whose cult centre was at Larak.
Sargon of Akkad (2234–2279)	King and founder of the Sargonic dynasty, he exercised control over most of Mesopotamia and neighbouring territories. He became a subject of legendary tales as the exemplary Mesopotamian ruler.
Ṣarpanîtu(m)	Babylonian goddess; consort of Marduk.
Šamaš	Babylonian sun-god; worshipped at Sippar and Larsa.
Sîn	Babylonian moon-god; main temple at Ur, equivalent of Sumerian Nanna-Suen.
Sumer	See Akkad.
Tašmetu(m)	Babylonian goddess, wife of Nabû.
Ur	City in southern Mesopotamia. Much of its wealth derived from trade, mainly by ship, along the Euphrates and the Arabian Gulf. Seat of the moon-god, important scribal centre. Capital of the Third Dynasty of Ur.
UrIII period	Abbreviation for the Third Dynasty of Ur (c.2113–2004), founded by Urnammu. Its most important ruler was Šulgi (2094–2047), subject of numerous royal hymns.
Uruk (modern Warka)	A city in southern Mesopotamia, seat of several dynasties during the third millennium. Important religious and literary centre, associated with An(u) and Inanna.
Ut-napištim	The flood-hero in the Gilgameš-epic.
Utu	Sumerian sun-god; brother of Inanna.
Ziggurat	Mesopotamian religious structure in the form of a pyramid composed of several stages.

NOTES

PREFACE

1   e.g. Pomeroy 1975; Devereux 1982; Detienne 1970; Dover 1978; Halperin 1989; Halperin and Winkler 1989; Winkler 1990; O'Flaherty 1973, also 1980.

INTRODUCTION

1   Especially in his *Address to the German Nobility* of 1520.
2   On writing and the history of decipherment, cf. Driver 1976; and on cuneiform, Walker 1987.
3   As in Wittgenstein's 'marked tools', see Wittgenstein, 1975: No. 15.
4   Although they can be ascribed esoteric value as a hindsight; see for instance the Kabbala or the sacred syllables of Buddhism.
5   Not in the strictest sense, the earliest sources date from the third millennium, but as there is only one short Sumerian text from Fara, and an Akkadian love incantation, I have integrated these in the relevant chapters.

1 THE COSMOLOGICAL ARTICULATION OF SEXUALITY

1   See Cassin, in Bonnefoy 1981 II: 228–35; Bottéro 1985; Brandon 1963.
2   Used by van Dijk 1964: 39ff. and in ibid. 1976: 125–33; also Lambert 1981: 220.
3   Jacobsen 1939.
4   Described, among others, by Thesiger 1964; for a detailed study of Eridu's place in Sumerian texts, see Green 1975.
5   Sumerian ama. tu. an. ki (*TCL* XV, 10) and ama palil ù-tu-dingir-šár-šár-ra-ke₄-ne (= *SEM* 116 I, 16 = *TCL* XVI, 71). According to Lambert 1981: 220, the name Nammu is the Emesal version of Imma, which may derive from *Nin, imma(imma) – 'River' [better 'element water'] that created everything'; Jacobsen 1987a: 155 proposed another, more fanciful etymology: *nin-imma>na, amma>nanma>namma*, and translates 'lady female genitals', an image derived from the impression that

276

NOTES

the dry riverbed evokes in the 'mythopoeic imagination': the 'great gash in the earth', 'the genitals of Mother Earth'.

6   Falkenstein 1953: 134. For the subject of 'Water as universal mother', see Eliade 1959: 191ff.

7   See Lloyd and Safar 1947–8.

8   Kramer, in Schmandt-Besserat 1976: 14.

9   As this particular list consists of en and nin pairs ('Lord' and 'Lady' respectively), the ki refers to 'Earth' and there is no connection with the Eridu deity, Enki. Cf. Green 1975: 110f. – that earliest texts differentiate Enki of Eridu from the Enki and Ninki as Enlil's primeval ancestors.

2 MASCULINE SEXUALITY IN SUMERIAN LITERATURE

1   For the most recent collection of texts concerning the god, see Kramer and Maier 1989; for a general discussion of function and historical development, see Galter 1981; for an analysis of some aspects, Bottéro, in Bonnefoy 1981: II, 102–11. On the relationship to sex, see Cooper 1989: 87–9.

2   They may well have been inserted here in a humorous way. Humour in Sumerian texts is only beginning to be appreciated as our familiarity with the language gradually deepens; see Jacobsen 1987a: 181; Hirsch 1983: 155.

3   A fairly short text, preserved on Sumerian and bilingual tablets from the Old Babylonian period. For an edition of the restored text: Benito 1969: 9–76; English translations: Jacobsen 1987a: 151–66; Kramer and Maier 1989: 31–7. It comprises some 140 lines with considerable gaps, especially towards the end.

4   This is also a theme of a number of later Babylonian compositions, notably Atra-hasis; see Lambert and Millard 1969.

5   Nammu is obviously not regarded as the 'Mother of Everything', the self-procreating matrix of the old Eridu system, in this text.

6   Many of the details are still poorly understood as the text is in bad condition; for an attempt at restoring the missing parts, see Jacobsen's translation (1987a: 155–8).

7   Line 51: 'a-a-tu-da-gin' (Benito 1969: 'like a corporeal father'; Jacobsen 1987a: 'like a father who has produced a son').

8   For foetal description in the physiognomic omen series, see Leichty 1970.

9   The same theme is used in the various flood-traditions, notably in the Atra-hasis epic and the 11th tablet of Gilgameš.

10   The Atra-hasis text also explains the origin of epidemics, fevers, natural catastrophes, etc. that threaten human life as a deliberate measure by the gods to keep mankind in check.

11   The creation of Man is also described in the Babylonian text Atra-hasis, but there the divine substance is the 'blood' of a slain god. The text is also concerned with the theme of reproduction and involves female birth deities, etc., and pays particular attention to the ritualistic aspects of pregnancy and delivery.

277

12 This theory of conception, which is unaware of the biological role of the ovum, remained practically unchallenged until 1877, when the Swiss biologist H. Fiol succeeded in observing the entry of sperm into the ovum of a starfish; see Lewinsohn 1958: 199–204.

3 ENKI AND NINHURSAGA: A MYTH OF MALE LUST?

1 For the Sumerian text and translation into French see Attinger 1985; for translations into English see Jacobsen 1987a: 183–204 and Kramer and Maier 1989: 23–30.

2 Jacobsen (1987a: 181) admitted to becoming aware of the humorous dimension only in his latest treatment of the myth; also Alster 1978: 9, although he singles out the last episode.

3 It was probably Bahrein.

4 The Sumerian is ki. sikil; see Jacobsen 1987a: 183 on the punning use of this name.

5 Cf. *Enki and Ninmah*, where the sleeping Enki had to be woken up by his mother. ná = i/utulu was a well-known euphemism for sexual intercourse, cf. Behrens 1978: 128f.

6 Notably *Enki and Ninmah* and *Inanna and Enki*.

7 She had the epithet ama-kalam-ma ('Mother of the Land') and was a well-known birth-goddess.

8 Note how the different scholars opt for one or the other possible reading of the sign a as 'water' or 'sperm'; the verbal forms are equally ambiguous.

9 Note the use of the verb dun = *harāru*, which means 'to plunge', 'to insert', as well as 'to water'.

10 See Uruhulake of Inanna, Cohen 1988: 123: nin-mu engur-ra giš hu-mu-ra-ni-du$_{11}$ ('My lady, may you have sex in the ENGUR'). For the erotic connotations of marsh and reed-thicket in Sanskrit poetry, see Merwin and Masson 1977: 137.

11 See Cohen 1988: 655, lines 121–2: 'We are joined twosome: indeed we have two heads and four legs, the fifth is thrust into the swamp.'

12 So in the fragment of unknown provenance; the other two texts have three repetitions.

13 lugal-gu$_{10}$ im-diri ga-ri im-diri ga-ri/ giri-ni AŠ-a ^{giš}má-a bi-in-gub/ min-kam-ma pár-rim$_4$-ma nam-mi-in-gub (Attinger 1985: 16) im-diri ga-ri is the equivalent of Akkadian *IM lil-lil*, a not unusual invocation in potency incantations (see Biggs 1967: Nos. 15–17), meaning 'let the wind blow' – a reference to the impeding cloud burst (= orgasm?). For similar metaphors see Alster 1993 'The Fowler and his Wife'.

14 See Ni 9602, obv. col. ii, 23 = Kramer 1963: 505 and Šulgi X, 32–3, Klein 1981: 150.

15 Only in the Louvre fragment.

16 lú, diš: another pun; diš (= no. 1) can be read as giš which sound the same as giš, the penis; Ea's divine number is also giš (= no. 60; cf. Gordon 1959: 257 n. 5).

17 See Biggs 1967, KAR 61, 2 for a ritual where a woman is given apples or pomegranates with a spell put on it; also the epithet of Inanna: 'Who loves "apples" and pomegranates.' Attinger translates 'apricots'. There is as yet no unanimity as to what fruit *hashur* (the Sumerian word usually translated as 'apples') really is; see Lambert 1987: 27–9.

18 This is of course a well-known folk-tale motive, especially the procurement of fruit; see, for instance, the Golden Apples of the Hesperides that Heracles had to bring to Aphrodite, as well as countless fairy-tales.

19 Line 167: úr-ra-ni bí-in-si-si. The fruit symbolize his potency in an obvious manner, as well as serving as a reminder that Enki controls the fertility of gardens with his supply of water.

20 Line 186: a ba-an-tag-tag-ge. For Jacobsen the whole scene is a rape (1987a: 184), involving some rough handling by Enki which makes Uttu cry for help. Alster 1978: 18 and Jacobsen 1987a: 200 opt for the translation 'to remove, take out' the sperm, implying that Ninhursaga intervenes and behaves 'unnaturally' by depriving Uttu of Enki's sperm (so also Kirk 1970: 97). There may be another explanation: the exclamation á is homophonous with a, 'sperm', 'water'. She may well have received a surfeit of the latter, which now covers not only her 'insides' but also her 'outside' and thighs; after all, Enki experienced some delay to his urge. This may well be another instance of a humorous *double entendre* about the watering capacities of Enki: just as the gardens were drenched to produce the fruit, so is Uttu swamped with the precious fluid.

21 This is an exact parallel to Enki's behaviour with the young goddess; 'to know their insides' recalls the biblical euphemism of 'knowing a woman' and it is also an interesting example of the congruence of eating and sexual activity.

22 See Jacobsen 1987a: 203 n. 26 for the puns.

23 See Jacobsen 1987a: 202 for a restoration of this rather fragmentary passage.

4 FROM ADOLESCENCE TO MATURITY: THE MYTH OF ENLIL AND NINLIL

1 This composition of some 150 lines is preserved on several tablets. Transliteration and translation: Behrens 1978; translations: Cooper 1980; Jacobsen 1987a: 167–80.

2 For age-categories, see Landsberger 1968: 55, Falkenstein 1966: 357, and Wilcke 1985: 213ff.

3 As Behrens (1978: 62–5) pointed out, the 'pure canal' is probably one used for purification purposes. The text presents a situation whereby the young women bathe after their first menstruation. We do not know whether this reflects common practice at Nippur at any one period or, indeed, if this was part of a coming-of-age ceremony. We know virtually nothing about the existence of such rites. Some authors, notably Jacobsen and Cooper, take the whole passage as a prohibitive

NOTES

and translate 'do not bathe'. The context of the passage, however, makes it clear that Ninlil will have to purify herself in the canal and that her mother warns her of the dangers of her new state.

4 The Sumerian word is tur, which means both 'small' and 'young'; the latter phrase about the lips being small, and not knowing how to kiss, is probably euphemistic.

5 Behrens (1978: 123) has drawn attention to a passage in the so-called Tummal inscription, which describes a ritual journey by boat 'towards the canebrake of Enlil's Tummal, towards Ninlil's place of joy' where Enlil, together with Ninlil sailed.

6 ki-šà-húl-la, literally 'the place of joy of the heart/womb'.

7 For a detailed discussion of this term, see Behrens: 150–8, also Geller 1990.

8 Behrens 1978: 170f., points out that this gate was known as the ká-gal ú-zah, a ritual gate; literally the 'gate of impurity'.

9 This short phrase (a-lugal-mu an-šè hé-DU a-mu ki-šè hé-DU) has caused some controversy. Kramer (1944b: 44) translated: 'The "water" of my king, let it go toward heaven, let it go toward earth.' Jacobsen (already 1970: 110) proposed quite a different reading; his latest translation (1987a: 176) has: 'May the sperm, my (future) master, go heavenward, and may my sperm go to the Netherworld instead of the sperm, my (future) master, come to the Netherworld.' He considered ki to signify the Underworld and concluded that this passage described the substitution of the doomed sperm (= Suen) by that of a subsequent ejaculation (Nergal, Ninazu and Enbilulu). He saw its aetiological purpose to explain the diverse functions of Enlil's sons – Nergal and Ninazu are chthonian gods.

10 The recurring phrase 'Enlil leaves, Ninlil follows, Nunammir [a title of Enlil's] went, the maid pursued him' might imply that Ninlil recognized Enlil despite his disguise.

11 *Contra* Behrens: 186–7, 253. Cf. Cooper 1989: 89, who credits Enlil with 'multiple rape' but does not consider him as having anything to do with fertility and irrigation.

12 She was eventually assimilated to Ninlil, but was originally an independent grain-goddess of the city Šurrupak.

13 Cf. in animals: giš-nu-zu ('which does not know the penis'); Akkadian equivalents were also used for women, such as *ša la naqpat* ('who is not penetrated'), *la petāt* ('not opened'), *ša zikāram la idû* ('who does not "know" a male'); cf. Finkelstein 1966: 58.

5 PHALLICISM IN SUMERIAN LITERATURE

1 We noticed an undercurrent of a matricentric model in the Eridu cosmology, in which the female alone was responsible for the whole process of childbearing, including conception. This concept was still unknown to the pre-Socratic philosophers, such as Empedocles, who described the woman as being as fertile as the man, if not more so,

'because she was able to produce life spontaneously' (M. Detienne in Bonnefoy 1981, II: 69).

2 *Enlil and Ninlil*, lines 148, 149 and 142; Behrens 1978: 218 and 226f.

3 The technical term is giš- du$_{11}$, literally 'to plant, insert the penis', rendered in Akkadian by *rehû* ('to fertilize'). The term is used specifically to describe the masculine act of penetration. It is interesting that it is practically never used in the love poetry, which is formulated primarily from a feminine perspective.

4 So Jacobsen 1987a: 168; also in *Enki and Ninhursaga* with Uttu!

5 *Enlil and Ninlil*, lines 45, 47, 49, *Enki and Ninhursaga*, lines 99, 120; also Ni 9721 (*Inanna and Šukalletuda*), see Kramer 1949: 401.

6 gaba im-ma-an-tab: *Enki und Ninhursaga*, lines 100, 120: Attinger 1985: 'lui saisit la poitrine', ibid., C 180: gaba šu im-mi-in-dab$_5$; Jacobsen 1987a: 196; 'clasped her to his bosom'; Behrens 1978: 136: 'faßte ihre Brust'.

7 E.g. *Enlil and Ninlil*, line 50: uš^{ki}-a tur-ra-šè im-ma-da-ab-ná-e ('he waited in ... (place) for the little one to lie with her'); 87, 113, 139; ^{d}en-líl-le nam-lú-ká-gal-la-ra da-ga-na ba-ná ('Enlil lay instead of the man of the gate in the chamber'); *Enki and Ninhursaga* 180: úr-ra-na nú-a ('s'étant étendu sur son sein' (Attinger 1985: 23)).

8 Quoted also by Civil, M. and Biggs, R.D., 1966, *RA* 60: 3 who translated: 'Tu n'abusera pas de la fille de l'homme libre, la "cour" le saura toujours.' The 'courtyard' probably refers to the large temple courtyard where legal disputes were being settled.

9 A new edition is currently being prepared by K. Volk (personal communication by J. Black).

6 FEMININITY AND EROTICISM IN SUMERIAN LITERATURE

1 See *CAD* under *ištaru*. There are several occurrences of the name in the Abu Ṣalabikh za-mì hymns and god-lists (see, for instance, Biggs 1974: 46–53 and Nos. 82, 83) and there are different cult places associated with a DINGIR. INANNA: not only Uruk-Kullaba, but also Zababa and other places. It is not certain whether these represent shrines for the same deity or whether they belonged to different local goddesses.

2 So in the so-called *Legend of Sargon*; see Lewis 1980, Falkenstein 1965.

3 'The Venus Tablets of Ammizaduqa'; see Reiner and Pingree 1975. It seems that in the cult at Ur, at least during the UrIII period, Inanna was primarily associated with the moon; see Sauren 1970: 21–2.

4 So already Winckler 1907: 81.

5 Line 41; in line 149 her mother Ningal is also mentioned.

6 ki-ága naturally denotes an emotional tie, such as that between parents and children, husbands and wives, etc. It was also a standard epithet in royal titles ever since the Early Dynastic period (see Seux 1967: 415–18).

7 So Kramer 1969: 579–82 and van Dijk and Hallo 1968: 50. Jacobsen 1987a: 6 prefers to translate it simply as 'the holy one', arguing that 'it designates a class of women the function and character of which is not clear'. It is one of the many Sumerian terms of office, the meaning of

which changed over the centuries. The relationship to the word níg gig. which means 'reserved, set aside (for a deity)', and more generally 'sacred' as opposed to 'profane', is not quite clear (cf. van der Toorn 1985: 43, also Geller 1990: 17); after all, nu often indicates negations, so for instance nu-sík ('orphan'), nu-mu-su ('widow'), in which case it would denote 'not sacred'. However, nu also prefixes other terms of office, such as nu-èš (a priestly term), nu-bànda (a military rank) and nu-ᵍⁱˢkiri₆ ('gardener'), nu-gig would then denote somebody who is 'set aside'. The connotation with sexuality that the term 'Hierodule' implies is based on late lexical lists which equate Akkadian terms for prostitute with this logogram (see *CAD*, *harimtu* and *ištarītu*) and on the fact that other goddesses of love, such as Nanâ and Ninisina, were described as nu-gig, so for instance in *Enki and the World Order*, line 402 and Römer 1965: 129, 15, etc. In one Early Dynastic votive inscription the wife of King Mesannepada is described as a nu-gig – see Sollberger and Kupper 1971: 41f. It is far from certain that this function implied a rank equal to that of the king, as van Dijk and Hallo 1968: 50 assume. To understand nu-gig-an-na to mean 'Hierodule of An' in the sense of an erotic relationship, as well as van Dijk and Hallo's contention that by becoming nin-gal it follows that Inanna became in fact the wife of An (van Dijk and Hallo 1968: 97), is also dubious in the given context, which establishes the offices and functions of the goddess as received by the greatest authority in the pantheon, An. Note that the following lines 3 and 4 also speak of the symbols of the office: nu-gig-an-na suh-kešda-gal-gal-la/aga-zi-dè ki-ága nam-en-na túm-ma (in van Dijk and Hallo's translation: '(you) of all the great ornaments/enamoured of the appropriate tiara, suitable for the high priesthood'. A sexual dimension to the title Nugig is, however, not inappropriate in other texts; we shall discuss this later.

8 So van Dijk and Hallo 1968: 21. The last line is interesting (57): nì-kù-ša-ga-na nam-mu-da-an-búr-re literally means 'What belongs to her holy inside/womb she would not reveal/loosen for him'. Both van Dijk and Hallo 1968 and Kramer 1969 avoid a euphemistic translation. The semantic range of šà that comprise inside/heart/womb is often obscured by the translation; Kramen 1969: 580 writes: 'Who revealed not to him the "holiness" of her heart.'

9 152: kur-gul-gul an-da me-ba-a/nin-mu hi-li gú-è. hi-li means more than just 'beauty' or 'allure' (as Kramer always translates it). It is part of Inanna's me and denotes an irresistible power to attract.

10 See for the former the hymn for Nanše (Heimpel 1981 and Jacobsen 1987a: 125–42) and that for the male deity Hendursanga (Edzard and Wilcke 1976).

11 Sumer and Akkad were referred to as kalam and uri respectively; the sign kur also means 'mountains' and denotes the non-Sumerian foreign lands at the periphery, especially when they are in a state of rebellion or aggression against Mesopotamia. For a somewhat idiosyncratic analysis of this complex term, see Bruschweiler 1988: 9–99.

12 garza =*parṣu*, cf. *CAD* under *parṣu* and Römer 1965: 188.

13 The translation is tentative, but the reference to 'canals and dikes' might

have something to do with purification rites, as in *Enlil and Ninlil*. Note also the contrast between the private sphere, the 'chamber' (ama₅), and 'broad market'!

14 We have as yet no proof that the historical person known as Enheduanna was indeed the author of these works, as the (much later) editions of these texts claim. It is therefore impossible to argue that the female perspective of Enheduanna is responsible for the strong emphasis on Inanna's 'masculine' qualities.

7 THE BRIDAL SONGS

1 Lines 16–24; cf. Sollberger and Kupper 1971: 130. In the Neo-Assyrian royal inscriptions Ištar of the Battle is said to march before the king into combat. On Inanna/Ištar's masculine side see also Groneberg 1985: 44f.

2 E.g. Uruhulake of Inanna, line 133: ama mu-gi₁₇-ib šul-da tuš-a-mên ('Mother, nugig, sitting with young men'; Cohen 1988: 655); in the Lugalbanda epic, Šara is said to be her son (cf. Wilcke 1969).

3 The portrayal of pastoralists in Sumerian literature would merit thorough investigation. Stereotypical descriptions are found in many texts of the nomad 'who knows no grain', and who does not share the aspirations and ideals of the settled agriculturalist. The irrigated fields were used for growing crops, while sheep, goats and cattle were pastured further afield, on less valuable land: either on the steppe during the spring, or on marginal land within the cultivated area. But while there was some appreciable difference of lifestyle between shepherd and farmer, the two were interdependent, and the produce of both was necessary to the general economy. We know from the UrIII texts that some areas specialized in livestock breeding, and I wonder whether Dumuzi's relationship with Badtibira also explains his pastoralist background, as the city was situated towards the periphery of the arable land. Generally on the impact of pastoral nomadism in the early period, see Zarins 1990; for Dumuzi and pastoralism: Heimpel 1972: 291; Jacobsen, 1983, *Journal of the American Oriental Society* 103(1): 195, where he suggests that the arali in which Dumuzi operates, lay between Badtibira and Uruk.

4 See, for instance, Sjöberg 1988: 168–9, a hymn of Inanna's, col. ii, 8–12: 'When I was living in (my) dwelling places, / when I was living in An's dwelling places, / my lover (mu-ú=-[d]a-na-mu), Ušumgalanna, was calling upon me to become his wife, in Badtibira, out of Emuškalama.' Also Sjöberg and Bergmann 1969: 29f., where the temple of Dumuzi in Badtibira is described as the 'house with herbs (lustrous as) lapis-lazuli, strewn upon the shining bed, . . of the holy Inanna'.

5 Lines 5–12; Ušumgalanna (literally 'great dragon of heaven') is a secondary title of Dumuzi's.

6 Lines 13–22; ma-la-mu ('my friend') can be masculine or feminine, as are the verbal forms. The translation 'girlfriend' and 'she' is a convention; the original makes it less of a straightforward lie, and more of a clever

excuse by pretending an innocuous context.

7   Line 49: ú-mu-un-mu úr-kù-ge hé-du₇. The verb du₇ means 'to be fitting, suitable'; úr can be 'lap' generally, or the genital area, of men or women; see *Enki and Ninhursaga* C 179: úr-ra-[n]a nú-a: 'He lay in her lap' (or, as Jacobsen puts it, 'her crotch'). In another erotic context (*CT* 42, No. 4, Kramer 1963: 501, line 20), the goddess is said to call for the 'bed of the sweet lap' (ki-ná úr-zé-ba); similarly BM 23666 = *CT* 58: 18–19: úrzi-le-en-na ('make the lap sweet for me'). The latter context of the word suggests the translation 'intercourse' (or 'embrace', as Jacobsen has it). 'To sweeten the lap' implies orgasmic intercourse for women. See also Römer 1965: 191 for further quotations.

8   Alster points out the *double entendre* of 'to make words' and 'casting a shade', a possible reference to the so-called 'missionary position'. But see also 'eme-ak an-bar an-dùl nu-gá-gá: 'Using the tongue (intercourse?) at noon without having a shade' (is a níg-gig, abomination) to Utu', cf. Geller 1990: 107. See also the Akkadian verb *šudbubu* in the context of love incantations, with the possible meaning 'to make (a woman) agree (to make love)' (Biggs 1967: 71).

9   tuku₄-e-da, here rendered as 'earthquake', comes from the verb tuku₄ = *nâšu*, 'to tremble'. Cf. also KAR 236 *l-lik* IM KUR-e *l[i-nu-šu* ('Let the wind blow, let the mountains quake') in a potency incantation (Biggs 1967: No. 17).

10 On hašhur, see Lambert 1987 and Powell, M., 1987, *Bulletin of Sumerian Agriculture* 3: 153ff.

11 See Lambert 1987a: 31, Jacobsen 1973: 207; also Wilcke 1976: 312. On *kharis*, see Winkler 1990: 77f.

12 Kramer 1963: 493–5; 1969: 72; Jacobsen 1987a: 3–7; Wilcke 1976: 293–7; Alster 1993: 23, 24.

13 Ninegalla ('Lady of the Great House') is a common appellative of Inanna.

14 See, for instance, Römer 1965: 78: (Ninisinna) unú-šuba-a šu hé-em-ma-an-ti nu-gig-an-na hé-em ('Ninisinna hat fürwahr das Gehänge als šuba-Stein in Empfang genommen, ist die Hierodule des Himmels'); Lambert 1987a: 31–3 derives šuba from Akkadian *šubû* 'which in origin was presumably a Sumerian borrowing from the Semitic *šupûm*' ('shining'). In BM 96936 (CT 58) Pabilsag is said to make the šuba-stones and plough with them. The stones in this text are said to come from Magan.

15 For the wedding symbolism in the enthronization of an *entum* in Old Babylonian Emar, see Dietrich 1989.

16 Wilcke 1967–8: 157 quotes the Old Akkadian text BIN VIII 164: '(… Urgal swore an oath on the King's name: "Ningula may marry the husband of her heart (= dam. šà-ga-na-ke₄). I shall not restrain her."' Interestingly, the Akadian equivalent of this phrase, *mutu libbiša ihassi*, is used several times in the Code of Hammurabi, but there it does not apply to the first marriage, but to remarriage following divorce (§ 137), seduction by the father-in-law (§ 156), or widowhood.

8 INANNA AND HER BROTHER

1 Note that in the famous Iddin-Dagan hymn to Inanna-Dilibad, the sheet for the bed is called túg-nì-bàra šà-húl-la (literally: 'the outer sheet of inside pleasure'), rendered by Reisman (1973: 191) as 'the cover which rejoices the heart'.

2 Alster (1985: 151) interprets this text as a dialogue between Inanna and her lover (Dumuzi).

3 Translation Jacobsen 1987a: 18; he also notes that the name Baba may be used as a 'pet-name' for Inanna, although he acknowledges that the song may have been taken from the cult of Baba, the city-goddess of Lagaš. In fact, no protagonists are named as such, only the colophon declares it to be a balbal song of Inanna's, which does not imply that it is necessarily about Inanna. At least by the Old Babylonian period, Baba was a common pet-name (see B. Landsberger, 'Zum "Silbenalphabet B"', in Çiğ, M., Kizilyay, H., 1959, *Zwei altbabylonische Schulbücher aus Nippur* (Ankara)): 102, 103.

4 An exception is UM 29-16-37, but there all members of the family on both sides, Inanna's and Dumuzi's, are enumerated and said to be equal to each other with the phrase 'My father is your father too' .. 'my mother is your mother too'; see Kramer 1963: 493–5; Jacobsen 1987a: 3–7.

5 So, for instance, in UM 29-16-8, which Jacobsen (1973: 199–212) reads as a dialogue between Geštinanna and Dumuzi and which Kramer (1963: 509–10) takes to be a dialogue between Inanna and Dumuzi.

6 An interesting parallel for the brother–sister mourning with erotic overtones is the little poem by the prē- or early Islamic poetess Safijja of Bahila, translated by the German Romantic poet Friedrich Rückert, 'Wir waren gleich zwei Stämmen aus einer Wurzel Grund', in Gundert, Schimmel and Schubrig 1965: 42.

9 INANNA REJOICING IN HER VULVA

1 Cf. *VAT* 8381 3–4; numun-zi-nam-lú-u$_x$-[ka] sà-ga ba-ni-in-ri e$_4$ (= A) -šà-ga-ri-a ka-kéš-du lú-ra dumu sum$_{šu}$-mu ('she (Nintur) had the rightful human seed ejaculated in (her) womb, semen ejaculated in her womb, contracted for (by marriage), giving the man a child'); for further quotes see Behrens 1978: 133ff.

2 Poems of self-praise were a feature of Sumerian culture, as in many traditional societies, cf. Black 1983–4: 110.

3 The gala, written UŠ. KU (Akkadian *kalû*), formed part of Inanna's temple personnel with special competence in the singing of elegies and lamentations. See chapter 14.

4 The 'duck-field', line 24 a-šà uz^{mušen} ne-en uz^{mušen} ha(?) .., is explained by Jacobsen 1970: 45 as follows: '(it is) a stubble field on which ducks have been put to be fattened, black hairs dotting it like ducks against the light dun soil'.

5   Note also Jacobsen's suggestion that it may form one proverb with the next two lines of the text, which seem to mention a sanitary towel; if one accepts this interpretation the woman supports her assertion by the fact that she still has periods (quoted by Lambert 1960: 248).

6   There are some proverbs where some 'food' is mentioned in connection with becoming 'ú-zug'; Gordon 1959: No. 1, 40, 1, 41, p. 60. But it is not clear whether this could refer to oral sex.

7   A much later, Arabic erotological work, supposedly from the twelfth century, defends the practice of cunnilingus: 'What fools are those who say that the vulva should not be touched and caressed by the lips of the man. Those unfortunates who miss this blessed caress of the man to the woman miss *touching and smelling and tasting the sweetest nectar.* They miss bestowing a gesture so exquisite and fine, which is the most loving gesture that a man can bestow on his beloved woman before entering her and fulfiling her' (my italics) (el Khalidi 1970: 38).

10 'MY CONSORT, MAID INANNA, LADY, VOLUPTUOUSNESS OF HEAVEN AND EARTH'

1   Both van Dijk 1954 and Kramer 1967a took this passage to be anticipatory and translated it in the *futurum exactum.* Klein 1981: 126 argued in favour of a past tense, on the assumption that the enclitic copula gim, which links the subordinate clauses in each statement, has a temporal function. There is still considerable disagreement on the subject of 'tenses' in Sumerian.

2   Römer 1965: 142 has an alternative version: 'Der König geht stolz erhobenen Hauptes zum heiligen Schoß, geht erhobeben Hauptes zum Schoß Inannas, Amaušumgalanna liegt bei ihr, kost getreulich ihren Schoß. Nachdem die Herrin mit (ihrem) heiligen Schoß das Lager voll ausgekostet, berät sie sich an der Lagerstätte mit ihm (und spricht(?): "Für Iddin-Dagan bin ich fürwahr ..."' Note that 'proudly' is literally 'with head up', often used in the sense of 'proud' but here surely also euphemistically for an erection. Römer's version brings out the emphasis on the satisfying performance of the king.

3   Kienast 1990 listed the passages in which the king describes himself as dam and proved that this title was only in use for a limited period from Amar-Suen of Ur until Sînmāgir of Isin (ibid.: 100). If we add Šulgi, who used the equivalent term *nitadam* for Inanna, this gives us a time span of some 220 years (accession of Šulgi c. 2046, end of Sînmāgir's reign 1818).

4   The writing of the king's name with the sign DINGIR, which is usually reserved for divine beings, was already introduced by kings of the Sargonic period. It does not represent deification as such.

5   From Šuruppak, see Biggs, 1966: 80, No. 50.

6   The highest deity of the Elamite pantheon during the third millennium was Pinenkir, a type of mother-goddess; see Hinz 1972: 42f.

7   Urnammu is quoted as having been en of Uruk, see Wilcke 1974: XIX R. I. A. (Paris), p. 185; see also Renger, *Zeitschrift für Assyriologie, NF*

24: 114–34 on the office of the en.

8   Berlin 1979: 58–9, lines 275–6: 'You are the beloved lord (=en) of Inanna; you alone are exalted;/Inanna has truly chosen you for her holy lap; you are beloved.'

11 'WORDS OF SEDUCTION': COURTLY LOVE POETRY

1   Šulgi B, line 14: dub ki-en-gi-ki-uri-ka nam-dub-sar-ra mi-in-zu, and line 156: nam-nar-ra gú-mu ha-ba-sum (Castellino 1972).

2   Ibid., line 306–15, pp. 62–6: 'My favorite songs, as (product of) a skilled master, (written) for the lasting of my name/may be proclaimed and engender brilliant renown./Down south, in Ur, in the holy place, they are sung,/in the "House of Learning" of Nidaba, the splendour, there are my songs!/Up north, in Nippur, they are entered into the "Large Place"/in order that my homage should be established in the Ekur./The scribe will go and take them in hand,/the singer will go and perform them./In the tablet houses they will last, things never to fail.'

3   For this title see Renger 1967: 149–79; also Jacobsen 1987b and the discussion here on p. 147f.

4   Babylonian law-codes tried to circumscribe polygamy. A man was only allowed to marry another wife if the first one was unable to bear children, see Driver and Miles 1955; for actual contracts stipulating that the marriage is to be monogamous, or that the woman marrying must not be treated as a concubine, see Paradise 1987.

5   Jacobsen 1987b: 60, n. 14. Note, however, that ^{giš}sa-bí-tum is a musical instrument, quoted in the context of the king's rite in Šulgi B, line 164: ^{giš}al-gar ^{giš} sa-bí-tum in-di lugal-la, see Castellino 1972: 165 for comments. Could the title *sabitum* in this text be a punning reference to such musical accompaniment?

6   Jacobsen 1987b: 60 n. 15 points out that the name Kubātum might also be read as Dab₅-ba-tum (following Falkenstein 1947). In which case the 'imagery taken from the loom and weaving may well have been prompted by the similarities of the name Dabbatum to the word da-ba-tum, a term for a special kind of cloth' (Jacobsen 1987b: 60 n. 15). But note also the use of the term 'my cloth of pleasure' (túg am-sa₆-ga-mu), which could also be an allusion to 'bridal' sheets, as in *SRT* 1, line 179: túg- nì-bàra šà-húl-la.

7   This paraphrases Alster 1985: 141. He translates lines 13–14 as 'Your gift is full of attractiveness, may it [catch] your eyes.'

8   Jacobsen 1987b: 59; Alster proposes 'a group of women' speaking in lines 19ff.

9   Cf. Inanna's self-laudatory hymn, Falkenstein 1953: 67; also Zimmern, *S.K.A.Z.* II, 199 III, 8–41 (all in Emesal). For Baba (or Bau), see also *UMBS* X, 14 in Römer 1965: 263–65; where she is said to have promoted Išme-Dagan's choice as king. Her connection with fertility is also accentuated: 'her sanctuary lets the seed go out' (line 19). For Baba as a sobriquet for Inanna, see also *UM* 29-16-8 and *SRT* 5.

NOTES

10 Jacobsen 1987b: 59, note 6 takes this to refer not to a status but to purification after childbirth.

11 Alster 1993: 16, note 9; see also Castellino 1972: 97 on the a-la, 'the praise, or the eulogy for Šulgi, detailing the blessings heaped upon him' – maybe this was any song addressing and eulogizing the king, praising any aspect of his life and personality and could therefore have been sung by a woman.

12 See also the text *UM* 29-16-37, referred to as the 'Lovers' Quarrel' by Jacobsen, especially line 23: inim bí-in-eš-a inim hi-li eš-àm (Jacobsen 1987a: 5: 'What they would be talking over was a matter for delight'); but see also Wilcke's translation (1976: 296): 'Die Wörter die sie gesprochen haben – die Wörter der Wonne sind dreißig', although he assumed that the reference to the number 30 originates from an ancient editor who counted the words (312). Alster 1993: 24, note 50 proposed that it 'may be an allusion to the rigid conventions to which an orally performed contest had to conform, like those of the German Meistersinger'.

13 There are stylistic echoes of the royal hymns which also include speeches by different voices.

14 *PBS* XII, translation follows Jacobsen 1987a: 91–92, except for lines 12–13 where he has 'whose words are as sweet as her vulva'; for a different translation, see Alster 1985: 135.

15 The pectoral worn by Inanna on her *Descent to the Netherworld*, line 22: 'the pectorals (named) "O man, come hither, come hither!"'; see also the reference there to the phrase in line 24, here said of kohl: 'O may he come, may he come' (Jacobsen 1987a: 207).

16 Atkins 1978: 178, 222, where he also points out that 'flowers and fruit are not so much symbolic of sex as sex itself'; see also Lambert 1987a: 27–9.

17 For the use of ama as the whole in relation to parts, cf. *Hh* III, 26–8 and 30 (Landsberger, B., 1957, *MSL* V: 95.

18 Winkler 1990: 183f. on Sappho's 'Like the sweet-apple ripening to red on the topmost branch, on the very tip of the topmost branch, and the apple pickers have overlooked it – no, they haven't overlooked it but they could not reach it' as a feminine symbolism.

19 M. Détienne in Bonnefoy 1981 II: 69 explains that the medicinal virtue of the plant was thought to encourage lactation and menstruation, while the heart of the lettuce, full of the white juices which resemble seminal fluid, was forbidden to them.

20 Atkins 1978: 188 thought that sweetness as a sex metaphor was 'a special contribution of the Arabs'; see there also the use of the word *zachary* ('sugar-stick') for the penis, also a pun on *zakar*, 'male'.

21 The adoption of the traditional trappings of high-class status is still a common feature in weddings in our societies, from the hired Rolls Royce to Moss Bros tails. In the modern Middle East, boys are dressed either as princes, complete with sword and satin cape, or as army officers in miniature uniform.

22 The text was first translated by Kramer, S.N., 1957, *Zeitschrift für Assyriologie 52*: 85f. and also in Kramer 1969: 104–6. Alster's new

version is to appear in *Zeitschrift für Assyriologie* 82. I was able to use a draft of his translation.

23 làl ama-ugu-na mu (so Alster *Zeitschrift für Assyriologie* 82). Jacobsen 1987b has ka-làl-ama-na-mu and freely translates this as 'mother's little honey-bun', ka-làl ('honey-mouth') is quoted in line 3. Both metaphors are hard to fathom; they could either be very general and banal appellatives, as Jacobsen suggests, or have a specifically erotic meaning.

24 Sefati 1990 and Jacobsen 1987b: 62 read 'you are a princess'. Alster points out that dumu-lugal is usually used for (male) princes. The term itself does not differentiate gender.

25 For women and gardens elsewhere, see Falkenstein 1964: 121: 'The maid, where she sits, it is a garden that carries delight', (Falkenstein 1964). Also said of Bau in Gudea's Cylinder B V 15: '(she) is a charming garden bearing fruit' (quoted by Sefati 1990: 61).

12 THE RITES OF DIVINE LOVE

1 Gudea, Cyl, B XVI, 19–XVII, 2. The expression ná =*itulu* is often used euphemistically for sexual intercourse, cf. Behrens 1978: 128.

2 Note also Jestin, 1949, 'Un rite sumérien de fécondité', *Archiv Orientalní* 17: 333–9.

3 Matsushima 1987: 131–75 includes data from the Late Babylonian and Persian period; mentioning the bed of Šamaš, the linen drapes for it, a bedroom of Aya, the wife of the sun-god, etc.

4 Matsushima 1987: 140: 'maybe a wooden tray'.

5 A phrase denoting that the statue is moved off its pedestal, *AhW* 842b.

6 Note the etymological connection between *hašādu-hadašu-kadašu*; *hadaššu* glossed *hašašu* 'to rejoice'; maybe related also to Arabic *hašada* ('assemble together')? (personal communication by Jeremy Black).

13 *L'AMOUR LIBRE* OR SACRED PROSTITUTION

1 It is likely that in these texts lukur is the short form of the full title lukur-kaskal-la.

2 Proto Lu 262–4, *MSL* 12: 2.

3 Malku I 131, 133, quoted by Lambert 1991: 138.

4 Arnaud 1973: 183 reminds us that women played an important role in economic and religious life in the third millennium and at the beginning of the second millennium, but that this situation changed; ibid., 115: 'la tradition savante et littéraire vehicula ensuite cet état de fait, l'importance cultuelle des femmes, dans une societé, à partir du 16ième siècle, qui ne connaissaient plus que dans les besognes vulgaires ou comme prostituées, autour des temples et même sur leurs parvis. Les scribes ont donc cherché à une éxplication en les chargeant alors du seul rôle culturel qu'ils pouvaient imaginer'; cf. also Renger 1967; Goodnick-Westenholz 1990: 516ff.; and Lambert 1991: 135–41.

5 A. Falkenstein, 1964: *Zeitschrift für Assyriologie* 118; see there also the

Old Babylonian PN: nin-éš-dam-(me)-ki-ága ('Lady who loves the tavern').

6 See W. H. P. Römer, *Orientalia, Nova Seria* 38: 110; van Dijk and Hallo 1968: 74.

7 Lambert 1960: 230, 235, 247ff., etc.; Gordon 1959: 116, 125, 129, 143, etc.; for riddles see Gordon, E. I., 1960, 'A new look at the wisdom of Sumer and Akkad', *Bibliotheca Orientalis* 17: 124 and 142; Biggs, R. D., 1973, 'Pre-Sargonic Riddles from Lagash', *Journal of Near Eastern Studies* 32, 26–33; and Alster, B., 1976, 'A Sumerian Riddle Collection', *Journal of Near Eastern Studies* 35: 263ff.; in the latter collection there are some riddles whose solution is said to be 'a vulva', 'a shrivelled penis' and 'lettuce'.

14 LIMINAL SEXUALITY: EUNUCHS, HOMOSEXUALS AND THE COMMON PROSTITUTE

1 Line 49: kuš-nam-dingir-ra kuš-bi-a mu-un-gál. Römer 1965 translates: 'liessen eine gottähnliche Körperlichkeit in ihrem Körper sein'. Reisman 1973 refuted this interpretation and thought that kuš-nam-dingir-ra was an article of clothing: 'they place on their bodies the cloak of divinity'; this is doubtful, especially as the verb gál does not mean 'to place' but 'to be'.

2 For *šugitum* as a type of 'priestess', see Römer 1965: 165.

3 Munroe, R. L., Whiting, J. W. M. and Hally, D., 1969, 'Institutionalized male Transvestism and Sex Disorders', *American Anthropologist* 71: 87–91. The authors investigated the influence of strong sex-role differentiation on the incidence of transvestism and found that 'Societies that tolerate the sharing of roles by the two sexes will also tolerate a role that enables a man to take over the functions of the female sex' and 'that societies that make minimum use of sex as a discriminating factor in prescribing behaviour and membership will have institutionalized male transvestism'. Too few ethno-historical data are available to check this hypothesis with respect to Mesopotamia. However, in view of the comparative equality between the sexes, at least in some sectors of Sumerian society, the report does not contradict the available evidence.

4 *CAD* AII *assinnu* refutes the notion that he was either a eunuch or a homosexual, but later volumes do translate the term as 'eunuch'. For the rather eccentric etymological explanation of kur-garra and pilpili as 'jemand der ein Häuflein macht' and '(jemand) der immer Pipi macht'; see Edzard 1990: 121.

5 Malku I *JAOS* 83, 1963, 82–7, 129–35; Proto-lu 262–4 and lú =sa 194–7 (*MSL* 12).

6 Cf. *ana ittišu*, *MSL* 1 96, 7; II 23–23e: nam-kar-kid-da-ni tillá-ta ba-an-da-íl-la ('as a prostitute he took her from a public place'), implying that the man was aware of her professional activities.

7 Protodiri, quoted by Falkenstein 1966: 362: Kar-kid =[wa]-ṣi-tum (lit, 'one who goes out', rendered by Falkenstein as 'Tramp')/ =[na]-a-

ak-tum '(one who copulates')/*[ha]-r-im-tum* ('prostitute').

8 For translations see Dalley 1989, Bottéro 1992; see also Foster 1987: 21–42 and Harris 1990: 218–30.

9 E.g. Maqlû, see Meier 1937; see also S. Rollin, 'Women and witchcraft in Ancient Assyria', in Cameron and Kuhrt 1983: 37–40.

16 BALLADS, HYMNS AND DIALOGUES: AKKADIAN LOVE POETRY

1 ᵈnin-an-na *šar-ra-tu₄ ša-ma-a-me*, so in *Šarrat Nippuri* III, 53; see Lambert 1982: 211.

2 Lambert 1987: 29 translated these lines as 'She/Goddess of joy, clothed with love – Adorned with fruit, cosmetics and sex-appeal'. He points out that *inbu* ('fruit') may stand here for the decoration of Ištar's statue with golden fruit-shaped jewellery.

3 Cf. Hirsch 1982: 'das Lachen der Liebe erfüllt sich an ihrer Erscheinung'.

4 Cf. also Gilg. VI, line 8 where Ištar asks to 'give me your fruit', which refers here to his sexual favour and vigour.

5 Cf. *K* 4355 10–13: *šá ina su-un mu-ti-šá ku-uz-ba la il-pu-tu*, 'who in the lap/embrace of her husband did not touch the voluptuousness' or, as Landsberger 1968: 45 put it, 'deren Körperfülle im ehelichen Beilager niemand berührt hat'.

6 Cf. *CAD* under *lalû*, *kuzbu* and *inbu* for references.

7 Cf. the *OB* god-lists, de Genouillac, *Revenue Assyriologique* 1923 20: 89ff. and *Revue Assyriologique* 1928 25: 133ff.

8 Cf. also Hruška 1969. The unclear references to Ištar's spouse in the 'Queen of Nippur' hymn – she seems to be assigned a rather obscure god called Amazilla – is discussed by Lambert 1982: 179.

9 See, for example, the prologue and epilogue of Hamurabi's law-code: Driver and Miles 1955: 7–13 and 95–107.

10 For the dual gender of Nanâ, see *K* 3933, lines 3–4: *i[ina]* UNUGᵏⁱ *ha-ri-ma-ku ina*ᵘʳᵘ *Da-du-ni tu-le-ia kab-bu-te/[ina] Bābili zi-iq-na zaq-[na-ku]* (Variant: *zik-ra-ku*) *a-na-ku-ma* ᵈ*Na-na-a* 'I am a hierodule in Babylon. I have heavy breasts in Daduni/I have a beard (Variant: 'a male') in Babylon, still I am Nanâ' (Reiner 1974: 221ff.).

11 E.g. Römer 1965: 77–82 (the Hymn to Ninisinna by Išbi-Erra), to Bau, (Ibid.: 236–65) and to Inanna (Ibid.: 266–78), both by Išme-Dagan.

12 Line 14: . . . *ku-uz-bi an-nu-ú ti-bi lu-ur-ta-a-ma; tebû* means 'to get up'. But in a sexual context, especially in potency incantations (Biggs 1967: 9) it means 'to have an erection', such a direct request in the imperative is unlikely to have been voiced as such – 'get it up' – hence Lambert's restrained translation, which fits the rather flowery tone better.

13 For the virtual identification of Nanâ with Ištar, see ABRT 1, 54, quoted by Livingstone 1989: 13–15.

14 New translation of these lines by Lambert 1987a: 35.

15 *ši mu-na-ti-ma*. Goodnick-Westenholz opts for 'morning of slumber'; her alternative suggestion is to derive the word from *menû* ('to love'), which might be more suitable here.

16 For Inanna at the sheep-stall see Hallo, *Bibliotheca Orientalis* 1966: 23, 5/6: 245, E I and II (also Römer 1965: 21f.). The erotic nature of this text has not been detected as far as I am aware. Römer, who incorporated the text in his edition of royal hymns, since line 34 of a variant refers to Išme-Dagan, admits that 'die kultische Funktion mir unklar bleibt'. Hallo saw it as a further proof for the identification of the king with Dumuzi (*op. cit.*, p. 244). Although there are general references to the fertility of the herds later in the text (especially II, 25–33), the choice of Inanna and Dumuzi (rather than Nannar, who is more often associated with flourishing herds) suggests an additional level of meaning, which is decidedly sexual; see especially ᵈinanna šakìr-e gù hé-em-me/(5) ᵈᵘᵍšakìr nita-dam zu gù hé-em-me/(6) ᵈᵘᵍšakìr ᵈdumu-z[i] gù hé-em-me (etc.), translated as 'Inanna, may you call to the (butter)-churn!/To the churn may your husband call / To the churn may Dumuzi call' and (9) búr-ru ᵈᵘᵍšakìr g[a]-mu-ra-an-tug-àm / (10) ᵈinanna ur₆-re ga-mu-u₈-húl-l[e] ('Let me be the one who gets the churning of the churn for you / let me make the "lap" (Hallo "reins") glad'). This is one of the few texts where there seems to be a definite connection between sexual activity and fertility.

17 I do not agree with Matsushima (1987: 148, 162) that this should be equated with the 'tablets of destiny'. After all, Nabû was the god of scribes and the lapis-lazuli tablet is a traditional emblem of scribal deities. It is the most precious object he can think of to compare her with, and there may also be an indirect allusion to the well-known lapis-lazuli, lozenge-shaped vulvas dedicated to Ištar.

17 LOVE MAGIC AND POTENCY INCANTATIONS

1 For Greek parallels see Winkler's 'The Constraints of Desire: Erotic Magical Spells' (Winkler 1990: 71–100).

2 BM 96569; see Alster's partial translation in Alster and Geller 1990: 11.

3 Line 7: ki-sikil dúr-an-ni kiri₆-hašhur-a ul-gùr-ru-àm; cf. *CBS* 8530, quoted by Alster 1993: No. 2, where we have GAM-emu 1½ gín-àm; 'When you bow down it is 1½ shekel', dúr-a-ni could also mean 'her buttocks'; maybe the three lines also, euphemistically or ambiguously, refer to different positions in lovemaking; *a tergo*, and lying down – can we possibly take sag-aka ('to make head') as a reference to fellatio? For 'casting a shade' as referring to the 'man on top of the woman', see Alster's remarks (1993: note 44); for ul-gùr-ru ('who carries lust, attractiveness (delight)' see Sefati 1990: 60.

4 Cf. the almost identical phrase in the Assyrian poem *TIM* 954, line 11: Ṣil kan-ni ša GIŠ, Ll pu-zar ᵈNa-bi-um-a-a mi-lul-la, 'The shade of a spring of juniper is shelter for Nabû and my 'games'' (Livingstone 1989: 35).

5 See Lambert 1987a: 37.

6 See Biggs 1967: 35, No. 15, line 15; *i-šá-ri lu SA-an sa-am-mi-e*, 'let my penis be a (taut) harp string'.

7 VAT 7847 + AO 6448 Rev. C, Seleucid tablet; see Weidner, F., 1967, 'Gestirnsdarstellungen auf babylonischen Tafeln', *Sitzungsberichte der Österreichischen Akademie der Wissenschaften, Phil.hist.Klasse* 254, 2 (Graz, Wien, Köln, 1967), p. 32; see also BM 34572, p. 37.

8 Cf. the Sumerian text of Dumuzi and Geštinnana in the sheep-fold; *CT* 15, 28–9, (Kramer, S.N., 1975, *Journal of Ancient Near Eastern Societies* 5: 243–53).

9 *KAR* 70, rev. 25–30 and *BM* 4691, 1–5, Biggs 1967: 25 and 41; but see his alternative translation of lines 28–30 *šá* NN A NN GIŠ-*šú lu-u* GIŠ, PA *mar-te-em-ma/li-duk* KÀ *šu-bur-ri šá an-na-ni-tu-ú-a/la i-šab-ba-a la-la-a-šá*: 'May the penis of NN son of NN be a stick of *martû*-wood, may it hit the anus of the woman NN whose desire is not satisfied.'

10 For the theory that 'societies with the greatest amount of sexual anxiety should develop love magic most exensively as an anxiety-reducing mechanism' see Shirley, R.W., and Romney, A.K., 'Love Magic and Socialization Anxiety', *American Anthropologist* 64: 1028–31.

11 I do not know of any references to intercourse between humans and animals from Mesopotamian sources. Hittite law, on the other hand, provided fairly detailed regulations for bestiality; see Friedrich, J., 1959, *Die Hethitischen Gesetze* (Leiden). Intercourse with mares, interestingly, was not a punishable offence.

12 Oberhuber 1972: 92 published the photograph of a tablet that has a couple embracing on one side and the sign ZI ('rise, have an erection') all over the reverse.

18 PROBLEMATIC ASPECTS OF SEXUALITY: SIN AND POLLUTION

1 Cf. SK 26, 27, 45; Jacobsen 1987a: 61–84; Kramer, S.N., 1982, 'A Sumerian Prototype of the Mother Dolorosa', *Eretz Israel* 16: 141–6. Cf. also Holst-Warhaft, G., 1992, *Dangerous Voices. Women's Laments in Greek Literature* (London, New York).

2 Cf. Kutscher 1990: 44. He also quotes Chwolson, D., orig, 1856, *Die Ssabier und der Ssabismus* (St. Petersburg) on the medieval survival of the Ta'uz =Dumuzi mourning among the Sabean women of Harran.

3 Falkenstein, A., 1955, *Comptes rendues de la Rencontre Assyriologique* III: 57.

4 Akkadian gloss: line 217; *i-ša-ra r[e-h]a il-ta-mad*, 'she has experienced the inseminating penis', so Cohen; Jacobsen 1987a: 33: 'came to know too the member plied there'; line 218: *na-šá-q[am il-ta-mad*; Jacobsen: 'learned too to suck the male member'. The Sumerian text has mu (Emesal for ĝiš) as the subject of both parallel sentences. Cf. Jacobsen, 1989: 75: 'sub basic meaning 'to suck' =*enēqu. .*', quotes the passage as reference to oral sex. But I cannot see anything that warrants this conclusion here. Instead of the usual ne we have an unexplained še, but this does not strengthen the argument for the verb being applied

specifically to mu, 'penis'. There is more of a case for fellatio in *Inanna and Enki*, I 35–6 giš-du$_{11}$-du$_{11}$ giš-[x-s]u-ub, some of the me that Inanna took from Eridu to Uruk. Cohen's translation 'she experienced phallatio' does not make grammatical sense either; if one takes *iltamad* to have a passive meaning then surely cunnilingus would be more suitable!

5 Line 215; ^{giš}gu-za-[kú-ga] dúr-mar-ra-àm 216 mu-rú-[kù-g]a ki-nú ba-nú, the Akkadian only has *ina ú-šib/ina it-ta-til*; cf. Volk 1989: 65 note 24 for his quote of SBH 39, Obv. 11–14; 'An jenen reinen Throne setzte sich der Feind, auf jenem Bett lag der Feind.'

6 For kù =*ellu*, see *CAD* E. The semantic relationship between kù, ZAG (=kù, dingir), níg-gig, níg-hul and nam-tag has to my knowledge not been systematically studied. Geller's review article (1991) took account of anthropological studies on the subject of purity and taboo, but he did not discuss kù, I suspect that there may be a gradient scale of relative purity behind these terms which the habitual translations 'pure', 'holy', etc. fail to convey. It is important to differentiate between an inherent quality of an object, a building, deity, etc. and the effect this state has if it comes into contact with human beings.

7 Geller 1991: 108; cf. on *arnu*: Reiner, E., 1970, *Šurpu*, (=*Archiv für Orientforschung, Beiheft 11*) (Osnabrück), esp. Tablet 11 and the *lipšur*-litanies: Reiner, E., 1956, *Journal of Near Eastern Studies* 15: 136–7.

8 Langdon 1913: 77 also pointed out that the text just mentions the punishment of a servant.

9 Although we also know from the omen texts that this did not necessarily imply chastity (see below).

10 Cf. *MSL* 12: 32–9.

11 I wonder whether the well-known ritual of the *šar puhi*, the 'substitute king' who was killed after the stipulated time, can be functionally related to this episode. Cf. Labat, R., 1945, 'Le sort des substituts royaux en Assyrie au temps des Sargonids', *Revue Assyriologique* 40: 123–42.

12 See Nötscher, F., *Orientalia 31*.

13 *CT* 39, 44f.; only the cuneiform text transcription is available.

14 Cf. *CAD* AII; 473.

15 Quoted by Oberhuber 1972: 99, there also the following quotes. Cf. Leviticus XV, 2–18 on the unclean properties of male sperm; in comparison the Mesopotamian text is much less strict on this issue. Note there also the functional parallelism with women's menstrual impurity: 16–33.

16 Cf. *CAD sub entu*.

19 WITCHES, DEMONS AND THE AMBIVALENCE OF LOVE

1 See also Abusch 1987 and 1991: 233–54.

2 Translation of lines 90–1 follows *CAD sub kadiddibu*.

NOTES

3   I 99:. .*ni-iš lib-bi-ia, i₅-ba-tu* ('meine Mannesskraft wegnahmen'
    (Meier 1967)). The technical term is *niš libbi*, a euphemism which
    literally means 'to take an interest in' but implies not only loss of libido
    but general inability to have sex (see Biggs 1967: 2).

4   Proto-diri: KAR, KID =*wa-ṣi-tum/ =[na]-a-a-di-tum/ =[ha]-ri-im-tum*,
    quoted by Finkelstein 1966: 362.

5   See also Cooper 1983: line 240: 'may the harlot hang herself at the gate
    of the hostel' (translation Jacobsen 1987a: 372).

6   Na'aman, N., 1980, 'The Ishtar Temple at Alalakh', *Journal of Near
    Eastern Studies* 39.3: 209–15; Speiser, E., 1954 'The Alalakh Tablets',
    Journal of the American Oriental Society 74: 23; Cohen 1988: 596; for
    castration as a punishment for adultery see, Middle Assyrian Laws §15,
    47–55: 'If he has taken and brought (him, i.e. the adulterer) either
    before the king or before the judges (and) charge (and) proof have been
    brought against him, if the woman's husband puts his wife to death,
    then he shall put the man to death, (but) if he has (only decided to) cut
    off his wife's nose, he shall make the man a eunuch and the whole of
    his face shall be mutilated.' (LÚ *a-na ša re-še-en ú-tar*), cf. Driver and
    Miles 1935: 389.

7   Cf. RLA 2, 1933: 485f.: cf. CAD *rēšu* and *anqnu*; also Kinnier-Wilson,
    J.V., 1972, *The Nimrud Wine Lists, a Study of Men and Administration
    in the Assyrian Capital in the Eighth Century BC* (London): 46 speaks
    in favour of real castration of officials known as *ša reši* (LÚ SAG) or the
    euphemistically named *ša ziqnu* (LÚ *ša* SU₆), 'The one of the beard'; the
    translation 'eunuch' for such persons is used by Fales, F.M. and
    Postgate, J.N., 1992, *Imperial Administrative Records, Part I* (Hel-
    sinki): *passim*, while Malbran-Labat, F., 1982, *L'armée et l'organisation
    militaire de l'Assyrie* (Paris): 131 is more cautious and prefers to regard
    it as a general title without necessarily implying any mutilation.

8   Cf. Maqlû III, 40–5: *kaššaptu nir-ta-ni-tum/e-il-ni-tum nar-šin-
    da-tum/a-ši-ip-tum eš-še-pu-ti/mušlahhatumᵗᵘᵐ a-gu-gi-il-tum/
    ᶠqadištu ᶠhadîtu/ ᵈištar-i-tum zêr-ma-ši-tum*; 'The witch, the
    murderess, "the one above",.../the female snake-charmer,.../the
    qadištu, nadîtu, the one dedicated to Ištar, the *zermašitu* . . .' 'Who kills
    men and does not spare women' (lines 52–3).

9   Farber 1977, see also p. 237f. and Maqlû V, 59 where Ištar, Dumuzi and
    Nanâ, 'the lady of love', are invoked in a ritual.

10 Also Maqlû VII, 92, 96.

11 The texts always speak of lapis-lazuli and golden ones. There may well
    have been such precious ex-votos, but archaeologists have so far found
    only cheap substitutes, made of clay or frit, with some blue paint
    on them.

12 E.g. Maqlû III, 31–2, and 64. This was not seen as a deviation. There is
    no Manichaean duality between forces of good and evil in Meso-
    potamian religion. The parentage of Anu merely suggests that some of
    his offspring are demonic.

13 See Ebeling, E., 1933–8, *RLA* 2: 107–13.

14 Thureau-Dangin, F., 1921, *Revue Assyriologique* 18: 161–98.

15 Krämer, K.F., 1928, *Mitteilungen der Altorientalischen Gesellschaft* 4:

108–21; see also Maqlû I, 138; II, 55. There was also a male *lilû*.
16 See Haas, V., n.d. [1976?], *Magie und Mythen im Reich der Hethiter* (Hamburg); Otten, H., 1964, *Handbuch der Orientalistik* VII.I.

20 THE ARTICULATION OF SEXUAL JEALOUSY

1 See also Egyptian love-songs from the Chester Beatty Papyrus: 'My disease cannot be identified./Only if somebody said: "She is here!", that would heal me./Only her name will relieve me./Only the coming and going of messengers will heal my heart./More useful is my sister to me than any remedy there is./She is better for me than all the medical knowledge.' (I, 7), translation after Vernus 1992: 68, see also 81–2.
2 Cf. Maqlû V, 166–8; VI 12–13, etc.
3 Verbs like *ṣabatu* ('to seize') are constantly used in incantations to express the intended control over the victim or the witch/demon.
4 This seems preferable to Held's 'the one who does not love'.
5 Cf. IB 1554 (Wilcke 1985: 38–41), a spell also directed against a rival woman.
6 It is not impossible that the missing parts of the text, between the columns, contained some ritual instructions; in which case it may have been a collection of similar spells like *IB* 1554, but as it stands, there is no evidence for that.
7 Cf. CH § 136, 137, 138–40, 146–7, 148–9; Driver and Miles, 1956: 55f.; also Driver and Miles 1935: 269–70.
8 Cf. *CAD qerû*; so Edzard instead of Lambert's 'Short silvery girl'.
9 *CAD sub singu* suggests a possible scribal error for *sinbu* ('loincloth'), but the verb *kaparu* ('to wipe') fits better with *singu*. According to the context of the lexical text Hh XIX, 301–5 a túg, nig, dara₄ was either a sanitary towel (line 303: tug-nig, dara₂ úš =*u-la-pu da-mi* and 305; túg, níg, dara₂, šul, lál =*da-me*, or strip of cloth worn by women as a cover for their genital region (see *AHw sinbu*, 'Schambinde'). The meaning suggested here could also signify the sort of cloth used by prostitutes to wipe off the secretions of lovemaking, and it is well known that male semen was considered highly polluting.
10 Might this refer to the width of her vulva, indicating slackness?
11 Or possibly: 'At night there is no such thing as a good housekeeper,/at night a man's wife offers no resistance' (*mu-šu e-muq-ti la i-ba-áš-ši/mu-šu alti améli la i-par-rik*.

21 LOVE AND EROS IN AKKADIAN NARRATIVE LITERATURE

1 Hurrian influence is quite clear in the 'Theogony of Dunnu', cf. Dalley 1989: 278–81f.
2 Dated after Hammurabi's conquest of Larsa in his 31st year (*c.* 1761).
3 For Ištar as a subject of satire see Foster, B.R., 1977, in de Jong Ellis, M. (ed.) *Essays on the Ancient Near East in Memory of J.J. Finkelstein* (New Haven: 79–84.

NOTES

4 *CT* 58, No. 16 (MB 96936), see Alster's summary on p. 15 (Alster and Geller 1990). The mother here is Gašannigarra; the nature of the transgression is rather obscure.

5 On the history of the text, see Tigay 1982. The following translations take into account the versions of Bottéro 1992 and Dalley 1989.

6 Cf. Harris 1990: 223 for quite a different interpretation: 'The predominant image [of Šamhat and Enkidu] is that of the mother and child.' And she adds in note 23: 'the consummate artistry with which the author(s) delineate the subtle and significant changes in the relationship, from worldlessness to dialogue: the importance of Enkidu's looking at and listening to Shamhat, beautifully replicating a child's development which ends with leaving the mother and home and entering a man's world.' While this is to a certain extent the case, I do not think it does justice to the text's inherent evaluation of sexuality in human development. After all, we would expect Aruru to have played a more signifiant role.

7 Cf. Finkelstein, J., 1970, *Journal of the American Oriental Society* 90: 250ff.; Cassin 1987: 353f.; Foster, *op. cit.*, 353f.

8 For *ha'iru* and the connection with marriage, see Wilcke 1985: 228, 297 note 211. In this respect Foster's remarks (*op. cit.*, p. 34) that Ištar proposes sex before marriage are dubious.

9 Here I agree with Harris 1990: 226.

10 *kappi* seems to be the bird's plaintive call.

11 Harris 1990 uses the structural principle of role reversals and 'inversion' as her main idea, cf. her evaluation of Ištar's behaviour, which comes to similar conclusions to those reached here (see especially p. 227).

12 For the former, see Jacobsen 1976: 219; Draffkorn-Kilmer 1982. For the latter position, see e.g. Foster 1987, also Lambert 1991: 156.

BIBLIOGRAPHY

Abdelwahab, B., 1975, *La sexualité en Islam* (Paris).
Abu Lughod, L., 1986, *Veiled Sentiments. Honor and Poetry in a Bedouin Society* (Berkeley, London).
Abusch, T., 1987, *Babylonian Witchcraft Literature* (Atlanta).
——, 1989a, 'The Demonic Image of the Witch in Standard Babylonian Literature', in Neusner, J. (*et al.*, eds) *Religion, Science and Magic* (Oxford, New York): 27–58.
——, 1989b, 'Gilgamesh', in Krstović, J.O. (ed.) *Classical and Medieval Literature Criticism* (Detroit, New York, Fort Lauderdale, London): 365–73.
——, 1991, 'The Ritual Tablet and Rubrics of Maglû: Toward the History of the Series', in Logan, M. and Eph'al, I. (eds)-*Ah! Assyria . . . Studies in Assyrian History Presented to Hayim Tadmor* (Jerusalem): 233–54.
Al Makhzoumi, Al Sayed Haroun Ibn, 1970, *The Fountains of Love. Sensual Secrets from Ancient Araby* (translated by Hateem el-Khalidi) (London).
Alster, B., 1972, *Dumuzi's Dream* (=Mesopotamia 1) (Copenhagen).
——, 1973, 'On the Interpretation of "Inanna and Enki"', *Zeitschrift für Assyriologie* 64: 23ff.
——, 1974, *The Instructions of Šuruppak* (Copenhagen).
——, 1975a, *Studies in Sumerian Proverbs* (=Mesopotamia 3) (Copenhagen).
——, 1975b, *Journal of Near Eastern Studies* 27: 216–19.
——, 1976, 'A Sumerian Riddle Collection', *Journal of Near Eastern Studies* 35(4): 263–6.
——, 1978, 'Enki and Ninhursag', *Ugarit Forschungen* 10: 15–27.
——, 1983, 'Dilmun, Bahrein and the Alleged Paradise in Sumerian Myth and Literature', *Berliner Beiträge zum Vorderen Orient* 2: 39–74.
——, 1985, 'Sumerian Love Songs', *Revue d'assyriologie* 79: 127–59.
——, 1992, 'The Manchester Tammuz', *Acta Sumerologica* 14: 1–47.
——, 1993, 'Two Sumerian Short Tales and a Love Song Reconsidered', *Zeitschrift für Assyriologie* 82: 186–201.
Alster, B. and Geller, M.J., 1990, *Cuneiform Texts from the British Museum* 58 (London).
Andrae, W., 1921, *Die jüngeren Ištartempel in Assur* (Wissenschaftliche Veröffnungen der Deutschen Orientgesellschaft 58) (Berlin).
Arnaud, D., 1973, 'La prostitution sacrée en Mésopotamie: un mythe historiographique?' *Révue d'Histoire des Religions* 183: 111–15.
Asher-Greve, J., 1985, *Frauen in altsumerischer Zeit* (=Bibliotheca Mesopotamica 18) (Malibu).

BIBLIOGRAPHY

*Asher-Greve, J.A., 1997, 'The Essential Body: Mesopotamian Conceptions of the Gendered Body.', *Gender & History* 9/3: 423–461.

*——, 2000, 'Stepping into the Maelstrom: Women, Gender and Ancient Near Eastern Scholarship', *NIN-Journal of Gender Studies in Antiquity.* 1: 1–22.

*Assante, J., 1999, 'The Kar.Kid/harimtu, Prostitute or Single Woman?', *Ugartit Forschungen* 30:5–96.

Atkins, J., 1978, *Sex in Literature, Vol. III* (London).

Attinger, P., 1985, 'Enki et Ninhursaga', *Zeitschrift für Assyriologie* 74: 1–52.

Attridge, H.W., 1976, *De Dea Syria* (Missoula).

*Bahrani, Z., 2001, *Women of Babylon: Gender and Representation in Mesopotamia.* (London and New York).

Bataille, G., 1987, *Eroticism* (London).

Battistini, Y., 1992, *Lyra erotica. VIe siècle de notre ère IXe siècle avant Jésus-Christ* (Paris).

Behrens, H., 1978, *Enlil and Ninlil* (=Studia Pohl: Series Maior 8) (Rome).

Behrens, H., Loding, D. and Roth, M.T. (eds.) 1989, *DUMU-e₂-dub.ba.a. Studies in Honor of Ake W. Sjöberg* (Philadelphia).

Benito, C., 1969, *Enki and Ninmah and Enki and the World Order* (Diss. Univ. of Pennsylvania).

Berlin, A., 1979, *Enmerkar and Ensuhkešdanna* (Philadelphia).

Biggs, R.D., 1966, 'The Abu Salabikh Tablets. A Preliminary Survey', *Journal of Cuneiform Studies* 20: 73–124.

——, 1967, *ŠÀ. ZI. GA, Ancient Mesopotamian Potency Incantations* (Locust Valley, New York).

——, 1974, *Inscriptions from Tell Abu Salabikh* (=Oriental Institute Publications 99) (Chicago and London).

——, 1977, 'Gilgamesh and Lugalbanda in the Fara Period', *Journal of Ancient Near Eastern Societies* 9: 1–4.

Bin Nun, R., 1975, *The Tawanannas in the Hittite Kingdom* (Heidelberg).

Black, J.A., 1983, 'Babylonian Ballads: A New Genre', *Journal of the American Oriental Society* 103: 25–34.

——, 1983–4, Review of Klein's *Three Šulgi Hymns* and *The Royal Hymns of Šulgi, King of Ur*, *Archiv für Orientforschung* 29–30: 110ff.

——, 1991, 'Eme-sal Cult Songs and Prayers', in *Festschrift Civil* (=Aura Orientalis 9): 23–36.

Bonnefoy, I. (ed.), 1981, *Dictionnaire des mythologies* 2 vols. (Paris).

Borger, R., 1956, 'Die Inschriften Asarhaddons, Königs von Assyrien', *Archiv für Orientforschung, Beiheft* 9 (Graz).

Bottéro, J., 1985, *Mythes et rites de Babylone* (Paris).

——, 1989, *Lorsque les dieux faisaient l'homme: mythologie mésopotamienne* (Paris).

——, 1992, *L'Épopée de Gilgameš* (Paris).

Brandon, S.G.E., 1963, *Creation Legends of the Ancient Near East* (London).

Brunner, H., 'Die Geburt des Gottkönigs', *Ägyptologische Abhandlungen* 10 (Wiesbaden).

Bruschweiler, F., 1988, *Inanna, La Déesse triomphante et vaincue dans la cosmologie sumérienne* (Louvain).

Burton, Sir R., 1989, *The Perfumed Garden* (London).

Cagni, L., 1969, *L'epopea di Erra* (=Studi Semitici 34) (Rome).

——, 1977, *The Poem of Erra* (Sources and Monographs of the Ancient Near East 1/3) (Malibu).

Cameron, A. and Kuhrt, A., 1983, *Images of Women in Antiquity* (London, Sydney).

Caplice, R.I., 1974, 'The Akkadian Namburbu Texts: An Introduction', *Sources from the Ancient Near East* I, 1 (Malibu).

Cassin, E., 1969, 'Pouvoirs de la femme et structures familiales', *Révue d'Assyriologie* 63: 144–5.

——, 1987, *Le semblable et le différent: symbolismes du pouvoir dans le Proche-Orient ancien* (Paris).

Castellino, G.R., 1957, 'Urnammu: Three Religious Texts', *Zeitschrift für Assyriologie* 18: 1–57.

——, 1972, *Two Šulgi Hymns* (Rome).

——, 1976, 'The Šamaš Hymn: A Note on its Structure', in *Kramer Anniversary Volume* (Alter Orient und Altes Testament 25) (Neukirchen-Vlyun): 71–4.

Chöpel, G., 1992, *The Tibetan Arts of Love* (New York).

Civil, M., 1964, 'The Message of LU-DINGIR-RA to His Mother', *Journal of Near Eastern Studies* 23(1): 1–11.

——, 1976, 'Song of the Plowing Oxen', in *Kramer Anniversary Volume* (Alter Orient und Altes Testament 25) (Neukirchen-Vluyn).

——, 1980, 'Les limites de l'information textuelle', *Colloques internationaux du C.N.R.S. 580, L'archéologie de l'Iraq* (Paris).

——, 1983, 'The Marriage of Sud', *Journal of the American Oriental Societies* 103: 64–6.

Cohen, M.E., 1974, *Balag-Compositions: Sumerian Lamentation Liturgies of the Second and First Millennium B.C.* (Sources and Monographs from the Ancient Near East 1/2) (Malibu).

——, 1988, *The Canonical Lamentations of Ancient Mesopotamia* (Potomac).

Cooper, J.S., 1971, 'New Cuneiform Parallels to the Song of Songs', *Journal of Biblical Literature* 90:

——, 1975, 'Heilige Hochzeit, Archäologisch', *Reallexikon der Assyriologie* III (Berlin): 259–69.

——, 1980, Review of H. Behrens *Enlil and Ninlil*, *Journal of Cuneiform Studies* 32.

——, 1983, *The Curse of Agade* (Baltimore).

——, 1989, 'Enki's Member: Eros and Irrigation in Sumerian Literature', in *Dumu-e₂-dub-ba-a. .in Honor of A. Sjöberg* (Philadelphia): 87–9.

*Cooper, J.S., 1993, 'Sacred Marriage and Popular Cult in Early Mesopotamia.' in Matsushima, E. (ed.) *Official Cult and Popular Religion in the Ancient Near East.* (Heidelberg): 81–96.

*——, 1997, 'Gendered Sexuality in Sumerian Love Poetry', in Finkel, I.L. and M.J. Geller (eds.) *Sumerian Gods and their Representations.* (Gröningen), 85–97.

Crapanzano, V., 1992, *Hermes' Dilemma and Hamlet's Desire* (Cambridge, Mass., London).

Dalley, S., 1989, *Myths from Mesopotamia* (Oxford, New York).

Dandamaev, M.A., 1984, *Slavery in Babylonia* (Northern Illinois).

Detienne, M., 1970, *Les Jardins d'Adonis* (Paris).

Devereux, G., 1982, *Baubo. Mystic Vulva.*

——, 1982, *Femme et Mythe* (Paris).

Dietrich, M., 1989, 'Das Einsetzungsritual der Entu von Emar', *Ugarit Forschungen* 21: 46–89.

Dover, J., 1978, *Greek Homosexuality* (Cambridge, Mass.).

Dowden, K., 1989, *Death and the Maiden* (London, New York).

Draffkorn-Kilmer, A., 1976, 'Speculations on Umul, the First Baby', in *Kramer Anniversary Volume* (Alter Orient und Altes Testament 25) (Neukirchen-Vluyn): 265–70.

——, 1982, 'A Note on an overlooked Word-Play in the Akkadian Gilgamesh', in van Driel (ed.) *Zikir Šumim Studies presented to F.R. Kraus* (Leiden): 128–32.

Driver, G.R. 1976, *Semitic Writing from Pictograph to Alphabet* (London).

Driver, G.R. and Miles, J.C., 1935, *The Assyrian Laws* (Oxford).

——, 1955, *The Babylonian Laws* (Oxford).

Ebeling, E., 1925, 'Liebeszauber im alten Orient', *Mitteilungen der Altorientalischen Gesellschaft* 1(1).

Edzard, D.O., 1987, 'Zur Ritualtafel der sogenannten 'Love Lyrics', in Rochberg-Halton, F. (ed.), *Language, Literature and History: Philological and Historical Studies Presented to Erica Reiner* (=American Oriental Studies 67) (New Haven, Conn.): 57–70.

——, 1990, Review of Jacobsen's *Harps that Once...*, *Journal of the American Oriental Society* 110: 119–122.

Edzard, D.O. and Wilcke, C., 1976, 'Die Hendursanga Hymne', in *Kramer Anniversary Volume* (Alter Orient und Altes Testament 25) (Neukirchen-Vluyn): 142–76.

Eliade, M., 1959, *Patterns in Comparative Religion* (London, Sydney).

el Khalidi, H. (ed.), 1970, *The Fountains of Pleasure* (London).

Fainzang, S., 1988, *La femme de mon mari: étude éthnologique du mariage* (Paris).

Falkenstein, A., 1947, 'Eine Hymne auf Šusin von Ur', *Welt des Orients* 1: 4ff.

——, 1953, 'Sumerische Hymen und Gebete', in Falkenstein, A. and Soden, W. von, *Sumerische und Akkadische Hymen und Gebete* (Zurich, Stuttgart): 59–231.

——, 1964, 'Sumerian Literary Texts', *Zeitschrift für Assyriologie, Neue Folge* 56: 113–29.

——, 1966, *Comptes rendues de la rencontre assyriologique* III: 61–62.

Farber, W., 1977, *Beschwörungsrituale an Ištar und Dumuzi: Atti Ištar šu Harmaša Dumuzi* (Wiesbaden).

Farber-Flügge, G., 1973, *Der Mythos 'Inanna und Enki' unter besonderer Berücksichtigung der Liste der me* (=Studia Pohl 10) (Rome).

——, 1984, 'Another Old Babylonian Childbirth Incantation', *Journal of Near Eastern Studies* 43(4): 311–16.

Fauth, W., 1985, 'Lilith und Astarten', *Welt des Orients* 16: 66–94.

Fernea, E., 1965, *Guests of the Sheikh: An Ethnography of an Iraqi Village* (New York).

Fernea, R.A., 1971, 'Southern Mesopotamia' in Sweet, L.A., *A Handbook of Anthropology and Published Research* (New Haven).

Finkel, I., 1988, 'A Fragmentary Catalogue of Lovesongs', *Acta Sumerologica* 10: 17–18.

Finkelstein, I., 1966, 'Sex Offences in Sumerian Laws', *Journal of the American Oriental Society* 86: 355ff.

Foster, B., 1987, 'Gilgameš, Sex, Love, and the Ascent of Knowledge', in Marks, J. and Good, R.M. (eds.), *Love and Death in the Ancient Near East: Essays in Honor of Marvin E. Pope* (Guildford, Conn.): 21–42.

———, 1993, *Before the Muses: An Anthology of Akkadian Literature, Vol. 1* (Bethesda, Md.).

Foucault, M., 1987, *History of Sexuality* (Harmondsworth).

Frame, G., 1984, 'A New Wife for Šu-Sin', *Annual Review of the Royal Inscriptions of Mesopotamia Project* 21: 3–4.

Frazer, Sir J., 1964, *The New Golden Bough* (ed. T. Gaster).

Frankfort, H., 1939, *Cylinder Seals* (London).

———, 1950, 'akiti-Fest und akiti-Festhaus', in *Festschrift Johannes Friedrich* (Heidelberg): 147–82.

Friedrich, P., 1978, *The Meaning of Aphrodite* (Chicago).

Fuller, C.J., 1980, 'The Divine Couple's Relationship in a South Indian Temple: Minaksi and Sundaresvara at Madurai', *History of Religions* 19: 321–49.

———,1984, *Servants of the Goddess* (Cambridge Studies in Social Anthropology) (Cambridge, London).

Gallery, R., 1980, 'Service Obligations of the *kēzertu* Women', *Orientalia, Nova Seria* 49: 333–8.

Galter, H.D., 1981, *Der Gott Ea/Enki in der akkadischen Überlieferung* (Graz).

Gelb, I.J., 1979, *State and Temple Economy in the Ancient Near East* (Leuven).

Gelb, I.J. and Kienast, B., 1990, *Die altakkadischen Königsinschriften des 3, Jahrtausends.*

Geller, M.J., 1990, 'Taboo in Mesopotamia', *Journal of Cuneiform Studies* 42(1): 105–17.

Gennep, A. van, 1969, *Les Rites de Passage* (reprint, Paris).

Gonda, J., 1969, *Visnuism and Sivaism* (London).

Goodnick-Westenholz, J., 1987,'A Forgotten Love Song', in Rochberg-Halton, F. (ed.), *Language, Literature and History: Philological and Historical Studies Presented to Erica Reiner* (=AOS 67) (New Haven, Conn.): 415–25.

———, 1990, 'Towards a New Conceptualization of the Female Role in Mesopotamian Society', *Journal of the American Oriental Society* 110: 510–21.

Gordon, E.I., 1959, *Sumerian Proverbs* (Philadelphia).

Green, M.W., 1975, *Eridu in Sumerian Literature* (Diss., Chicago).

Greengus, S., 1969, 'The Old Babylonian Marriage Contract', *Journal of the American Oriental Society* 89: 529–53.

Groneberg, B., 1985, 'Die sumerisch-akkadische Inanna-Ištar, Hermaphroditus?', *Welt des Orients* 16: 25–46.

*Groneberg, B., 1997, *Lob der Istar: Gebet und Ritual an die altbabylonische Venusgöttin.* (Grönigen).

*Guinan, A., 1997, 'Auguries of Hegemony: The Sex Omens of Mesopotamia', *Gender and History* 9/3: 38–55.

Gulik, R.H. van, 1975, *Sexual Life in Ancient China* (Leiden).

Gundert, W., Schimmel, A. and Schubig, W. (eds) 1965, *Lyrik des Ostens* (Munich).

Gurney, O.R., 1960, 'The Sultantepe Tablets', *Anatolian Studies* 10: 105–31.

Güterbock, H.G., 1951-2, 'The Song of Ullikummi: Revised Text of the Hittite Version of a Hurrian Myth', *Journal of Cuneiform Studies* 5,6.

*Haas, V., 1999, *Babylonischer Liebesgarten: Erotik und Sexualität im Alten Orient* (Munich).

Hallo, W.W., 1966, *Journal of Cuneiform Studies* 20.

——, 1975, 'Towards a History of Sumerian Literature', in *Sumerological Studies in Honor of Thorkild Jacobsen* (=Assyriological Studies 20) (Chicago, London): 191–4.

——, 1987, 'The Birth of Kings', in Marks, J.H. and Good, R.M. (eds.), *Love and Death in the Ancient Near East: Essays in Honor of Marvin H. Pope* (Guildford, Conn.): 45–52.

Hallo, W.W. and Simpson, W.H., 1971, *The Ancient Near East: A History* (New York, Chicago, Atlanta).

Halperin, D.M., 1989, *One Hundred Years of Homosexuality and Other Essays on Greek Love* (New York).

Halperin, D.M., Winkler, J.J., Abusch,T., Huehnergard, J. and Steinkellner, P. (eds), 1989, *Before Sexuality: The Construction of Erotic Experience in the Ancient Greek World* (Princeton).

Harris, R., 1964, 'The nadītu woman', in *Studies presented to A.L. Oppenheim* (Chicago).

——, 1990, 'Images of Women in the Gilgamesh Epic', in Abusch, T., Huehnergard, J. and Steinkellner, P. (eds)*Lingering over Words: Studies Presented in Honor of William C. Moran* (Atlanta).

Heidel, A., 1951 *A Babylonian Genesis*, 2nd ed. (Chicago).

Heimpel, W., 1972, Review of Kramer's Sacred Marriage Rite, *Journal of the American Oriental Society* 92(2): 288–91.

——, 1981, 'The Nanshe Hymn', *Journal of Cuneiform Studies* 20: 65–139.

Held, M., 1961-2, 'A Faithful Lover in an Old Babylonian Dialogue', *Journal of Cuneiform Studies* 1: 1–26, 2: 37–9.

——, 1976, 'Two Philological Notes on the Enuma Elish', in *Kramer Anniversary Volume* (=Alter Orient und Altes Testament 25) (Neukirchen-Vluyn): 231–40.

Hermann, A., 1959, *Altägyptische Liebesdichtung* (Wiesbaden).

Hibbert, P.M., 1985, 'Liebeslyrik der arsakidischen Zeit', *Welt des Orients* 15.

Hinz, W., 1972, *The Lost World of Elam* (London).

Hirsch, H., 1982, Über das Lachen der Götter', in Driel, G. van, Krispijn, T.J.H., Stol, M. and Veenhof, K.R. (eds), *Zikir Šumin: Studies Presented to F.R. Kraus* (Leiden): 110–20.

——, 1983, 'Spaß mit der Sprache', in Seybold, S. (ed.), *Meqqor Hayyim* (Graz): 155ff.

Hrouda, B., 1971, *Vorderasien* (Munich).

Hruška, B., 1969, 'Das spätbabylonische Lehrgedicht "Inannas Erhö-hung"', *Archiv Orientalní* 37: 473–521.
Hutter, M., 1985, *Altorientalische Vorstellungen von der Unterwelt* (Göttingen).
Ichiro, K., 1979, *Deities in the Mari Texts* (Ann Arbor).
Jacobsen, T., 1939, *The Sumerian Kinglist* (Chicago).
——, 1970, *Towards the Image of Tamuz* (Cambridge).
——, 1973, 'The Sister's Message', *The Journal of the Ancient Near Eastern Society of Columbia University* 5: 199–212.
——, 1976, *Treasures of Darkness* (New Haven, London).
——, 1984, 'The Harab Myth', *Studies in Ancient Near Eastern Societies* 2/3.
——, 1987a, *Harps that Once. . .* (New Haven, London).
——, 1987b, 'Two ba-bal-e Dialogues', in Marks, J.H. and Good, R.M. (eds.), *Love and Death in the Ancient Near East: Essays in Honor of Marvin H. Pope* (Guildford, Conn.): 57–63.
——, 1989, 'Lugalbanda and Ninsuna', *Journal of Cuneiform Studies* 41(1):69–86.
Jones, S., 1993, *Language of the Genes* (London).
Jones, H.W. and Scott, W.W., 1971, *Hermaphroditism, Genital Anomalies and Related Endocrine Disorders* (Baltimore).
Jordan, R.A. (ed.) 1985, *Women's Folklore, Women's Culture* (Philadelphia).
Kang, S.T., 1972, 'Sumerian Economic Texts from Drehem', *Archive Urbana* 261ff.
Kienast, B., 1990, 'Naramsîn mut ᵈInanna', *Orientalia, Nova Seria* 59(2): 196–206.
Kinnier-Wilson, J.V., 1974, 'Further Contributions to the Myth of Etana', *Journal of Near Eastern Studies* 32: 237ff.
——, 1985, *The Legend of Etana* (Warminster).
Kirk, G.S., 1970, *Myth: Its Meaning and Functions in Ancient and Other Cultures* (Berkeley, Los Angeles).
Klein, J., 1976, Šulgi and Gilgameš: Two Brother Peers', in *Kramer Anniversary Volume* (Alter Orient und Altes Testament 25) (Neukirchen-Vluyn).
Klein, J., 1981, *Three Šulgi Hymns* (Ramat-Gan).
Klein, J. and Skavist, A. (eds) 1990, *Bar-Ilan Studies in Assyriology Dedicated to Pinhas Artzi* (Ramat-Gan).
Kluckhorn, C., 1965, 'Myths and Rituals: A General Theory', in Lessse, W.A. and Vogt, Z.E. (eds), *Reader in Comparative Religion* (New York, Evanston, San Francisco, London).
Knudtzon, J., 1915, *Die El-Amarna Tafeln* (Leipzig).
Kramer, S.N., 1944a, 'The Epic of Gilgamesh and its Sumerian Sources', *Journal of the American Oriental Society* 64: 7–23.
——, 1944b, *Sumerian Mythology* (New York).
——, 1949, *Archiv Orientalní* 17: 399ff.
——, 1952, *Enmerkar and the Lord of Aratta* (Philadelphia).
——, 1963, 'The Sumerian Sacred Marriage Texts', *Proceedings of the Society of Biblical Archaeology* (London) 107: 485–525.

——, 1967a, 'The Death of Urnammu', *Journal of Cuneiform Studies* 21: 104ff.

——, 1967b, 'Shulgi of Ur: A Royal Hymn and a Divine Blessing', in Neuman, A. and Zeitlin, S. (eds) *The Seventy-Fifth Anniversary Volume of the Jewish Quarterly Review* (Philadelphia): 396–480.

——, 1969, 'The Dumuzi–Inanna Sacred Marriage Rite: Origin, Development, Character', *17ième Rencontre Assyriologique Internationale* (Leiden).

——, 1976, 'Poets and Psalmists', in Schmandt-Besserat, D. (ed.), *The Legacy of Sumer* (Malibu).

——, 1985, 'Bread for Enlil, Sex for Inanna', *Orientalia. Nova Seria* 54: 117–32.

——, 1990, 'A New Dumuzi Myth', *Révue d'Assyriologie* 84: 143ff.

——, 1993, 'The Marriage of Martu' in Klein and Skavist 1990: 11–28.

Kramer, S.N. and Maier, J., 1989, *Myths of Enki, the Crafty God* (New York, Oxford).

Kraus, F., 1974, 'Das altbabylonische Königtum', *Le Palais et le Royauté, XIX Recontre Assysriologique Internationale* (Paris).

Kutscher, R., 1990, 'The Cult of Dumuzi/Tammuz', in Klein and Skavist 1990: 29–44.

La Barre, W., 1984, *Muelos: A Stone Age Superstition about Sexuality* (New York).

Lacan, J., 1991, *Le Séminaire de Jacques Lacan, Livre VIII. Le transfert* (Paris).

Lambert, W.G., 1960, *Babylonian Wisdom Literature* (Oxford).

——, 1966, 'Divine Love-Lyrics from the Reign of Abi-ešuh', *Mitteilungen des Instituts für Orientforschung* 12: 41–57.

——, 1975a, 'The Cult of Ištar of Babylon', *20ième Rencontre Assyriologique Internationale* (Leiden): 104–6.

——, 1975b, 'The Problem of the Love Lyrics', in Goedicke, H. and Roberts, J.J.M. (eds), *Unity and Diversity* (Baltimore): 98–135.

——, 1981, *Reallexikon der Assyriologie. VI* (Berlin) 218ff.

——, 1982, 'The Hymn to the Queen of Nippur', in Driel, G. van. Krispijn, T.J.H. (et al. eds.) *Zukir Šumin: Assyriological Studies presented to F.R. Kraus* (Leiden): 173–218.

——, 1987a, 'Devotion: The Languages of Religion and Love', in Mindlin, M., Geller, M.J. and Wansbrough, J.E. (eds), *Figurative Language in the Ancient Near East* (London): 25–39.

——, 1987b, 'Gilgamesh in Literature and Art: The Second and First Millennia', in Farhar, A. (ed.), *Monsters and Demons in the Ancient and Medieval Worlds* (Mainz).

——, 1991, 'Prostitution', in Haas, V. (ed.), *Außenseiter und Randgruppen* (Xenia, Konstanzer Althistorische Vorträge und Forschungen, Heft 32) (Konstanz): 127–57.

Lambert, W.G. and Millard, A.R., 1969, *Atra-hasîs: The Babylonian Story of the Flood* (Oxford).

Landsberger, B., 1968, 'Jungfräulichkeit', in Ankum, J.A. (et al., eds.), *Symbolae iuridicae et historiae Martino David dedicatae*: 41–105.

Langdon, S., 1913, *Babylonian Liturgies* (London).

——, 1915, *The Sumerian Epic of Paradise: The Flood and the Fall of Man* (Philadelphia).

Leichty, E.V., 1970, *The Omen Series šumma izbu* (Texts from Cuneiform Sources 4) (Locust Valley, NY).

Leick, G., 1991, *A Dictionary of Ancient Near Eastern Mythology* (London, New York).

Lerberghe, K. van. 1982, 'New Data from the Archives found in the House of Ur-Tutu at Tell-ed-Dēr', =Comptes rendus de la Rencontre Assyriologique Internationale (*Archiv für Orientforschung, Beiheft* 19: 281–3.

Lewinsohn, R., 1958, *A History of Sexual Customs* (London).

Lewis, B., 1980, *The Sargon Legend* (Cambridge, Mass.).

Limet, H., 1970, 'L'organisation de quelques fêtes mensuelles à l'époque néo-sumerienne', in Finet, A. (ed.), *Actes de la XVII Rencontre Assyriologique Internationale, Bruxelles* (Ham-sur-Heure): 59–74.

Livingstone, A., 1986, *Mystical and Mythological Explanatory Works of Assyrian and Babylonian Scholars* (Oxford).

——, 1989, *Court Poetry and Literary Miscellanea* (Helsinki).

Lloyd, S. and Safar, F., 1947–48 'Eridu', in *Sumer* 3 and 4.

Ludwig, M.C., 1990, *Untersuchungen zu den Hymnen des Išme-Dagan von Isin* (Wiesbaden).

Lurker, M., 1980, *The Gods and Symbols of Ancient Egypt* (London).

Malinowski, B., 1963, *Sex, Culture and Myth* (London).

Matsushima, E., 1987, 'Le Rituel Hierogamique de Nabû', *Acta Sumerologica* 9: 131–75.

——, 1988, 'Les Rituels du Mariage Divin dans les documents Accadiens', *Acta Sumerologica* 10: 95–127.

Meier, G., 1967, 'Die assyrische Beschwörungssammlung Maqlû', *Archiv für Orientforschung, Beiheft* 2 (Osnabrück).

Merwin, W.S. and Masson, S.M., 1977, *Sanskrit Love Poetry* (New York).

Michalowski, P., 1976, 'Royal Women of the UrIII Period: I The Wife of Šulgi', *Journal of Cuneiform Studies* 28: 169–72.

——, 1979, 'Royal Women of the URIII Period, Part II', *Journal of Cuneiform Studies* 31: 171–6.

——, 1981, 'On "The Fowler and his Wife"', *Revue d'Assyriologie* 75: 170.

——, 1982, 'Royal Women in the URIII Period, Part III', *Acta Sumerologica* 4: 129–42.

——, 1989, *The Lamentation over the Destruction of Sumer and Ur* (Winona Lake).

Mieroop, M. van der, 1992, *Society and Enterprise in Old Babylonian Ur* (Berlin).

Mitchell, J. and Rose, J., 1982, *Feminine Sexuality* (Houndsmill, Basingstoke).

Myerhoff, B., 1974, *Peyote Hunt* (Cornell).

Na'aman, N., 1980, 'The Ishtar Temple at Alalakh', *Journal of Near Eastern Studies* 39(3): 209–14.

Nanda, S., 1986, 'The Hijras of India: Cultural and Individual Dimensions of an Institutionalised Third Gender Role', in Blackwood, E., *Anthropology and Homosexual Behavior* (New York).

———, 1990, *Neither Men nor Women: The Hijras of India* (Belmont).

Neusner, J., Frerichs, E.S. and Flesher, P.V.M.C. (eds), 1989, *Religion, Science and Magic* (New York, Oxford).

Nissen, H.J., 1988, *The Early History of the Ancient Near East, 9000–2000 BC* (Chicago).

O'Donoghue, B., 1982, *The Courtly Love Tradition* (Manchester).

O'Flaherty, W., 1973, *Śiva: The Erotic Ascetic* (Oxford).

———, 1980, *Women, Androgynes, and Other Mythical Beasts* (Chicago).

Oates, J., 1960, *Iraq* 22.

Oberhuber, K., 1972, *Die Kultur das Alten Orients* (Frankfurt am Main).

Oettinger, N., 1976, *Die militärischen Eide der Hethiter* (Wiesbaden).

Paglia, C., 1992, *Sex, Art and American Culture* (New York).

Parker, W.H., 1988, *Priapea: Poems for a Phallic God* (London, Sydney).

Parrinder, G., 1980, *Sex in World Religions* (New York).

Picchioni, S.A., 1981, *Il poemetto di Adapa* (Budapest).

*Pinnock, F., 1995, 'Erotic Art in the Ancient Near East', in Sasson, J.M. (ed.) *Civilisations of the Ancient Near East.* (New York): 2521–2531.

Pomeroy, S.B., 1975, *Goddesses, Whores, Wives and Slaves: Women in Classical Antiquity* (New York).

Pomponio, I., 1978, *Nabû* (Studi Semitici 51) (Rome).

Pope, M.H., 1964, *The Song of Songs* (New York).

Pritchard, J.B. (ed.), 1975, *The Ancient Near East, Vol. II. A New Anthology of Texts and Pictures* (Princeton).

Redman, C.L., 1978, *The Rise of Civilization: From Early Farmers to Urban Society* (San Francisco).

Reiner, E., 1970, 'Šurpu: A Collection of Sumerian and Akkadian Incantations', *Archiv für Orientforschung, Beiheft 11* (Osnabrück).

———, 1974, 'A Sumero-Akkadian Hymn of Nanâ', *Journal of Near Eastern Studies* 33: 221ff.

———, 1985, *Poetry from Babylonia and Assyria* (Chicago).

Reiner, E. and Pingreen, D., 1975, 'The Venus Tablets of Ammisaduqa', *Bibliotheca Mesopotamica* 21 (Malibu).

Reisman, D., 1973, 'Iddin Dagan's Sacred Marriage Hymn', *Journal of Cuneiform Studies* 25: 189–202.

———, 1976, 'A "Royal" Hymn from Išbi-Erra to the Goddess Nisaba', in *Kramer Anniversary Volume* (Alter Orient und Altes Testament 25) (Neukirchen Vluyn): 357–66.

Renger, J., 1967,'Untersuchungen zum Priestertum in der altbabylonischen Zeit', *Zeitschrift für Assyriologie* 58:110–89.

———, 1975, 'Heilige Hochzeit', in *Reallexikon der Assyriologie* III (Berlin): 251–9.

Roberts, J.J.M., 1972, *The Earliest Semitic Pantheon* (Baltimore).

Römer, W.H.P., 1965, *Sumerische 'Königshymnen' der Isin-Zeit* (Leiden).

———, 1966, 'Studien zu altbabylonischen hymnisch-epischen Texten.2', *Journal of the American Oriental Society* 86: 138–47.

———, 1969, 'Eine sumerische Hymne mit Selbstlob Inannas', *Orientalia, Nova Seria* 38: 97–114.

———, 1976, in *Kramer Anniversary Volume* (Alter Orient und Altes Testament 25) (Neukirchen-Vluyn): 371–8.

Rollin, S., 1983, 'Women and Witchcraft in Ancient Assyria', in Cameron, A. and Kuhrt, A. (eds), *Images of Women in Antiquity* (London, Sydney).

Rosengarten, Y., 1971, 'L'origine de Dilmun', in *Trois aspects de la pensée religieuse sumérienne* (Paris): 7–38.

Roux, G., 1964, *Ancient Iraq* (Harmondsworth).

Rundle-Clark, R.J., 1959, *Myth and Symbol in Ancient Egypt* (London).

Sasson, J.M. (ed.) 1984, *Studies in Literature from the Ancient Near East by Members of the American Oriental Society Dedicated to Samuel Noah Kramer* (New Haven, Conn.).

Sauren, H., 1970, 'Les fêtes néo-sumériennes et leur périodicité', in Finet, A. (ed.), *Actes de la XVII Rencontre Assyriologique Internationale, Bruxelles* (Ham-sur-Heure): 11–29.

Scheil, V., 1927, 'Contraste féminim', *Revue d'Assyriologie* 24: 34–7.

Schmandt-Besserat, D. (ed.), 1976, *The Legacy of Sumer* (Malibu).

Schretter, M.K., 1990, *Emesal Studien* (Innsbrucker Beiträge zur Kulturwissenschaft, Sonderheft 69) (Innsbruck).

Scurlock, J.A., 1989–90, 'Was there a 'Love-Hungry' Entu Priestess named Etirtum?', *Archiv für Orientforschung* 36/7: 107–12.

Sefati, Y., 1990, 'An Oath of Chastity in a Sumerian Love Song', in Klein and Skavist 1990: 45–63.

*Sefati, Y. 1998, *Love Songs in Sumerian Literature: Critical Edition of the Dumazi-Inanna Songs.* (Bar Ilan Studies in Near Eastern Languages and Culture, Ramat Gan).

*Seidel, U., 1998, 'Nackheit B; in der Bildkunst', *Reallexikon der Assyriologie* 9 (Berlin): 140–173.

*Selz, G.J., 2000, 'Five Divine Ladies: Thought on Inanna(k), Istar, In(n)in (a), Annunitum, and 'Anat, and the Origin of the Title "Queen of Heaven", *NIN-Journal of Gender Studies in Antiquity.* 1: 29–62.

Seux, M.J., 1967, *Épithètes royales akkadiennes et sumériennes* (Paris).

Sharma, S.K., 1989, *Hijras: The Labelled Deviants* (New Delhi).

Shattuck, R., 1980, *The Forbidden Experiment: The Story of the Wild Boy of Aveyron* (London).

Sherfey, N.J., 1973, *The Nature and Evolution of Female Sexuality* (New York).

Shulman, D.D., 1980, *Tamil Temple Myths: Sacrifice and Divine Marriage in the South Indian Saiva Tradition* (Princeton).

Sjöberg, A.W., 1960, *Der Mondgott Nanna-Suen in der sumerischen Überlieferung* (Uppsala).

——, 1973, 'Die göttliche Abstammung der sumerisch–babylonischen Herrscher', *Orientalia Suecana*, 21: 87–9.

——, 1976, 'in-nin-šà-gur₄-ra. A Hymn to the goddess Inanna by the en-Priestess Enheduanna', *Zeitschrift für Assyriologie* 65: 163–253.

——, 1977, 'Miscellaneous Sumerian Texts II', *Journal of Cuneiform Studies* 29: 3–45.

——, 1988, 'A Hymn to Inanna and her Self-Praise', *Journal of Cuneiform Studies* 40: 165–86.

Sjöberg, A.W. and Bergmann, S.J., 1969, *The Collection of Sumerian Temple Hymns* (Locust Valley, NY).

Sladek, W., 1974, *Inanna's Descent to the Netherworld* (Ann Arbor).

Soden, W. von, 1938, 'Altbabylonische Dialektdichtungen', *Zeitschrift für Assyriologie* 10: 31–44.

——, 1950, 'Ein Zwiegespräch Hammurabis mit einer Frau', *Zeitschrift für Assyriologie* 49: 151–94.

——, 1953, 'Akkadische Hymnen und Gebete', in Falkenstein, A. and Soden, W. von. *Sumerische und Akkadische Hymnen und Gebete* (Zurich, Stuttgart).

——, 1974, 'Duplikate aus Ninive', *Journal of Near Eastern Studies* 33: 340–4.

Sollberger, E., 1978, 'A Note on the Lyrical Dialogue SRT 23', *Journal of Cuneiform Studies* 30: 99–100.

Sollberger, E. and Kupper, J.R., 1971, *Inscriptions royales sumériennes et akkadiennes* (Paris).

Spycket, A., 1981, *La Statuaire du Proche Orient* (Paris).

——, 1992, *Les Figurines de Suse* (Paris).

Stamm, J.J., 1968, *Die akkadische Namensgebung* (Darmstadt).

Steinkellner, P., 1981, *Acta Sumerologica* 3: 77–92.

Thesiger, W., 1964, *The Marsh Arabs* (London).

Thureau-Dangin, F., 1921, *Rituels Accadiens* (Paris).

——, 1925, 'Un Hymne à Ištar', *Revue d'Assyriologie* 22: 169–77.

Tigay, H.H., 1982, *The Evolution of the Gilgamesh Epic* (Philadelphia).

Toorn, K. van der, 1985, *Sin and Sanction in Israel and Mesopotamia* (Assen).

——, 1989, 'Female Prostitution', *Journal of Biblical Literature* 108(2): 193–205.

Ungnad, A., 1941–4, 'Besprechungskunst und Astrologie in Babylonien', *Archiv für Orientforschung* 14: 250–84.

Van Dijk, J., 1953, *La sagesse suméro-accadienne* (Leiden).

——, 1954, 'Le fète du nouvel an dans un texte de Šulgi', *Bibliotheca Orientalis*, 11: 83ff.

——, 1964, 'Le motif cosmique dans la pensée sumérienne', *Acta Orientalia* 28 I: 1–59.

——, 1975a, 'Existe-t-il un "Poème de la Création Sumérien?", in *Kramer Anniversary Volume* (Alter Orient und Altes Testament 25) (Neukirchen-Vluyn): 125–34.

——, 1975b, 'Incantations accompagnant la naissance de l'homme', *Orientalia. Nova Seria* 44: 52–79.

Vernus, P., 1992, *Chants d'amour de l'Égypte antique* (Paris).

Volk, K., 1989, *Die Balag Komposition úru-am-ma-ir-ra-bi. Rekonstruktion und Bearbeitung der Tafeln 18, 19, 20 und 21 der späten, kanonischen Version* (Freiburger Altorientalische Studien 18) (Stuttgart).

Walker, C.B.F., 1987, *Reading the Past: Cuneiform* (London).

Westenholz, A. and Westenholz, J., 1977, 'The Old Akkadian Love Incantation MAD V 8', *Orientalia. Nova Seria* 46: 198–219.

*Westenholz, J.G., 1995a, 'Heilige Hochzeit und kultische Prostitution im alten Mesopotamien: sexuelle Vereinigung im sakralen Raum?', in Stähli, H.-P. (ed.) *Wort und Dienst.* (Bethel): 43–62.

*———, 1995b, 'Love Lyrics from the Ancient Near East.' in Sasson, J.M. (ed.) *Civilizations of the Ancient Near East.* (New York): 2471–2484.

*———, 2000, 'King by Love of Inanna – an image of female empowerment?', *NIN- Journal of Gender Studies in Antiquity.* 1: 75–89.

White, J.B., 1978, *A Study of the Language of Love in the Song of Songs and Ancient Egyptian Poetry* (Missoula, Mont.).

*Wiggerman, F.A.M., 1998, 'Nackte Göttin A.Philologisch', *Reallexikon der Assyriologie* 9 (Berlin): 56–53.

Wilcke, C., 1967–8; 'Einige Erwägungen zum § 29 des Codex Lipitestar', *Welt des Orients* 4: 153–62.

———, 1969, *Das Lugalband Epos* (Wiesbaden).

———, 1970, 'Die Akkadischen Glossen im THNF 25 und eine neue Interpretation des Textes', *Archiv für Orientforschung* 23: 84–7.

———, 1973, 'Inanna und Sukalletuda', *Archiv für Orientforschung* 29: 86.

———, 1974, 'Zum Königtum in der UrIII Zeit', *XIX Rencontre Assyriologique Internationale* (Paris).

———, 1975, 'Formale Gesichtspunkte in der sumerischen Literatur', in *Sumerological Studies in Honor of Thorkild Jacobsen* (=Assyriological Studies 20) (Chicago and London): 205–316.

———, 1984, 'Liebesbeschwörungen aus Isin', *Zeitschrift für Assyriologie. Neue Folge* 84: 188–209.

———, 1985, 'Familiengründung im Alten Babylonien', in Müller, E.W. (ed.), *Geschlechtsreife und Legitimation zur Zeugung* (Freiburg, Munich).

———, 1987, *33ième Rencontre Assyriologique International* (Paris): 179ff.

*Winter, I.J., 1996, 'Sex, Rhetoric, and the Public Monument: The Alluring Body of Naram-Sin of Agade', in Kampen, N. (ed.) *Sexuality in Ancient Art* (Cambridge): 1–26.

Witzel, M., 1946, 'Enki und Ninhursag', *Orientalia. Nova Seria* 15: 239–85.

Winckler, H., 1907, *Die babylonische Geisteskultur* (Leipzig).

Winckler, J.J., 1990, *The Constraints of Desire: The Anthropology of Sex and Gender in Ancient Greece* (New York, London).

Wittgenstein, L., 1975, *Philosophische Untersuchungen* (Frankfurt am Main).

*Wyke, M., 1998, *Gender and Body in the Ancient Mediterranean.* (Oxford).

Zarins, J., 1990, 'Early Mesopotamian Pastoral Nomadism and the Settlement of Lower Mesopotamia', *Bulletin of the American Society of Oriental Research* 280: 31–65.

*additional works included in the 2003 paperback, which were unavailable for the original edition.

INDEX

INDEX